ELVIS AND GLADYS

By the same author

NOVELS
The Dud Avocado
The Old Man and Me
The Injured Party

PLAY
My Place

BIOGRAPHY
Finch, Bloody Finch

Elvis
and
Gladys

Elaine Dundy

Macmillan Publishing Company
New York

Macmillan Publishing Company
866 Third Avenue, New York, N.Y. 10022
Collier Macmillan Canada, Inc.

Library of Congress Cataloging in Publication Data
Dundy, Elaine.
Elvis and Gladys.
Bibliography: p.
Includes index.
1. Presley, Elvis, 1935–1977. 2. Presley, Gladys
Love, 1912–1958. 3. Rock musicians—United States—
Biography. I. Title.
ML420.P96D78   1985   784.5′4′00924 [B]   85-3014
ISBN 0-02-553910-8

Macmillan books are available at special discounts for
bulk purchases for sales promotions, premiums, fund-raising,
or educational use. For details, contact:
Special Sales Director
Macmillan Publishing Company
866 Third Avenue
New York, N.Y. 10022

10   9   8   7   6   5   4   3   2   1

Printed in the United States of America

To Roy Turner
and
to Anna Brooks

Contents

A Note to the Reader

To what must be the main question in the reader's mind in being presented with this book—namely, Is there anything in it about Elvis that hasn't already been said?—my answer is a resounding yes. For one thing, it seems extraordinary in Elvis' case that his maternal line has not been thoroughly explored in view of the fact that it is now accepted that his mother, Gladys, was the pivotal force in his life. By "thoroughly explored" I do not mean the usual swift "begat" romp through the centuries but a penetrating, detailed, and on-the-spot investigation that brings to life and to reason the personalities as well as the times, customs, and traditions as they developed from the American Indian Wars which led Gladys' great-great-grandparents, William Mansell and his wife, to migrate to northeast Mississippi, and the subsequent Mansells, via the neighboring counties of Itawamba and Pontotoc, to Lee County where in Tupelo, its county seat, Elvis was born.

Also lacking has been any detailed, documented illumination of what Gladys was actually like growing up, as a child, an adolescent, and a young woman prior to her marriage to Elvis' father. Nor, for that matter, have Elvis' formative years—from his birth to the age of thirteen when the family moved to Memphis—been given anything close to the attention they deserve. Here, as with his mother, people who have never before allowed themselves to be interviewed spoke out for the first time. Many facts hitherto unknown came to light along with events previously mentioned but glossed over which now assume their proper, devastating importance.

New information, providing a far firmer foundation than has been laid before, enabled me to rebuild Elvis' character and, as I followed him and Gladys through their lives together, to project a portrait of each of them in far sharper focus and more vivid colors. I have come to believe it is only through this kind of historical approach—with its emphasis on the interweaving of families, generations, and cultures—that the true meaning of Elvis' life unfolds. For me, at least, there is no other way.

I arrived in Tupelo, Mississippi, Elvis' birthplace, in April 1981, to remain there, with frequent side trips to Memphis and to the University of Mississippi, at Oxford, for five months (until that August)—knowing no one and never having been in Mississippi before. Although my knowledge of the South was not exactly negligible, having spent my university years at Sweet Briar College in Lynchburg, Virginia, my awareness of the mores and manners of the South was broad and superficial rather than deep and concentrated. In any case, that was a long time ago. If any of my college mates had come from Mississippi or Tennessee, as they undoubtedly did, I had forgotten them. I wanted to enter a strange land, free and unencumbered, to await what would befall me.

There must be something in a willingness to meet one's luck halfway, for I arrived in Tupelo on a Friday and by Sunday I was listening to a sermon delivered by Brother Frank Smith, who had been the preacher at the First Assembly of God Church during the last years that the Presleys were members of its congregation. Afterwards I was invited to join the Smiths for their Sunday meal prepared by Frank's wife, Corene—Corene Randle, as she had been before her marriage, who though six years older than Elvis, had grown up in the same neighborhood. Becoming friends, Corene and I soon fell into the habit of meeting for afternoon or evening coffee two or three times a week. During these meetings I questioned her avidly on every aspect of her childhood and adolescence in East Tupelo—the sights, sounds, smells, the weather, the work, the clothes, the schooling, the recreations, the First Assembly of God Church, the Depression and the recession—and, as we talked, she found herself becoming as absorbed as I in the reconstruction of this particular past. She showed me her photograph album and generously loaned me several pertinent pictures. For her information and her considerable and consistent help (it was entirely through her good graces that Annie Presley, who had previously refused to be interviewed, agreed to talk to me) and for her lucid descriptions of those bygone times, I owe special thanks.

My next important friend in Tupelo was Phyllis Harper, feature editor and writer of the deservedly popular "It Seems to Me" column in the *Tupelo Daily Journal,* whose work has recently found its way into prestigious southern anthologies. She, too, was a native of the area, having been raised at Fawn Grove, a farm in Itawamba County, which is touched on in relation to Gladys' forebears. It was Phyllis who urged me to contact Professor Vaughn Grisham when I visited the University of Mississippi. He had just completed a definitive sociological treatise, "Tupelo, Mississippi: From Settlement to Industrial City, 1860–1970." For his letting me read it before publication and for his several enlightening discussions with me on the subject afterwards, I am deeply obliged. Phyllis Harper also wrote an article about me in the *Tupelo Daily Journal* under the fine-sounding title, "Established Writer in Tupelo to Research Presley," which, as well as including my past published work, emphasized that the biography I planned on Presley would be a serious one. She added in closing that I was interested in talking not only to those who knew the Presleys but others who could tell me something of the local history and times of his early years in Tupelo. This article opened many doors for me, not only ones that might have been shut had I attempted to storm them "cold," but doors I had no way of knowing even existed.

Herman Irwin, manager of a large insurance company in Tupelo, was one of the people who contacted me in response to Phyllis' column. His father and mother, Len and Lily Mae Irwin, had been friends of Gladys' mother and father, Robert and Doll Smith, and had worked shares alongside them on Burk's farm. Both of Herman Irwin's parents were still living. Herman, after first driving me—or "carrying" me (to employ the eighteenth-century term still in usage there)—to the exact place where the Smiths had made their home for that tragically short time (of which nothing is left to mark it but rosebushes rambling wild), then carried me further around the environs pointing out the various landmarks which had anecdotal bearings on the Smiths and their way of life. Finally he took me to his parents' house. There both Len and Lily Mae Irwin reminisced in a very lively manner not only of the Smiths but the many Smith children, of whom Gladys was the fourth. Lily Mae Irwin further helped me by writing down, at her son's request, a résumé of her own life, which included more reminiscences of the Smiths, the invalid Doll and the sudden death of Bob.

I have much more to thank Herman Irwin for: notably his wife, Billie Dale, who runs the Senior Citizens' Recreation Center and who took time from her busy schedule to assemble those particular people who had personally known the Smiths and the Presleys so that I might interview them separately and at length. Through the years the Presleys had kept close contact with old Tupelo friends. Much valuable information came out of these meetings.

Again it was Herman who arranged for me to meet Mertice Finley Collins, whose family had farmed across the way from the Smiths in the Gilvo community before they moved to Burk's farm. To her, especially for the accuracy and precision of her memory for names, dates, and places as befits an ex-schoolteacher, my awed appreciation.

Further, it was Mrs. Collins who led me to Roy Turner.

For about a month now, though information had been coming at me hard and fast, I had been feeling the increasing need of solid, tangible things like documents. I had also decided that in order to tell the story best I must concentrate on only one particular branch from which Gladys had directly descended. Gladys' father was a Smith, her mother a Mansell—which side would I choose? As it turned out, the records chose it for me. Roy Turner, when I first met him on a Sunday afternoon in May 1981 in his pleasant house with his wife, Debbie, and his two children, was a brilliant twenty-eight-year-old. A fifth-generation Tupeloan, he then held the title of corresponding secretary of the Northeast Mississippi Historical and Genealogical Society, of which he is now president. He had at the time two publications under his belt, *Lee County Marriage Records, 1867–1900* and *Lee County Cemeteries,* and was just finishing his third, *Itawamba Settlers.* The Turners' workroom—they work as partners—was a formidable affair of the tools of his trade: genealogical tomes, photographic equipment, and a huge duplicating machine, but it was over the breakfast table that we sat, according to my journal, from 4 P.M. till 10 P.M. that day, while he pored over marriage records, census records, school records, cemetery records, old city directories, maps, and plats. At the same time he attempted to crash-course me into the arcane ways of genealogy and the clues and the intuitive leaps you had to take before turning up a documented solution. It was better than a detective story. Was it then we decided to follow the Mansell line? I think so. Tupelo is full of Mansells, one of whom, Elzie Mansell, Roy knew well, and their migration was from nearby Alabama, while Gladys' great-grandfather Smith, according to the 1880 census, was from South Carolina, farther away. When we discovered that Gladys descended from Mansells on both her maternal and paternal line, that clinched it.

There was a moment in June I won't easily forget. I was in Memphis and had just spent an exhausting and irritating day in high summer— one contact had failed to turn up, another had proved worthless, still another was out of town for a month. In the passivity this sort of frustration provokes, I sat in my air-frozen room at a Holiday Inn wondering if it was all worth it. Suddenly I was ringing Roy in Tupelo to see how he was doing down there. "I've been waiting for you to come back," he said. "You remember I told you I traced our Mansells back to Marion County, Alabama? Well, I got in touch with Dorothy Stalcup, the head of the Genealogical Society in that area and she got me in touch with Joel Palmer in Hamilton who's working on his Mansell line and we matched up the lines with our charts, and ... Elvis' great-great-great-grandmother was a full-blooded Cherokee called Morning Dove White!"

My special thanks, then, to Joel Palmer who, when we visited him, showed us his documents, conducted us around the Mansell and Mansell-Palmer graves, introduced us to some Alabama Mansells, and imparted to us much valuable information about the family.

For the rest of my stay Roy and I worked as a team. He showed me through many cemeteries where Elvis' ancestors lay, searched out many people who had known Elvis and the family, aided and abetted me during many interviews, and conducted others on his own. For only a portion of what I owe him, I refer the reader to my dedication.

Roy was also with me when I first visited Gladys' eldest sister, Lillian Smith Mann Fortenberry, whom I was to see and correspond with often.

If it is true, as I had been told, that there was a family likeness between the two sisters, it is easy to see wherein lay Gladys' charm. Lillian Fortenberry, at 78, is a woman of striking appearance. Her easy directness and openness of manner, together with a native dignity that never conceals a sense of fun, even of mischief, immediately sets off sympathetic vibrations. I always looked forward to seeing her. As with many elderly people, she speaks with great clarity about the distant past and of Gladys' last few years with frankness, forcefulness, and feeling.

I would also like to express my gratitude for the contributions of the following: Bill Mitchell, the late Cully Mitchell, Vera Turner, Ernest Bowen, the Reverend Frank Smith, Mavis Cristil, Grace Reed, Buddy and Kay Bain, Mrs. David Gallentine Jr., and Shirley (Jones) Gallentine, Era and Oscar Tackett, Bob Tackett, John Allen Cooke, Magnolia Clanton, Becky Martin, Carrie Hall, Catherine (Hall) Gardner, Janis McCoy, Randy McCoy, Raymond McCoy, Elzie Mansell (to whom special thanks are due for his help on the Mansell line), Ellis Mansell, Mrs. J.C. Grimes, Charles Farrar, Erlene Horton, Terry Wood, Joy Harris, Mrs. Novie Clarke, Bill Parham, Archie Mackay, Marcus Kelly, Maxine Williams, John Marcy, Ed Smith, Jimmie Palmer, Wayne Earnest, Corinne Richards Tate, the late Leona Richards, Eloise Bedford, Francis Patterson, Dorothy Rutledge, Marshall and Vona Mae Brown, John Cannon, Ruth Love Lucas, Hod Harris, Pid Harris, Ophelia Harris, Analyn Kirksey, Vernon Hood (nephew of Minnie Mae Presley) and his wife Gladys Hood, Charlie Boren, Curtis Robinson, Mrs. Wink Martindale, Gay McRae, Reggie Bell, Mildred Merchent, Shirley Lumpkin, Shirley Wheeler, Mary Joe Eades, Roland Tindall, Maude Dean Cook, Kitty and Carolyn Brewer, Jean Aberbach, Freddy Bienstock, Shelley Winters, Maureen Stapleton, Mike MacGregor, Professor Vaughn Grisham, Professor Columbus Hopper, James Ausborn, Marion McCauley, Olivia Holmes, Donald Johnson, Cathy Osment, Martha Wallace, Jimmy Velvet, Aaron Kennedy, Louis and Sherry Black, Philip Dunne, Sidney Lumet, Mickey Knox, Barry Brown, Tony Sloman, John Crippen, Sandy Lieberson, Todd Slaughter, Judy Rehak, (researcher), Dr. J.C. Cowen, MA, MB, B.Chir., Terence Gray (handwriting expert), and my lawyer, Anthony Rubinstein. I would like to single out for very special thanks Dr. and Mrs. Lester Hofman.

Anna Brooks, my assistant throughout the actual writing of this book, came to me planning to stay two months and remained two years to become my right hand and extra head. Her considerable managerial, organizational, and research skills made her invaluable and, but for her aid, I sometimes believe this book would never have been completed.

And finally, I am grateful to my editor, Robert Stewart, for his help and skill.

PART ONE

ONE

Captain Marvel, Jr.

By the time Elvis was in first grade, he and his schoolmate Wayne Earnest had evolved a system that would both double their money and their reading pleasure. They swapped comic books—Elvis sometimes walking the mile over to Wayne's place on Saturday afternoon to complete the transaction.

Elvis was already immersed in the adventures of the Lone Ranger, Hopalong Cassidy, Tarzan, Batman, and Superman when his secret life suddenly took a dramatic new turn. He discovered Freddy Freeman in the comic book series *Captain Marvel's Adventures*. There, on page 267, young Freddy made his entrance—and very nearly his exit—fishing off a boat with his grandpa:

"Look, Grandpa! Somebody fell in the water over there!"

"Put about and we'll rescue him," says Grandpa.

In fact they have rescued the diabolical Captain Nazi who repays their softheartedness by socking old Grandpa overboard and then, grabbing the oar out of Freddy's hand, whacks him into the briny deep as well.

By the time Captain Marvel flies to the rescue, Grandpa has drowned and Freddy is no more than a symbolic hand stretching up from the sea.

Swooping down and sweeping up Freddy's almost lifeless form in his arms, Captain Marvel says, "You're in bad shape, youngster. I'd better get you to a hospital right away."

Easier flown to than entered. Unimpressed by the astounding figure cut by the Captain and the desperate condition of his charge, an officious hospital attendant bars their way. "This is highly irregular," he splutters.

"This is a private institution. You can't come in."

Responding with a simple "Nuts," Captain Marvel walks through a wall and into an operating room where he curtly orders a surprised doctor to "get to work" on the young boy. Then, uttering the magic word "Shazam!" the Captain is transformed into plain, everyday Billy Batson sitting in the waiting room anxiously asking a nurse, "How is he? Will he live?"

"The doctors say there's no hope. Even if he lived, he'd be a cripple for life. We're doing all we can, but we don't expect him to last the night out."

Billy waits till midnight to sneak into Room 15, hoists Freddy in a fireman's haul, carries him downstairs and out and...

Spellbound, six-year-old Elvis read on as Billy walked down the "long ancient underground hall where he first met the sorcerer Shazam" and stared with interest at the panel depicting Billy carrying the dying Freddy on his shoulder through a tunnel lined with gargoyles labeled Pride, Envy, Greed, and Hatred. Billy laid Freddy before an empty, dust-covered throne. He lit a long-extinguished torch and as the flame flared up there was a rumbling sound, a lightning bolt, a crash of thunder, and the ghost of the dead wizard appeared.

"Who calls old Shazam from his thousand years of sleep?" asks the wizard.

"I, Billy Batson, call you. There is a man loose above—a man called Captain Nazi who is destroying everything. I've brought you a boy who is dying as a result of Captain Nazi's cruelty. You must help him as once you helped me!"

Rising from his throne, the wizard pronounces, "What has already come to pass cannot be changed by any power of mine. *But you, as Captain Marvel, can, if you will, pass on to this boy some of the mighty powers I once gave you.* Billy Batson, speak my name!"

Billy complies. "Shazam!"

And the last panel of the page is filled with black clouds and yet another lightning bolt.

Elvis turned the page and read on:

"The wraith of Shazam vanished and in his place stands the familiar red-clad figure, *Captain Marvel.*" The dying boy lies at his feet.

In the second panel Freddy springs miraculously back to life exclaiming simply: "Why it—it's *Captain Marvel!*"

And the third panel on that page gives itself over to a third lightning bolt.

The next panel stretches clear across the page: Captain Marvel stands astride in his familiar snappy red body suit trimmed with the yellow arm bracelets and his familiar yellow boots and belt, and sporting his familiar yellow lightning bolt emblem on his chest. His flowing white cape flares rakishly on one shoulder. An enormous Book of Knowledge rests on the wizard's throne, and the brazier is still aflame.

In the foreground, profiled in an aura of light, stands Freddy—whole, healed, and triumphant. His hair is shining black; a lock falls over his forehead. He is wearing sideburns and his hair grows down the base of his neck. Although his body suit is blue and his cape red, his outfit is otherwise an exact replica of the Captain's in every detail including the yellow lightning bolt emblem.

"I'm all well again! I—I'm like you!" he exclaims in wonder.

"That's right! You're *Captain Marvel, Jr.!*"

Looking at them standing together—the Captain and his junior—we are instantly struck by the differing techniques used in the drawing of Freddy/Captain Marvel, Jr., from that of Billy/Captain Marvel. Billy/Captain Marvel is drawn in the stylized cartoon strip tradition. As the Captain, he is beetle-browed, pin-eyed, muscle-bound and lockjawed, while as Billy, his features suggest that a child of eight has delineated them on the blank oval of his face. Freddy/Marvel, Jr., on the other hand, has been obviously and sensitively copied from a most appealing adolescent life-model.

He looks in fact *exactly* as Elvis, from adolescence to the end of his life, strove to make himself look.

On the last page, Captain Marvel and Captain Marvel, Jr., are flying through the air deep in conversation.

"Now you have all the powers I have. Use them to fight the forces of evil wherever they appear," says Captain Marvel.

"And do I change back to my own shape, too, like you do to Billy Batson?"

"Yes, you will have to go through life in your own form, but whenever you need me, speak my name and as Captain Marvel, Jr., you will be able to do the things I do. Now go back in the hospital and get well. And then I'm going to send you into *Master Comics* to take care of Captain Nazi."

"Goodbye, *Captain Marvel*," replied Jr., stalwartly.

And with the lightning bolt panel that precedes all changes in psyche and geography, Freddy wakes up in the hospital exclaiming:

"Gosh! I wonder if it's all really true! Well, I'll be out of here tomorrow and then I'll find out!"

And he does find out. It is true. Although, as a caption points out, "The poor boy is destined to carry on with a crippled leg as a souvenir of his

encounter with Captain Nazi." Yet what the evil Captain does not know
is that the innocent lad he crippled is now "the most powerful boy in the
world! *Captain Marvel, Jr.*"

Thus Captain Marvel, Jr., began starring in his *own* series beginning
in January, 1942. It was six years to the month after Elvis was born.

On the chill afternoon of Tuesday, January 8, 1935, Catherine Hall was
walking briskly back home. At the end of Lake Street she slowed down
looking right and left before crossing Highway 78 like her mama was
always cautioning her to, but resumed her stride past Kelly Street and
up to the corner of Berry when she brought herself to an abrupt halt.
There on the Old Saltillo Road where she lived, right across from the
Methodist church, she saw a crowd of neighbors collected around both
Presley houses. Something interesting must be going on. Mama would
know. She hurried past the people to her own front porch. But Mama
was already waiting for her, and even before the thirteen-year-old girl
could get out her question she was told to quickly change into her clean
dress and tidy herself up because one of the twins young Mrs. Vernon
Presley next door had given birth to that morning had passed away and
they were going to pay their respects.

When her mother told her she was actually going to see a little baby
who had died, Catherine prepared herself to see it looking all funny and
twisted and deformed like that little calf that had come out all wrong.
Once in the small front room, Catherine took no notice of the people or
the food, or of Gladys Presley and the little live baby in bed with her, but
slipped away from her mother and went straight to the small, open casket
standing by the window. Fearfully she peered into it. Then her fear changed
to puzzled astonishment. The tiny baby lying there was perfectly formed.
It didn't even look dead; it just looked asleep. She glanced around at the
grownups. Perhaps they'd made a mistake.

Later on Catherine just couldn't help telling her best friend that in her
opinion they could've made a mistake putting that little infant in the
casket. That baby didn't look to her like he had anything wrong with
him. Couldn't he be alive and just real quiet, resting or something?

But Catherine's best friend was one of Vernon Presley's younger sisters
and therefore, being infinitely better informed about the whole matter,
was in a position to put Catherine right. She told her not to be so simple;
of course the baby was dead. Wouldn't Mrs. Edna Robinson, who'd mid-
wifed most of the babies in East Tupelo, and Dr. Hunt, whom Vernon
had fetched because of the emergency—wouldn't they be expected to

know everything there was to know about these things? She went on to tell more: that the second twin—the one who was all right—hadn't come out till a whole half-hour after the first and that he hadn't arrived till 4:30 in the morning. They'd already named him Elvis Aron.

"But what about the other?" Catherine timidly queried. "Do they name babies who are...like that, or what?"

She received an impatient look. Of course they did; they already had. How would he get into heaven without a name? He was named Jesse Garon and he was going to be buried near all the Presleys in the cemetery at Priceville so that he wouldn't be lonely.

Hearing about the arrival of Gladys' twins, Mertice Finley, a thirty-year-old schoolteacher who was surviving the Depression by working at the Tupelo Garment Center where Gladys had worked before her confinement, drove over that evening to see her.

At the Presleys', Mertice was not concerned with the dead baby who still looked alive, nor even the live one who in fact did not look that lively. She was too shocked at the sight of Gladys herself. Wan, weak, and in obvious, persistent pain, she had begun hemorrhaging again. She looked, in Mertice's words, "close to death," and they were getting ready to take Gladys and her baby to the Tupelo hospital. There they would both remain in the charity ward for over three weeks, Gladys recovering with difficulty.

Gladys was of special concern to Mertice. She had watched the Smith children grow up hungry. There had been six or seven of them at the time—she never could keep count—and they had lived on the Wilburn farm across the road from the Finleys in a small community called Gilvo. Gladys Smith, the darkest and chubbiest of them, was to Mertice the prettiest and her special favorite. Images of the Smith children tumbling over each other into the Finleys' farmhouse now came back to her. They were strictly relegated to the kitchen. Only there would they be fed scraps by Mertice and her mother because her father could not bear the sight of those poor, pitiful, importunate little things swarming around his dinner table; their hungry faces upset him so. Then Mertice had gone up to Memphis to a training college for teachers, and the Smiths moved off someplace else. Mertice hadn't set eyes on Gladys for about eleven years when they met up again at the Tupelo Garment Center in 1934.

It was about the beginning of November, as Mertice describes it. The noon whistle shrilled and she was just walking down the steps of the factory to go to lunch when a very pregnant, pretty young woman with smooth, neatly arranged black hair and huge swollen legs all wrapped up in ragged bandages, smilingly approached her and asked if she wasn't Mrs. Vertie Finley's daughter—she'd heard she was working there.

"Why, it's Gladys Smith!" exclaimed Mertice, giving her a big hug. "Mama told me you'd gotten married."

"That's right. I married Mr. Vernon Presley a while back. I'm going to have my baby soon," she added unnecessarily.

Mertice was waiting for some friends and she invited Gladys to join them for lunch. Gladys paused a bit and then declined because, as she explained, she didn't happen to have any money along with her that day. Mertice registered this grimly but without surprise.

After getting her teaching degree in Memphis, Mertice came back to Mississippi to the little town of Mooreville, not far from Tupelo, and began teaching. In the Depression the banks faltered, then failed, and were finally shut down in March 1933 by Roosevelt, leaving Mertice with fourteen teacher's certificates and no banks to honor them. In spite of this she continued teaching for another year until she reluctantly got herself a full-time job at the Tupelo Garment Center. Factory wages were notoriously low, but the Great Depression, the great economic leveler, stimulated great fellow feeling. Mertice reissued her invitation to Gladys, promising that she and her friends together would share the cost of Gladys' midday meal. The truth was that Mertice could not have afforded to pay for Gladys' meal alone.

Over lunch, as Mertice observed Gladys' ponderous body and the haggard expression on her face when in repose, she recalled her mother saying to her about a year ago, "Guess who I saw the other day in town? Gladys Smith! Wearing a blood-red dress and looking so pretty and so pleased. Told me she'd got herself married to one of those Presley boys from East Tupelo. *You* know, the ones from Above The Highway."

Mertice's mother, by capitalizing the first letter of those three words, gave the phrase a nuance that anyone living in Lee County at the time would have caught. Of course all of East Tupelo was the wrong side of the tracks but that particular little community of five short streets lumped together under the phrase "above the highway" was the wrongest: It was the dwelling place of the poorest white laborers.[1]

However, Gladys' face that lunchtime was rarely in repose. Mostly she was her cheerful, chattering self, so pleased she was at this reunion with

[1] Small as Tupelo was, it was still able to accommodate two other wrong sides of the tracks—Shakerag, where the black people lived, and South Tupelo, where the factory workers lived.

her childhood friend—this friend who, together with her mother, Miss Vertie, she had the best reason in the world to be grateful to, and who even this very day was keeping her hunger pangs away.

Twenty-one years later, in 1956, when Elvis would return to sing at the Mississippi–Alabama Fair, when the mayor of Tupelo would declare it Elvis Presley Day with marching bands and banners, Gladys would make sure that tickets had been sent to Mertice's mother along with a special invitation to attend the occasion. She would search for her diligently in the crowd and would greet her with a great embrace, declaring, "Miz' Vertie, if it hadn't been for your beans and potatoes we would have starved!"

But now Gladys chattered on, catching Mertice up with her story of the intervening years. She told her about her daddy's sudden death on Burk's farm, about them moving in with Granny Smith in Eggville for a spell; about first going in to Tupelo to work at the Garment Center and traveling to and from the country every day by school buses that the municipal government had requisitioned and about her decision, now that she was the head of the family, to move them all into East Tupelo on Kelly Street so as to be nearer the Garment Center and nearer their Mansell kinfolk—especially Uncle Gaines who was a preacher at their church. She told about her mama, still doing poorly, still an invalid— well, as comfortable as could be expected—being looked after by Gladys' youngest sister Clettes (she'd arrived just after Mertice's time). And she told about meeting Vernon Presley who lived close to them on the Old Saltillo Road and who went to the same church that she did. She told how they'd gotten married and built a little house of their own right next to her in-laws and how she was so happy she was going to have a baby though she was so big she was sure she was having twins. She began to talk about how much trouble her legs were giving her. The trouble was, she'd been shifted from the sewing section to the ironing section about three months back and she had to stand there all day every day pushing those big heavy steam irons. It really made her feel bad, she said, to have her old friend see her with her feet in this condition. And then suddenly she broke into one of her big smiles again and said she'd spoken up that very morning to her supervisor who promised they'd shift her again—this time to the sorting and folding, and that wouldn't give her any trouble at all. Privately Mertice decided to have a talk with Gladys' supervisor herself to make sure this was done, but when she went to see him, he told her Gladys had had to quit work because of the difficulties of her confinement.

* * *

When Mertice heard that Gladys and Elvis had been discharged from the hospital and learned more about their straitened circumstances at home, she got together with some of Gladys' friends and co-workers and between them they raised a collection of thirty dollars.

"Don't give it to her in money," they were warned. "*He'll* only drink it up."

Even then, at the age of nineteen, Vernon Presley seemed fated never to have a good word said about him. But perhaps whoever did the cautioning was drawing too hasty a conclusion. True, he was not a good provider. But this was the Depression and jobs were scarce, especially for male laborers. The garment mills' employment rolls were over ninety percent female—factory girls. Vernon had a milk delivery route for a while and then people couldn't afford having milk delivered regularly. He worked here, there, and yonder in the fields and doing odd jobs. The trouble was he didn't work very hard or very steadily. He had not been able to pay for his own marriage license or for Dr. Hunt for the delivery of the twins or for the hospital expenses. He had been known all his young life as a "jellybean"—by definition weak, spineless, and work-shy. This was certainly the assessment of his father, J. D. Presley, who in a fit of temper had kicked his fifteen-year-old son out of the house, sent him down to Pickens, Mississippi, to a relative's farm to shape up and received him back a year later not so much as a prodigal son as a bad penny. In his entire life Vernon probably did not perform a single noble action. Nor, having a skill, did he choose to develop it. Briefly he worked in Ernest Bowen, Sr.'s carpentry shop and Mr. Bowen said that Vernon could do just about anything in the world with wood. He might have known the self-satisfaction—even the dignity—of a craftsman. He might have had a trade. "My father was a common laborer," Elvis said early in his career, "he didn't have no trade, just like I didn't have." Why did Vernon abandon it for driving a truck? Because he liked driving a truck. That's the way he was. What he really liked best of all was just plain loafing. But this did not prevent him from having a tender heart. Like his father, J. D., he was extremely handsome. Unlike his father, he was pleasant, polite, easygoing and happy-go-lucky. And also—unlike his father—he was not a drunk. He genuinely loved his wife, after his fashion, and he worshipped his baby child. A month after Elvis' birth, Mrs. Lily Martin, the lady of the house whose fence Vernon was repairing came upon him in tears. When she asked him what was the matter he told her he couldn't stop grieving over the dead twin. She pointed out that one of her children had lived and turned out to be a helpless cripple in mind and body—so perhaps it was for the best. But Vernon was inconsolable.

Instead of giving Gladys the thirty dollars in cash, her friends gave her a baby shower: baby clothes and linen, baby food, baby toys, a high chair. Gladys was overjoyed. It was not the first nor the last time in her life that Gladys would be grateful for the charity of friends. To the poor of the South, it was a way of life.

TWO

Gladys' Roots

So far nothing of detailed, accurate information has been published about Elvis' maternal forebears, yet it is this side of the family's story that is the most enthralling—its roots going back to embrace much of American history: the War of Independence, the Indian Wars, the Civil War, the expansion of the southwest and, not least of all, the American melting pot.

It is odd that most biographers and genealogists concentrate entirely on the paternal line, the maternal side only dropping in when the subject's father marries his mother. In Spain, in breeding fighting bulls, it is accepted that the qualities of courage and bravery are transmitted through the female genes and there are regular trials held at bull ranches in which the bravery of the young cows is tested. The bridge between brave bulls and brave human beings is not one that at present can be crossed, but under the harsh conditions of the new land in the American southwest, with its constant family migrations, with the men so often gone to war—"from war to plough to war again" as the expression ran—the survival of the next generation was expected to be the sole responsibility of the mother.

John Steinbeck, in his *The Grapes of Wrath*, has written of the mother's position in the frontier family in this way:

It was a great and humble position. They looked to her for joy so she laughed. From her position as defender, she gave dignity. As healer, her hand had grown sure and cool and quiet; from her position as arbiter, she was faultless in judgment. She knew if she swayed the family shook. If she ever wavered or despaired, the family would fall and the family will to function would be gone. In short she was the person of the greatest power.

Whether or not every pioneer mother lived up to this is another matter. Nevertheless it is revealing to trace Elvis through his maternal line to discover what brave blood, as well as what circumstances, produced the kind of person Gladys was, and what enabled her to produce the phenomenon of Elvis.

The earliest female that can be traced with certainty in Elvis' maternal line was his great-great-great-grandmother, Morning Dove White. A full-blooded Cherokee Indian, she was born in about 1800, and died certainly in 1835, and is buried in Hamilton, Alabama.

The man she married was a William Mansell. He lived in western Tennessee where the Cherokee nation occupied land as they did in Georgia and North Carolina. His father, Richard Mansell, from South Carolina, had been a soldier in the Revolution. One can go farther than that, though only in a general way. The name Mansell is of French origin. It means, literally, the man from Le Mans. During the Norman Conquest there were many men from Le Mans. They went all over England: the home counties, the north country; they went to Scotland where our particular Mansells intermingled with the Scots. And from Scotland they went to Ulster, where they multiplied mightily, and from Ulster to America in the mass migration which began in 1718 and where they became known as Scots-Irish.

In William Mansell's time no purebred Indian bore a surname, but when the new Americans discovered that even within the separate Indian nations there existed conflict and dissension, they were quick to emphasize these divisions by affixing the word "White" to the names of those Indians who were friendly to the Americans and the Revolution, and the word "Red" to those who sided with the British, and were not. Wisdom and peacefulness came to be associated with the Whites, while the Reds became big warriors, big war chiefs, and from the settlers' point of view, big troublemakers.

Intermarriage with a friendly White Indian maid was not unusual in the southern states, where the pioneer men by far outnumbered their womenfolk. In Elvis' antecedents this is substantiated by the fact that Morning Dove's sister, Mapy, also married a white man, Moses Purser. Paradoxically, some of the children of these "friendly" marriages would turn out to be far wilder and fiercer than any that could be produced by either pure white or pure Indian strain. A good case in point was the militant Creek chief, Red Eagle (christened William Weatherford), who was the son of an Indian mother and a Scots trader.

What adds piquancy to this story is that before Morning Dove and William Mansell married, he had fought two wars against the Indians under Andrew Jackson—as did his friend Moses Purser.

In the first, as a nineteen-year-old raw recruit from Tennessee, Private Mansell fought in the harrowing Battle of Horseshoe Bend in Alabama. It was the final battle of the Creek war and it started as an Indian civil war with Jackson's invasion fitting perfectly into the pattern of the Indians' own warfare.

The Creek war had begun with Chief Red Eagle and his Red Sticks (so called because they painted bright red clubs all over themselves) massacring Fort Mims, owned by Samuel Mims who like Red Eagle was also part Creek. Mims was a wealthy merchant who lived as a white man. His stockade housed 120 militia men, three hundred other people who were white, or of mixed blood, or friendly Indians, and about three hundred black slaves.

At midday August 30, 1813, with its gates open and children playing, Red Eagle and his Red Sticks stormed the fort. The fort's commander was clubbed to death in his attempt to close the gates. A few whites managed to escape but the rest of the people within the fort at the time— some two hundred and fifty—were butchered in the most brutal manner.

It was this that brought Jackson from Tennessee. The specific aim was to avenge Fort Mims but there is no doubt that Jackson's overall goal was to cut a road through the middle of Alabama from Tennessee to Mobile, slicing the Creek nation in half, defeating them and driving them out, thus giving the United States a chance to expand.

All through that year Jackson, "Old Hickory," America's first Common Man, fought the Indians in Alabama with varying degrees of success and with increasingly ragged troops but with himself ever gaining in popularity, fame, and notoriety. Finally, much to his relief, he gained support from the War Department of the U.S. government and by the middle of March 1814 Jackson—still only a colonel in the militia—was in command of four thousand men. As well as Private Mansell, the troops included many Creek allies.

It was then that Jackson felt himself ready to chance all on an assault on the dangerously placed Indian fort at Horseshoe Bend. This stronghold, to which Red Eagle's Red Sticks had rallied to defend some thousand Indians, was a hundred-acre wooded peninsula almost completely surrounded by the Tallapoosa River and fortified, where it connected with the mainland, by a cleverly arranged wall of curved breastwork scalloped in such a fashion that no army could advance upon it without being

exposed to deadly crossfire from its portholes. It was an engineering feat
that surprised the white men who did not believe savage Indians capable
of such skill. To Jackson it was "a place well formed by Nature for defence
and rendered more secure by Art." To Jackson's troops it was pure hell.

The Battle of Horseshoe Bend started at ten o'clock on the morning of
March 27, 1814, and ceased only when it became too dark for the troops
to see any more Indians. It was the decisive victory against the Creeks.
At the end of the day there were nine hundred dead Indians—the Americans cut off their noses to keep accurate count—and three hundred
captives taken. All but four of these were women and children. Jackson
said he regretted the lives of the two or three women that had been lost.
He said he "never made war on females."

On April 18, Jackson raised the American flag at an old French fort at
the juncture of the Coosa and Tallapoosa rivers, renamed it Fort Jackson
and its environs Hickory Ground. It was here that he accepted the dignified surrender of Red Eagle on behalf of the Creek nation. By May,
Colonel Jackson had become Major General Jackson in the regular United
States Army. He then proceeded by the terms of his treaty with Red Eagle
to relocate the Indians. In plain English it meant that Jackson, running
wild over the indecisive President Madison, highhandedly took it upon
himself to snatch the Creeks' land and force them westward.

The die was cast. Over the next few years, the wild general from
Tennessee would relentlessly pursue his policy of Indian removal, ar-
ranging treaties that involved the acquisition of valuable land in virtually
every southern state—almost one-third of Tennessee, three-quarters of
Florida and Alabama, one-fifth of Georgia and Mississippi, and one-tenth
of Kentucky and North Carolina for the new Americans to settle in.
Naturally, this did not make him unpopular with the new grass roots.
Naturally, this caused him to have a few run-ins with the government of
the United States. In 1815 it went so far as a trial—*The United States
Government* v. *Major General Andrew Jackson*—with Judge Hall com-
menting that "the only question was whether the law should bend to the
General or the General to the Law." Jackson bent to the law only to the
tune of $1,000, and was off on his merry way. The truth was that Jackson,
like Napoleon—his junior by two years—was a law unto himself.

In November 1817 there was a border incident involving Spanish Florida and American Georgia; a matter of the Florida Seminole Indians (a
branch of the Creek nation) crossing the line and massacring some Americans who had insisted on their right to settle in Georgia under Jackson's
treaty with the Creeks of three years before. This time General Jackson

was officially ordered (as if that were needed) by his ally, President James Monroe, to raise a force of Tennessee militia, and pursue the offenders into Spanish Florida if necessary.

Twenty-two-year-old William Mansell, back in Tennessee by then, turned again from his plough to answer his general's clarion call. Along with some thousand other volunteers who included, as always, troops of friendly Indians of every tribe, Private Mansell followed Jackson from Tennessee down through Georgia. Jackson had destroyed Seminole villages along the way and in retaliation the Seminoles had ambushed and massacred an army detachment of Jackson's. When he learned of this, Jackson burst into Florida like an avenging demon. The Florida Seminoles, terrified, sued for peace. But Jackson was not through. He went on to take Pensacola, to eject its Spanish governor, and to garrison its fortress with Americans. For the Spaniards it was the beginning of the end of their possessions. Three years later Florida would be part of the United States with Jackson as its governor.

In the spring of 1818, William Mansell was back home in Tennessee, now ready to find himself a wife. Should we be astonished that having fought the Indians so bitterly he would now turn around and marry one? Had the Indians' proximity into which he'd been forced by these battles so gotten into his bloodstream that he could not live without one? Or was there, by now, such a deep schism between the Red and White Indians as to render the question pointless? Still—Red or White—they did belong to the same racial family.

In strictly practical terms, the marriage was a fair exchange. In marrying William Mansell, Morning Dove White was giving herself the chance for a decent life. With Jackson's Cherokee removals, the Indians who remained—both men and women—soon melted in with the white people. As early as 1800, many Cherokees had been converted to Christianity; their sunburned skins were not that much darker than the whites', nor were their features that dissimilar. In this way they covered their identities, for the laws of the southwest had become harsh against the Indians and they could be mistreated very badly. In marrying her he would gain her age-old Indian knowledge of the American terrain: of forests and prairies; of crops and game; of protection against the climate; of medicine lore, healing plants as well as something in which the Indians were expert—the setting of broken bones. In the Cherokee tradition of women she would be humble, devoted, and hardworking—in the fields as well as in the house. Nor by tradition could she complain if he took another wife or wives to live with them, for not only Indian chiefs but the common Indian had all the wives he could get if so inclined. William Mansell did not have this inclination. That in succeeding generations the names of Morning, Dove, and even White would flutter through the leaves of the family tree seems proof that he loved and honored his wife.

The age of American expansion had begun in earnest. Andrew Jackson's exploits had loosed in the settlers a new wave of restlessness, adventure, ambition, and patriotism. William Mansell had no sooner returned to Tennessee than he yearned for the Alabama territory whose rich, cheap lands he had come to know as part of the conquering army. It must have seemed to him nothing short of traitorous to have fought there with Jackson but not to have taken advantage of the spoils of war.

In the winter of 1820, together with Morning Dove's sister and brother-in-law, Mapy and Moses Purser, the Mansells, traveling by ox-cart, crossed the frozen Tennessee River into Alabama.

They were not alone. They were taking part in a huge migration begun some five years before. Alabama fever had broken out. Ex-Indian fighters from Tennessee were joined by blacksmiths, wagonmakers, machinists, and other laborers of every description from that state. Pioneers came streaming out of the valley of Virginia, out of the piedmonts of North and South Carolina, out of the swamps of Georgia. The fever spread far and fast until it was caught by farmers in every state of the Union seeking to better their lot and ambitious enough to uproot their families for the long trek to the uncertain future. Many migrants trudged on foot, their wagons packed with children and rude possessions, a milk-cow bringing up the rear. An English geographer recording land conditions in Alabama also recorded encountering twelve thousand travellers *within a single day*.

The predominant settlers in Alabama were the Scots-Irish like William Mansell, and since by their very numbers they would set the tone of the southwest, it is well to clear up this term before it leads one into thinking incorrectly that they were a mixture of the two countries when, in fact, they were Scots who had settled in Ulster before coming to America. As peasants in Scotland in the sixteenth and seventeenth centuries they were dirty, illiterate, superstitious, robust, and cheerful; a scrapping, swearing, swaggering, swilling people who kept themselves notorious by cattle-stealing and feuds. John Knox and the Presbyterian Church had won them over in 1560 by "uplifting their morals and improving their literacy." They were a fecund people living in a barren land, so when James I decided to conquer Papist Ireland by settling these Presbyterian Scots in Northern Ireland, they readily acquiesced. By 1690 some fifty thousand lowland Scots had settled in Ulster.

In the three to five generations they spent in Ulster before migrating to the New World, they kept their identities entirely separate from their Irish neighbors, and they thrived, so much so that Scots-Irish products became serious competition for the English. This was summarily dealt with by the English Parliament by prohibiting export of their wool and linen, raw or cloth, to England or any other country. And when in the beginning of the eighteenth century the Scots-Irish Presbyterians were excluded from legal or military office and the English absentee landlords more than doubled their rents, the New World beckoned and the Scots-Irish emigrated in droves.

By the time of the American Revolution, one-tenth of all Americans were Scots-Irish; they continued to be as fecund as they had been in the Old Country. We have a record in the form of an eighteenth-century journal by a priggish Anglican, the Reverend Woodmason, who, shocked and excited, views young Scots-Irish women in the southwest for the first time:

They wear nothing but thin shifts and a thin petticoat underneath. They are sensual and promiscuous. They draw their shift as tight as possible to the body, and pin it close, to shew the roundness of their breasts, and slender waists (for they are generally finely shaped) and draw their petticoat close to their hips to show the fineness of their limbs—so that they might as well be in *puri naturalibus*.

The Reverend Woodmason also seems to have stubbed his toe hard against the touchy emotionalism of the Scots-Irish about their new frontier religion (Presbyterianism had been replaced by the less intellectual, more hope-giving Methodist and Baptist denominations):

They delight in their present low, lazy, sluttish, heathenish, hellish life, and seem not desirous of changing it. These people despise knowledge, and instead of honoring a learned person ... they despise and ill-treat them ...

No conversions to the Church of England that day.

On the other hand, James Hall from Philadelphia, at his first sight of a Scots-Irish frontiersman, was struck with admiration:

He strode among us with the step of Achilles.... I thought I could see in that man, one of the progenitors of an unconquerable race; his face presented the traces of a spirit quick to resent—he had the will to dare, and the power to execute; there was a something in his look which bespoke a disdain of control, and an absence of constraint in all his movements indicating an habitual independence of thought and action.

In short, they were as wild and as rough and tough a bunch as ever you would be likely to meet in a month of Saturday nights in Glasgow.

Andrew Jackson, the people's hero, might be said to be the Scots-Irish to end all Scots-Irish; he was, in Captain Marvel's parlance, the Big Red Cheese. Other settlers—tamer—were mainly of English and German stock.

William Mansell and his wife settled in Marion County in northeast Alabama not far from the Mississippi state border. Many of his comrades-in-arms would be there before him. According to Joel Palmer, who is related to Elvis through the Mansell line (Joel is the great-great-grandson of William and Morning Dove), almost all the first settlers of Marion County had been with Jackson when he came through there in 1814. Joel says: "The land was up for grabs and the men came back as soon as they got out of the army. I remember an old man called Uncle Philip Barns when I was small telling Dad and me that his pa said Jackson crossed the creek just above where my father still lives. You can see the ruts in the creek bank yet."

Sometime in 1820, William Mansell registered his land claim No. T9–R16–S13 at the courthouse in Pikeville. The Mansells settled down to farming. As the years went by they prospered and William was able to build a substantial house some three miles from the town of Hamilton on a gentle rise in the land, near a main road and with rolling fields in back. It exists today as a picturesque ruin overrun with brush and bramble, having long been abandoned and then struck by lightning some years ago. But one can still see evidence of what a pleasant home it must have been. To the basic structure of a good-size woodframe house, Mansell had added on wings and sloping roofs as the family enlarged.

William and Morning Dove had three surviving children. John Mansell, born in 1828, was the eldest. Next came Morning Dizenie Mansell in 1832, and finally James J. Mansell born in 1835. As it was in this year that Morning Dove died, it can be presumed it had to do with giving birth to him. William, who survived his wife by seven years, did not remarry.

By then the Mansells' position and property in the community were such as to enable their daughter, young Morning Dizenie, to marry the town's leading doctor and large landowner, Dr. Russell Palmer, some fourteen years her senior. They both lived to a ripe old age and had twelve children. Of the boys, three of them, George, Lafayette, and Grant became farmers, one became a minister, and one a merchant. And of the two that became doctors, Dr. Benjamin Palmer had a town named after him and Dr. Alexander Sherman Palmer—a surgeon who practiced in Hamilton—had a distinguished enough career to merit over a page in William S. Biddle's *Notable Men of Alabama* (1893).

Naming a child "Lafayette" means something. It means Liberty, the Declaration of Independence, the American Revolution, and union of the United States. Naming a southern child "Grant" *after* the Civil War in honor of the victorious Union general takes it a step further. It shows us where Russell Palmer's sympathies lay in the conflict. In fact he was outspokenly opposed to secession and loyal to the Union throughout the war, though this did not stop him from tending wounded Confederate soldiers nor looking after families whose fathers and sons had gone to fight.

As for Morning Dizenie, she grew, with age, into something of a matriarchal martinet. Remarks Joel Palmer, "My father said she was very tight on her grandchildren and it seems you walked very softly behind her or she would tan up your behind. My dad thought her to be a nut about cleanness, too." When she died, she was buried in the Palmer family cemetery outside of Hamilton in the Cherokee tradition, with large smooth stones arranged in an Indian mound over her grave.

But much as these descendants of William Mansell's daughter flourished and prospered, and happy as we are for them, they are only next door to Elvis' story.

It is the Mansells' eldest son John who directly concerns us. For he is the great-great-grandfather of Elvis; and his is a very different chronicle. The oldest of the three and therefore the inheritor of the Mansell farm, one would have expected him to have been the soberest, the most responsible. One would have been wrong.

John Mansell, half Scots-Irish, half Indian, seems to have grown up wholly "wild Injun." Although by the time he was twenty-two he had married Elizabeth "Betsy" Gilmore and they would have some nine or ten children together, "settling down" can hardly be the phrase for what he was devoting his life to. John was one of those sexually overactive men who seem intent on populating the universe with children. Both his legitimate and illegitimate descendants still abound in northwest Alabama and in northeast Mississippi. There is much evidence that at some point John added Betsy's sister Rebecca and her children, or rather *their* children, to his ménage.

Joel Palmer comments on the population explosion caused by John Mansell: "All the old people had Indian ways. And Morning Dizenie's sons also carried on the same business, including my grandfather who had at least one illegitimate son. My great-uncle George had fifty, it was said, but I'm not sure of that being true. And having common-law wives was a common thing with my people. This same great-uncle George had several. And his illegitimate children took his name Palmer and go by it now. My great-grandfather, Russell Palmer, took advantage of this sport, too."

If it is going too far to suggest that sexual promiscuity can be inherited, we nevertheless have to look at the fact that the tradition of sexually permissive behavior for men was a legacy of these southwesterners and, as such, accepted by their womenfolk.

By 1880 John Mansell had abandoned the Mansell farm. Through inattention to some country matters—and too much attention to others— he had sold, or had taken away, or had slip away from him, the farm. And his sons, fed up, had years before struck out over the red clay cliffs into northeast Mississippi to seek their fortunes in that new country and homestead near the town of Saltillo, formerly in Itawamba County, but by 1880 part of Lee County, whose county seat—Tupelo—would be the birthplace of Elvis.

So what did the amorous John Mansell do? Why, he takes Betsy and some of their younger children, *and* he takes his other "wife" Rebecca and their children, and he dumps them *all* on his son White Mansell there near Saltillo to make out as best they can. And then he promptly runs off with young Mandy Bennett to Oxford, Mississippi, where he will be born again as 'Colonel' Lee Mansell.

White Mansell (sometimes referred to in records as A. W., but White was what he was always called), who by the abdication of his daddy was to become the head of the Mansell clan, was the third son. When he came to northeast Mississippi at the age of around eighteen to homestead, his farming neighbors were a family called Tackett, originally from Tennessee. Among their children—and there were six—the one that caught his eye was sixteen-year-old Martha who had a twin brother, Jerome.

When Martha turned eighteen and White twenty they were married, on January 22, 1870. She was the daughter of Abner and Nancy J. Burdine Tackett and though Abner was to marry several times after, Nancy is of particular interest to us. According to Elvis' third cousin Oscar Tackett (who shared the same ancestors, Abner and Nancy), Nancy was Jewish. She and Abner had met as schoolmates in Tennessee. Again, names often tell a story and two of Martha's brothers were given Jewish names, Sidney and Jerome.

Ten years later when the census man came around to White's place near Saltillo, here is what greeted him:

Head of the house:	White Mansell
Wife:	Martha (Tackett) Mansell
Children:	Melissa
	Ida

	Jehru
	Lucy (Octavia Luvenia,
	Elvis' maternal grandmother)
Mother:	Betsy (Gilmore) Mansell
Sisters:	Edy Mansell
	Mary Mansell
Aunt:	Rebecca Gilmore
Aunt's children:	Dukie Mansell
	Senna Mansell

In other words, a wife, a mother, four children (more to come), two sisters plus an aunt and her two children (who have the surname Mansell)—that's twelve people White was looking after—quite a full house even for a kin-conscious southerner. Quarter Indian, he was, like his name, the great White Father of the Mansells. Next door to White and his gang lived his brother William and his family, and next door to him, brother George and his family.

And then there was White's sister, Ann Mansell, who had stayed on for a while in Alabama. There seems to have been some confusion as to whether she was indeed White's sister, but Elzie Mansell, Ann and White's great-nephew, confirms it. Sometime in the early 1870s she appears to have popped up to visit her brother and his young bride, Martha. Perhaps she was bored in Alabama; perhaps she missed this particular brother, the White Hope; perhaps she wanted to see what the possibilities were in Mississippi. She was a bright young girl, sassy and spirited. She would become a lofty matriarch and live to a great old age.[2]

An essential to marrying someone is first meeting them. In the 1870s in northeast Mississippi this was almost entirely dependent on geographical proximity. The children of neighbors married each other.

Up around Saltillo way near the Mansell clan lived a Steven S. Smith and his wife Mary and their children Elizabeth, Ann, Wesley (this name turns up with relentless frequency in southwestern genealogies as homage to John Wesley, father of Methodism, who arrived in America in 1736 and by the time he left in 1737 announced that all Georgia was his parish), Pelham, and Leila Love. This youngest daughter, born in 1870, would give Elvis' mother her Bible and her middle name. Boarding with the Smiths was Steven's elder brother, Milege Obediah ("Obe") Smith. Steven Smith ended up as a respected citizen: a Mason and the proud owner of

---

[2] Genealogist Roy Turner's comment on Ann Mansell Smith's photograph (facing p. 112): "The pose is not typical of the times. And does Ann ever appear to be in command of her life! I was really surprised to see the expression and general theme of the picture—it's so posed; it's more of a glamor shot than a lady of that day and age would have taken. It's certainly not the thing you usually find in the ancestors' rogue."

a cotton gin. Obe, alas, did not. And it was Obe, unfortunately, who would set off sparks in Ann Mansell's sunbonnet.

Obe Smith married Ann Mansell on December 13, 1874, when she was twenty (she said) and he was thirty-seven. Perhaps Ann missed never having her daddy around.

Mertice Finley would describe Ann Smith in her later years thus: "What was she like?" And jumping up in demonstration: "The Queen of England! Always stiff, straight, and dignified. Granny Smith never stepped out of her house without a little black hat perched straight on her head, level with her eyes." She was dark-skinned and, when young, her hair was pitch-black.

In twelve years Obe and Ann produced seven children. This seems to be about all Obe ever did produce. Could he read and write? His name is signed on the wedding license with an admirable flourish, but perhaps it was written by an official of the ceremony. In any case, he was never able to give his family a house of their own; they always boarded with others. Six years after their marriage they and their children were still boarding at Thomas Winter's house in Saltillo. After some twenty years of boarding Ann Smith had had enough. Taking her younger children Robert, Hal, Belle, John, and Tabby with her—the older boys Jim and Will could look after themselves—she left Obe, star boarder, and went twenty miles south to a farm in Fawn Grove near the little town of Richmond in Lee County. Obe Smith goes blithely on living and boarding, now with Cindy and Mary Mansell, sisters of Ann and White who apparently took pity on him and let him loaf about their house.

Twenty-five years after her marriage Ann would firmly describe herself as widowed in the 1900 census when in fact the same census reveals a husband perfectly alive and well. And if you look at her gravestone in Unity Cemetery where the Mansells are buried you can make out that she was born 25th Oct. 18—and then it's very hard to read but the third digit looks suspiciously like a four. Eighteen forty-something, perhaps nine, 1849. Could she be being skittish about her birthdate as well as her widowhood? She rigidly gives it as 1854 in all the census reports but until late 1912 births were *not* recorded in either northwest Alabama or northeast Mississippi, so you could tell the census man you were any age you wanted. Neither are birth dates on gravestones always accurate. When an elderly woman died in those days who was around to say exactly how old she was?

At any rate, sassy and grand, Ann Smith, eighty-six or eighty-one years old, is buried next to her husband Obe Smith—who outlived her "censured" wish of 1900 by nine years. Whatever strife they experienced with each other in life they lie demurely together in Unity Cemetery in Lee County surrounded by kin. Ann gets a nice send-off. Her inscription reads:

A precious one to us is gone
A voice we loved is stilled
A place is vacant in our home
That never can be filled.

Ann's move near Richmond was obviously inspired by her brother White's move in that direction at the same time. For, as has been noted, he is the head of the family, the patriarch, and it is he who will always initiate the Mansell moves. By 1900 not only White and his family but also his brothers William and George and their families have moved to the Hussey farm near Richmond where they were working shares. White's wife Martha had died in 1887 and his two eldest girls were married. A widow called Sarah Cordelia ("Dealy") Kemp and her daughter Ann moved in with the fifty-year-old widower and family, and White and Dealy later got married.

There is more than a suggestion of hard times in this move. Eighteen ninety was the year of a nationwide panic, which had a crippling effect on agriculture in the South and specifically on Mississippi's main crop, King Cotton. From homesteaders the Mansells were reduced to that dreaded fate—sharecropping. Living conditions on the Hussey farm were hard. Huge families were sometimes jammed into very small shacks. The young people were too poor to get properly married and sometimes lived together for years before they could put aside even the small sum that the wedding license cost. Yet in this case the image of the wicked land-owner, squeezing his tenants for his own profit, seems not to apply, as the Hussey brothers themselves had nine children each before they could afford to marry their wives.

Life, however, was not unrelievedly grim. Like anyone else, these farm-ers had fun. There was a lot of rousing preaching and a lot of rousing singing. There were also parties and picnics. There were square dances for which the front room of one of the larger dwellings on the Hussey farm would be emptied of its furniture for the occasion. And always there would be at least one fiddle and one guitar livening the festivities as the caller shouted out the figures. "Do-Si-Do," "Four in the Middle," "Weaving the Basket," and "Crow's Nest" were particular ones that these Hussey farm dancers passed down to their descendants.

And the gayest of all the girls at these gatherings, the acknowledged beauty, was the slim, exquisite, tubercular, porcelain-featured, spoiled third daughter of White Mansell, the apple of his eye—Octavia Luvenia

Mansell, who in 1902 had reached the age of twenty-six without being able to decide on whom to bestow her gifts in marriage. As a child her name had been shortened to Lucy and then to Loo. But at the time we are speaking of, at the height of her delicate and intense radiance, there was only one name on earth that could fully express both her physical and incorporeal essence. It was the name by which she was now called, and would be called, for the rest of her life: Doll.

Doll—how the name suited her. A china doll; a broken doll. It suggests pleasure, it suggests coyness. It suggests handle with care. It suggests neatness, a fondness for ornamentation. It suggests someone who would spend a great deal of time and thought on herself, on her appearance. And "Dollie," as she was sometimes called, suggests something too: an essential childishness. Her sister Ida's husband, John King, told his children that she was "the prettiest woman I ever laid eyes on!" But today, a ninety-year-old granny who had been raised on the Hussey farm, and to whom old times are as vivid and clear as the present is dull and muddy, says—her eyes on fire with an indescribable glitter, and in a voice that brooks no doubt that it was making something clear once and for all— "Doll Mansell was a...*flirt*!"

But in the spring of 1903 Doll went from being twenty-six years old to twenty-seven. Perhaps it was the widow Dealy moving into her father's house, and his heart, that gave her the extra push; but she could not put off getting married any longer. Although reluctant to begin this grown-up life of which she was so afraid, she had, in fact, already chosen someone. Perhaps she had chosen him a long way back—or rather, chosen him a long way back to *fall back on*; for in her choice of this man can be seen the evidence of all her anxieties. At least there would be no terror of the unknown. He was a man she had known all her life, a man she had grown up with who had never been far away from her either in the Saltillo area when they were children or in the Richmond area now. He was Obe and Ann Smith's third son, Doll's first cousin. He was Robert Lee Smith, known as Bob.

"Of course Ashley'll marry Melanie," Scarlett O'Hara is told—or told off—"the Wilkes marry their cousins." And true, those fancy folk the Wilkes were forever marrying their cousins. And true, those plain folk, those Mansells (and those Tacketts and Plunketts and Kings all around Lee County), they were bad to marrying their cousins, too. A peculiarity of the old South, we say, endemic on whatever level of wealth or lack of it; and as if that weren't enough, sisters of one family were always marrying brothers of another. Like *Seven Brides for Seven Brothers,* only that took place in the American West. And, going up north, those intermarrying Roosevelts. Or further up to Boston, those intermarrying Cabots and Lowells and Lodges.

So if Elvis' genes are supposed to be (as it has been suggested), too similar for health to Gladys' through cousinship in her generation, there were also—not too many generations back—infusions of blood of two very different races whose strength might be said to be *doubled* by this cousinship.

Genetically speaking, what produced Elvis is quite a mixture. At the beginning, to French Norman blood was added Scots-Irish blood. And when you then add to these the Indian strain supplying the mystery and the Jewish strain supplying spectacular showmanship, and you overlay all this with his circumstances, social conditioning, and religious upbringing—specifically his Southern poor white, First Assembly of God upbringing—you have the enigma that was Elvis.

Bob Smith was a nice young man; actually he was a little younger than Doll—which only proved that in her determination to be babied, age meant nothing. He was strikingly handsome, with his Indian blood coming plainly in his noble brow, his good bone structure, his straight even features, his dark deep-set eyes, and his hair black as water shining in moonlight. He was a powerful-looking man but in fact he was very gentle and very devoted; and he had loved Doll all his life. He was a hard worker but not a skilled one except in the one thing that he had a most definite talent for—and that was not farming. He was, says everyone in Lee County who knew him, a *good* man.

On September 20, 1903, Doll Mansell and Bob Smith were married by the Reverend Martin. (Along with everything else Doll was very religious, and twice on Sundays and twice during the week she went to Church of God meetings in Union Grove.) For her wedding she wore a white embroidered dress, a high starched collar, and a corsage of flowers pinned above her left breast. Bob also wore a high starched collar and a white bow tie. And to emphasize the formality of the occasion he donned a waistcoat under his jacket. On the lapel of his jacket was pinned a button whose legend read GRIT. Actually, *Grit* was the name of a national Sunday newspaper sold in the Richmond area, but one cannot overestimate the significance of Bob wearing this button on his wedding day. It was as if he already knew that grit was going to be needed in large doses for the rest of his life.

As Bob and Doll stood on the threshold of their future, we may wonder how differently they viewed it from William and Morning Dove Mansell. How wide was the gap between the Indian fighter and his Indian wife starting out in 1820 and Bob and Doll starting out in 1903? Leaving aside actual living conditions, for in both cases they may be said to be fairly primitive, one sees the gap between these two generations' hopes and expectations. William Mansell and his generation shared an unquench-able belief that their lives would be rewarded with prosperity and hap-piness if they worked hard enough. But the Smiths could hardly share this confidence. During the intervening eighty years the South had been visited by every conceivable disaster. First there was the Mexican War in 1846–48, with four times as many volunteers from this "new country" (as they called it) as were furnished by all the rest of the states together. The eccentric, swashbuckling dandy, General Winfield Scott of Virginia, had led these troops to a victory for the U.S. government and to a disaster for the soldiers; nearly seven times as many died of disease in Mexico as in battle. Saltillo, in fact, was named after one of the battles, in memory of the returning soldiers' comrades who died. In a diary that recently turned up in Itawamba County, Henry Jackson Lentz (1819–69), a jus-tice of the peace first in Limestone, Alabama, then in Itawamba, Missis-sippi, records over and over again such items as: "25 February 1848: Captain Higgins, 13th Regiment, was discharged in Mexico and died in Vera Cruz."

Yellow fever in Alabama and Mississippi could be depended on to break out every few years. Lentz records in July 1851 twenty-eight deaths within nineteen days; in August 1852, five deaths, in September ten, and in the midst of recording deaths, he states simply, "It is the sickest time I ever saw."

In 1833 in Itawamba County there was a plague of it. A generation later yellow fever devastated the area again; and again in 1878, forty-six towns in Mississippi were hit and three thousand lives lost. One form of the disease was called black vomit and was always fatal. Brown vomit, another form, it was hoped could be overcome. An anguished note of the time has been preserved: "It is not alone to see loved ones die; it is to dread their dying kiss. It is not to watch the dear dead face until the coffin-lid is closed above it, but to turn, shuddering, from the face where you can see a yellow, transfigured mask. Their forms are changed to a poison so deadly that death can be tasted in the air around them."

And then in 1861 came the Civil War with the crushing defeat of the Confederacy and the looting and burning of Southern towns. Lentz notes:

1862, 17th Dec.:   The Yankees took Tupelo about the 17th.
1863, 26th Feb.:   Sam J. Warren's mill was burned by the Yankees the 14th.
1863, 1st March: The Yankees tore up Hardin Patten and Old Man Lastley and others in Itawamba Co., Miss.

1863, 8th May:	Yankees at old Bob Colliers'—took nearly all his and several of his neighbors' horses.
1863, 18th June:	Yankees at Lem Truloves'—burnt his store and gin and Masonic Hall.
1863, 19th June:	The Yankees tore up John Warren; at Dock Davis'. At Jim Bailey's took all of his tobacco—broke Riley Bounds' gun; at J. T. Parkers'; at Eliza Spearman's.
1863, 14th Aug.:	The Yankees at old Bob Collier's—tore him up.
1863, 23rd Dec.:	A raid of 250 cavalry encamped at old Jim Bailey's place—they took J. T. Parker's horse, corn and fodder the night of the 23rd.
1864, 16th July:	Battle near Tupelo, 14th, 15th, 16th.
1864, 18th July:	Battle near Harrisburg.
1865, 1st Jan.:	Yankees took 20 wagons at Parsons Deavors and burnt them. Yankees took 100 wagons and burnt them at the Acock old place and killed 60-odd mules.

Tupelo was said to be one of the last battlefields. Reconstruction followed with the northern exploiters from without and the southern exploiters from within. And, of course, there was King Cotton, causing the exhaustion of the soil. Ironically, Lee and the neighboring counties were in a very fertile area and would have been able to produce anything: fruits, vegetables of all kinds; things you can eat. You cannot eat cotton.

Profoundly paradoxical, not to say downright illogical, are the whims of nature. How else to explain the small-boned, narrow-hipped, childish, consumptively ailing Doll giving birth to nine children, eight of whom would survive? The emphasis should be on the last word of that sentence. In those days of high infant mortality Doll's score was way above average. Should we be surprised that she promptly took to her bed after her first child and remained there for the rest of her life, rarely leaving it and finally exchanging it only for her grave in her fifty-ninth year?

Psychologically speaking, there is a certain type of tubercular woman. The consumptive Marguerite Gautier is well known in fiction as the Lady of the Camellias. And in reality, there was Vivien Leigh. Beauty and charm and sexual desire seem to be inextricably woven into this disease.

Doll, unlike the fashionable European consumptive of her time, was not able to benefit from holidays in the Alps or smart watering places during the summer heat, though perhaps the hilly air of Lee County might have been of some aid to her, if she had gotten out of bed often enough to breathe it. But the summers are long—April to September—and they are faintingly, inescapably, 96°F-in-the-front-porch-shade hot. Was it the salubrious hill climate that kept her so long alive, that kept her childbearing for an incredible twenty years—her last child being born when she was forty-six? Perhaps it was Bob's love that kept her alive.

People in the area were very frightened of TB. It was thought to be as infectious as yellow fever, and known TB victims were hustled off in quarantine—huddled together in specially built compounds where they stayed on in dreadful conditions until they recovered or died. It would have been unthinkable for Bob even to have considered doing this to Doll.

But there is a family's own reaction to invalidism, and there is the outsider's reaction to it. And it must be said that to most people who knew the Smiths, Doll seemed merely to be "enjoying bad health," a common enough term used to reveal healthy people's impatience with a bedridden woman who does not prove her illness by dying within a reasonable length of time.

THREE

Gladys

After their marriage Doll and Bob moved in with his mother Ann. Their first child, a girl, was born ten months after their marriage and died a year and two months later. Her name was Effie. Next came Lillian in 1906. And after her came Levalle in 1908.

By then White Mansell had moved from the Hussey farm to his own farm in Pontotoc County, the county next to Lee. Soon after followed the Smiths: Granny Ann Smith, with her twenty-four-year-old Johnny (who would remain with her, unmarried, for the rest of his life) and the sickly twenty-one-year-old Tabby who would die in 1919, and Bob and Doll with their two children Lillian and Levalle also moved—lock, stock and barrel— to shelter once more under White's protective wing. In 1910 Doll gave birth to another girl, Rhetha.

And then on April 25, 1912, she gave birth to yet another girl—Elvis' mother—Gladys Love Smith.[3] Four girls in a row for a farming family with an invalid mother did not augur well for the future. They would work in the fields along with the men but they would not be able to start as young nor work as hard as boys would. That was a fact of life.

Lee County is a pretty county with winding, sand-colored roads and clumps of green trees so still they look sculptured. An abandoned shack stands on the brow of a hill, stark and weathered and, because of the purity of its outline, it takes on a primordial significance. A lone chimney

---

[3] Both Elvis and Marilyn Monroe, the two most potent sex symbols of this century, had mothers named Gladys.

of red brick—all that's left of a house that burned down—still stands on a green slope, its gothic lines slicing the sky; and settles itself immovably in one's memory. There is an abundance of woods, of trees along the roads, and silver shining lakes, and streams that shine and blink like mica in the hot sun. But you cannot see very far in any direction you look in Lee County; the contours of the land prevent this. The horizon meets a tree, a house, a hill, the vista ends abruptly.

Pontotoc County is different. It is flat land and you can see its cultivation. In the glitter and deep stillness of a southern afternoon you can see stretching before you sunlit fields and pastures and orchards glistening with fruit. And you feel a sense of peace and calmness and harmony contemplating these free reaches. In the summertime there is a scented profusion of flowering shrubs: purple althea, bright pink crepe myrtle, lilac, honeysuckle, and the trumpet creeper catalpa. There are fields of red clover. There are pine trees and native cedar and native walnut trees and dogwood and magnolia, elm, silver poplar, wild cherry, and plum trees. The cotton bolls in the fields smell like sweet dust. An onlooker watches a silver silo as the setting sun turns it into icy blue flames. Everything is still, silent. The yellow-green light of the dying sun lingeringly pales to a rose lavender and the trees blacken into silhouettes against the glow. At last the twilight falls in a soft dusty blue. Pontotoc is a beautiful county.

To the onlooker Gladys' first sight of the world would have been an entirely pleasant one: lovely landscape and picturesque poverty. The Smiths' house—you would have to call it a shack—would have been made of Mississippi pine—the outside walls built of boards put together by the tongue-and-groove method. These closely joined boards produce a wall that is airtight and watertight. Inside, it would have a "breezeway," a hall running through the center from the front door to the back door. The front room would contain only one proper iron bedstead covered with a patchwork quilt. The bed would be placed diagonally against two walls, this being the position in which it would take up the least amount of space, while at the same time allowing room on either side of the bed to get in and out of it. All the children, except the youngest, who always slept in the same bed with its parents, slept on what were called "made beds" on the floor. Pallets were stuffed with clean soft crabgrass and sewn into what they called a thicket. And they all slept in the same room. What would they feel witnessing the primal act? Did they merely ignore it as a grown-up activity and therefore no concern of theirs? Did they think they had discovered the secret of life? Or did they, like children all over the world catching their parents at it, get it all wrong?

In 1915 Doll gave birth to her first boy, Travis. In 1917 she gave birth to another boy, Tracy.

There were now six Smith children on White Mansell's farm. There were other Mansells there, too, of course. Gains Mansell was there. He was White's nephew. He had married his cousin, Ada, Doll's sister, and had become a preacher.

Abruptly in 1917 the Smiths—all of them, Granny Smith, Bob and Doll and their children—went back to Lee County, again to the Richmond area, this time to the small community of Gilvo, some four miles from Tupelo. Lillian, the eldest Smith girl, was eleven at the time and remembers the journey in an open wagon because she was fascinated, passing them on the road, by another family traveling in a wagon in which she counted twenty little children, their heads like a row of watermelons.

White had made his last Mansell move and would stay on in Pontotoc for the rest of his life—living, as befits a patriarch, well into his seventies.

Why then were the Smiths making this long move?

Mertice Finley remembers the Smiths simply turning up one day out of the blue and settling into the Whitehead house, "the sorriest shack on the Wilburn farm," across the road from the Finley farm. It had only two rooms. Next door to it, adorned in her little black hat, lived Granny Smith with her son Johnny. They were sharecroppers.

Bob Smith, Mertice remembers, was just no good at farming, hard as he tried. She remembers watching him one day with a new horse, trying to train it to the plow and not being able to direct it into the furrows and losing control over it, having the horse escape from the yoke, and having to chase after it and get it back. And then starting all over again, trying to hitch it up and not being able to master that, and finally giving up. She thought maybe he hadn't been brought up to farming but then Johnny came over and was able to manage the horse all right.

What *were* the Bob Smiths doing in Gilvo and where did they come from, a lot of people wondered. One man now a senior citizen, and originally from those parts, did not have to wonder; he knew. "Run out of Alabama, Freedom Hill district. Caught moonshining." He was only geographically wrong. For the one thing Bob Smith could do, the one thing he had an incredible knack for, was moonshining. Bob Smith, a poor farmer, made good moonshine.

Making moonshine (bad moonshine tasted like kerosene, good moonshine like bourbon; peach brandy, which Bob also made, tasted like brandied peaches with the kick of a mule) was illegal in Mississippi even before Prohibition, but to a certain voluble sector of the public it was *not* unlawful. It was lawful as hell, and no handful of government or state legislators were going to tell them what to drink and what not to. And that was *their* law, their higher law, if you like, of independence! Was it, or was it not, a free country?

"February 14, 1868: Old Bill Parker began to make whisky," noted that old busybody Lentz. But moonshining was illegal—no getting around that—and most people would much rather have drunk it than made it. Those government men would come down from the north and you could get caught, and then you could be in big trouble, if not dead. The only thing to do when you got wind of a raid was to "git." So Bob got out of Pontotoc.

Cully Mitchell lived in Parkertown a few miles away from Gilvo and fondly remembered the moonshining days. He was just a youngster at the time and Bob Smith, the master, taught him and his friends the art. First you had to make sure that the still was buried in the hills with a good solid surrounding wall of bushes, brambles, and briars thick and fierce enough to discourage discovery, and a nice dank swamp full of water moccasin snakes was not a bad idea to have in back. Bob would retire to his still for a week at a time. The recipe for moonshine was simplicity itself: corn, sorghum molasses, and sugar thrown into a vast cauldron over a fire and allowed to ferment for three or four days—he would make forty gallons at a time. But it was the distillation of it that separated the men from the boys. Carefully you ran it through a copper worm pipe over and over and over again till all the impurities were distilled out and what you had left was a pure searing draft of "white lightning."

But while Joe Kennedy and Al Capone were getting rich and building empires out of bootlegging, Bob Smith was only meagerly supplementing an already meager income. During Prohibition the Mob came down and tried to organize the moonshiners, but the proud Scots-Irish independence asserted itself and the hoodlums were told to go home. They went.

From time to time pressure from the government would be put on the farm owners of the county. Cully Mitchell's father-in-law, Farmer Parker, told six men on his farm who were making moonshine to quit making it. They didn't. It was the early days of Prohibition and it was getting doubly dangerous but they kept right on moonshining. So he rounded up the men thinking they would be tried locally and let off with a stiff warning. Instead, the first thing he knew the whole thing snowballed into a regular trial at the Lee County courthouse in Tupelo. Farmer Parker had a sky-blue fit.

He was subpoenaed as a reluctant witness and watched the proceedings with mounting horror. On the first day he took a couple of nips to steady himself. On the second day, still not called, he took a couple more.

By the third day, well into his cups, he hit the witness stand, roared out, "I know a lot more than I'm going to tell you!" and was thrown in jail for being drunk. The six men got a year in jail.

"People did it," said Cully Mitchell, "because there was nothing else to do. But some got in the way of it. They moved to Freedom Hill across the border where most of the moonshining went on. They got used to being outlaws, got a taste for stealing cars and the rest of it. They ended up bad. Dead or in jail."

This did not happen to Bob Smith. He never "got in the way of it" nor did he end up in Freedom Hill or in jail. This was probably because moonshining was not his sole occupation, and he only did it irregularly in a desperate attempt to support his ever increasing family. In 1919 Doll gave birth to a girl, Clettes, and in 1922 to a boy, John.

Bob and his family worked shares on the Wilburn farm for four years. That was the longest they ever stayed in one place. But it was a bad time perhaps because he wasn't supplementing his income by moonshining—the precariousness of this occupation having been brought home to him by having so nearly gotten caught in Pontotoc—and also because, besides his brother Johnny, the only field hands in his family were Lillian, Levalle, Rhetha, and Gladys who, by the time they left, were fifteen, thirteen, eleven, and nine respectively.

After they left the Wilburn place, the whole Smith family, including Granny Smith and Johnny, moved every two years, each time with the hope that things would be better; that the soil would be better, the cotton crop better, the shack they lived in better, that they might be able to make ends meet at the end of the year. The Smiths were still enough of an early American family to have an unquenchable belief that the next move would somehow present them with the prosperity that had escaped them before.

They moved to Marion Parker's dairy farm.

They moved to Isom Parker's place (Bob Smith's sister Belle had married a Parker).

They moved to Marvin Lamb's place.

They moved to Jim Love's place.

They moved to Luther Lummus' place.

They moved to Dennis Brook's place.

They moved to Harry Hallmark's place and their shack burned down and Griffin Barber's family took them in. And all the time from Parkertown to Eggville to Mooreville to Nettleton to Spring Hill they never moved beyond a radius of ten miles. Sharecroppers did that. And whenever they moved the people whose farm they were moving to would come for them in their wagon and load up all their furniture and animals and children and deposit them on the land they were going to work.

Throughout his life, besides sharecropping and moonshining, Bob worked at anything he could find. Lily Mae Irwin particularly remembers Bob walking seven miles to the Hebron community and seven miles back every day for weeks in winter to dig a ditch through a bottomland on Will Herring's place. He made crossties for railroad tracks. He swept— or, as they say, he scratched—cemeteries; graveyards had no grass in those days and they had to be kept weeded. The one he had the most liking for was the cemetery next to the Presbyterian Church in Spring Hill. He tended it with special care and told members of the congregation he would like to be buried there. He got his wish: he and Doll are buried there along with their daughter Rhetha and Lillian's first husband Charlie Mann—all in unmarked graves. "Bob was a good man," says Lily Mae Irwin. "He worked hard but the large family and the invalid wife—he just could not make it. You never saw Doll unless you went into the house." "Everything would go out of that house as quick as it went in," adds her husband Len. In other words, any money Bob brought in would immediately be used to purchase Doll's necessary luxuries. Doll would send one of her daughters to Saltillo to buy material to make herself dressing gowns, fancy side combs for her hair of which she was especially fond (the collection is now in the possession of one of her nieces), lavender water to cool her fevered brow, peppermint drops, and medicines prescribed by Dr. Pyle. Under her pillow she kept a mirror and comb in readiness for receiving visitors.

From her temperament, from her character, from her occasional TB flare-ups and constant invalidism, Doll had unquestionably abdicated the role of John Steinbeck's pioneer mother. Emotionally this had a profound effect on all her children. They would "look to her for joy" and she would give them sorrow and anxiety. They would "look to her to defend them" and she would lie helplessly in bed. Instead of having the "sure, cool, quiet hand of a healer," her hand was nervous and distraught. Yet, still, she was the person of greatest power; ruling through weakness, her bed her throne. "When a girl has no mother to palpitate for her she must needs be on the alert," wrote Edith Wharton.

What chance would Gladys have in life?

Says Herman Irwin, Len and Lily Mae's son: "In all of Lee County there was no girl brought up under more adverse conditions socially, economically, and intellectually than Elvis' mother."

How would Gladys survive? By what doggedness, perseverance, persistence, diligence, tenacity, and assiduousness would she surmount the
adversity of her conditions?

According to her sister Lillian, Gladys as a young child was languid
and listless. "Hog-lazy; that's what we called her. We'd be shaking out
the beds and you'd turn around and there'd be Gladys lying across one
asleep." Could Gladys have been childishly, unconsciously emulating her
mother, the attention-getter, the central focus of the family when inside
the house? Very likely, for she presented an altogether different picture
to the outside world. To outsiders she was, above all, sweet. That is the
word most often used in describing her. Mertice Finley: "She was a sweet,
chubby, attractive little thing." Vera Turner, Cully Mitchell's daughter:
"She had the sweetest disposition of all the Smith girls." Lily Mae Irwin:
"She was a very sweet person." She was by other people's descriptions
lovable, winsome, and winning. How nicely and politely she would ask
the Finleys for food. How politely and willingly she would run back home,
as Mrs. Finley directed her, to fetch a bucket so that Mrs. Finley could
fill it with their leftover scraps. She was not at all boisterous or demanding
or importunate like the other Smith children. Hunger had taught Gladys
manners, just as it taught her to show the friendly, pleasant, outgoing
side of her nature, the side that depended on other people for its very
existence.

It was Lillian, the eldest, who took over the role of the mother in the
Smith family. She did the cooking and cleaning, looked after the housekeeping, took care of Doll and supervised the children. It is her observations of Gladys—inside and out—that are the sharpest. "Inside, Gladys
was very highly strung, very nervous, very scary. She was frightened by
all kinds of things—by thunderstorms and wind. She was always hearing
noises outside at night and imagining there was someone in the bushes."
A legacy from her moonshining daddy? "But she was stubborn, too. You
couldn't make her do anything she didn't want to. Headstrong, you could
say she was."

From her earliest years there was a deep gap between Gladys' private
fears and her public face. And so it would be throughout her life until
the last three years when the gap would close and there was nothing but
fear.

Like all the other children from the area, Gladys went to school only
four months out of the year—in the winter. For the rest of the year she
was needed in the fields: hoeing cotton, chopping cotton, picking cotton,
pulling corn. Gladys was not "good with books," as they say, and though
she took them home at night to do her homework, she rarely looked at

them; they didn't interest her. Nevertheless Gladys loved school because of the chance it gave her to be with other boys and girls. And especially she loved the one sport that girls were allowed to play: basketball. In this she triumphed. She may have had less materially than any of her classmates but none of them could match her in her physical skills, in dribbling and passing and faking. So formidable a forward was she on her team that there was only one person adroit enough to guard her and that was no less personage than the basketball coach herself, Miss Mary Harville.

Classmates remember Gladys at thirteen, a large girl for her age, exactly the same size as her coach. They were a dexterous duet: Miss Harville chasing the laughing Gladys up and down the court, the latter deftly outmaneuvering her teacher as she suddenly ducked under her arms and scored a basket. After a game of basketball, Gladys had a gaiety about her that was close to ecstasy. She also liked to play party games like hide-and-seek. She loved blindman's buff and was always suggesting they play it in the school yard. What did she get out of the game? Two things—first, when "it," she was good at it, and though blindfolded, her fingers had a sensitivity that could immediately identify which of her playmates she was touching; and second, as a player, she liked being chased and caught.

That would be about the time the Smiths were at Marion Parker's dairy farm. Gladys' early morning chore was milking the Parker cows. For this she would receive half a pail of sorghum molasses which she would drink on the way to school.

Alderman John Marcy, himself a poor orphan until Farmer Jim Love took him in, is nevertheless not uncritical of the Smiths and likes to dwell on the more lurid aspects of their poverty: "They were so poor they wore hog rings in their shoes—wore 'em on every toe to keep the soles of their shoes on. They were like a mule train—they just kept on moving." Then he remembers his own hard times: "Everybody in this county like to starve to death when the banks failed in 1932. You carried ashes from the fireplace to the stove and back again because if you let the fire go out you didn't have a nickel to buy matches to start the fire again." Then back to the Smiths: "Sometimes they were asked to move on," he says ominously. According to him, they weren't popular; they were charity cases. He was also outspokenly against the idea of having the Bankhead Highway—Highway 78 which runs near Elvis' birthplace—being renamed Elvis Presley Highway. After all, he points out, it was Senator Bankhead of Alabama (Tallulah Bankhead's father) who built the highway—not Elvis.

Against her background of hardship and deprivation Gladys, at sixteen, threw herself into life with a ferocious energy. Several things happened which successfully kept the dark side of her nature at bay. Her nubile adolescence flowered into beauty; her chubbiness was transformed into graceful curves. Her straight hair, black as her father's, which she parted on the side, lay across her high, clear forehead smooth and sleek as a wing. Her dark eyes were round and large and shone under her dark arched brows. The contours of her face were still childishly round but her features had emerged from her puppy fat. Her nose was small and delicately carved, as was her mouth, and her sweet smile deepened the voluptuous curve of her cheeks—that special whorl of the cheekbone that would so enhance Elvis' smile.

The Smiths were now living in a small log cabin at Luther Lummus' farm. It was in the Spring Hill community a few miles southeast of Saltillo. Grace Reed and her husband lived on her Uncle Luther's farm as well. She had five children and badly needed someone to help her out. "Gladys Smith," she says, "was just my answer." Gladys came every afternoon after school. She did the laundry and the household chores and sometimes in the evening attended the children.

"I can see Gladys coming down this road now," says Grace, "her arms swinging away at her sides. Her little deaf brother Tracy would be with her, too. Only he'd be walking on his *hands*." Tracy's deafness was the result of whooping cough when he was two. Somehow he was able to talk but very indistinctly. "Johnny makepit! Johnny makepit!" was his way of telling someone that his brother Johnny had just been bitten by a snake. He compensated for his disability by developing his prowess as an acrobat and it was said (surely with southern hyperbole) that he could easily walk the twelve miles from Saltillo to Tupelo on his hands.

One afternoon, when Gladys arrived at work at the Reeds', there was something that had not been there before: a brand new Victrola! Grace had also bought some Jimmie Rodgers records and she was playing them. Gladys promptly fell in love with the Victrola, with the music and with the famous Jimmie Rodgers, a Mississippian. Rodgers mostly sang, suggestively, about love—love gone bad and love that was good; sometimes he sang yearningly about faraway places, or knowingly about trains and departures. His attitude would switch from a bubbly arrogance to mournful heartbreak—and underneath (though never mawkishly) there would be undertones of massive anguish, for he was dying of TB.

Grace showed Gladys how to play the Victrola and told her she could play it whenever she wanted to, for she saw how much it livened her up and quickened her work. For days at a time Gladys only played "Mean Mama Blues." It was her favorite. Then "Any Old Time" took its place.

Then she favored one of the "Blue Yodels." Then another. And then she went back to her first love, "Mean Mama"; any record-lover knows how it goes.

One evening when Luther and Maude Lummus and Grace and her husband and two other friends, who had dropped in for a visit, were all there, Grace put on Jimmie Rodgers' "Corinna, Corinna," and Gladys began dancing to it. At Cully Mitchell's not long before, she had watched Joe Green, who always knew the latest dance steps, do the Charleston; and now Gladys flung herself into a Charleston: her shoulders shaking, her hips rolling, her knees flashing, her legs kicking so high and fast there seemed to be ten of each of them; her hair came loose and tumbled over one eye; her shoe flew off and she kicked off the other one. Then her bare feet really got a grip on the floor. Gladys threw herself into the Charleston with the same energy that she had thrown herself into basketball when she was thirteen. But there was a great difference. She was not playing a sport now, she was *dancing*.

When one says she was dancing, one is not talking about tap, toe, or ballet; or ballroom or square-dancing, or "round dancing," which is what they call it in Mississippi when two people dance together; one is talking about "buck" dancing which is one person dancing alone. Gladys revealed her innermost self to Jimmie Rodgers' rhythm and melody and suggestive words in such a way that although it was for the appreciation of other people, it was still the expression of Gladys' most private impulses of personal freedom and eroticism. Buck dancing—really good buck dancing—is done only by switching off your mind and allowing your body to take over; and stepping into the rhythm, rejoicing and jubilating in the surrounding shower of notes and obeying the words of the song. Gladys could do it.

The words of "Corinna, Corinna" are a masterful balance of yearning and bawdiness, and Gladys' dance matched them:

> *Corinna, Corinna*
> *Where you been last night?*
> *Cause your hair's all messed up*
> *And your clothes don't fit you right.*
>
> *Corinna, Corinna*
> *Where you been so long?*
> *I ain't had no loving*
> *Since you been gone....*

Grace says whenever she watched Gladys dance to "Corinna, Corinna," she was so stirred up she began to cry.

By the end of the evening, Gladys was feeling very different from the way she had at the beginning. There was Miss Grace in tears and everybody else who had watched her dance was smiling at her in a way they never had before. These smiles were not like the smiles she had hitherto been awarded for being a "good girl"—that is, for getting all the ironing done in one day. These smiles had in them a touch of surprise instead of a touch of condescension; a touch of awe, and more than a touch of enjoyment. It made Gladys feel good to see everyone feeling so happy. For a young girl who knows her family has always been an object of pity—if not scorn—the thrill of having the power to cheer people up cannot be overestimated. For that's what Farmer Lummus himself said— and meant it. He said that he would go over to the Smiths every night in his truck especially to pick up Gladys and take her over to his place, the big farmhouse, so that she could dance for them and cheer them up.

Many years later when they watched Elvis on television doing *his* buck dance they would say, "Elvis got it honest. Gladys had rhythm."

Has anyone ever successfully described what it does to a young girl when she discovers she can *dance*? How it transforms her? For you can see it happening before your very eyes, like a moonflower opening at moonrise; you can actually see how this kind of coordination gives her confidence; changes her posture, the way she holds her head, points her feet. And you can see dancing becoming a craze with her and hear the record player on from the minute she comes home from school until her father, reaching the end of his rope, shouts out, "Shut that damn thing off!"

Now when Gladys went to parties everyone asked her to Charleston— and even if they didn't, she did anyway if she felt like it. "She was fast and fun," says Hod Harris. "She didn't miss a step." "Hot as a pistol," says John Marcy. "She was just crazy about buck dancing," says Ophelia Harris, lowering her voice as if she were saying something not quite nice.

Gladys Smith had the same real name that Mary Pickford, America's sweetheart, was born with. But they didn't call her Mary Pickford. They called her after America's favorite hoyden—Clara Bow. It was easy to see why. There was something about Gladys that instantly attracted one at first sight, something passionate that could not be ignored. They called her Clara Bow because she had *It*.

Yet Lillian remembers how frightened Gladys was at the first boy who asked her if he could walk her home. Apparently she took off her shoes and ran. When he caught up with her she made him walk on one side of the road while she walked on the other. But that was when she was a mere child of fourteen. From the age of sixteen on, the blossoming Gladys dated a lot.

The Charleston dance craze had invaded America. Fourteen-year-old Ginger Rogers, the Charleston champion of Texas, had Charlestoned her way to New York. Seventeen-year-old Lucille LeSueur from Missouri had Charlestoned her way to Joan Crawford and Hollywood.

Movies were shown every Saturday night in Saltillo right in the center of town, hoisted on a flatbed truck. Did sixteen-year-old Gladys Smith, watching Joan Crawford in *Our Dancing Daughters*, dream of going to Hollywood? Did she not? Didn't every American girl in the twenties who had been told more than once (and Gladys was told a lot), "You ought to be in pictures," think—Well, why not? Movies still didn't talk and there were only the odd (very odd) sound effects and musical scores, so you didn't have *words* to worry about. Wasn't some nobody almost every single day magically transformed into a somebody by a once-in-a-lifetime break? Of course, Gladys' dream would only last the space of the film and then ... after all, you lived from day to day, you got by, you didn't make plans about a never-never future. So it was back to housework and the fields. The dream sank, but *not* without a trace. She would pass her Hollywood dream on to her son.

Meanwhile, one by one, Gladys' older sisters were getting married. The third sister, Rhetha, was the first one. In 1929 she ran off with a man called Loyd, a field hand who hadn't been in the area very long. Then Lillian, after a proper courtship, married Charlie Mann. Then Levalle married Ed Smith (no relation).

In about 1930 Bob Smith heard through his friends the Irwin family— father Dave, son Len, and wife Lily Mae—who ran a general store and a peddling wagon on Burk's farm and also worked shares, that there was a house and twenty-five acres of cotton land plus five acres of corn land right next to theirs that was now untenanted. Miracle of miracles, Bob was able to get a loan from the bank and gave the money to the Irwins' store for credit to buy flour, sugar, coffee, snuff, and side meat, and he and his family moved in. "It seemed like the Promised Land to him," says Len. The house was of a good size and in good condition; the nicest house the Smiths ever had. It even had hedge roses growing around the front door.

Gladys had been dating Pid Harris. Then she began dating Rex Stamford. It was developing into a serious courtship. "Rex claimed Gladys but she didn't claim him," states Vera Turner. "He wanted to marry her. He was crazy about her. It wasn't his fault they quit. It was hers. She turned him down." Gladys turned Rex down and then, hot as a pistol, she turned around and walked herself up Fool's Hill—which means exactly what it sounds like it means. Gladys had fallen head over heels in love with a young farmer on Burk's place and she ran off with him and, swiftly tumbling down Fool's Hill, returned home again. It seems that the young farmer was married. And had second thoughts about it all. On the second day. Nobody knew of this escapade—well, not for sure. There was some talk, of course.

But Gladys, without a mother to palpitate for her, was on the alert. So that when one of Jessie Bell's daughters, who for some time had been quietly watching the progress of this romance and had noticed when they were picking cotton that Gladys always somehow or other contrived to be not only in the same row as this young married farmer but also as close to him as possible—practically on top of him—began to make some pointed remarks to Gladys, one thing led to another. Accusations were leveled—and hotly denied; accusations were reasserted—and met with personal remarks of a highly disparaging nature. Words then turned to blows. The two girls began slapping each other and pulling each other's hair until, says Hod Harris, people had to step in and separate them. A girl without a mother to defend her, without even an older brother to protect her, learns early to stand up for herself.

Gladys kept her head high. And her clothes neat. "Gladys always looked nice," says Lily Mae Irwin. "She always wore pretty dresses." Erlene Horton remembers girlishly admiring Gladys when she came round to show off a new dress she'd just made. Vera Turner still has the sewing machine (and it still works) with which she and Gladys used to make dresses. It was common practice at the time and would continue to be throughout the forties that if one family had a desired object—a sewing machine, or a camera, a Victrola, a radio—they would share the use of it with the neighbors.

So Gladys looked nice. And bought things. Lily Mae Irwin remembers Gladys and her twelve-year-old sister Clettes in and out of the store sixty times a day. They would only buy one item at a time—snuff, for instance, which temporarily stills the pangs of hunger—and then they would come back again for a rope of licorice. And then they would come back again for a bottle of Nehi. And then come back for a bottle of Grove's Chill Tonic for Doll. And then come back again for peppermint sticks. Why should the rich have a monopoly on life's pleasures?

Bob made one crop on Burk's farm. And he made some moonshine, too. Rather daringly—or desperately (this was in winter when food was low)—he didn't go into the hills to make it, he made it in the storm shelter in back of his house. Dave Irwin, Len's father, caught on to it when Bob put in a big order for sugar at the store. "You moonshining?" he asked. Bob admitted it. "Well, just don't sell it around here," he warned.

Bob, alas, did not sell it anywhere. A few weeks later a deeply troubled Dr. Pyle spoke to Len Irwin: "I've just been over to Bob Smith's. He's got pneumonia and I can't do a thing about it. He won't last the week."

Bob died the next day. He had not been sick long. It was completely sudden, completely unexpected. They didn't even have time to pray for him. And it was, of course, a shock to everyone who knew the Smiths that it was Bob who had died, not the sickly Doll.

To the family it was a catastrophe which, in practical terms, they could not deal with. "They didn't even have a winding sheet for him," says Lily Mae Irwin. She had to bring one of her own sheets over to the Smiths to wrap poor Bob's body in.

Bob Smith, lover of Doll, tenant farmer, moonshiner, odd-job man, who had pinned the button GRIT to his lapel on his wedding day, had been the keystone of his family's rickety structure, and when this keystone, though worn and eroded, who had supported the family walls all this long time was brusquely punched out by death, the walls caved in.

But first there was the family's grief. It was intense, deep, and protracted. Strangers are always surprised at how much southern families touch one another, hug one another, kiss and squeeze their children's cheeks. Each other was really all the Smiths had—day in, day out, and in the closest proximity. To have wrenched away from you so abruptly the father you have lived with in the same two (though ever-changing) rooms, have worked in the same fields with, have eaten at the same table with every single day of your life, is grave indeed.

All these southerners held life most dearly; took death most seriously. This would be considered a paradox in view of the sometimes fatal testiness and touchiness of those Scots-Irish-Indian hills. Of the previous century the indefatigable Lentz reports:

1850, Aug. 13:	David B. Holis had three men and seven women taken with a peace warrant.
1850, Aug. 21:	Kelly Stigall hit William Lanman on the head with a long bullet.
1851, Jan. 15:	Alex A. Whitehead stabbed David B. Foley in Rogersville till he died.
18—, Feb. 18:	Joshua James and William Lentz' son had a fight.
1852, Dec. 25:	Dorn Patton's son-in-law was stabbed and died.
1856, Feb. 6:	John Parker fought his old gray-headed father (Micajah Parker, Sr.)
1856, Apr. 30	Elizabeth A. Parker stuck adze in J. T. Parker.
1857, Aug. 28:	Mr. Gray killed Robert Abernathy in Pontotoc County, Miss.

1858, Jan. 18:   Parson Sparks stole John Dulaney's daughter to marry her and Jim Dulaney and Parson Sparks had a fight.

1858, Dec. 2:   John Bess stabbed Wright Acock on the evening of the first and he died the evening of the second.

1859, May 28:   Jack Warren shot at Bob Collier and did not hit him.

1861, Mar. 20:   Mr. Bohanen killed Agrippa Pearce, a boy.

1861, June 17:   Burzeala Stone knocked down old man Parker and hurt him very bad.

1861, Nov. 25:   The Lees and Samples fought with sticks and knives and some of them got hurt.

Hotblooded—say violent—and warmhearted—say tender—perhaps best explains the paradox.

In any case the Smiths were, by the testimony of a neighbor, Bill Parham, "very poor people but good and peaceful."

All the people in the area who had known Bob in his fifty-odd years and who were still around, came to the Smiths to view the body and pay their respects to the widow. This was a tradition that was strictly observed.

Mr. Raper, the undertaker who also ran a dry goods store, supplied— or rather donated—the casket. Bob Smith was buried in an unmarked grave in the Spring Hill Cemetery.

It was one of the few wishes granted to him in his entire life.

The bereaved family, however, were not granted their wish of continued tenure at Burk's farm. An invalid mother, nineteen-year-old Gladys, her three younger brothers, and her twelve-year-old sister were not going to be able to bring in the crop. So after Bob's death they had to go.

But where was there to go? The economics of the situation were as follows: Someone had to look after Doll. But whoever was to do it would not at the same time be able to earn a full-time living, which was essential to their situation. Thus Doll went to live with her second married daughter, Levalle, and her husband, Ed. Travis found work as a hired hand and the rest of the Smiths, with Granny Smith and Johnny, moved back to Eggville to stay with another of Granny Smith's sons. The family, though fragmented, was not split; it would reform in different patterns down through the years.

But at this sudden alteration of her life, Gladys slipped back into her early listlessness and lethargy, becoming almost childish. All her previous existence had been lived on the cutting edge of poverty but always with the same members of her family and under the same familiar circumstances. Her one rash grab at the pursuit of happiness had been a notable failure. She was crushed by her father's death. If only she'd been more noticing of her daddy... even though it had all happened so quickly...

On top of it all, there was the pressing necessity of earning a living.

She must get herself a job—and a full-time one—not just seasonal field work or part-time cleaning and looking after children.

"Gladys got herself into such a state," says a friend, "that her legs would start shaking every time she was fixing to go out of the house. It was pitiful. The only way she'd get out was when we'd go to a church meeting."

Very near Eggville was the Church of God and Prophecy in Union Grove, Parkertown. It was the church the family belonged to: Bob had taken them to it whenever they lived close enough. Both as a little child and as an adolescent, Gladys had attended.

This church, in Gladys' time, used to have what they called "poundings." It was their way of welcoming new people of their sect who had just moved into the community. Each family of the congregation was given a letter of the alphabet and they would supply the food or household staple of that alphabet letter to the newcomers at a housewarming. Gladys had responded gratefully to this warm and filling gesture and began to go to church regularly.

When Gladys had attended church as a youngster her mind no doubt was elsewhere. But now she listened to her preacher with the desperation of the lost. And if she had heard what is heard in that same church today, she no doubt must have felt that he was talking directly to her:

We see people who has misfortunes and say, 'I wonder what they did wrong.' But their greatness is in their misfortune. Their greatness is in holding their confidence in God. Joseph still maintained his greatness in God. Our spirit today will have a lot to do with what we have to do tomorrow. How should we respond to the past? Forget the past and look to the future. We're all going to make it, aren't we? We all need to be lifted up by the Word of God. I've been raised up—I've been healed and that's because I'm serving God. If you feel alone, we have got a heaven full of angels. Oh, glory to God. It's great going to bed at night and to know, thank God, that we are covered up with the blood of Jesus. The most surest thing to know is that your life is in the hands of God. And it is not wrong to cry for help—and it is not wrong to cry for mercy—and it is not wrong to cry for love—and it is not wrong to let God in on your planning.

Gladys must have responded, as the rest of the congregation, with "Amen to that," "Oh God, I love you," "Hallelujah!," "Praise the Lord from whom all blessings flow," and "Thank you, Jesus."

And then, the *singing* at these Holiness churches! To say a southerner can sing is like saying a southerner can breathe. Nevertheless, attending an all-day sing at the Presbyterian church at Spring Hill (with an hour out for a sumptuous buffet on the grounds), one hears a marked difference. The singing there is excellent—professional; each voice true to its range and key and all blending together in mellifluous harmony. But it is churchy-hymny-organy music. A typical hymn: "O careless soul, oh

heed the warning ... oh how sad to face the judgment to meet the Lord."
The singing in the Holiness churches is, well, something else. Typical
hymns: "Love Lifted Me" and "He Took My Sins Away and Keeps Me
Singing Every Day." They are singing to Jesus, but they are singing the
blues. The rhythm is syncopated, the notes are blue notes—there is
the transitional flattening of thirds and sevenths in the melodies, and the
emotion is as powerful as that of black music, but drier. It is as if matter-
of-factness were pushed to its ecstatic extreme. Like black sanctified
music, there are always rhythm and tempo changes, and a voice—usually
soprano—often makes a rondo entrance and goes sailing off on its own
for a while into the blue; all of which tends to give the music a deceptively
free and easy improvisational quality, which is not the case at all. These
singers and musicians practice daily and in the results, the ear can detect
their discipline. The "joyous noise" they make is sad as well as happy,
and hopeful as well as yearning. This was Gladys' music as much as the
music of Jimmie Rodgers was hers.

The Church of God, which includes the First Assembly of God, and
the Church of God and Prophecy as they are sometimes called, is a
charismatic fundamentalist sect. It is the oldest of the Holiness churches
and was founded in the nineteenth century in Anderson, Indiana, where
it still thrives. They insist on the reality of the supernatural and particularly of the Holy Spirit on which they place their main emphasis; they
feel man's sanctification is the direct work of the Holy Spirit. They are
Utopian; they are urged to separate themselves from the world to be *in*
the world but not *of* it. Their doctrine is that the key to holiness is love.
Love is normally present in every virtuous act and it is the fulfillment of
all the precepts. An extraordinary power (as of healing) given by the Holy
Spirit is what they mean by the word charisma (from the Greek *chairein*:
to feel tenderness, passion). "The congregation is characterized by exuberant emotionalism and physical agitation," says the *Dictionary of
Religion*.

The congregations of the Churches of God were more exuberant and
emotional, and more "physically agitated" in the 1930s through 1950s
than they are now. Martha Jetter, whose father, Columbus Jetter, had
been a preacher at a First Assembly of God Church, is disgusted with its
new conservatism. "If you went to an Assembly of God meeting today
you would think you were in a Baptist church," she deplores. "That's why
I go to the Pentecostal now." So, for an exact replica of what Gladys and
later Vernon and Elvis were experiencing in their Church of God days,
you must today go to the Pentecostal church. For, however much a Union
Grove preacher may now try to activate his congregation, none of them

is actually going to execute one of those astonishing dramatic jumps that start at one end of a pew and land the jumper clear over the other side literally rolling in the aisle and speaking in tongues. Not nowadays. For that, as I said, you have to go to the Pentecostal church.

But in duets, trios, and quartets, the Church of God congregation will still today be singing like angels. And so will the preacher who often has a guitar and always has a good voice. And there will be, whenever possible, a visiting preacher and he will prowl the platform getting all fired up in search of his inspiration, the Holy Spirit, and when he finds it he doesn't quit. Throwing off his jacket, rhythmically suiting words to his agility, he makes a sudden step, then a deliberate three-point turn which he follows by an abrupt landing which brings him face-to-face with the congregation, arm extended and index finger pointing at *you*. Then he lets you have it: "Let's get down to where the rubber meets the road. The lust of the eye and the lust of the flesh is the way the Devil gets in... but just hang loose for a minute!"

He uses a personal example, demonstrating how he outsmarted Temptation by jumping quickly three times sideways as if leaping from one bank of a narrow creek to another, his face red, his shirt wringing wet, his handkerchief flourished, as he crows triumphantly at the Devil: "I made it! I made it! I made it!" Suddenly through his movements and timing, one sees Elvis clearly. They will sing hymns such as "It's a Grand and Glorious Feeling"; "At the Meeting in the Air"; "I Heard Somebody Calling My Name"; "I'll Fly Away"; "The Old Account Was Settled Long Ago"; and "He Died on the Cross for Someone and I Just Realized I'm the One." They will sway their bodies, and will raise their hands in a graceful gesture that seems at once pleading and placating. They will clap their hands on the off-beat and praise the Lord. They will listen without astonishment to the preacher telling them about going to a meeting in Memphis and then on the way back: "The Holy Ghost was so strong in that car we don't really remember getting from Memphis to Tupelo. I saw a blue haze setting down and my hair stood straight up on my head. We just got here without knowing what happened...."

At this point it is probably useful to correct some misconceptions about the Church of God. One is that it is God-fearing. It is not. It is God-loving. God does not punish you. He loves you. Another is that it is obsessed with hell. Whatever sermons on fire and brimstone, with the Devil stoking the coals in readiness for your descent, other churches may indulge in, one does not hear hell even mentioned in a Church of God. As far as one could learn over an extended period, hell isn't even a place and the Devil is not down there ready to grab you at the final reckoning; he is right here on earth beside you so you better watch out, though God will wash your sins away. Another misconception is that this religion is grim, humorless. In fact its humor is as much an American commodity as its evangelism. And the atmosphere in the church is positively jolly.

"Y'all have to pray for me," smiles a pretty young singer stopping in mid-phrase, "I lost my key." A few beats later she resumes her singing in the right one. And the preacher to a mother whose six-month-old baby is screaming its head off, "That's all right, ma'am. I can outshout him," or "If you think *I* preach a long sermon, you might remember the Bible tells us about Paul in this here town he came to, and he preached all day and he preached all night and someone listening to him fell asleep and fell out of the window and he kept right on a-preaching—and he was just *passing through.*"

The Church of God in Union Grove always served punch and cookies after its Sunday morning services. And after its Sunday evening services there would be a church supper, its various dishes supplied by the joint effort of the women in the congregation.

At these suppers, Gladys did what she always did: she ate and made friends. A few of the girls she had known from her sporadic stabs at school, some she had not met before. But gregarious Gladys soon made the interesting discovery that most of these farm girls were not working on the farm anymore but were getting jobs in Tupelo. Tupelo—why, that was a town of almost six thousand people; it made her head swim to think of it. Yet here were these farm girls just like her, perfectly able to work at the cotton mills, at the textile plants, at Long's Laundry, at Reed's Department Store, and at the Tupelo Garment Center.

Of the twelve hundred women working in garment factories, eighty-five percent of them lived in the surrounding country districts and traveled back and forth in specially chartered school buses. That meant instead of starving on their farms in the Depression—the inexorable fate of the South—they had been able to work in factories at two dollars a day "and glad of it," as the expression goes. One Monday morning in December, 1932, Gladys got on the school bus with the other farm girls and went to work at the Tupelo Garment Center as a sewing machine operator. At two dollars a day. And glad of it.

FOUR

A Romance

In 1832 the land from which Tupelo and Lee County was eventually to be carved was transferred by treaty from the Chickasaw nation to the United States. The establishment of a land office in Pontotoc was the signal for launching one of the wildest and most spectacular periods in the history of the South. By the 1850s this territory could be seen as a reservoir of enterprise and adventure: a boiling cauldron of glittering greed into which bubbled a mad mixture of redskins, ruffleshirts, and rednecks.

"What country could boast more largely of its crime?" wrote J. C. Baldwin in 1853. "What more splendid roll of felonies! What more terrific murders! What gorgeous bank robberies! What more magnificent operations in the land offices and in Indian affairs! The poetry of theft! The romance of wild and weird larceny!"[4]

Out of all this emerged the town of Tupelo, first called Gum Pond because its big mosquito-infested pond was surrounded by gum trees. In 1858 the Gulf Mobile & Ohio Railroad decided to run its glinting tracks through this particular dismal swamp and that seemed reason enough for its hundred inhabitants to fill in the muddy swampland, lay down a couple of streets, build a train depot, two churches, a schoolhouse, a deer lick, a pigeon roost, and to change the town's name. Tupelo is a Chickasaw word meaning, some say, a lodging place (Topa-la)—others, the name of

---

[4] *The Flash Times of Alabama and Mississippi, A Series of Sketches,* J. C. Baldwin, New York, 1853.

that gum tree (Tupela), and still others, a pole that magically bends either north, south, east, or west, in whatever direction the Chickasaws would then decide to settle (Ta-pole-a).

However open to question is the derivation of its name, there is no question that Tupelo's guiding and driving spirit was, is, and always will be *boosterism*. Boosterism, which in general means merely any activities by which enthusiastic supporters promote a cause, came to have a rather special meaning in the nineteenth century. It meant the imaginative practice of creating impressive city plans which, in fact, existed only on paper—"town-building" being the surest way to increase the value of the land. This swindle was used throughout the southwest. For instance, in 1860 Tupelo's plan indicated a courthouse, a college, and a number of churches, none of which existed in reality. We must now wonder about Gum Pond's deer lick and pigeon roost—we have after all only their boosterical word.

Another booster ploy to attract settlers to the area was to testify to the richness of Lee County soil by emphasizing that the site had earlier been occupied by Indians. This was true, but what was not mentioned was that the Chickasaws were hunters rather than farmers.

The fountainheads of boosterism were the various local newspapers which sprang up in Tupelo and in the surrounding hamlets of Lee County (all the incorporated towns in northern Mississippi had newspapers by 1840), which gushed forth fantasies of the impossibly bright prospects of the town—while, at the same time, their editorials admonished the local citizens that it was only by hard work that they could achieve these prospects. Widely distributed pamphlets full of bombast did their bit as well.

In 1870 when Tupelo became incorporated, the streets, mostly dirt roads, were bad. As in the outlying districts, schools were poor and only lasted four months of the year. Fires spread causing damage, danger, and loss of lives as did the malaria-carrying mosquitoes of Gum Pond. Already there were slums. Saloons abounded, as did shootouts. Drunken men rode into stores and smashed them up. Night travel was dangerous. Although Tupelo's marshall warned, "We advise all those contemplating getting drunk and cutting up in Tupelo to be very careful, the marshall won't scare worth a cent," it fell on deaf—or drunken—ears. And the newspaper, the *Tupelo Standard*, even printed someone's comment that "Tupelo is a very uncorporated town with a very bad name and nothing to recommend it." Nevertheless, Mississippi Congressman John Allen, from Tupelo, the wittiest booster of them all, declared in Washington: "When Horace Greeley and others petitioned President Lincoln to let the states that wanted to secede do so, the President answered, 'Secede not Mississippi for then we would lose Tupelo.'"

By 1880 a number of the population, disillusioned, decided to move on—only delaying long enough to scrawl the initials G.T.T.—Gone to Texas—on their abandoned front doors.

Yet by some strange miracle the little town, overcoming both the hazards of sudden drifts westward and sudden occupational switches of those that remained, managed by its peculiarly American combination of optimism and stretching the truth, not only to boost itself into survival, but into something of a success story. The railroads helped mightily. Trains going through—and stopping off—at Tupelo gave the cattle and cotton-growing community ("cattle in Tupelo today is in the stockyards of St. Louis tomorrow") a big lift economically. Front Street, ending at the railroad station, was called Cotton Row. A banner across it said, "Tupelo City Beautiful."

In the 1880s there was another life-giving boost: the St. Louis–San Francisco railroad.

Judge C. P. Long's account of Tupelo in the years 1885–87 has a Twainian twang. First he bathes us in a sleepy pastoral glow of the town:

There were no sidewalks, nor cement, nor gravelled roads, but there was some mighty fine shade trees located at different intervals on Main Street under which a large majority of the inhabitants discussed politics, played dominoes and checkers and cut up goods boxes and cut up each other if it became necessary. There were three small restaurants.... Land between Main Street and the courthouse was used for hitching yards and hitching posts from twenty to twenty-five yards apart.... In summer and early fall after heavy rains, pools of green water caused by the horses being hitched so long that they became restless and pawed until they dug out these holes, were to be seen. Some holes were larger than others because some riders forgot to unhitch their horses when they got ready to go home. They rode the horses 'round the post all night going as far one way as the bridle reins would allow, unwinding and winding all night. On occasions riders were found around eight and nine o'clock the next morning....

Then he wakes us up: Tupelo wants the Frisco railroad badly.

At one time it looked as if Verona would win the contest... but certain business people at Tupelo, being more active and alert and more liberal in the way of inducements such as the right of way and other facilities, the road was built through Tupelo instead of Verona or Saltillo, and from this date Tupelo really took on new life and began to build in a substantial way, growing and expanding in size and magnitude.[5]

5. Paper on Tupelo's past by J. C. Long, from Archives of Mississippi Room, Lee County Library, Tupelo.

In 1889 Tupelo found this railroad could be employed for other county jollifications. Public hangings were advertised in its newspapers with the information that for this purpose "excursion trains from Tupelo to Aberdeen leave Tupelo at 8:00 A.M."

"Wanted!" trumpeted a pamphlet at the turn of the century, "Five thousand enthusiastic, thrifty, loyal people to move to Tupelo and Lee County within the next five years and make this their home. Brilliant opportunities loom for people who come to Lee County which promises to be the greatest and the best county in Mississippi."

By 1919 Tupelo's Main Street, "composed of ornamental posts with clusters of high-powered electric lights," was proudly photographed as "a section of the longest White Way in the State . . . part of that unequalled path of progress—the Bankhead Highway, which extends through Lee County from Alabama to Tennessee."

Nor did boosterism flag throughout the twenties. A pamphlet, "Tupelo, Premier City of Northeast Mississippi," was distributed throughout the South boasting of its excellent public schools, government fish hatchery, Tupelo cotton mills, fertilizer factory, fire and sewage system, its handsome courthouse, its beautiful post office, sixteen passenger trains daily, a beautiful Confederate monument, the annual Mississippi-Alabama State Fair that was to have such an effect on Elvis' life; two railroad systems, a cotton market, a well-organized police station, an ice factory, a creamery, the mills, a hospital, and a Coca-Cola bottling plant. As an extra boost of xenophobia, the pamphlet added: "In the city of 6,000, 5,999 are boosters in every sense of the word. Citizenship is composed of 100 percent Americans, and the city does not encourage half-hearted patriots." By then, it is evident, the impossible dream of this little town stuck out in the middle of nowhere had become a functioning reality. Even up in Tennessee, the Memphis newspaper, the *Commercial Appeal,* contributed its boost with: "Lee County soil will grow just about everything. It is a delightful sight to notice kept orchards and good gardens near every farmhouse. It shows enterprise." Grit, guts, and greed is the way one contemporary Tupeloan journalist summed up their enterprise.

There was, it now becomes plain, nothing further away from Tupelo, Mississippi, than the never-never (or rarely-rarely) land of that southern town of fable, fringed with large crumbling plantations at which Ole Massa sits on the verandah, ever brooding about old times, up to his eyeballs in mint julep, while his kindly Missus still tears up their best curtains for forgotten Confederate bandages and their southern belle daughter spends the mornings putting on layers of petticoats and darkies strum in the cotton fields and poor white trash roll down the hills ravaged with pellagra and hookworm.

Tupelo and its environs had, in fact, always been notably health-conscious. In the late thirties a Sunday article in the *Tupelo Daily Journal*, entitled "Lee County, the Model Health County," proceeded to prove that it should at least get "A" for effort:

For healthiness, few sections of the U.S. surpass Tupelo and Lee County. A recent campaign was waged to show the people the way to happiness is through health. On numerous highways of Lee County there is a signpost to each mile which carries instructions for the care of health. The signs carry a twofold benefit— one for the convenience of the traveller and the other to tell them how to live. Thousands of dollars was [sic] expended in teaching persons how to care for their bodies and how to live a clean and wholesome life. The campaign resulted in Lee County becoming healthier.

Just as Congressman John Allen had said in establishing the Federal Fish Hatchery in his hometown, "A fish will travel for miles to get into the water we have in Tupelo," similarly in 1932 the notorious Machine-Gun Kelly, at a time when banks were going bankrupt, chose out of all the banks in all the cities in the U.S. at his disposal to rob the Citizens' State Bank in Tupelo—and make off with $17,000.

Boosterism discourages questioning; it encourages optimism. Working as a factory girl in Tupelo, Gladys inherited, along with many other traditions associated with the South, the one that is not—the tradition of optimism. She soaked it up from the very air.

Gladys entered the Great Depression and the Roosevelt era in work. On her first day in the vast room on the second floor of the Tupelo Garment Center, with the sun streaming in from the tall windows, Gladys' ears were assaulted by the clicking, whirring buzz of what seemed to be hundreds of motors running, and her eyes by what looked like hundreds of rows of spindles of thread feeding into hundreds of sewing machines, at which sat hundreds of young women primly side by side twisting and turning the ready-cut patterns of men's shirts under the machines. Gladys found it all tremendously exciting. It only took her a few days to get the hang of it. Everyone was so helpful and, after all, operating a sewing machine in the factory was not so different from running her friend Vera's machine except that here you did it all day long.

Nor, in the close proximity of her co-workers, did it take Gladys long to make new friends. The factory girls were all about her own age (no girl under sixteen was hired) and among them there existed that atmosphere of breezy good fellowship that is always found when a number of more or less the same kind of people are assembled in the same place to do the same thing. Gladys didn't feel shy. With her boundless cheerful chatter, she was soon accepted. The first thing she noticed about the town girls was certain details of their clothes. She very much admired the flaring cut of their collars and their smart slim-knotted ties and the gaily colored belts they wore to liven up their dresses and in these flourishes she strove to emulate them.

What was of primary importance to her in this new situation was that for the very first time in her life she was an equal. Not only were hundreds of girls doing exactly what she was doing, but Gladys was getting exactly as much money for it as they were. She was no longer the hired help or a field hand or (delivered with a sigh and shake of the head) "one of them Smiths." She was not now in the humble position she had been all through her growing up that would enable one old-timer to refer back to the Smiths of yore with a dismissive, "I remember the whiskey but I don't remember the girls," or Oscar Tackett to contribute: "Everybody in these parts was down in them days. But the Smiths was more down than we was."

It is clear that even in the great American agricultural democracy where everyone did indeed help everyone else to get in the crops and help their neighbors to raise their houses and barns, social distinctions *were* made— and if they were fine, they were also sharply drawn. And so even unto the next generation. Said an active committee woman recently, "If the Presleys were to come into my house right this moment, I'd be just as *nice* to them as I could be but I wouldn't invite them to tea at the country club." To which Herman Irwin murmured in an aside, "If my grandma heard that she'd turn in her grave."

In the Smiths' time the girls Gladys knew at school often gave parties and picnics to which they only invited their specially "picked" friends— and from these she was definitely excluded. At the factory popularity depended simply upon how good you were at your work, and how pleasing you were in your looks and your personality. Gladys passed on all three counts. The girls that Gladys was friendliest with all lived in East Tupelo and sometimes invited her to their houses.

Looking at the map of Tupelo and East Tupelo one can see how readily the east side was born to be the wrong side. "It was only a mile away from Main Town," says Corene Randle Smith, "but it was a *long* mile." East Tupelo was separated from Tupelo not only emotionally and economically but physically as well, by a levee, by cotton and corn fields, and by being on the eastern side of both the Gulf Mobile and Ohio and the Frisco railroad tracks.

There always seems to have been a stigma surrounding the word "east"

—perhaps because original sin began eastward in Eden. Automatically it becomes the part of town where the poor reside, the part of town that is known as the slums and the wrong side of the tracks: the East End of London, the East Indian Docks, the sprawling East End of Glasgow, the East End of Boston, the Lower East Side of New York, and... East Tupelo.

Even today, when it is called Presley Heights, Janis McCoy writes apologetically about it in her sociological paper, "Many residents of Tupelo used to regard, and some still do, the east side of the town as the 'other side of the tracks.' This is an image citizens of the east side have worked hard to overcome...."

On the other hand—and this will play a central part in Elvis' character—what is always overlooked is that although the poor want to be rich, it does not follow that they either like the rich or that they in any way want to emulate their characters which, in fact, they despise. Both the poor and the rich have always found precisely the same grounds on which to complain about each other. Each feels the other has no manners, is disloyal, corrupt, insensitive—and has never put in an honest day's work in its life. "A coldblooded businessman" is a phrase that Elvis learned early and well.

Gladys loved East Tupelo, especially the part above the highway. There were only five streets and the little woodframe houses were all right next door to each other—not spread out like they were in the country. It gave Gladys a safe, comforting feeling. And each house had its own front porch facing the road so that the neighbors passing to and from Roy Martin's grocery store, or just strolling by, chatted with everyone else rocking on their porches. Gladys instantly felt at home.

Riding on the wave of confidence she had gained with her equality, Gladys soon decided to move herself and her family to this little community. It struck her forcibly, now that she was working and earning regularly, that she was the head of the family and must do some thinking for herself.

It is a pattern in large families that all the older members do your thinking for you; and are always on hand ready with unasked-for advice about what you should or should not be doing. This is especially true if you have three older married sisters living in the country and they are all the time talking about what seems to be everything else under the sun, such as them having so much housework now that the new baby has come that they don't know how they'll ever get it done, and had you heard that the Weathers' youngest daughter was quitting Reed's Department Store to come back and help out at her brother's farm.... But really all the time you know that these remarks were being specially aimed at *you*.

Gladys resisted having her family do her thinking for her and insisted on doing her own. She found the process gave her much satisfaction. She was determined to put her country days behind her. Already two of her uncles were living in East Tupelo: Uncle Sims and the preacher, Uncle Gains Mansell, who, along with Brother Edward Parks, shared the pastoral duties at the First Assembly of God Church, at this point only a tabernacle (tent) in East Tupelo. With the help of these relatives, Gladys found a small house on Kelly Street that suited her. She had noted also that there were several farms bordering the little community, of which one was Orville S. Bean's dairy farm. Bean's property included most of the houses in the small community which the occupants rented from him. That meant there would be work for Gladys' brothers on these farms and, though her sister Clettes was still too young to work at the mills, she was a good girl and would look after her ailing mother. For now that Gladys was head of the family, she would of course have her mother back under her roof again, too. And this would work out fine because Doll was getting more and more frail and relying more and more on the comfort of preachers visiting her, and as Brother Gains was her sister Ada's husband she'd have the comfort of her, too.

And so, once more, the Smiths were on the move. This move involved very little technical difficulty and required only the loan of a neighbor's wagon, the collecting of their meager possessions, and the trussing up of the legs of their chickens so they couldn't escape along the journey. And yet, for Gladys, it was the most significant move of her life.

Gladys hardly had time to settle down in East Tupelo—though some of the night sights, the lightning bugs and the field mice, and some of the night sounds, the whippoorwills, the frogs, the crickets, and the hoot owls—were familiar to the country girl. She could hardly get used to the firetrucks clanging day and night because some house or store or factory was always burning down. And she could hardly get used to the rumbling of the trains as they rushed by; they sounded so close they might be right in the same room with you. But just as she was starting to learn not to jump out of her skin as the shrill shriek of the laundry whistle pierced through the dawn at six o'clock every morning, and just as she was starting to get to know her neighbors and to find her way around Mr. Roy Martin's grocery store on Lake Street and Miller's candy store which specialized in homemade chocolate-covered coconut and nut candies, when one day it was spring, it was April, it was around her twenty-first birthday. . . . Gladys saw a young man. He was beautiful, tall, and fair-haired, and she didn't know who he was. He was the one thing lacking in her new and optimistic horizon, the one person she had to see daily walking along one of those five streets, the one person she had to see every Sunday in the small congregation at the First Assembly of God Tabernacle; he had to appear. She didn't know who he was but they told her he was one of the large Presley clan and that he lived with his mother and father on the Old Saltillo Road and that his name was Vernon.

The whirlwind romance of Gladys and Vernon and their elopement, not two months after they met each other, bear all the earmarks of your usual pair of thunderstruck young lovers caught in the coils of an uncontrollable physical passion that temporarily stultifies the brain.

Nevertheless, the elopement of these particular thunderstruck young lovers must go on record as being the most totally unthought-out elopement of the year... at least in East Tupelo. When they ran off it was by impulse, not even by sudden plan.

There are three conditions essential to getting married: two that *must* obtain and one that *should* obtain. First, the interested parties must have the money necessary for the marriage license; second, both parties must be of legal age; and third, they'd better have a place to live together. Between them Gladys and Vernon were not able to fulfill even one of these conditions. They did not have the three dollars for the license. Though Gladys was twenty-one, Vernon had just turned seventeen on April 10, and was under legal age. And they had not the slightest notion of where they were going to live.

By going back over their brief pre-elopement courtship and their activities during it, it is possible to find a clue as to how they happened to find themselves short of those three so very vital marriage license dollars.

Gladys and Vernon spent most of those evenings at the rollerskating rink on the edge of Main Town. Swooping, swirling, wheeling, or just lazily circling around the large rink hand-in-hand with Vernon while the colored lights played on their faces, every alteration of tint making them look more beautiful in each other's eyes than the last, the swinging music blaring out from the loudspeaker—all this was pure rapture for Gladys; the union of motion with music was one of her great sensuous delights.

So perhaps in this enhancement of their mutual bewitchment they blew all their scanty earnings on rollerskating. But certain other things contributed to their lack of money. Gladys, as the head of the Smith family, was also its main support. As for Vernon, the fact that people remember him doing so many different things at the time—a milk delivery route (though with the Depression fewer and fewer people used this service), helping his father on Orville Bean's dairy farm, hauling for various grocery stores whenever they needed an extra hand, and any odd job he could find here, there, and yonder—meant that he didn't have a regular job and he was not the sort of person to go out looking for one.

It was left to Marshall Brown, a good friend of Vernon—just how good a friend will be seen later—to supply the three dollars for the marriage license. This obstacle hurdled, they were now faced with the fact that they could not get married in Tupelo, where everyone knew everyone else and would therefore know that Vernon was only seventeen. This was overcome by them going to Pontotoc County and getting a license there. Pontotoc was, of course, the county of Gladys' birth.

On Saturday, June 17, 1933 (hard to believe they actually waited for the weekend), Gladys and Vernon, along with Marshall Brown and his wife Vona Mae (née Presley), took off for Pontotoc. All in one day they: made out an application for a marriage license, made out a marriage license and certificate, and then, "by virtue of a license from the Clerk of the Circuit Court of said County of Pontotoc (the Circuit Clerk Mr. J. M. Gates) this day celebrated the rights of matrimony between Mr. Vernon Presley and Miss Gladys Smith."

"Vernon," says Vona Mae Brown, "was very nervous and Gladys smiled right through the whole thing; in fact, she smiled right through the rest of the day." Vernon gave his age as twenty-two and Gladys gave hers as nineteen. The Browns would have known that Vernon was seventeen but they would have had no way of knowing that Gladys, a newcomer to East Tupelo, was not nineteen. Nor would there have been a tell-tale birth certificate to betray her. As mentioned previously, the law requiring births to be registered and certificates to be issued was not passed in Mississippi till *late* 1912; Gladys, born in April, was not registered. And that is how she wanted it. Gratefully she shed her two past years—those two hard, discouraging years filled with more than their share of heartbreak and sadness.

For all her fooling herself about her age, which she would do till the end of her life, and for all her inveterate romanticism, Gladys did not fool herself for a moment about Vernon. He was not going to make life any easier for her; he was not going to make anything of himself. Of course she must have thought, as all women do, that *she* might make something of him, but she wasn't counting on it. She simply accepted him for what he was: a ravishingly handsome, tenderhearted, unambitious young loafer. She loved him passionately and, without question, he returned her love. Impetuosity and impulsiveness played a large part in her makeup. One cannot ignore the fact that this was the second time she had eloped. She knew nothing of moderation or half measures, nor was there anything halfhearted or self-protective about her. "We just ran off like a couple of kids," was the way she later described it. This was accurate; she did not feel like a twenty-one-year-old woman, she felt like a kid. Elvis would inherit from Gladys her unpredictable impulses.

The newlyweds had no place to stay. The Smiths had been living six in their little house on Kelly Street, and the Presleys: father J. D., mother Minnie Mae, Vester the eldest son, Vernon, and the four young sisters, Delta, Nashville, Lorene, and Gladys (a popular name of the period— henceforth she would be known as Little Gladys and Elvis' mother as Big Gladys), lived on the Old Saltillo Road in what they called the big house, as it had four rooms. Around this time, the Presleys also had lodging with them the Reverend Edward Parks of the First Assembly of God Church and his wife. The situation was that although each house had accommodated Gladys and Vernon separately, neither could accommodate both. Again they were indebted to the philanthropy of Marshall and Vona Mae Brown. For weeks thereafter they were their house guests— sleeping on the floor in a made bed.

Vernon was not looking forward to having to tell his daddy about his marriage. J. D., he knew, would be angry. And he was. It probably had nothing to do with Gladys personally, it was just that everything Vernon did (or didn't do) made him angry. In J. D.'s eyes, Vernon could never do anything right. And his harsh treatment of Vernon from childhood on may have contributed to Vernon being the way he was. As we have seen, he kicked him out of the house when he was fifteen and sent him to Pickens. Marcus Kelly remembers Vernon living in constant fear of J. D.'s wrath. In the middle of some after-school sport he would suddenly stop playing and say, "If I don't get home in time to feed the stock, Daddy's going to whip the hide off me." It is no fun being raised by a terrible-tempered father who either spends his nights in the one-room jail on Lake Street sleeping it off or with some woman he's picked up at a "pig-stand," a dive like the Bloody Bucket, which sold booze.

Many forces could have gone into forming J. D.'s abrasive character, some of which may go as far back as his grandfather, Dunnan Presley, Jr. (1827–1900). Like John Mansell (born a year later), he was a real cut-up. He was married several times—four times, to be exact... simultaneously. He had also, according to the distinguished historian William Wright, deserted twice in the Civil War. He was caught the first time and dragged back. William Wright, incidentally, spent some time with Elvis in 1955 in Vicksburg, Mississippi, at a gas station while they were both getting their motorcycles fixed. What was his assessment of Elvis? "He knew a lot about motorcycles. I think he knew more about motorcycles than he knew about people."

The Presley family tree, according to the genealogical research of the *National Enquirer*, goes back to 1745 when an Andrew Presley, a Scots blacksmith, emigrated to North Carolina. His son Andrew Presley, Jr., fought in the Revolution; his son Dunnan Presley wandered around Tennessee, which brings us to Dunnan, Jr. This is probably the place to add that *A British Dictionary of Surnames*, by P. H. Reaney, gives the following sources and variations for the surname Presley: "Priestley, Priestly, Presley, Preslee, Presslie, Pressley, Prisley ... 'dweller by the Priest's wood or clearing,'" along with the following comment: "Priest: in early examples denoting office but later usually a nickname for a man of 'priestly' appearance or, no doubt, often for one of a most unpriestly character."

Martha Jane Wesson of Fulton, Itawamba County, was one of playboy Dunnan, Jr.'s wives. He loved her and left her with two daughters, Rosalinda and Rosella. Rosella Presley (1862–1924) was J. D. Presley's mother. One of her daughters, Mrs. Robbie Stacy, interviewed in 1977, had this to say: "My mother told me that when she and her sister were just little babies, their grandparents had taken them to church on Sunday and when they came back their father Dunnan was gone. He went back to his other wife and child." Rosella never really knew her father, and the ten children she subsequently had did not know their father—or fathers. But, says Vernon Hood, the nephew of Minnie Mae Presley, "They say she had some children by a man called Steele who was part Cherokee." Says her last-born son, Joseph Presley, "She was a sharecropper. She was a very strict disciplinarian but she was a loving mother. Despite the hardships she always managed to give each of us a little present at Christmas—even if it was only a piece of candy or a secondhand pair of shoes." She had very little education but insisted that her children go to school. She died at the age of sixty-three without ever revealing the identity of any of her children's fathers.[6] This was a pioneer woman with a mind of her own and as much a taste for polyandry as her father for polygamy. According to Bill Parham there were "goings on" at the Griffins' farm in Itawamba County and "nobody could tell which was Griffins and which was Presleys."

With eight children (two died early), the Presley family contained the usual amount of good apples and bad apples common to every family. Jessie D. McClowell Presley (1896–1973), J. D., early put himself into deadly competition with his brother Noah. Noah became metaphorically

[6.] *National Enquirer*, September, 22, 1977.

the "good boy" and Jessie the "bad boy". What happened was that J. D. decided if he couldn't be the goodest apple, he was going to be the baddest. As a young man, Noah moved to East Tupelo, opened a grocery store and ran a school bus. He was kind, generous, and public-spirited. On January 7, 1936, he became mayor of East Tupelo, and Janis McCoy, in her paper, says, "It was under the leadership of Presley that East Tupelo made its greatest strides in improving its physical facilities." As a treat for the children of East Tupelo on Sundays, Noah would take them in the school bus to the zoo in Memphis. Janelle McCombe remembers these excursions with pleasure as her first trips out of the state and a widening of her horizons.

J. D. on the other hand, besides drinking, was "mean as hell," according to all reports. He pocketed the key when he locked up his whiskey so his wife, Minnie Mae, could not get at it to have a friendly nip with relatives, and he told her when folks came calling just exactly how many pieces of cheese to slice and how many biscuits to offer them.

J. D. was also very good-looking. Gay McCrae, who was brought up in East Tupelo as a child, remembers, after she'd grown up into an avid Elvis fan, her mother saying: "That Mr. Presley was the handsomest man I've ever seen in my life. All the women just couldn't help staring at him as he walked down the road. He was miles better-looking than Elvis." To which Gay replied with some heat, "Vernon better looking than Elvis? Don't be foolish, Mama." "Oh, I wasn't talking about *Vernon*," said her mother, "I was talking about J. D." But he was a vain man and his younger son's good looks and fine physique would have posed some sort of sexual threat to him that his elder son, Vester, who was short and scrawny would not.

J. D., at seventeen, married Minnie Mae Hood from Fulton. She was skinny, peppy, and peppery. She was eight years older than he and several steps above him socially. She may even have brought a dowry to the marriage. When they moved to East Tupelo, J. D. first worked shares on Dr. Feemster's land and then on Orville Bean's dairy farm.

Eventually blood prevailed—or more probably Minnie Mae, as Vernon was her favorite son. And so, in the fullness of time, Vernon was forgiven by J. D. for doing exactly what J. D. had done at the same age. All were convinced that Vernon would now settle down to being an upright, mature, responsible, industrious, married man.

Vernon and Gladys now only needed a house of their own to complete their bliss. The site chosen was the empty lot next door to the Presleys' home on the Old Saltillo Road. It was on Orville Bean's property, and Bean loaned Vernon $180 (with interest) to build the house and then charged him rent until he repaid it. He did this with all the tenants on his property.

J. D. and Vester are supposed to have helped Vernon build the little shotgun house. Probably they did; but as we know he could have done it on his own. One thing he did know about was carpentry. In this case, he did a fine job and if you walk in it and around it today—never mind that it's been prettified by paint and wallpaper and various added touches— the basic bones of the little two-room house, after some fifty years of rain, floods, violent storms, and tornadoes, are still sound and upright. The windows and doors are well placed and well made, as are the chimney and floors. The tongue-and-groove boards that comprise the outside walls show first-rate workmanship and are in excellent condition. Like all houses built at the time, it was raised on stone piles to allow for drainage during the spring flood. Vernon also built a barn on the property. And an out- house. Some people remember that the Presleys had a cow of their own— and some that they shared the cow with their in-laws. They also had chickens running around the yard. None of the yards of the houses above the highway had grass. No one could have afforded a lawnmower and besides, the chickens would have scratched a lawn to bits. Grass was the enemy. Every day Gladys was out with her dogwood broom sweeping the dirt yard clean and tidy.

In November 1934 President Roosevelt came down to Tupelo to open the Tennessee Valley Authority and strangely enough, of all East Tupelo only the area above the highway was wired for electricity. Strange because they were the people least likely to have afforded it. The Presley house was wired but it was never hooked up during their time. They used oil lamps.

Gladys continued working at the Tupelo Garment Center. She was a married woman with a husband and a house all her own and she gloried in it. Now her friends at the factory were also young married matrons— Faye Harris and Annie Presley, in particular. Annie Presley was the wife of one of Noah's sons, Sales. Twice a week Annie and Sales and Gladys and Vernon would visit with each other, sit on their porches, and sing hymns. "That's about all there was to do in those days. Vernon and Gladys both had fine voices," says Annie Presley. "Gladys sang alto."

Sometimes, as was the custom of the day, Annie and Gladys without their menfolk would sit on the front porch and they would take a twig from a black gum tree, chew it to the consistency of bristles, then dip it into a tin of sweet Garnett Green Label snuff, put it on their lower back gums and hold it there for about an hour before they spat it out. That was something else to do, and it also killed the appetite.

About the end of June 1934 Gladys knew she was pregnant. Sometime around her fifth month she was sure she was having twins. It has been suggested that this knowledge came to her in the form of a spiritual visitation but there were far more realistic reasons for her to expect twins. Not only was she unusually large early on in her pregnancy and, at a more advanced stage, could feel two babies inside her kicking separately, but the family had histories of twins on both sides. Sales Presley had a fraternal twin brother, Gordon, and Gladys had identical twin cousins, Elzie and Ellis Mansell. Annie Presley's daughter has twins.

Gladys had been as impatient to begin her married life as her mother, Doll, had been reluctant. She doted on Vernon. The very sight of him filled her with pleasure. She wanted him near her at every possible moment.

There was still that side of her that was nervous and highly strung: that, when alone at night—even in that tight little community—became anxious and frightened. She disguised this by being the life and soul of the party, always laughing and dancing, the person whom everyone sought out when they needed cheering up as they had on the Lummus farm years ago. This was her purpose; to be so gay and so lively that people would always seek her out, always drop by and visit with her or ask her to come round and see them when Vernon had gone off to the pool hall or the bowling alley or Clyde Reese's café. Cheering up other people calmed her nerves and lightened her fears.

Now she was pregnant, and even though it was a difficult pregnancy, what with being so heavy and so tired and her legs all swollen up, she was glad. From the minute she had married Vernon, she had wanted to have not just children but *his* children who would look like him, and *their* children that they would share and yes, *her* children who would be around her all the time.

FIVE

The Live Twin

Just exactly who was present at Elvis' birth early that frosty morn in January of 1935? Accounts are so various we shall probably never know.

According to Vernon, in an interview for *Good Housekeeping* in 1977, besides himself there were J. D., Minnie Mae, the midwife, Edna Robinson, a friend, and the doctor. According to Vester, there were only Minnie Mae and the doctor. According to Faye Harris, there was the whole first cast plus some other neighbors. But then Faye Harris had Elvis inaccurately born in the early *afternoon* as she had him inaccurately born *before* Jesse; whereas actually he arrived at 4:35 a.m., a half-hour after Jesse.

What amuses East Tupeloans is the Legend of the Disbelieving Doctor who has to be convinced against his will that Gladys is having twins. With many variations it has been endlessly repeated.

The late Faye Harris told Jerry Hopkins for his biography of Elvis: "All along Gladys told everybody she was going to have twins, but the doctor wasn't having any of it. Elvis was borned...and she said she was still in labor. The doctor said he didn't think so. Gladys said, 'Well, there's still the same pain.' Finally a neighbor said, 'Doctor, there's another baby got to come out of there.'" (And out comes Jesse—in the wrong order.)

Vernon, still in *Good Housekeeping*, said, "After what seemed to me an eternity a baby was born—dead. But then my father put his hand on my wife's stomach and announced, 'Vernon, there's another baby there.' At the time Elvis was born medicine hadn't advanced enough for the doctor to predict twins, so his arrival took us completely by surprise."

It makes a good story, but: "As if Dr. Hunt and Edna Robinson couldn't tell for themselves that there were twins!" says Corene Smith.

The simple straightforward fact of the birth of twins is, was, and always has been as follows: in the case of a single baby when the mother discharges the afterbirth, her uterus contracts into a hard nugget; if she is having twins, the uterus will stay swollen. Dr. Hunt would have had to have been a very inexperienced, not to say incompetent, doctor—and he was neither—to have failed to notice that after Jesse's birth Gladys' uterus was still swollen.

One of Parkinson's laws should read: The accuracy with which an event is remembered varies inversely with its importance.

Elvis was born a twin, possibly—it was too early to say for certain— an identical twin. The fact that the mystery of death was attendant at his birth, that the very beginning of his life marked the end of his brother's, affected him throughout his life in a way that people who are not twins would find hard to understand.

There is a phenomenon called "twin bonding." A recent book, *Twins on Twins* by Kathryn McLaughlin Abbe and Frances McLaughlin Gill, gives many examples of twins who are separated at birth and yet grow up in mysteriously similar ways. One pair of male twins was placed for adoption at four months old. Unknown to each other, both couples named their sons James. The twins remet at the age of thirty-nine. They found that they were both divorced from women named Linda and remarried to women named Betty. Both named their first sons John Alan. Each had a pet dog named Toy. Each had had law-enforcement training and was a part-time deputy. Both did mechanical drawing and carpentry as hobbies. Both did well in math and poorly in spelling. Each drove a Chevrolet. Both were six feet tall and weighed 180 pounds. Both suffered from tension headaches.

Another set of twins was separated at six months and reunited at the age of forty-seven. They were reared in different countries and spoke different languages and were exposed to entirely different kinds of child-rearing, but they had great similarities of behavior. They had the same style of walking, of sitting, and of eating. Their rate of speech was similar. Both liked spicy foods, fell asleep after eating, and were absentminded. Both stored rubber bands on their wrists, read magazines back to front, and flushed toilets before and after using them. Both wore double-breasted suits to their initial meeting, had clipped moustaches and large rectangular glasses. Both were married and had two children.

There is also the phenomenon of the death of one twin from medical causes which is followed, after a short space of time, by the death of the other for no apparent reason other than that he or she has lost the will to live.

As for the case of a live twin and one that has died at birth, *Twins on Twins* has this to say: "Eerily, twin bonding has been reported among people whose twin died before or shortly after birth. One physician says he always felt oddly attuned to twins to the point of dreaming that he was a twin. Upon finally questioning his mother, he learned that a 'mass of tissue' had been born with him. He believes that 'mass of tissue' was in fact the lost twin who has haunted his dreams."

Actresses playing Viola in *Twelfth Night*—one half of a twin, the other presumed dead—find the melancholy side of her character constantly at odds with the play's farce and comedy. The longer the play runs, they say, the more deeply they are affected. They have only to pronounce those two mournful lines at the beginning:

> And what should I do in Illyria?
> My brother he is in Elysium.

for them to feel that whatever happens to Viola during the rest of the play—her love for the Duke, the mistaken identity tangles—is secondary to the deep sense of loss for her twin whose sameness she describes while looking in a mirror:

> ...I my brother know
> Yet living in my glass. Even such and so
> In favor was my brother, and he went
> Still in this fashion, color, ornament
> For him I imitate.

Shakespeare would have seen twin bonding at first hand, for he himself had twins—Judith and Hamnet. And Hamnet died.

There is a theory that Narcissus, who fell in love with his reflection in the water and drowned, had a twin brother who died at birth. In any case, Elvis would look long and hard into mirrors while growing up—and see there the image of his dead brother.

The naming of the Presley twins was highly significant. The first-born was named Jesse after Vernon's father with whom, as we know, Vernon was always on uneasy—not to say bad—terms, but whom he nevertheless needed to placate. It was a gesture then—but an empty one, as the child was dead. To the live child they gave the middle name Aron. This was in honor of Aaron Kennedy, the friend Vernon most admired. Aaron and his wife Mattie Sue were living at J. D. Presley's house at the time. To the dead Jesse, they gave the middle name Garon which rhymed with Aron in keeping with a tradition in that area of giving twins either rhyming or assonant names: Rhonda and Shonda, Merrill and Sherrill, Randall and Darrell, Carol and Cheryl—and Gladys' cousins, Elzie and Ellis.

To the live child they gave the first name of Elvis. It was Vernon's middle name and his mother Minnie Mae had chosen it simply because she liked its sound. It was not a common name. The Mormon Church's genealogical society says: "It is the first time it has ever come up before us in all our extensive genealogical research." Be that as it may, the name was not unique in Lee County. At Elvis' birth there were already two men named Elvis: an Elvis McCoy and his son. There was also an Elvis Heaperly, an Elvis Gordon, and an Elvis McCall—all born before Elvis Presley. And by a strange stroke of coincidence there lies in Libertyville Cemetery in Lee County, an Elvis Smith (1906–67).

So far this is in the realm of the explainable. Entering the realm of the metaphysical, however, one notes with wonder that Gladys and Vernon should choose, when naming their live son, such an obvious anagram for "lives." When Elvis worked it out for himself he was delighted.

One has dwelt on Elvis-the-twin's sense of loss; one could go further and theorize on his sense of guilt. Corene Smith, six years older than Elvis, remembers that the speculation going around in those days was whether the doctor, if he hadn't been so busy saving Elvis' life, might have been able to save poor little Jesse's. Life and death were major topics in front-porch society and this supposition was still being discussed when young Elvis' sharp ears were able to pick it up.

Even as late as the age of thirteen, Elvis signed his name Elvis aron Presley with a small "a". According to handwriting expert Terence Gray this space for the missing capital "G" of his brother's middle name indicates how strongly Elvis felt his brother's death.

So Elvis felt loss and he felt guilt. But he also felt something else— something without which, unless we are aware of it, we cannot begin to fathom Elvis' character. He felt *triumphant*. He was, after all, the one who had survived. Did this not prove that he was the strongest, the most powerful? Would it not be necessary for him to prove this all his life?

The division in Elvis' soul was not between good and evil but between power and powerlessness. Elvis might relate to friends and lovers with the intimate dependency of a twin looking for his other half, but he would always be the dominant one. And placed where he was in his station of life, he would always see himself as "buying in" rather than "selling out."

The belief in magic is inherent in us all. We are born with it, grow up with it, and secretly never really abandon it. As often as we thrust down this illogical belief, it pops up again, and always when we least expect it—quite suddenly we find ourselves colliding into a car in the street in order to avoid walking under a ladder on the pavement. Or wishing on a wishbone.

We have all, at one time or another, accepted magic: coincidences, superstitions, miracles—call it what you will. What is interesting is the direction in which some particular person's faith in magic may lie.

"I was the hero of every comic book I ever read," said Elvis in the 1970s.

His belief in his supernatural strength and power was reinforced by his reading matter. The golden age of the Comic Book was from 1939 to 1954. Growing up, our folk hero was immersed in this special form of folk art. Many of the most popular of these books shared the same theme— the twinship that resides within one person. The heroes had two identities: one powerful, one powerless. In his powerless identity the young man led a normal everyday life. But within him existed his secret powerful self who, through various devices, emerges as a magical being with various super powers, the most important of which, in Elvis' mind, was the ability to fly.

Superman was the first of the double-identity heroes to appear in comic book form. Then came Batman who, by day, was a lightweight playboy called Bruce Wayne and, by night, donning a menacing cat mask and a black cape, buzzed around striking fear in the hearts of evildoers, catching criminals and putting the world to rights.

Another thug-thwarter was called the Spirit. This calmly powerful hero had perhaps the most interesting powerless double identity of all of them. He was called Danny Colt. And he was officially dead. He used Wildwood Cemetery as the base of his operations. As the Spirit, he wore ordinary street clothes and only the slightest of masks. His approach to crime-fighting scorned dramatics and it was his very nondescript appearance and no-nonsense methods that made him impressive.

The elastically powerful Plastic Man could stretch his limbs like rubber bands... for *miles*. He began as a failed gangster called the Eel, whose chums ran out on him when he was wounded in a robbery. He was nursed back to health by a sympathetic monk, at which time he discovered that a chemical that had entered his wound gave him the ability to distort his body into any shape. In his double identity he became the Plastic Man, sporting a very odd bathing suit with a plunging décolleté and a pair of goggles.

Elvis loved all these comic books. He not only kept them, he took care of them as scrupulously as any bibliophile. His cousin Harold Loyd remembers that when Elvis was in high school in Memphis he and Harold would swap comic books. "Sometimes I would go over and borrow some books from him. He would let me have them because he knew I would return them in good shape when I finished reading them. He had a large bookrack made out of wire to keep the books in and he always made sure they were in neat order and not out of place."

But the Captain Marvel series, and in particular, Captain Marvel, Jr., was Elvis' unquestioned favorite. Adding greatly to the popularity of the series were the characters that derived and that sprang up from the stories. A sort of family eventually surfaced—some self-appointed and eager to get in on the act. "Wilfred Batson from Arkansas figured we must be cousins. We really aren't, but I hadn't the heart to tell him..." says Billy Batson/Captain Marvel. And, "Uncle Dudley pretends to be our uncle and to turn into Uncle Marvel. We aren't related but we all love him anyway." On the other hand, "Mary and I have only one living relative ... our Uncle Ebenezer Batson. But we'd just as soon forget him... he's a crook."

Mary Batson is the real thing. She turns up out of the blue as Billy's twin sister. "She'd been raised by wealthy Mrs. Bromfield," explains Billy. "Mary has the power to turn into Mary Marvel." Apart from being a delightful-looking adolescent, fresh-faced with shoulder-length brown hair softly curled below her ears, Mary is innocent, good, sunny-natured, and so full of spunk and adventure that she and her superpowers are soon awarded a comic book series all their own.

Freddy Freeman, another of these derived creations "...isn't a Batson at all... but he is a member of the Marvel family, as Captain Marvel, Jr.," confirms Billy. Like Mary, he too made an enormous hit on his first appearance and was immediately sent into his own comic book series.

Elvis' twin-fusion with Freddy/Captain Marvel, Jr., was total, and it was from reading his adventures that the young Elvis secretly began to create himself. The power of Captain Marvel, Jr., symbolized by his ability to fly high over the earth, was twinned with his external powerlessness in the form of his other identity, the poor crippled newsboy (symbolizing for Elvis his own "crippling" by the death of Jesse?) whose name *is* nevertheless *Free*man.

Millions of other children, of course, were reading this same comic book in bright, primary colors at the same time, but Elvis' specific background and temperament made him singularly susceptible to its magic. He must have felt it drawn and written for his eyes only.

It was Captain Marvel, Jr., who helped mold Elvis' personality, humble and humorous, and who crystalized his desire to save the world and his family. It was Captain Marvel, Jr., who sculpted Elvis' authoritative stance, legs exultantly wide apart, the graceful gestures of his hands, palms flat, fingers outstretched, thumbs extended. It was Captain Marvel, Jr., who styled Elvis' glistening hair, side-parted with the forelock falling over his brow, the sideburns, the hair growing down his neck. Much later would come Elvis' Captain Marvel, Jr., cape and lightning bolt emblems on the TCB (Taking Care of Business) and TLC (Tender Loving Care) jewelry he would give to his special friends. There were no clasps on the TLC necklaces. There were no catches to his feelings, Elvis explained to a close friend, Sterling Hofman, the wife of his Memphis dentist, Dr. Lester Hofman, to whom he presented one. The necklace was meant to describe a continuous and eternal circle of affection with no reservations, no qualifications.

Elvis used the lightning bolt emblem so often—on the tail wing of his airplane, the *Lisa Marie*, it shows up hugely as it did on the wall of his gameroom at Graceland—that it became a sort of signature and everyone speculated as to what it symbolized and where he had gotten the idea. Everything possible has been suggested from the Memphis weather— given to violent electric storms—to the emblem of the West Coast Mafia to which it is said to be similar. But one wonders if it were not something seen long ago and long submerged that sprang suddenly into Elvis' consciousness in the early 70s. Lightning bolts abound in the panels of the Captain Marvel, Jr., series—not just on the young hero's chest. What did the lightning bolt mean to the grown-up Elvis? Precisely, what did it mean to the child? It meant power.

After Elvis' birth—with Gladys, as we have seen, "close to death"—they were both taken to the Tupelo hospital. Perhaps it was not only Gladys who was fighting for her life. Perhaps her frail little infant "no bigger than a minute" who had had such a difficult passage into the world was fighting for his life, too. Conceivably it was this that made Gladys instantly love him more dearly. But it is more likely that it was the primitive, or animal, or biological drive that swept Gladys into the extremes of maternal devotion. The forces of passion that caused her to cast her lot with Vernon with such reckless abandon had reassembled themselves, had multiplied a hundredfold, and were now focused on the love and care and protection of her son.

This was noticed immediately by friends and neighbors when Gladys and Elvis came back to the little house on the Old Saltillo Road. Dot Rutledge used to come over to look after Elvis while Gladys went to the grocery store. She remembers that when Gladys said, "I'll only be gone five minutes," she meant just that. Generally she meant even less than that. Gladys positively raced to the store and back; it was agony for her to leave her child even for a moment with *anyone* else, to let anyone else touch Elvis. Maternal love was not for Gladys a prettily sentimental attachment. Rather it was a passionate concentration which deepened into a painful intensity when her son was not there, directly in her sight. She imagined all sorts of horrors. She imagined he was being tortured and she was not there to stop it. It was physical torment for her to be separated from him.

Maternal devotion is constantly misrepresented as either grasping, clinging, stifling or pathetic. It is none of these things. Every mother of a very young child has the primordial conviction, deeper than reason, that as long as her child is within her eyesight she will be able to protect him from all harm. Generally the mother outgrows this as the child grows up but Gladys all her life remained anxious over each one of Elvis' separations from her.

That year saw the death of the ailing Doll and her burial at Spring Hill next to Bob Smith in an unmarked grave. It also saw Granny Smith's death and her burial next to her husband Obe in the Mansell part of Unity Cemetery. And in September, Vester, Vernon's older brother, married Clettes, Gladys' younger sister. Kinship carried on.

On April 5, 1936, when Elvis was a year old, a tornado twisted through Tupelo at 9:04 P.M. on a Sunday evening causing massive damage. Tupeloans even to this day have a way of dividing time and events into B.T. and A.T.—Before the Tornado and After the Tornado.

The tornado killed 235 people in Tupelo, injuring 350, and leveling forty-eight city blocks. "It sounded like a bunch of freight cars running together," says Magnolia Clanton. "It just hit and you heard people screaming in the streets and you didn't know which way you were going or which way you were going to go because you went crazy."

The giant black spiral tinged with fiery red twisted its way over Tupelo and out of the southwest. The evening had been sultry, the wind blowing restlessly. Lightning bolts began flashing. Evening church services were over. Most people were at home. The tornado only lasted a few minutes— from 9:04 to 9:09—yet whole families were killed. It destroyed the black settlement at Tank Hill, hurling bodies into Gum Pond. Fires broke out. An estimated nine hundred homes were splintered. Chickens were shorn of their feathers and cows dehorned.

The courthouse, churches, and cinemas were all transformed into hospitals. Roosevelt sent in national aid and the Red Cross set up in boxcars at the stations.

Where was Elvis on this dangerous night? Fortunately we know exactly where he was and it was fortunate for him that he was where he was, because it could have been a close call.

Catherine Hall had taken Vernon's sister, Gladys Presley, along with her that evening to the service at the Baptist Church. Suddenly Little Gladys' father, J. D., appeared at the back and signaled them to hurry out. There were storm warnings. They hurried into the school bus, together with Gladys, Vernon, Elvis, Minnie Mae, and the rest of her children. Uncle Noah drove them to his house, which was stronger and larger and where they could all be together. The menfolk lined up against the south wall of the house to brace the planks against the worst that was to come. Minnie Mae kept fainting, Catherine remembers, then she would be revived, then she would faint again. Gladys, her baby in her arms, sat quietly huddled in a corner. The tornado twisted through East Tupelo. The house remained intact. When it was over they could see fires lighting up one after the other all across Main Town. Uncle Noah said to the men, "Let's go. They're going to need help." And the men piled into the school bus and headed across the levee to Tupelo.

When Gladys and Elvis got home the first thing they saw was that the tornado had totally razed St. Mark's Methodist Church *directly across the road* from them. It had not touched their own home.

The closeness of the disaster could be thought not to have made too much of an impression on a year-old child. But the church would not be rebuilt for over several years and every day, looking at its splintered foundations, Gladys and Vernon would talk of the miracle that had saved their home—and their lives. Would this not have added to little Elvis' feelings of triumph at having survived yet again?

For years after that, folks kept scanning the skies for warnings. Children would be gotten up, often in the middle of the night, in March and April and May, to go to their storm shelters—the Presleys had a storm shelter in the hills behind them—to spend the rest of the night.

In late September when the crop was ready, everyone in East Tupelo, men, women, and children, got out into the fields and picked cotton. For the first years of Elvis' life, Gladys was out there, too, her six-foot duck sack trailing along the ground, picking cotton on Capp Shirley's place on the Reese farm. It was arduous work plucking the soft white bolls, two rows at a time, grappling with stalks and burrs. One dollar and fifty cents for a hundred pounds of cotton was the going rate. Elvis, one may be sure, was not left at home. To his delight, Gladys set him on her sack and pulled him with her up and down the rows.

In 1937 Brother Gains Mansell became the sole preacher at the First

Assembly of God Church. He had, in fact, built the small two-roomed, wood-framed building covered with brick veneer with his own hands. It was on Adams Street and over its door was printed the word 'Welcome.'

Perhaps it was the feeling of security caused by this familial association with the church that emboldened the shy two-year-old Elvis one Sunday morning to leave his mother's side in the congregation of sixty-odd people, scramble up to the platform, and join in with the other singers—although he did not yet know the words to the hymns he was singing. It was more likely that his musical ability had simply manifested itself at what seems an astonishingly early age—as did his need to express it.

What is known about the aspects of the preciously musically gifted? Anram Scheinfeld has this to say in *Your Heredity and Environment* about singers and instrumentalists: "In no other field of human achievement do the young so strikingly scale the heights and so easily outdistance great numbers of competing adults." This raises the question of whether musical *performance* is a special type of achievement which does not demand full intellectual development or even full physical development and is therefore not out of reach of a child. Musical talent as revealed through performance, continues Scheinfeld, is unique among other human talents in that the achievements can be measured one against another. Exactly the same song or piece of music can be sung by singers or played by instrumentalists of different ages, backgrounds, and nationalities, and the listener does not have to be an *expert* to distinguish the superlative performances from the mediocre or inferior ones. No such easy method of comparison is possible in any other field where creativity—writing, painting, musical composition (relative judgments of these by contemporary critics are often wrong)—as opposed to interpretation, is the determinant. Since interpretive musical talent *is* measurable, scientists are in a better position to calculate the part played by heredity or environment in it than in any other of the arts.

Scheinfeld conducted a vast survey of artists which included thirty-five outstanding pianists, violinists, and conductors of world acclaim; thirty-six principal singers of the Metropolitan Opera Company; and a group of fifty students selected as the most promising from the Juilliard Graduate School of Music. The findings were as follows: In almost every case musical talent expressed itself at an early age. The instrumentalists began at four and three-quarters. The Juilliard group at five and a half. The Metropolitan singers at nine and three-quarters. Great musical achievement is invariably correlated with an extremely early start. By the time a child is ten, his or her future musical performance can be quite clearly determined. And at sixteen an individual is musically set.

The differences in family backgrounds, or the presence of talent in both parents, or in one parent, or in neither parent, often seem to have little to do with the caliber or quality of musicianship displayed by the individual. Some of the greatest virtuosi came from the humblest and least musical homes where neither parent had talent. There seems, therefore, a lack of direct and consistent correlation between musical achievement and background which suggests that musical talent does not necessarily arise from musical home environment.

Of the artists interviewed, however, the majority (seventy percent) had talented parents, one or both. Yet on the other hand quite a number reported no talent in either parent. And since some of these are such distinguished examples, they should be noted: Toscanini's family history revealed no musical talent whatever in either his parents, or his brothers and sisters, or his own children. Artur Rubinstein, the twentieth-century virtuoso pianist, born in a ghetto in Poland of a very poor family where no musical instrument was to be heard, at the age of one and a half spontaneously began singing little songs of his own to express what he wanted or to designate various members of the family. Nor was there any musical history in Schnabel's family. Nor in that of Leonard Bernstein, who may have been a child prodigy—but no one knew it. This was because there was no piano in his home until he was ten.

The biological basis of musical aptitude, however, can be measured and broken down into sense of pitch, timing, harmony, rhythm, and tonal memory, interval discrimination, mode (or chord) discrimination, melodic sequences, and musical imagery, and these are governed by the structure of the vocal cavities, the lips, teeth, tongue, soft palate, jaw muscles, and the thickness and length of the vocal chords. After running a series of tests with thousands of individuals, Professor Carl E. Seashore reached the conclusion that musical aptitude appears to have a *constitutional* basis. Training, it was concluded, can only develop these senses to the degree that the capacity is inherent in the individual. No amount of training can make an unmusical person musical.

As for Elvis, he had a fair start. Vernon had a very good voice. Gladys had not only a good voice, she had rhythm—and the instincts of a performer. Nevertheless, though they did provide somewhat of a musical environment, even without it, one wonders if Elvis, with his biological musical equipment, would not still have become a virtuoso.

Elvis' musical talent, it appears, was born in him. But again, what of all the millions of other children born at the same time? Could there not have been at least—well, at least a dozen of them born with similar powers? Would not Elvis need a little something extra to assure him of success?

"If a man has been his mother's undisputed darling, he retains through-out life the triumphant feeling, the confidence in success, which not seldom brings actual success along with it," pronounced Freud; a dogma which caused Alfred Adler to observe, "Freudian psychology is the cre-ation of a spoilt child."

It would seem then that Elvis, cherished by his mother beyond all ordinary limits, was also to be a son spoiled beyond all ordinary limits. But it was not quite that simple.

The rapport between the mother and her small son, as observed by the neighbors, seemed one of total harmony. Gay McCrae's mother has an image of them, "when Elvis was just about three," which stays with her to this day. It is that of Elvis and Gladys on the front porch. Gladys is sitting on the swing and Elvis is sitting at her feet. His arm is resting on her knee. A neighbor stops by for a chat. Elvis sits quietly listening, silent and still; only his eyes follow whoever is speaking, going from Gladys to the visitor and back again. His arm remains always on Gladys' knee.

This is, however, not only a picture of a small child completely depen-dent on his mother, it is also (extraordinarily enough for so young a boy) a picture of a small child *protecting* his mother.

The fact was that from the age of three, Elvis regarded himself as head of the family, and conducted himself in that manner. An actual event explains this behavior.

On November 16, 1937, when Elvis was nearly three, Vernon, along with Gladys' brother Travis, and a man called Lether Gable, was indicted for forgery. A check that Orville Bean had made out to Vernon had been altered, and the culprits stood accused by Bean.

Vernon had sold Bean a hog and received for it (it is said) a check for only $4—a sum much less than he had expected. Vernon was furious; he knew the hog was worth much more. And he had been counting on that money, he was desperate for it. He talked it over that night with Travis and Lether, and helped along no doubt by several drinks and the fact that all three men felt hard done by Bean, what with one thing and another, an idea emerged: since Vernon had been sold short, why not make the check closer to the amount he deserved?

Courthouse records of the indictment and the sentencing do not in-clude the details of how large a sum of money the check was altered to, so, going on people's memories, it seems to have been either fourteen or forty dollars.

According to Vernon's old friend, Aaron Kennedy, who is still living in Gordo, Alabama, and who says he thinks Travis "put Vernon up to it," the check was not altered but forged by putting a blank check form over Orville Bean's one, holding them up to the light, and tracing his writing on to it, with both Vernon and Travis working on it together. If it seems odd that two young men who could only write with difficulty would try their hands at forgery, a look at Orville Bean's signature reveals that he formed his letters no better than they did.

Whether this is correct or whether they simply altered the 'four' to make fourteen or forty, Vernon, one had to conclude, was not taking a long view of things. But then, people do not eat in the long view, they eat every day. The recession had set in. The crops had been gathered far back in September. The winter months stretched out jobless. His family was hurting for food.

In any case, what had looked at the start of the evening like not much more than an idea became by the end of it, accompanied by that rush of blood to the head which floods the brain and jams the gates of reason, a workable reality. They had reached the point of no return.

None of these young men had a very clear idea of how a bank operates to cover the possibility of forgery or misrepresentation. They were paid their wages in cash. To them a dollar bill was a dollar bill and that was legal tender and worth what it bought. But a check was simply a piece of paper on which you could write any amount. If it came right down to it they would all three simply support each other. It would be their word against Bean's as to how much he had made the check out for.

They were caught. And not long after they'd done it.

As arranged, they pleaded not guilty. They were nevertheless thrown into the Tupelo jailhouse. Great pressure was put on Orville Bean by the community in East Tupelo to show leniency towards the offenders. Gladys was especially active at rallying everyone from the preacher and the congregation of the First Assembly of God, to alderman, to Noah Presley, mayor of East Tupelo—anyone she could approach on Vernon's behalf. She went to Orville Bean herself, pleading extenuating circumstances in the family, their hunger, and the age of their small boy.

But nothing could slake Bean's anger. His view was that he had only bought the hog from Vernon in the first place to help him out—and look what Vernon turned around and did to him! If he couldn't trust his workers, how was he going to run his farm? But behind this official view, according to Aaron Kennedy, there was another reason for Bean's pressing charges for so small a sum. It was Bean's way of getting even with Noah Presley for muscling in on what Bean considered his territory.

And then Bean was heard to call Vernon something shocking, something that was considered in those lean years to be a very grave insult. He called Vernon "long hungry," and there were many witnesses to this. To be long hungry meant that you were a glutton, a hog at the trough; it meant that you were capable of taking the food out of your own family's mouths in order to gorge yourself. Elvis was to hear reverberations of this insult all the years of his growing up. Skinny and scrawny all through his childhood, it was noted that no matter how much Gladys plied him, he was a poor eater. It was as if by eating as little as possible at the family table he would not be taking their food away; as if he would not eat until he felt he had earned the right to.

A bond for bail was fixed for the culprits for the stiffish amount of five hundred dollars each. But on January 4, 1938, only *two* bonds were filed. C. E. Biggerstaff and J. H. Gable stood as sureties for Lether Gable, and J. D. Presley and J. G. Brown stood as sureties for Travis Smith.

The Lee County courthouse records do not list anyone posting bail for Vernon. It must therefore be concluded that Vernon spent the next six months before the trial in custody. This refusal to post bail for his son was either J. D.'s choice or his necessity. His son had turned just as bad as he'd always prophesied. Let him cool his heels in jail. Teach him a lesson. And J. D., it must be remembered, was farming on Orville Bean's land; Orville Bean was his landlord, and it behooved him to stay on the right side of the landowner. But who can say what malicious pleasure he might have putting up bail for Travis and not Vernon?

Aunt Lillian vividly recalls visiting Elvis and Gladys during those bad winter months. Elvis had been walking and talking for some months now and when she came to visit she would find him energetically dashing back and forth through the two rooms of the little house. But each time he came to Gladys where she sat he would pause, reach up to pat her on the head, and tenderly say, "There, there, my little baby." Neighbors at the time also have stories of Elvis' precocious solicitude towards his mother. He was always inquiring of her anxiously, "Mama, do you need anything?," "Do you want a glass of water?," "Do you want a chair?"

In so small and so poor a community, where there is an intense interest in other people's affairs, the news of Vernon's arrest had not spread slowly. It says much for the young Presleys' popularity and the community's understanding of the situation that Gladys had the sympathy of all; that her neighbors flocked around her saying (as they still do to this day): "I would have done the same thing as Vernon if I'd been in his place." They did not, and had not, but this expression of their loyalty and solidarity was genuine and would remain so. For they never mentioned the affair until it made headlines in several tabloids after Elvis' death.

On May 24, 1938, the trial took place. The three men had by then changed their plea to guilty. Judge Thomas H. Johnston sentenced them to three years in Parchman, the Mississippi state penitentiary.

Vernon and his buddies had a deep and fatal misunderstanding of the law. English law, and by the same token American law, goes back to medieval law when the barons were running their feudal estates. It has always valued property over people. In other words the little clerk who fiddles the books for some trifling sum will get a stiffer sentence than if he had run over a child. The punishment, says the law, must be greater than the reward of the ill-gotten gains. So it was not just a matter of paying back the money, as had been naively proposed.

Still the harshness of the punishment in relation to the crime might be further explained by the antifraud mood of the time induced by the recession and reflected, on the same day as Vernon was sentenced, in the *Tupelo Daily Journal's* editorial:

When times are good the public apparently doesn't give a hang how much money is stolen from the city, county, or state funds, or how much bribery goes on behind the political scenes to protect vice rings. When business pinches, however, when the local treasury begins to empty, it is an old custom of democracy to call for a house-cleaning and slap the offending officials behind bars. The present slump will prove a real blessing if it spurs voters to cast corrupt political rings overboard and demand honesty in city, county, and state government.

Hard times everywhere.

The best-known photograph of Elvis as a child, usually captioned "between the ages of two and three," the one most reproduced—it even adorns the cover of one of his albums—is the one of him dressed in overalls and a small hat standing between his seated parents against what looks like a stark gray cement background. It is an odd photograph for many reasons. First of all it is a "posed" photograph yet it is without a studio backdrop or studio lighting. Second it is the only photograph of Elvis taken at so early an age *indoors*—all the other photographs of young Elvis are Kodak snapshots with outdoor settings. Most important is the palpable tension emanating from the figures in the photograph. All three are grim-visaged. Gladys, dark and beautiful, neat and slender, is all eyes, all character. Vernon is handsome and terrified. Elvis is pudgy, cupid-lipped and stiff-fingered with strain. Fear and panic leap out of their eyes as all three glance sideways (no one is "looking at the birdie") focusing on ... catastrophe. Something about the way Gladys, her cheek pressed against Elvis' little hat, has extended her arm behind him and is gripping

Vernon's shoulder makes one wonder if this photograph was not actually taken at the police station and at Gladys' insistence that she and Vernon and Elvis have this remembrance of them all together to cherish in the harsh months to follow.

SIX

Elvis and Gladys

In the wake of this Elvis grew up fast—though not overnight. It took some time for the three-year-old to grasp, for reasons that only much later would become clear to him, that his father was not coming home. But at the time "he nearly lost his mind with his daddy away," say neighbors, attributing a too adult reaction to the child; nevertheless it was part of Elvis' temperament—an inheritance, no doubt, from Gladys—to take things hard, and reports of seeing him daily "bawling so hard he couldn't catch his breath," are very likely accurate.

Throughout his life Elvis would take things hard; until he found something else to do. The very fact of his taking things so hard meant that he must search the more ardently for the next thing to do. What he found then was to look after his low-spirited, suffering mother. It seemed to him both in his mind and his heart that their survival was wholly dependent on his taking charge of the situation. Thereupon he became the father and Gladys the child who needed him to get her a drink of water, to fetch things for her, to pat her gently on the head, stroke her face, and smooth her eyebrows; to watch her and comfort her: "There, there, my little baby."

This strange reversal of roles between the parent and the child often takes place when one parent is absent and the other is either physically or emotionally wounded. A typical example of this role-reversal is the alcoholic mother looked after by the child who takes over the complete running of the household. It had already happened, to a degree, in the Smith family, with Lillian stepping into the mother's role in place of the tubercular Doll. For this role-reversal to have taken place as early as the age of three with Elvis means that it took place, of course, mainly in his imagination. Nevertheless take place it did, and out of the emotions this engendered in Elvis' heart came that quality of feeling that was to serve him for the rest of his life.

He was also making his twin adjustment: The powerful must take care of the powerless. He had, in fact, what psychologists call a "saving complex." The confusion of his being at the same time both father and son was to exist all his life. Any account of Elvis having been, in those post-Freudian times, such an outspokenly shameless mother-lover is not complete without pointing out his pride at being not only a good son to her but a good—and providing—father. Vernon and Gladys were always "his babies," which was how the adult Elvis referred to them when from the age of nineteen he became the sole breadwinner and support, not only of his immediate family but also of many of his kin. In an early interview at the age of twenty, Elvis would say, and not seem to think it odd to say it, "I made my father retire a few months ago. There's not much sense in his working because I can make more in a day then he can make in a year."

On the other hand he was in constant need of the kind of love and attention that is lavished on a small child. And the ambiguity of this double role not only existed within him but within Gladys and Vernon as well.

But that summer of 1938 Gladys herself fought hard against collapse, summoning up her considerable strength. And there was no one in the community who was not impressed by her quiet display of pride.

Across the way from them the St. Mark's Methodist Church, blown away in the tornado, had been rebuilt and was holding a week-long revival meeting. In the middle of the week a woman member of the congregation, who had been noticing the mother and her little boy sitting alone evening after evening on their porch, went up to Gladys and invited her to the revival.

Gladys thought it over. "I don't think so," she finally said. "I would have come along if you'd asked me on the first day, but now I think I'll just go to my own little church on Adams Street."

Gladys and Elvis "went every time the door was open," says Carrie Hall, Catherine's sister. Gladys and Elvis in church: one sees them by the dozens even today in First Assembly of God churches all over northeast Mississippi: the mother and her small son sitting close together in their pew, the mother rapt, safe, saved; rocking her snuggling child throughout the service. And every little boy is a replica of Elvis at that age—solemn-eyed with a wax-pale complexion and a stoic, expressionless face under an equally pale mop of straight, short-cut hair. Watching them, it becomes easy to visualize the sense of refuge and peace Gladys and Elvis shared through these meetings; as it does the emotional exaltation released within them when they sang. As Elvis was later to say in the documentary *Elvis on Tour*, "It [gospel singing] more or less puts your mind to rest. At least it does mine, since I was two."

For Gladys it was time suspended from the grim reality she had to face each week when she walked to the welfare office for her "commodities"— canned butter, rice, flour, lard, and cheese—a walk which so humiliated her and which she so dreaded she would beg her friends to accompany her. And still, "She could not bring herself to leave Elvis in the care of anyone else," says Dot Rutledge. "I never looked after Elvis then for more than half an hour."

But church meetings were more than merely a caesura between the realities and the problems of the world outside. There was real warmth and friendliness there. And there were of course the church lunches that would follow the Sunday morning service and the refreshments after evening services. Perhaps these were almost as important to Gladys and Elvis in their straitened circumstances as the sense of community and support extended to them by the congregation. No wonder Gladys— and therefore Elvis, too—left these meetings feeling, as she herself put it, "renewed and restored."

Meanwhile Vernon was serving time in Parchman in Sunflower County, where he would find that hundreds of other young farmhands like himself, imprisoned for whatever crimes from moonshining to mayhem, had left work in the fields outside only to go to work in the fields in prison; for Parchman, set in rich delta farmland, is a vast penal plantation. The men are divided into separate units or camps each of which is overseen by a sergeant responsible for the work as well as discipline and order.

Parchman is no summer camp. Being sentenced to hard labor there means exactly that. Or as Columbus Hopper, Professor of Penology at the University of Mississippi, puts it, "Unlike many prisons, idleness among prisoners has never been a problem at Parchman. Rather they work from daylight until dark in the woods and fields of the plantation frequently under threat of floggings and a variety of 'unofficial' techniques such as beating with chains and blackjacks and even shooting." It is therefore all the more surprising to learn that this prison, which had "established a national image as rife with exploitation, brutality, and degradation," allowed its prisoners—even as far back as 1938—full conjugal rights.

The conjugal visit at Parchman is apparently unique in U.S. penal practice. In every camp there is a little building called the Red House located near the main camp building. When an inmate's wife comes to visit him, he is permitted to go with her into one of the rooms of this building and here they engage in the physical phase of the conjugal relationship. "Officials and staff members," says Professor Hopper, "consistently praise the conjugal visit as a highly important factor in reducing homosexuality, boosting inmate morale, and... comprising an important factor in preserving marriages."

Every other Sunday, as soon as Vernon had visiting privileges, Elvis would embark with Gladys upon a long, strange journey across Mississippi that must have left an indelible mark on him. They would be up very early that morning, Gladys taking special care over their clothes and appearance; then they would either board a bus or get a ride with friends like F. L. Bobo, who ran the local hardware store, or any of Gladys' relations who were willing, and drive for over five hours until they finally arrived at what looked like endless cotton fields.

Then, somehow, Elvis would suddenly find himself inside a red-brick house and there would be his daddy who would hug him and play with him for a while, but then his daddy and mama would go off somewhere and leave him alone in the outer room among strange children.

Five hours there and five hours back; for Gladys these trips were not merely labors of love, they were labors of necessity. She was a woman with an unquestioning thirst to prove her devotion.

And uppermost in her mind was how to get Vernon out.

Mississippi did not develop a parole system until 1945, well after Vernon left. No records were kept in 1938. Prisoners could even serve sentences under assumed names.

Prior to that time the authority to pardon, commute sentences, and grant early releases rested with the governor of the state. Most people felt that you could buy your way out of prison if you bribed the right people, but in most instances in the thirties hardship (the wife's and children's economic situation) was important, as was the total family situation—that is, whether the family was considered a good influence. Mothers, fathers, wives, preachers, and other community members could write to the governor and prison officials and plead for pardon. The camp sergeant's opinion was crucial. If he thought a man deserved to be set free he could just about get it done.

"I suspect," says Professor Hopper, "that Vernon was a good worker, was polite to the sergeant, did not get into trouble, and that the community members in Tupelo wrote letters and persuaded the authorities to let

Vernon out in nine months to a year. That's about as good a scenario as you can get."

Professor Hopper's good-as-you-can-get scenario turns out to be accurate down to the last detail. Hardship was considered, his family was considered a good influence, the sergeant gave his OK, and Mrs. Novie Clark remembers signing along with the rest of the community a petition to the governor pleading for Vernon's early release. Vernon was freed on February 6, 1939. He had served nine months.

Vernon went back to Tupelo but he did not go back to the little house on the Old Saltillo Road. Understandably, in view of J. D.'s attitude towards his son, Gladys, as the long months passed, had grown more and more uncomfortable living next door to her father-in-law. At some point during Vernon's prison sentence Gladys did what family custom dictates she do when faced with a situation economically and emotionally beyond her control: she moved in with blood kin. All her sisters were now living out in the country, but Lillian came to town and helped Gladys pack her few belongings along with Elvis' toys. Gladys moved in with her first cousin, Frank Richards, his wife Leona, and their children, who lived on Maple Street in South Tupelo. Frank was the son of Doll's oldest sister, Melissa.

Always secure in blood ties, Gladys was at last able to leave the now four-year-old Elvis with Leona and her children and work in the nearby Mid-South Laundry. Elvis could still be seen from time to time on the Richards' porch "crying his eyes out because his daddy was away."

When Elvis was finally reunited with his daddy, all three stayed on at the Richards'. It was during this time, Leona Richards reports, that the Presley family had what she calls "action nightmares" either separately or all together. One night Gladys and Vernon and Elvis took the mattress and sheets off the bed and remade it on the floor and went back to sleep. When Leona found them the next morning they remembered nothing. Another night Gladys woke up having hurt her head badly. She had dreamt, she said, that she was on the bank of Mud Creek. She had apparently stood up in bed and dived off it and knocked her head against the chest of drawers.

Elvis' sleepwalking, which became something of a problem at the age of five and was to continue intermittently until late in his teens, would seem to have been influenced by these episodes. It caused Gladys much anxiety, and when Elvis had his own bedroom in his adolescence she took the precaution of removing the doorknob from the inside of his room.

Considering that sleepwalking is not uncommon with children, it is odd that apart from the sensational revelations of Lady Macbeth, next to nothing is known about this state of nocturnal suspension or its underlying causes. In former times it was believed that sleepwalkers were simply acting out their dreams, but with the advent of the EEG (electroencephalogram) as an agent for the study of sleep, this concept has been proved erroneous.

Somnambulism, we are now told, takes place just *after* the dream stage when sleep is deeper, the blood pressure lower, the heart rate sharply decreased, and the body temperature declined. It is only then that the sleeper's eyes mysteriously open and his body begins to move. Somnambulists are in a curious amnesiac state in which their eyes see, their hands feel, and their legs walk. Yet while all voluntary powers, all organs and senses of perception, memory, and imagination are in full activity, the operation of the power of judgment is torpid—partially, if not wholly, obscured.

Although somnambulists do not actually go out of their way to execute acts of great skill such as balancing on precipices, the ordinary acts they do perform—going downstairs, walking out the front door, opening windows, cooking a meal—can, because of their diminished state of judgment as well as their diminished state of vision, create a danger. And unlike the dream state, which can sometimes be recalled by the dreamer, the somnambulist experience does not register in the conscious thoughts of the sleepwalker.

At present the medical view of this phenomenon is that sleepwalking appears to have a family history of similarly affected persons (Gladys and Vernon obviously had bouts of it after their reunion, and one of Annie Presley's daughters used to go into the front room and play the piano in her sleep) and that it also may be caused by some family upset or disturbance.

Families of a somnambulist are warned never to awaken the sleepwalker in mid-action but instead try to get him back to bed where he will promptly relapse into a normal state of sleep. But what if he should suddenly awaken by himself in mid-action and alone?

Harry Crewes, in his recollections of his childhood in Georgia as a sharecropper's son, vividly describes his experience at the age of five:

I woke up sometime in the middle of the night. An enormous and brilliant moon shone over the cottonfield where I was standing still in my gown. It was not a dream and I knew immediately it was not a dream. I was where I thought I was and I had come here by walking in my sleep. I came awake that night the way I always have when I've gotten up in my sleep and walked. Terrified. Terrified almost beyond terror because it had no name and it was sourceless. My heart was pounding and I was soaked with sweat and my gown was soaking to my freezing skin.

When he goes back to his house his father tells him, "You was dreaming, boy. You walked in your sleep. It ain't nothing to worry about. You probably got it from me. I was bad to walk in my sleep when I was a boy."

However, whatever somnambulistic traumas the return of Vernon may have caused Elvis and the Presley family group at night, Elvis—by day and awake—was joyfully sure that his father had come back home in answer to his and his mother's prayers.

Nineteen forty found Vernon, Gladys, and Elvis, along with their cousin, Sales Presley, his wife Annie, and their children living in Pascagoula, a port near Biloxi at the southernmost tip of Mississippi on the Gulf of Mexico.

The expanding of the Pascagoula shipyards was a Works Progress Administration (WPA) project begun in 1938 which was urgently in need of unskilled labor. Handbills, posters, and columns in the Lee County newspapers all advertised large numbers of openings for shipyard workers in this area. Pascagoula was being enlarged to service ships from the port of New Orleans as well as from its own, and the increased activity was accelerated by the war which had broken out in Europe in 1939.

According to Annie Presley the two families stayed there for about eight months in the relentless, oppressive heat, living next to each other in a jerry-built row of one-room cabins, the walls of which were comprised mainly of screening.

While the men labored long and hard in the shipyards, Annie and Gladys, strangers to the rest of the community and thrown into constant proximity with each other, cemented their friendship, sharing cups of coffee at ten every morning, looking after their children together, and sitting and talking under the trees in the afternoon. Even on this very intimate basis, Gladys, says Annie, was always easy to get along with, while Elvis played with her children, especially her baby Diane to whom he'd taken a shine and would carry around on his hip.

By the end of the eight months Sales had had his fill of the broiling heat and the shipyards of Pascagoula, and told Vernon he was quitting. Vernon reckoned he might as well stay on a while.

As the other Presleys drove off early that morning Annie remembers that though she was not sorry to leave anything else in Pascagoula, she was very sorry to be leaving Gladys.

They stopped for lunch at a roadside café on their journey homewards. They had not been sitting there long (or so it seemed to Annie) at a table outside, when to their utter astonishment along came a car. It stopped and out came Vernon and Gladys and Elvis. Gladys, in the lead, explained the situation. "We're not staying down there alone," she declared firmly, "watching all those uptown folk eating shrimps and oysters."

Happily reunited, the couples drove back to Tupelo and once there Vernon and his family moved back in with the Frank Richardses long enough for Elvis to skid on the ice in the winter and break his arm.

Then they returned to East Tupelo where for some time they shared a two-family house on Reese Street with Vester and Clettes and their newborn daughter, Patsy. This frame house with two front doors, sloping roof, and gabled attic window, now a peeling faded yellow in color, tongue-and-grooved throughout—floors and ceilings as well as walls—still stands today, though only just, and its water pump, equidistant between the Presley house and their neighbor's, still works.

It was around this time that, according to Annie, "J. D. sold Vernon's house on the Old Saltillo Road out from under him." Although this is corroborated by several of her contemporaries, as the deeds of this transaction, presumably between J. D., Orville Bean, and a third party, have not turned up, it raises the question of how the house became his to sell in the first place. Perhaps J. D. had been paying rent on the house all the time Vernon was in jail and that gave him the right. Or perhaps when he sold it he gave the proceeds to Vernon. Perhaps. But it does not sound that way from the people who remember it. Whatever may or may not have transpired, the outcome was that Vernon, Gladys, and Elvis never returned to the little house on the Old Saltillo Road that Vernon built himself.

Vernon's problems, those of being a recently returned jailbird in so small a town, did not easily blow away. How many employers, distinctly aware of his criminal record but only vaguely of the details, were reluctant to hire him? From how many jobs might he have been automatically debarred?

After all, how many people are there in the world like Vernon's old patron Orville Bean, so eager to spring to the aid of a needy comrade that they will cheerfully purchase from him a hog at only half its worth and then make sure that this same needy comrade remain safely behind bars until such time as he has learned the invaluable lesson of gratitude?

Much later, when Elvis was famous, Bean, in another outburst of his celebrated generosity, swore to friends that he was going to dismantle Elvis' birthplace and sell the boards—one by one—to fans.

But if employers were wary of Vernon, his old pals were not. They welcomed him back with open arms confiding to him eloquently and frequently that in their opinion he had more than paid his debt and mended his ways and changed them and straightened his path and that, if he took their advice, he'd put the whole thing behind him and start fresh and that even though everybody knowed it hadn't been his fault in the first place they wanted to tell him right out that they thought it must have took an awful lot of *guts* to come back and settle down here after all what happened, and that was a *fact*. It was invariably at this point that a gleam would come into the speaker's eye and with an air of innocuous spontaneity, as if the thought had only that minute occurred to him, he would say to Vernon in a voice of suppressed excitement, "Listen, fellow, tell me one thing... what's it *really* like inside, huh? I mean, what'd they *really* do to you in there?"

It was, needless to say, a tale Vernon did not enjoy telling. The glamour of being such an object of interest did not balance for him the stigma that went with it. As a result he withdrew further into himself and his family and into his natural passivity. And he got into the habit of viewing himself as something of a martyr.

Meanwhile such jobs as he got continued to wear their air of perpetual impermanence, as they had before he went to jail. He worked, in the main, on public projects in and around Tupelo, one of them being the building of public lavatories. And just as he was resigning himself to never hearing the end of it he found that the good old boys' interest in his former predicament had cooled off and that they had gone on to concern themselves with fresher events.

Gladys reacted to all this somewhat differently from Vernon. It can be argued that it is sometimes the person closest to the afflicted, the one who has to stand by watching, who suffers more keenly than the victim who is so involved in his circumstances that he is too busy marshaling his defenses to have much time left over for surplus emotion. In any event, so it must have been with Gladys and Vernon, and would have had much to do with her resolve that this was never going to happen to her son.

All this the child Elvis—no common observer—observed: their feelings of helplessness, their feelings of undeserved humiliation, and the habit of looking upon themselves as victims. To Gladys' resolve that this would never happen to her son, Elvis added his own.

SEVEN

The Horizon Widens

When six-year-old Elvis began school in 1941 he may be said to have, at last, entered upon a more normal childhood than the one to which he had previously been exposed.

The school he went to, East Tupelo Consolidated on Lake Street, south of the highway, not five minutes from where Elvis lived, was something of an anomaly in that part of the world. It was an exceedingly well-run school in an exceedingly poor area. This school in Elvis' time consisted of two buildings: one housed the elementary school and the other the high school. The elementary school, though a woodframe building, had conveniences most of the children had never seen before—certainly not in their homes—in the way of heating, lighting, and plumbing. It had ample classrooms, comfortable desks, and its own auditorium. A large gymnasium was shared with the high school. The entire school's seven hundred pupils and thirty-six teachers were divided into classrooms of thirty pupils each.

Its surprisingly large number of students was accounted for by the fact that it drew its students not only from East Tupelo but from the surrounding areas of Priceville, Briar Ridge, Oak Hill, Moore's Crossroads, Bissell, Beach Springs, Auburn, and Mooreville. Its numbers had further increased in 1936 when the school building in Tupelo was destroyed by the tornado and its students transferred to East Tupelo until it was rebuilt.

East Tupelo Consolidated School, built in 1926 on the wrong side of the tracks, was the result of the determined efforts of its citizens to locate a modern school with all grades within the precincts of their town. It was an objective for whose existence these citizens had fought, legislated, raised bond issues, and contributed money out of their own pockets. It was their most visible and most shared source of pride and joy, and it is no exaggeration to say that it was the one tangible asset on which the hopes and aspirations of the community for their children centered. It was considered the best-run school in Lee County.

In 1936 East Tupeloans took great personal satisfaction in knowing that their school was the first in Lee County to add a business department. The next year a vocational agricultural department and a home economics department was added to the curriculum, as well as a lunchroom operated under the WPA. The community was proud when the school won the Lee County Literary Association contest three years running and prouder still at the successes of its football team and the school band when it was chosen for the honor of playing in the Cotton Carnival in Memphis. Tupelo's famous boosterism and optimism would seem to have traveled across the levee via this school to Elvis.

The guiding spirit of East Tupelo Consolidated School was its superintendent, Ross Lawhon (later the school was renamed Lawhon after him, as was a street in Tupelo). He was a strict disciplinarian, deeply respected in the community and county for his ability to raise public funds and then get things done with them. He had an instinct for engaging committed teachers to make up his staff and a ferocious determination that every child in the school, however poor, got the best education possible while under his supervision. He was, in short, a man who believed in education.

Although J. D. Cole was principal of the school during Elvis' years, it was Lawhon, from the vantage point of his office window which overlooked the school grounds, who ran the show. Uncomfortably, soon the children came to know that his eye was unblinkingly upon them. Any boy or girl he glimpsed walking down the street together holding hands was forthwith hauled into his office for a severe dressing down. Any boy caught on or even (it is insisted) too near his beloved flowerbeds was paddled.

Elvis was fortunate in beginning his school education, along with many other children of his age and background, in an environment of order, concern, and firmness of purpose. It could only have been a relief for him, this daily escape from the anxieties of his mother—added to which was the death of her sister Rhetha from severe burns when her stove, touched off by an overturned kerosene can, caught fire and burned down her house—and the perplexities of his father.

It is interesting to speculate how regular Elvis' school attendance might have been had his parents settled in the surrounding county areas as so many of their relatives had; how often in bad weather the school bus might not have turned up or have broken down; how often he might not have been spared—as Gladys had not been spared—from the priorities of farm and household chores.

As it was every morning during the school term, Gladys got Elvis out of bed, scrubbed his face, neck and ears with homemade soap, gave him breakfast, put him in clean overalls and, along with Annie Presley and her children, marched him off the short distance to school in the morning and the short distance back in the afternoon.

And so began the daily ritual of Gladys walking Elvis to and from school; a ritual she was to observe whenever possible almost to the end of Elvis' school days. That it was to cause him much embarrassment, annoyance, and frustration, not to say anger (he finally insisted she walk behind him and on the other side of the road, hidden in the bushes if possible), did not prevent him from understanding the motives for her persistence and—in the main—from being sympathetic with her ultimate aim.

For the truth of the matter was that as late as Gladys and Vernon's generation, book learning was still considered irrelevant, and education— even in its most basic forms of simple reading, writing, and "figuring"— inessential to the welfare of the poor agricultural worker in the South. The imperatives stressed were the daily practicalities in this most practical of all lands, and you didn't need to read a book to learn how to do them— your father or your boss *showed* you how. But with the migration of the agricultural laborers to towns it was becoming ever more impractical for even those doing the most unskilled work not to have a grasp, however tenuous, on the Three Rs—and for those over school age it was, by then, too late. One old Tupeloan, a former truck driver, recalls that he had to turn down the lucrative offer of a job involving the delivering of goods from Tupelo to Chicago because he couldn't read the road signs.

Against this background Gladys' continual monitoring of Elvis' school attendance can no longer be interpreted as the activity of a dementedly possessive mother. By the age of ten—like all the boys and many of the girls in East Tupelo—Elvis had learned to drive a car. At twelve, Vernon and Gladys were allowing him to be the driver of their old secondhand car on their various outings. Young Elvis was often seen behind the wheel chauffeuring his family to revival meetings around Lee County and, a few years later, driving them down from Memphis to Tupelo. As a high school student in Memphis, the sight of Elvis in the battered family car with its piece of cardboard in the place of a window was so familiar to his schoolmates that they assumed it was his very own.

Surely no mother, as will be seen, who allows her son at the age of eight to hitch rides from East Tupelo to Main Town on his own; who lets him drive a car at ten; who later allows him to take jobs in the evening that finish well into the night, is going to be idiotic enough to think him physically incapable of getting to school under his own steam.

The reason she accompanied him so often is as obvious as it is moving. Her walking him to and from school was for her a ceremony, both celebratory and cautionary. She was celebrating that he was going to have the education neither she nor Vernon had had, and she was cautioning him from slipping away from school—as she had sometimes caught him—by collecting him at the end of the day. Gladys was making sure that Elvis was going to get his high school diploma. And she had good reason to be afraid of him playing hookey.

Vernon did not care so much if or when Elvis quit school. He might, secretly and understandably, grudge his child the education he'd never had and, wearying of employment offices, welfare offices, social security checks, and work itself, might feel the sooner Elvis started earning regularly and contributing towards the family income the better.

Elvis himself, especially in his last year in high school, was strongly pulled away from school and impatient to get on with his life. But it is a fact that in later years when Elvis took friends around his trophy room the first thing he showed them was his high school diploma prominently framed on the wall. "I never thought I'd make it," he said. Gladys thought differently.

"Gladys was foolish about Elvis—just foolish," all her friends, relatives, and neighbors agree. "She never let that boy out of her sight," they said.

It is the last part of that statement that must be questioned because, on closer examination, it proves to be demonstrably false. That Gladys was foolish about Elvis was true but that he was regularly out of her sight from as early as eight years old on was also true. And where he went when out of her sight is of the utmost significance.

When Elvis was six years old the first local radio station, WELO, was built in Tupelo. It was installed over the Black and White Store on Spring Street. Charlie Boren, its first announcer, claims to have helped lay the cables with his own hands as well. That it would be the *only* radio station in northeast Mississippi powerful enough to have signals into Memphis is easily anticipated. The station was, after all, in Tupelo (the call-sign used the last three letters of Tupelo, while the next local station to be built, WTUP, used the first three). A lot of country bands appeared on it—Mrs. Billie Walker, Pappy Stewart, and the Two Arkansas Cowgirls, the Nicolas Brothers, Dan Whitney, Mississippi Slim, the Lee County Ramblers. "We had them all," says Charlie Boren, "the whole six yards." Above all, for Elvis, there was Mississippi Slim.

Charlie Boren now lives in Amory, Mississippi, where he runs a dry-goods store and still organizes screenings all over the state of old movies from his famous library. His motto: Old movies don't fade away, they just get better. It was he who had brought the movies to Saltillo, on a flatbed truck, and captivated Gladys and the other country girls with *Our Dancing Daughters* and other Joan Crawford movies.

Charlie Boren must be what they call "a card." In any case, here is his:

New cars	Call girls	Jury bribes	Wheel chairs
Bed pans	Elections rigged		Black market surplus
Cotton pickers	Chicken pluckers		Pickle packers
Trash haulers	Horse trading		Manure broker
Baby sitting	Artificial Insemination		Lawns mowed
Dickerer	CHARLIE BOREN		Printer
	BOX 15–AMORY, MISS.		
NIGHT: 601-256-3984			DAY: 256-5685
Hotel Reservations	Tequila	Beer	Steaks
Anything wholesale	Articles for sale		Brassieres
Perfumes	Railroad tickets one-way		Wrenches
	Also an assortment of odds and ends—mostly ends		

Charlie well remembers Elvis from the age of eight onwards at the Tupelo courthouse every Saturday afternoon. It was from there that WELO broadcast its "Saturday Jamboree," an amateur program which started at 1 P.M. and went on till 4:30 and had live audiences composed of up to a hundred and fifty people.

"The way you got to sing or play was just to walk up and say, 'I want to go on,'" says Charlie. "It was first come first served and it was a big thing, those kids standing in line waiting for their chance, so if you were smart you got there early." He remembers Elvis getting to sing there as often as every other Saturday a fairly wide selection of songs from Gene Autry to gospel and, later on, a World War II song entitled "God Bless My Daddy, He's Over There." But others only remember his persistent renderings of Red Foley's "Old Shep," the ballad about a boy and his dog: the boy's heart-wrenching reminiscences of their long friendship, how Old Shep saved him from drowning, how in the end he has to shoot Old Shep and "wished they had shot me instead" and how he knows that "if

dogs have a heaven Old Shep has a wonderful home." It had hundreds
of verses which Elvis included as he mastered them.

Reggie Bell worked in a garage in Mooreville in those days and in the
late afternoon, if there weren't many customers, he would take off to play
with the Lee County Ramblers on WELO. On his way to Tupelo he would
often pick up young Elvis waiting on the corner of Canal Street in front
of the C & A Cleaners and together they would drive off to Spring Street
where Elvis would sit quietly in the studio watching and listening to the
Lee County Ramblers and his first musical hero, Mississippi Slim.

Carvel Lee Ausborn—Mississippi Slim—came from East Tupelo where
Elvis made a point of getting to know him, says Ernest Bowen, another
former radio announcer, by the simple expedient of "following him
around like a pet dog." Tall, slender, long-nosed, red-faced and beady-
eyed, Slim was very much the archetype of the southern country singer.
He played guitar, sometimes harmonica, and sometimes sang duets with
his kinsman Clinton. But on these last occasions he was not always to
be relied upon and often he had to be telephoned frantically from WELO
and told to get the hell on over there as Clinton was sitting on his own
lap.

Slim drifted from Tupelo to Memphis to Nashville. He was married at
least four times and was a lively chronicler of these events. When Ernest
Bowen inquired after his latest wife he replied, "I says to her one day,
'I'm hungry,' and she went out to get me a hamburger, and the next thing
I knew it was twenty-four hours later when a car pulls up and there she
is sitting between two sailors. I said, 'All I got to say to you is *where's my
goddam hamburger?*'"

Mississippi Slim began singing on WELO when it first came on the
air and stayed there, on and off, for about twenty years. First he had a
fifteen-minute Saturday show called "Singin' and Pickin' Hillbilly." Elvis
would ride up with him from East Tupelo and sit adoringly in the studio.
The program was soon increased to thirty minutes once a week, and
finally to five times a week for an hour. That is an awful lot of Mississippi
Slim.

How good was he? He has four tapes in the Country Music Hall of
Fame in Nashville, and while not everyone agrees that they should be
there, all are unanimous in one respect: he was an original; he had a
style all his own. It just depended on whether you liked it or not. Ernest
Bowen did not. He thought Slim strictly hillbilly. According to Ernest, a
big-band addict, there were only two kinds of country music in those
days—the best and the worst. Slim he considered at the bottom of the
worst. On the other hand young Elvis worshipped him. Certainly, on the

evidence, Slim had a very large audience. From his records, "Honky Tonk Woman," "Tired of Your Eyes," and "I'm Through Crying Over You" (Tennessee Label), he reveals himself as having one of those plaintive, cajoling, wistful, wheedling, maddening, endearing, tin-shack, sun-setting voices whose reedy richness can probably only be fully captured on an old wind-up Victrola.

An Australian listening to these records said, "Oh God, it takes me back to all those terrible songs I used to hear on the radio in the outback when I was a boy. I expect him to break into a ballad about Ned Kelly any minute."

Yet others consider the sly subtlety of Slim's timing and phrasing one of the wonders of the world, as was certainly the jazz piano accompaniment on his records, courtesy of one Del Wood—female and white.

From Mississippi Slim, Elvis' first professional musical mentor, he learned a lot. Though Slim tolerated his young fan's adoration and indeed was not at all displeased by it, he was slightly taken aback, he confided to fellow musician Archie McKay, by this shy boy's insistence that Slim accompany him on one of WELO's Saturday afternoon amateur shows. Finally he consented. "Hell, I got to play for him," he told McKay. "His timing's all off but he's doing a good job for an eight-year-old." Though after the performance he could be observed muttering with a discouraged sigh, "The kid can't keep time."

At the age of nine it was Mertice Finley—now Mrs. Mertice Collins—who gave rides into town to the young boy standing on Canal Street every Friday afternoon on her way from Mooreville to Tupelo, where she worked after hours at Penney's. She remembers Elvis as a painfully shy, almost tongue-tied child whose only conversation with her during her initial drive was their exchange of names, though there were so many Presleys she didn't connect Elvis with Gladys. "My mama says she knows you," he got up the nerve to tell her one day and mentioned he was going to WELO. She dropped him there and showed him where she would be parking her car and told him if he waited for her inside it after the show, she'd carry him back to East Tupelo after work.

It was winter and bitter cold but Mertice always found Elvis waiting for her outside the car. In spite of her urging he never once got in till she arrived.

Later, after Elvis got his famous first guitar for his tenth birthday and he learned to play it well enough to accompany himself singing "Old Shep," he sang the song every place and at every opportunity permitted so that it became a joke among his schoolmates—"Oh no! Not another round of 'Old Shep' today." Mississippi Slim told Elvis he was good but must keep practicing. He taught him additional chords—minor chords, sharps, and flats. According to Slim's younger brother, James Ausborn, who was a schoolmate of Elvis' in sixth grade, he listened attentively but just didn't seem to learn, at least not quickly.

When Elvis was twelve, Slim occasionally had the boy on his shows. There was a slight skirmish over his first appearance. Slim had announced that a young lad, Elvis Presley, would be on the following week. But when the time came Elvis had such a bad attack of stage fright he couldn't do it. Shy people set themselves difficult tasks. He went on the week after.

Elvis and James would meet up at Slim's shows on Saturday mornings, following which would take place such amiable exchanges as Elvis telling Slim he wished he could sing just like him and Slim replying, "You're good to be as young as you are—you just keep on working."

Elvis looked up to Slim the way kids in the future would look up to Elvis. But though James and Elvis were close friends for two years Elvis never once expressed to him his own desire to become a professional singer.

Yet there was young Elvis following Mississippi Slim around, regularly turning up for the "Saturday Jamborees," and singing whenever and wherever he got the chance. Vividly Archie McKay remembers one such occasion at the courthouse with Elvis "in a little white suit and his chewing gum guitar—we called them that because they looked like you'd sent off a chewing gum wrapper to get it"—actually getting a standing ovation for his rendition of "Old Shep." But, he adds, "I don't think it was that he was so good but that he was so little."

Gladys is conspicuously absent from all these events. She is not standing on the corner of Canal Street summer and winter with Elvis and she is not sitting in the studio with him. The people who were so sure she never let Elvis out of her sight seemed to have been looking the wrong way.

What is to be concluded from this? That he sneaked off for these regular outings only to catch hell from her upon his return? What is far more likely is that from earliest days there was a pact between them—in some form or other—about this aspect of his life, and that there was not only an understanding, or a collusion, or an appreciation, or a sympathy, but a trading, a swapping, and bargaining for certain freedoms, a not unusual part of a child's relationship with his mother.

Just how clearly defined and stated Elvis' aspirations were to become a country singer or when they crystallized or whether he made or even intended to make a more specific declaration of it to his mother than the oft quoted "When I grow up, Mama, I'm going to take care of you" would be impossible to say. In any case as far as serving his apprenticeship to his vocation, he was certainly going about it the right way. Nor, quite remarkably, knowing of Gladys' painful separation anxieties, did she ever try to prevent him. Perhaps she preferred him safely in the radio station to getting into fights with other boys. The Above the Highway bunch was a rough crowd.

The year before Elvis took his first active steps into the World of WELO was 1942. The United States had entered World War II. Vernon, with his family entirely dependent on him, was not drafted. Instead, he went back to prison. *Not*—it must quickly be interpolated—to be incarcerated therein, but, ironically, to help *build* one.

Under the WPA, a prisoner-of-war camp was being constructed in Como, Mississippi, one hundred and seventy-three miles from Tupelo. It was called Japtown, although as it turned out it was to hold only German prisoners.

It was during this time, with Vernon miles away, that Gladys suffered another emotional heartbreak and physical tragedy. Mrs. Leona Moore, now a retired nurse who was working at the Tupelo Hospital at the time, offers the following story:

One day Gladys was brought to the hospital on a stretcher with seven-year-old Elvis at her side, holding her hand and crying. As Nurse Moore quickly made preparations to admit her, Gladys began objecting. She couldn't afford the hospital, she had only ten dollars to live on until her husband returned, and what would she do with her young son? Nurse Moore assured her that in this emergency "people like her" would not have to pay the hospital fees; further, she arranged for Elvis' Uncle Noah to come and get the child. Only when Noah arrived for Elvis did Gladys agree to be admitted. What was Gladys admitted for? Says Mrs. Moore today, "The truth is she had a miscarriage."

This traumatic event, besides rendering Elvis and Gladys more precious to each other than ever, finally puts at rest the constant speculation of why Gladys never had another child. She had tried, and failed. It was as commonplace as that.

Shortly before Japtown's completion in May 1943, Vernon went up to his friend and fellow worker, Bill Parham, and said he'd been given his notice and wanted to know if Bill had, too. No, said Bill, he hadn't. There it was again; Vernon always the first to be let go. "Well," said Vernon to Bill, "Guess I'll be going up to Memphis now to look for work."

In the War Boom, Vernon found factory work in Memphis. There he stayed, receiving higher wages during this period than he ever had in his life and returning home only on weekends until the war was over and the factories closed down. Elvis and Gladys were better equipped to cope with this separation from Vernon. For one thing more money was coming regularly and for another his past notoriety was running out.

Elvis was armed now with the regularity of school days and the widening of his horizons. He had found his escape not only into what was to become his art—his music—but also into what was to become an important part of his fantasy life: his reading.

If the shy boy had set himself the difficult task of learning to sing and perform, it was far easier for him to learn to read, motivated as he was by his desire to follow more closely the thrilling adventures of the heroes and villains he had discovered in comic books. From *The Long Ranger* to *Superman*, apart from double identities, the golden age of comic book heroes all shared one other interesting feature in common: They were all exhilaratingly free from parental tension, for they had neither fathers nor mothers. This further enabled the young reader to break loose from the complicated constrictions imposed on him by childhood into a dream of self-reliance—aided in his triumphs only by some godlike magic, or a horse.

Elvis was able to exist for hours, adventurously, independently, and happily in a world without his mother, flying high above her with the Marvels, the Batmans, the Supermans, free from all his responsibilities to her until, brought back to earth with a bang by a look on her face, he would feel the guilt and danger of his desertion resurface and would subside again into the constant components of love, placation, and reconciliation which counterbalanced these flights.

It was in third grade that Raymond McCoy first registered his classmate Elvis. He remembers him as a skinny, energetic boy, scrappy, "not looking for a fight but not turning it down." But it was something else about Elvis that fixed him firmly in his mind.

At the end of each school day the children had a thirty-minute rest period. Then their teacher, Mrs. Bell, would have them put their heads down on their desks and either go to sleep or listen quietly while one of them told a story. What made Raymond so vividly recall the eight-year-old Elvis was that, unlike the other children's stories that ended with each rest period, the story he told was a series which continued day after day. "He kept us fascinated for weeks with the hero's adventures," says Raymond. "It was about a tin man."

The Wizard of Oz, the best-known, best-loved American children's book, had become even better known when it was made into a film in 1939 and was also appearing in the form of newspaper comic strips and a series called *Big Little Comic Books* during Elvis' childhood. The connection between the Tin Woodman in *The Wizard of Oz* and Elvis' Tin Man seems obvious although Raymond didn't make it.

The initial reason for Elvis' being so powerfully affected by this tale surely must lie in its beginning when, following a great shriek of wind, Dorothy's house shakes so hard that she loses her footing and sits suddenly on the floor. And then a strange thing happens. The house whirls around two or three times, rises slowly in the air and Dorothy, caught up in the cyclone—or what in Tupelo they would call a tornado—is catapulted into Oz.

There was also the Tin Woodman's striking appearance; shining in armor like knights of old—but not too like them, funny and homely as well, with an overturned oil can for a cap; yet still cutting a dashing figure as he uses his unique skills in constructing rafts to ford the rivers, or—in his finest hour—wielding his flashing silver-bladed, gold-handled ax about him as he cleaves through the terrifying Forest of Fighting Trees.

For Elvis, the sight of his father, relatives, and neighbors chopping up trees in East Tupelo's thickly wooded hills, chopping wood to build with, chopping wood for stoves and fireplaces, was a familiar one, a chore not without danger to fingers, toes, and limbs.

It was around this time also, Corene Smith recalls, that with Vernon in Memphis, Gladys had begun to feel "scary" about all the bushes that surrounded their house. They increasingly made her feel isolated and she became convinced that dark things were moving in them. Finally she insisted they be chopped down.

Elvis' Tin Man and his adventures might also be said to reflect fairly accurately Elvis' view of himself at this point, of his surroundings and that other world outside Tupelo, "over the rainbow."

In the book *The Wizard of Oz*, of all Dorothy's companions—the Cowardly Lion, the Scarecrow, and the Tin Woodman—the only one ever actually to have been human once is the Tin Woodman.

He is tin because his ax kept slipping and chopping off parts of him, and as each part was replaced by a tin one he gradually became entirely composed of tin. But his heart was not replaced and he keenly feels the loss of it. It is to seek one from the Wizard that he joins up with Dorothy and her friends on the road to the Emerald City.

The Tin Woodman can be seen as a true hero with a tragic flaw: He is without a heart. Or alternately as a comic hero, since the Wizard corrects this defect and gives him one (in the book a silk pincushion stuffed with sawdust, in the film a big, round, red, ticking clock), although not without a quibble: "I think you are wrong to want a heart. It makes people most unhappy. If you only knew it, you are lucky not to have a heart," he says. To which the Tin Woodman, rising to the occasion in the best chivalric tradition, replies: "For my part, I will bear all the unhappiness without a murmur, if you will give me the heart."

Notably it is not the Scarecrow's lack of a brain nor the Cowardly Lion's lack of courage that seems to have fired Elvis' imagination, but the Tin Woodman's lack of heart.

A case could be made that Elvis, missing his dead twin, sometimes saw reflected in the Tin Woodman a feeling of his own emptiness. And also that he recognized in his hero his own need for armor. And that he harbored a fierce desire for a gold-handled, silver-bladed ax with which to lay about the world in all directions. Apart from the Tin Man episode, schoolmate memories of Elvis' first years are unexceptional.

According to Mrs. Mildred Merchent, now school secretary of Lawhon, formerly East Tupelo Consolidated, Elvis was an average student from first through fourth grades. And although there is ample proof that Gladys loomed large as ever in his foreground, oversupervising, overprotecting, and overdefending him, Elvis himself put his feelings about the general situation in a nutshell when he said in an interview on September 22, 1958, "I used to get very angry with her when I was growing up. It's a natural thing when a young person wants to go somewhere and do something and your mother won't let you, you think, 'Why? What's wrong with *you*?'" (His emphasis on *you* clarifies the meaning: What was wrong with his mother was what puzzled him.) And Annie Presley tells the following revealing anecdote: "Once, on account of a mix-up over who was to pick up the children from school, they walked home by themselves and Gladys saw the Hand boys ganging up on Elvis. She jumped off the front porch and went after them with her dogwood broom. She didn't use the steps." Still, Gladys did not seem to be able to prevent Elvis from doing what most of the young boys did in East Tupelo besides fight with each other.

Elvis not only swapped comic books with Wayne Earnest and other classmates, he also swapped colds and other childhood illnesses. According to Vernon in *Good Housekeeping*, when Elvis was about six years old "... he had developed acute tonsillitis with such high fever he was on the verge of convulsions. Gladys and I were afraid that we were going to lose him." The doctor, says Vernon, had given up on him and suggested they call another. Instead, "My wife and I turned in prayer to the greatest healer of all, God. I do believe in miracles, so that day I prayed to God that he would miraculously heal our child. My wife and I prayed together and separately, and by that night I could see that Elvis was better." With or without prayer Elvis also recovered from whooping cough and measles.

Besides the numerous children of his Mansell, Smith, and Presley relations, Elvis numbered Charles and James Farrar, Guy Harris, Odell Clarke, and Becky Martin among his friends. Like them, he played marbles which he kept in a tobacco sack, and wore longjohns which scratched in the winter and which he looked forward to taking off on the first day of spring.

Charles Farrar remembers that Vernon built Elvis a flying jenny in his front yard—a sort of upright pole with two boards attached to it that they all swung around in, and Odell Clarke remembers that a boy made a guitar out of a five-gallon lard can and traded it to Elvis and that Elvis "banged on that thing for quite a while."

According to F. L. Bobo—the same Mr. Bobo who used to drive Gladys and Elvis to visit Vernon in Parchman—it was for Elvis' ninth or tenth birthday that he received his first real guitar.

Mr. Bobo, who ran the hardware store where it was bought, describes the event:

Elvis and his mother came in one morning. He was anxious to buy a rifle, his mother was trying to persuade him to buy a guitar. I showed him the rifle first and then I took him and showed him his guitar and I sat him down behind the counter on a shell box and he enjoyed that, too. He told his mother he didn't have enough money to buy the guitar and so she said, "I'll pay up for you, but I can't pay up if it's to buy you a rifle. You're liable to kill all your little playmates." So Elvis convinced himself about the guitar. The papers always said it was $12 but it wasn't—you got a real good guitar back in those days for $12—but this was only $7.75, I believe. Of course, we had a 2¢ sales tax.

Two things stand out in this narrative: first, that Elvis himself had saved up his own money toward his birthday present (by doing yard work for other people and accepting empty Coke bottles in payment which he cashed in) and second, with "you're liable to kill all your little playmates," Gladys vividly reveals that recurringly apprehensive state of her mind.

Mr. Bobo continued his reminiscences of Elvis:

He came back to the Mississippi-Alabama Fair in 1956, I think it were about then. So he came back to Tupelo and we had supper after at the Thompson's— that's on Wayside Street—and I guess I was late because when I left he was going to Dallas, Texas, and he promised that night, "If I make good I'm going to buy you a steak dinner." He made good but he didn't make the supper. I don't hold that against Elvis. I'm proud of Elvis. He made good; he always tried to do right, he loved his neighbors, he loved all his playmates in school, he loved his fans—he just loved people, that's all. Elvis, he'd always come back and see his people—always at night. He was never proud. He had a wonderful mother; she was a very nice woman.

People come here, I tell them my tale. One woman from Florida, said she was a distant cousin, wanted to know if I'd take her out there to see the house where he was born. I told her OK. She said she wanted something that he'd touched. So we was walking down the driveway and I found a little ole rock. I picked it up, I told her, I said, "Now here is a rock; Elvis wore that rock down with his feet, I'm sure." I said, "Take it and keep it. You can tell them where it's come from and if anyone wants to see it you can charge them a nickel." And do you know, she turned around and before you know it, she made a dime off two boys who could have walked down there and picked it up for themselves. I said she might be a rich woman with a rock like that.

Charles Farrar remembers that he and Elvis went to the Strand Theater in Main Town to the movies, and to special children's shows on Saturdays in a room above a store in East Tupelo where they saw Flash Gordon, Sunset Carson, and Gene Autry films. "It cost a dime to get into the Strand and Coca-Cola and popcorn were a nickel each. A dime would be like a birthday and fifty cents looked as big as a wagon wheel. Me and Elvis and some of the other boys would get together in an empty shed or we'd dig a large hole in the ground and that would be our clubhouse for a while. I can't remember much what we did there except tell stories and jokes. When it was hot in the summer everyone slept out on the front porch—just get a blanket and lay out on it."

He remembers going for a hike in the woods with Elvis and the new young First Assembly of God preacher, Frank Smith, who took an active interest in the kids, and that they came across a dead lizard and buried him and Brother Smith held a funeral service over it. Elvis' recorded memories of his poor but happy childhood, "There wasn't much money but there was a lot of love," would seem to tally with the forceful conviction with which Charles ends his recollections. "Them," he says, "were joyous days."

Entering the fifth grade, Elvis, along with the rest of the boys, hoped that of the two homeroom teachers he wouldn't get Mrs. Grimes. She had the reputation for being the hard one, the one with whom you couldn't get away with anything. But Mrs. Grimes was who he got.

At the beginning of that school term, during morning devotions, Mrs. Grimes asked her pupils if any of them could say a prayer. Elvis got up and said one and then went straight into his rendition of "Old Shep." Mrs. Grimes was highly impressed. "He sang it so sweetly," she says, "it liked to make me cry." And it gave her an idea.

She took him along to the school principal, Mr. Cole, and again Elvis sang "Old Shep." Mr. Cole was similarly impressed. It was a few weeks before the Mississippi-Alabama Fair, held annually at Tupelo's fairgrounds, which included among its many attractions a Children's Talent Contest. Each school in the area selected its contestants. Elvis was promptly entered.

EIGHT

The Short Happy Months

The intoxicating aroma of diesel fuel mingled with food, smoke, sizzling grease, and sawdust is the first thing Tupeloans recall about the annual Mississippi-Alabama Fair and Dairy Show of their childhood which opened the last week in September on a Tuesday and closed the next Saturday night. And those special fairground tastes of candied apples, roast corn-on-the-cob, cotton candy, footlong hot dogs smothered in mustard and sauerkraut, and fiddlesticks (a stick of vanilla, chocolate or strawberry ice cream dipped into chocolate sauce and then into chopped walnuts)—they were the ones you would never be able to reproduce either in a kitchen or, for that matter, anywhere in the world, however similar the ingredients used.

Then there were the thrilling rides: the Ferris wheel, the merry-go-round, the Mad Mouse, the Dodgem', the Scrambler, the Octopus, the Whip, and the Tilt-a-Whirl.

There was the Mirror House and the Fun House and the Haunted House.

There were the carnival barkers outside the tents of the various hoochie-koochie shows, belly dancers, snake-charmers, tattooed ladies—Children Not Admitted but sneaked in anyway—peep shows and freak shows.

There were the shooting galleries and booths at which a well-aimed ball would win you a giant stuffed panda.

There were, of course, dairy product and livestock exhibits from all over Mississippi and Alabama and horse shows and cattle auctions. But far more exciting to the children were the daredevils on motorcycles who climbed the walls of a pit. Lottery tickets, whose prize was an automobile, went on sale at least a month before the Fair opened. Every school in the surrounding area had a booth, a band, and a parade.

The fairground grandstand had a seating capacity of two thousand. During the fair it held shows that included a rodeo with a clown; any number of beauty contests at which were chosen Miss Tupelo and Miss East Tupelo and even Lil' Miss Mississippi as well as Miss Mississippi and Miss Alabama for the national Miss America contest; live singers, live comedy acts, live bands.

Not half a mile from where he lived, all these wonders would bloom annually for Elvis all the years of his childhood—would bloom, you could say, right there in his own backyard. And all he needed was something he did not often have—the price of admission.

The children of East Tupelo saved up for the fair. Without compunction small boys stole nickels and dimes out of their older sisters' pocketbooks for those five glorious days in autumn. For them it was much better than Christmas; it lasted longer. Along with all the other children Elvis dreamed about it for weeks in advance. When it arrived he dreamed of running away from home and joining it. For weeks after it closed down and left town he went back to the fairgrounds; walking around it, staking out in his mind where everything had been, remembering and savoring it all over again.

"It stood for mystery, glamour, maturity, independence," says Roy Turner. "It was the best thing that happened every year."

Every year at the fair there was a photography booth where, against the same painted background of a western sky, snowcapped mountains, a few cacti and a corral fence to lean on, you could be photographed dressed in the cowboy suit they supplied—hat, chaps, gun holster, and gun. Elvis was photographed there at thirteen. So was his friend, James Ausborn. So were Uncle Vester and his family. Practically every family album in East Tupelo contains a photograph of one of its members in that same outfit that Elvis wore against those same mountains.

Every so often the corporate conscience of the leading citizens in Tupelo would act up and committees would be formed to discuss the advisability of closing down the fair for good. There was a moral issue at stake, it was argued. The fair was leading the poor of the county into temptation and calamity by causing them to throw their hard-earned money away, recklessly grabbing for themselves and their children that One Good Time, only to feel the pinch for the rest of the year. It followed that the fair was a bad thing, a dangerous thing, and should be abolished. But inevitably when The Conscience got around to weighing this against the glory of Tupelo being the site of the biggest and best goddamn fair as they put it, in the whole South, and that they sometimes even cleared a profit on it—the first consideration faded away and Tupelo today still remains host to the Mississippi-Alabama Fair.

On Wednesday afternoon, the second day of the 1945 fair, when he was ten years old, Elvis, wearing overalls and accompanying himself on his guitar, stood on a chair to reach the microphone on the stage of the grandstand and sang "Old Shep" in the children's singing contest. He won second prize—$5 and free admission to all the amusement rides.

He had sung "Old Shep" of course, many many times before. But as this can be considered his professional debut—he got money for it—it is worth noting that it took place not in a little theater, or in an actors' studio, or in an obscure nightclub, but at a country fair in front of a live audience of his own people—and in a grandstand that seated two thousand.

As the prizes were gauged by audience applause, Elvis' reaction to his success must certainly have been a magnification of Gladys' reaction to *her* success dancing to Jimmie Rodgers. But if Gladys had tasted pleasure, Elvis—it might be said—had tasted blood. For, however many people were actually seated in the grandstand to watch a children's talent contest, his child's eye must have it filled to capacity.

What had happened during and after his performance that memorable day was a turning point or, to be more accurate, a go-ahead signal for Elvis to continue along his chosen path.

To Elvis the whole experience of that day at the fair—of his euphoria at being appreciated, applauded, and awarded, of being in twinship with a large audience, of having his triumph capped off with a prize (he who had till then climbed over the fence just to sneak in)—was something he would never get over. From this experience stemmed his lifelong devotion to Liberty Land, Memphis' amusement park. He would become its most dedicated patron and its biggest spender, taking possession of it after hours with his friends and admirers and frolicking there till dawn.

To Mrs. Grimes, the hard fifth-grade teacher, must go the honor of being Elvis' first academic booster. It is impossible to overemphasize the importance of her encouragement at that moment in Elvis' life. If she had not singled him out, if her enthusiasm for his talent had not led her to take the immediate practical step of calling him to Mr. Cole's attention, Elvis would not have been entered in the contest. Of this Elvis was aware not only at the time but also in retrospect. When he later returned to East Tupelo he often visited Mrs. Grimes.

Once he turned her classroom inside out by being caught peeking in at its window.

"He was a good student," Mrs. Grimes almost mechanically repeats when asked about Elvis. "I knew him that well, I'd remember that. Sweet. That's the word. Sweet and average." She is also quoted as saying, "I didn't think Elvis'd ever amount to much, of course."

Mrs. J. C. Grimes—her husband, Clint, had a furniture store—was the former Miss Oleta Bean. She was, and it is here recorded for the first time, the daughter of Vernon's tormentor, Orville Bean.

But back in 1945 on that day of the Mississippi-Alabama Fair, who won first prize? As with many other important events in Elvis' life, a certain amount of confusion surrounds it.

In 1977 an article in the *Tupelo Daily Journal*, and subsequently reprinted in many other publications, had a Becky Harris of Bissell, aged six, winning with "Sentimental Journey." The only trouble is that she won it in 1946, a year later. When Shirley (Jones) Gallentine read the article, she called the journalist who wrote it and asked for a correction. It was she who had won first prize at the 1945 contest. A year younger than Elvis and also a pupil at East Tupelo Consolidated School, she had ridden over to the fair in the school bus with Elvis. She wore an off-the-shoulder white dress her mother had made for her and sang "My Dreams Are Getting Better All The Time," and won first prize—a $25 war bond.

In school assemblies for the rest of that year she and Elvis often sang duets together: "Deep in the Heart of Texas," "Blue Moon Over My Shoulder," "My Blue Heaven," and a lot of other Gene Austin songs.

As early as fourth grade, Elvis' interest in girls was conspicuous if not reciprocated. In fifth grade, now, he sought out Eloise Bedford and was able to make his attentions official by taking her to the school Halloween party. Then one day not long after, just as she was boarding the school bus in the afternoon, he handed her a note. It read, without preamble or postscript, "I have found another girl."

It is doubtful whether Eloise lost too much sleep over his abrupt desertion. Painfully shy but with an irritating show-off streak, and always getting up to crazy antics that made him look a fool, Elvis had what Eloise describes as a "permanently silly grin on his face—not a smile, a grin. The one you see in all his movies, he kept it up all his life. It was like he was saying, 'I know something you don't.'" Elvis, though you had to admit he sang pretty well, was hardly the beau ideal, nor by any standards the town catch at the time.

A certain lordliness in picking and discarding girlfriends that year would seem quickly to have accompanied his new-found confidence as a performer. Caroline Ballard had preceded Eloise in Elvis' affections, and Magdalen Morgan would follow. In later years the girls would not be sequential but concurrent.

Whether or not such promiscuity is usual in so young a boy, it was certainly not unusual in the man that young boy was intent on emulating—Mississippi Slim.

In later years when Gladys would confide to her friends how much she wished she and her family "could just go back to being poor again," it was those months, from the late summer of 1945 to the early summer of 1946, to which she returned most often in wistful, haunted memory.

Although the war plant in Memphis had closed down with the end of the war and Vernon was again out of a job, it meant that he would return to Tupelo and that the family would again be reunited. Gladys would have her husband back and Elvis his father, not just for the odd weekend but on a regular, daily basis.

Best of all, in its last years the war had not only provided the Presleys with the increase in Vernon's wage packet at the war plant, it had also, by the reduction and rationing of consumer goods then in force, effectively reduced opportunities for spending it. Of major importance was the fact that the Presleys had not during those years suffered any "bad luck"— to use that universal phrase that includes fire, accident, ill health, death, and other acts of God as well as sudden reversals in fortune.

And now the Presleys had managed that miracle; they had managed to put by enough to think in terms of re-realizing the dream they'd had when Vernon built the little house on the Old Saltillo Road, the dream that had been so abruptly snatched away by Vernon's bad luck. At last they were going to become *homeowners* and have that Ⓗ after their names in the city directory. A new house had just been built on Berry Street. A brand-new house with four rooms; and they would *buy* it. At least, hoped Vernon, they would make a stab at it.

It was therefore quite a day for the Presleys on August 18, 1945, when Vernon paid $200 cash in down payment for lot 18, 19, block 2, northeast quarter of section 33, township 9, range 6 east on Berry Street—this exact description will be most significant to this story—and completed his first step towards purchasing the house for $2,000 from its owner, Orville Bean.

One says "quite a day," for is not $2,000 quite a price to pay for a four-room woodframe house in this poor working man's neighborhood? Is not this price in fact quite extraordinarily high? Yet records show this was not unique. For instance, on October 11, 1945, Orville Bean sold a lot on Kelly Street, the same size as the one on Berry Street, for $2,150.

There was an acute housing shortage after the war—even in Tupelo. You couldn't get material fast enough to build. There was even a country-western song at the time that Elvis would have known, which went: "My heart beats slower when I read on the do-ah—no vacancy," followed by lines and lines of "no vacancy, no vacancy" in the chorus. It was a doleful ditty about men returning from the war and unable to find a place to live—a real tear-jerker about homeless heroes and their homeless wives and homeless little children. It was a situation of which the owner of the house on Berry Street would be only too aware—that the seemingly outrageous price of $2,000 he was demanding for the house was, in fact, a price he could easily get.

That the owner was Orville Bean should not surprise anyone now aware of the feudal aspects of the Above The Highway community.

The deed was spelled out in the following terms: installments of $30 were due the first of every month to which was added a monthly rate of 6 percent. Vernon also had to pay the ad valorem. With this step he hoped he had crossed forever the line dividing his family from being, in the Shavian phrase, the "undeserving poor"—that is, welfare and public works employment—to "deserving poor"—that is, private employment, no debts, and most important of all, the putting-by of enough against their luck so that never again would they have to go back across that line.

That winter Vernon took another big step towards becoming one of the deserving. He accepted the honored position of deacon in the First Assembly of God Church.

Elvis, too, had taken a big step—musically.

By making frequent use of the pianos at both his church and his school he had made an important discovery. He had discovered that his first instrument, the guitar, was not his real one. Elvis' real instrument was the piano. Elvis learned to play the guitar slowly and painfully, and in his early life he had many teachers: his uncles Johnny and Vester; Brother Frank Smith, the young preacher; and, of course, his mentor Mississippi Slim.

But nobody had to teach Elvis how to play the piano. He was entirely self-taught. He played it easily and well, with immense satisfaction and pleasure. It is ironic that the guitar would become so identified with him and his music for, as he often remarked in public, though he certainly could play it he never rated himself very highly as a guitarist. Through most of the legendary early "Sun sessions," the records cut with Bill Black and Scotty Moore under Sam Phillips' direction, Elvis often uses his guitar like a drum simply to drive on the beat. But one of the first things he bought with the first money he made was something he had wanted passionately for a long, long time—a piano. Early on in his career he played piano on his recording of "Lawdy, Miss Clawdy" (Fats Domino had played piano on the one originally recorded in 1952 by Lloyd Price), "Wear a Ring Around Your Neck," and "One Sided Love Affair." Later at concerts he accompanied himself on piano when he sang "Unchained Melody." On his album *How Great Thou Art*, he played piano on some of the cuts. In the *Million Dollar Quartet* cover photograph of Elvis, Carl Perkins, Johnny Cash, and Jerry Lee Lewis, it is Elvis seated at the piano. He was lucky in discovering his right musical instrument as early as he did. A talented child begun on the wrong instrument can suffer great frustration and his musical progress be seriously impeded unless he is changed to the instrument best suited to him. One must not be fooled by the Captain Marvel, Jr., aspect of Elvis' meteoric rise to fame: one way or another, a very great deal of both musical training and musical theory was instilled as well as ingrained in the young Elvis.

At school and at church he was taught to sing by what is known as the tonic sol-fa (sometimes called fa-sol) system. This particular method of teaching singing, prevalent in Mississippi when Elvis was growing up, had its origins in seventeenth-century England. Having crossed the sea with the early settlers, the sol-fa system appears in many musical introductions of collections of metrical psalms in the American colonies. By the eighteenth century, this method was in such widespread use in America that in the first edition of the *Bay Psalm Book*, the first book to contain musical notation (Boston, 1700), sol-fa names (do, re, mi, fa, sol, la, ti) were printed under the staff notation.

But it remained for America to add a visual innovation to the sol-fa system. This aid to sight-reading music was called "shape note printing," later nicknamed "buckwheat notation." The sol-fa syllables were now shown on the page of music by a musical type which gave differently shaped heads to each each syllable—a triangle for fa, a rectangle for la, a diamond for mi, and so on. It probably made its first appearance in *The Easy Instructor, or a New Method of Teaching Sacred Harmony* (Philadelphia, c. 1798), and is found in such books as *The Western Lyre* (Cincinnati, 1831) and *The Missouri Harmony* (1837).

The stranger quickly makes the discovery that even today in Tupelo all hymnals in the First Assembly of God churches and, indeed, most of the other churches, are still printed in Buckwheat Notation.

For a clear description of the tonic sol-fa system in action with all its fascinating musical implications and reverberations, there is no more lively account then the one in W. C. Handy's autobiography, *Father of the Blues*, of his first music lessons at the turn of the century.

There was no piano or organ in our school, just as there were few instruments in the homes of the pupils. We were required to hold our books in our left hand and beat time with our right. Professor Wallace sounded his A pitch pipe or tuning fork, and we understood the tone to be la. If C happened to be the starting key, we made the step and a half in our minds and then sang out the key note in concert. We would then sound the notes for our respective parts, perhaps do for the basses, mi for the altos, and sol and do for the sopranos and tenors, depending of course on the first note of the sopranos. Before attempting to sing the words of any song, we were required to work out our parts by singing over and over the proper sol-fa syllables. In this way we learned to sing in all keys, measures, and movements. We learned all the songs in gospel hymns, one to six. Each year we bought new instrument books and advanced to a point where we could sing excerpts from the works of Wagner, Bizet, Verdi, and other masters—all without instrumental accompaniment.

When passing a certain field near the railroad tracks John Allen Cooke, a black former truck driver, often points to it saying: "This is where I used to see Elvis laying around. Killing time. He was real quiet. Thinking about his music, I guess..."

The picture this evokes of the eleven-year-old Elvis surely parallels another of W. C. Handy's accounts of learning music:

When I was no more than ten, I could catalogue almost any sound that came to my ears, using the tonic sol-fa system....Whenever I heard the song of a bird and the answering call of its mate, I could visualize the notes in the scale. Robins carried a warm alto theme. Bobolinks sang contrapuntal melodies. Mocking birds trilled cadenzas. Altogether, as I fancied, they belonged to a great outdoor choir.

There was a French horn concealed in the breast of the blue jay. The tappings of the woodpecker were to me the reverberations of a snare drum. The bullfrog supplied an effective bass. In the raucous call of the distant crow I would hear the jazz motif. The purple night would awaken a million crickets with their obbligatos of mournful sound, also the katydids, and down the lonely road the hooves of the galloping horses beat in syncopation. I knew the gait of horses by the rhythm of their hooves. As I grew older I added the saxophonic wailing of the moocows and the clarinets of the moody whippoorwills. All built up within my consciousness a natural symphony. This was the primitive prelude to the mature melodies now recognized as the blues. Nature was my kindergarten.

The musician's ear is clearly different from the ordinary person's ear. Friends of Elvis have noted how disconcerting it was that Old Super Ears, as they called him, had the ability to be speaking to someone while at the same time hearing what others were saying across the room.

Great voices, too, reflect their early sounds down to the very ground their singers walked on. Elvis' rich southern voice is like the beeswax soil of Mississippi—stab a shovel in it and when you pull it out the soil surges and roils together again—as Sinatra's urban voice is like the pound and scrape of shoe-leather against the unyielding concrete of a city sidewalk.

The awareness of music can also be perceived in a musician's handwriting. According to handwriting expert Terence Gray, a sample of Elvis' work at age ten shows "several symbolic examples that the writer is interested in music even if there is little to indicate his eventual success. If you look at the letters M in Mary, V in violet, M in married, and less clearly the M in make, W in when, and E in Elvis, their curlicues all resemble, even if badly formed, a musical note."

But Elvis, for all his knowledge of music and the laws that govern rhythm and harmony, would never become what he called a "sheet musician." Early on he said in an interview: "For my recording sessions I work with ear musicians and not sheet musicians. They're great. You just hum or whistle or sing a tune for them twice and then they get to work, and inside a minute or two the joint is jumping."

Elvis had perfect pitch. When he said, 'Give me an A,' that is precisely what he meant and what he would get. Like other well-known musicians and even composers (Irving Berlin and Paul McCartney being the most famous examples) he had a prejudice against reading music. "It don't look the way it sounds," he once complained to a friend. Could he have been disappointed by the boring regularity and monotony of the usual cough drop-shaped notes after the delightful variety of triangles, lozenges, diamonds, rectangles, and wedges of buckwheat notation?

Elvis' eleventh year got off—literally—to a shrieking, screaming start. On the day before his birthday, Monday, January 7, 1946, at 5 A.M., a tornado ripped northeastward through Lee County. This one, small and freakishly out-of-season, wreaked nothing like the damage the big one had in 1936, only touching the edge of Tupelo at Clayton Avenue. Still, there again was that frightening sound—the sound of a hundred freight cars crashing into each other and a hundred train whistles going off together—to send terror through the hearts of the inhabitants and speed their feet toward their storm shelters.

One could view this small freak tornado as a premonition of the winds of change that would later in the year blow the Presleys out of their new house on Berry Street and, via a short stop on Commerce Street, into a broken-down old shack on Mulberry Alley in downtown Tupelo, near the city dump.

Elvis Presley's great-grandfather, the patriarch White Mansell. (*Corinne Tate*)

Sassy and spirited Ann (Mansell) Smith, Elvis' great-grandmother (Gladys' father's mother). (*Virginia Boughman*)

Henry and Melissa (Mansell) Richards, Elvis' great-uncle and aunt on Gladys' side. (*Corinne Tate*)

Leona and Frank Richards, Gladys' cousins who helped her and Elvis while Vernon was in prison. (*Corinne Tate*)

Sims Mansell, another great-uncle of Elvis on Gladys' side. Elvis seems to have inherited the Mansells' soulful good looks. (*Corinne Tate*)

Gains and Ada Mansell. Ada was Doll's sister. The Rev. Gains Mansell, a distant cousin, built the First Assembly of God Church in East Tupelo. (*Corinne Tate*)

Gladys' parents, Bob and Doll Smith, on their marriage, September 19, 1903. Note the Grit button on Bob's lapel. (*Corinne Tate*)

Elvis' birthplace on the Old Saltillo Road, East Tupelo, now a tourist attraction on Elvis Presley Drive. (*A.P. Wide World Photos*)

Gladys, Elvis and Vernon. Elvis is three years old and Vernon is about to go to prison. (*The Official Elvis Presley Fan Club, P.O. Box 4, Leicester, England*)

Vernon, Gladys and Elvis in East Tupelo. Elvis is eight or nine years old. (*Syndication International*)

Corene Smith gets busy with her Box Brownie

The Rev. Frank Smith and his wife Corene in front of the welcoming First Assembly of God Church 1945.

Elvis' preacher, the Rev. Frank Smith in 1945. He still uses his guitar in his sermons.

Corene snaps ten-year-old Elvis and girlfriend Magdalen Morgan after church service.

Elvis in 1946 takes up his new position at Milam School, far right in overalls. (*Roland Tindall*)

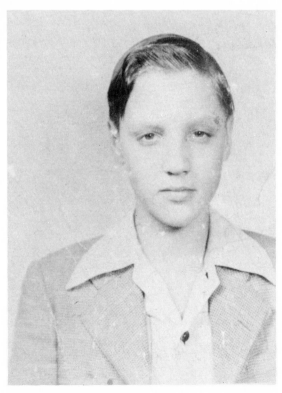

A determined Elvis on the brink of leaving Tupelo for Memphis, aged 13 (1948). (*Roland Tindall*)

Captain Marvel Jr, Elvis' first fantasy hero.

In the 1970s the lightning bolt resurfaced in solid gold often as 'Taking Care of Business' necklaces for special friends ... and on his private plane. (*Private Collection*)

In order to become The Most Powerful Boy in the World Elvis learned to keep his double identity secret.

Aunt Lillian, Memphis 1960.
(*Private Collection*)

LEFT Elvis' first musical hero,
Mississippi Slim, whom he
"followed round like a pet dog."
(*James Ausborn*)

Celebratory photograph of Gladys and Vernon in 1954. They were still living on Alabama Street.
(*Graceland Picture Library*)

Just eleven months after Vernon had signed the deed purchasing his house on Berry Street—on July 18, 1946, to be exact—he sold it. The buyer was his friend Aaron Kennedy and as property values were apparently still booming, along with the booming post-war economy, Vernon was able to sell it for $3,000.

There is no way not to marvel at just how Vernon, having made this sale "for and in consideration of $3,000 to Aaron Kennedy" as the warranty deed so plainly states—and which assumes a profit of $1,000—could still find himself and his family in circumstances far worse than before. How is this possible?

Was Vernon Presley a profligate father on the scale of those notoriously insolvent fathers of Bernard Shaw, James Joyce, and Charles Dickens? Fathers whose fecklessness, misguided energies, and grandiose but faulty visions made them so adept at landing their families so regularly and steadily in the soup?

To conclude this would be interesting but unfair. Although Vernon undoubtedly shared with these other fathers the inability to support his dependents, there is no evidence he ever disrupted the family finances such as they were by being a big spender, a drunkard, a gambler, an imprudent investor—or even an easy touch. For this last family trait we must look elsewhere.

Shaw's reaction to his father was to become a teetotaler; Joyce's to become an exile; and Dickens' to turn his father into some of his greatest fictional characters. These reactions might be expected. But Elvis' reaction to his father's improvidence—he made Vernon his personal business manager—seems inexplicable until we take into account the fact that Vernon's reputation for being parsimonious was almost equal to his reputation for being lazy.

Vernon's first job when he returned home was to work in the Leake and Godlett lumberyard on East Main Street for which he earned no more than $18 a week. Since out of that the Presleys were going to have to put by almost half for their monthly installments to Bean, they were already walking a very tight rope—without a net.

Soon after Vernon returned, his father J. D. took off again. This time he took off for good. He left Tupelo and, working his way northwards, ended up in Kentucky where he later became a nightwatchman at a Pepsi-Cola plant in Louisville. In 1947, J. D. suddenly filed for divorce from Minnie Mae claiming desertion, and although Minnie Mae's counterstatement read, "I didn't desert my husband, as a matter of fact, he deserted me and hasn't sent me any money in over a year and I'm not able to make a living," the Circuit Court Judge Lawrence granted J. D. the divorce. Minnie Mae, by now in her late fifties, moved into Berry Street with her son and daughter-in-law.

Sixteen-year-old Harold Loyd, Elvis' cousin, also came to stay with them on Berry Street from time to time. After the death of his mother Rhetha he ran away from home and grew up living with various aunts and uncles, though never staying with any too long to keep from being a burden on one family. "Elvis' mother," he has written, "was a great woman—she was like a mother to me."

Gladys did not work during this time. "The Presley men," says Annie Presley, "didn't want their women to work. They wanted them to look after them and to be there when they came home." And Gladys herself did not want to work. As much as both her Presley men, Vernon and Elvis, she too wanted to stay home and look after them.

The time has come to face the truth about Gladys. Good at cooking, excellent at cleaning—wherever the Presleys found themselves, the interiors of their dwellings were invariably described as spotless—she was hopeless as a manager. Generous, emotional, loving, softhearted and a soft touch, she was, in Corene Smith's phrase, "a neighbor and a half." But she was also a consumer and a half, and had been since her earliest days back in the country on Burk's Farm where Lily Mae Irwin had watched her and her sister Clettes go in and out of the Irwin store "sixty times a day" buying one item at a time, clearly enjoying purchasing almost as much as the purchase.

Down the years Gladys had clung stubbornly to that notion of hers that life's pleasures were not only meant for the rich. During the war her consumer gratifications for herself and her family had been held in check by the government. But postwar America was a consumer's Babylon and Gladys was unable to resist the seductiveness of the goods that flooded the stores full of groceries and clothes, cosmetics and toys.

Gladys had noticed a few gray strands in the dark hair of which she was so proud. She began going to the Tupelo Beauty School where, since it was a hairdressers' training school, you could have your hair done for much less than at a regular beauty shop. It cost some; but it was worth every cent. Pretty, plump, and pleasing at thirty-three, she felt it vital to sustain the fiction begun when, as a newcomer in East Tupelo, she had run off and married Vernon; the harmless fiction that she was the same age, if not a little younger than he.

They had, of course, a radio and listened often to WELO, their Tupelo station that had the signal to Memphis. From Memphis via WELO, Elvis would have heard a lot of country-western music, the Grand Ole Opry particularly, a lot of big-band music, and some Negro spirituals. "He would *not* have heard race music—black rhythm and blues," emphatically states Ernest Bowen. "WELO did not broadcast it at the time." In any case, the Memphis black station, WDIA, did not begin until 1948.

Even so, the picture of Elvis with his ear glued to the radio twenty-four hours a day, picking up tricks from famous country singers, becomes extremely dubious. To begin with, radio batteries at the time were very expensive and very shortlived. Listening to radios was still confined to social occasions; families and friends gathering at each other's houses to hear their favorite programs.

But the most important reason that Elvis was not constantly glued to the radio in his youth was that he himself was too busy out singing with his mother and father at various churches, camp meetings, revivals, and conventions. Short biographies of Elvis written for his early albums and given in early interviews describe him and his family as having been a "popular singing trio" in Tupelo. This description was quickly suppressed as his fame grew—possibly because the professional ring suggested by this phrase was inaccurate but most certainly because it was unaccept-able to the myth everyone wanted to be awesomely true (and it must be remembered that it is only great feelings of awe that inspire great myths), unacceptable to the image of a phenomenon who, simply by stepping out of a delivery truck and into a recording studio, becomes a singing sen-sation. If that sensation turns out to be merely part of a small group of family singers, where is the magic in that?

Nevertheless, the Presleys were known for their good voices and, like many family groups in the area, enjoyed some reputation for singing. The level of performance was extremely informal and never involved payment. Marie Lummus Kate, for instance, remembers a typical singing held at the Free Will Baptist Church in Tupelo. Mrs. Kate was called upon to sing and as both Vernon and Elvis were there in the congregation, they were called upon to join her. Mrs. Kate sang soprano, Vernon tenor, and Elvis "hit the alto on the chorus." They sang, she remembers, a recently written hymn, "If We Never Meet Again This Side of Heaven." The Presleys were not singing for their supper but for their own plea-sure—and without question for the chance of getting up to sing in front of a lot of people.

But Elvis was not only singing in church, he was also listening.

The new preacher at the First Assembly of God Church (who for a while co-pastored it with Uncle Gains) was the nineteen-year-old Brother Frank Smith from Meridian, Mississippi. His father had been a drunkard and Frank had been saved by hearing his mother praying nightly to

God for the salvation of her sons. He married the fifteen-year-old neighbor of the Presleys, Corene Randle, who became Corene Smith. Frank had already become a good friend of the Presleys. Today a bald, rosy-complexioned, bespectacled man in his late fifties, a food salesman in the daytime, Brother Frank preaches with a big guitar, interspersing his sermons with hymns in a fine singing voice. He gives emphasis to the words by an upward swing of his guitar at the end of each phrase.

The sermon he preached in April 1981 in Vernona, Mississippi, was on revival. This sermon and its message is as age-old a tradition as the legend to a beloved mother found on many gravestones in Tupelo and Saltillo, "She was the sunshine of our home," which Elvis had inscribed on Gladys' tomb. Said Brother Frank:

There is nothing wrong with weeping, it's a way of emptying your heart. If you break down and cry, you can empty your heart of grief. Strong men weep. Hear me, I said strong men weep in the presence of God. A superintendent of Sunday School, a strong man, an automobile mechanic and a good one, wept and said: "I'm crying but don't pity me. I'm crying because I'm in the presence of God." By crying you empty your heart of all that emotion.

During the service a group came down to the front of the church to be healed and then later on requests were made from the congregation:

"I want to pray for grandma, she cut her hand real bad."

"I want you to pray for my daddy, he's had a heart attack."

"I want y'all to pray for my sister, she's having surgery tomorrow."

Then Brother Frank prayed: "Lord, *melt* my heart! *Melt* my heart!"

One heard no mention of hell or fire or brimstone in his service.

In the same month and the same year at Elvis' own church, the First Assembly of God on Adams Street, one heard this sermon:

"What's wrong with Christianity today? We're still *of* this world, not *separated* from it as we should be. *Separate yourself from the world!* We've got to *separate* ourselves from the world before we have a revival in our hearts! Get to where nothing matters but God!"

Not only in his last years but all through his life, Elvis would heed this advice in his dark and confused hours.

Though Tupeloans remember Elvis singing outside the Tupelo Hotel on Spring Street, when Jack Connor was proprietor, for nickels and dimes and quarters, their memories are vague about which of all the talent shows and contests Elvis did enter as a child and as an adolescent. Talent shows were such a regular feature throughout the South that their participants would have attracted very little attention. In fact, the known quantity (and unknown quality) of these shows is revealed in the thumbs-down showbiz expression, "It was like amateur night in Dixie," when describing a showbiz shambles.

In any case, during those eleven months from August 1945 to July 1946, Elvis and his mother and father were at their happiest—though it would seem so to them only in retrospect. They not only loved each other, they got along with each other. As one close neighbor summed it up: "Nobody ever heard *them* Presleys making a racket."

When Elvis came home from school in those days Gladys would merrily have "boocups" to tell him—or he her. As with much of their conversation that has been reported as baby talk, "boocups"—though it may sound unbearably coy to some—was in lighthearted usage in Tupelo at the time and still is. As for baby talk in general, both Bernard Shaw's and Dean Swift's love letters reveal them guilty of it.

"Boocups," from the French *beaucoup*, descends from the line of Elizabethan borrowings as the Shakespearean "kickshaws" for *quelque chose*.

What other pleasures were available to the Presleys besides singing in church? There was a bowling alley. There was the favorite country spectator sport, cockfighting. Though Mississippi was "dry"—"Mississippi will be dry as long as we can stagger to the polls to vote"—beer and moonshine were always available at the local fish-bait shop and the pigstands. Vernon shot birds, rabbits, and squirrels for food. Squirrels are still considered a delicacy—there is not much meat on them—but they have to be shot in season.

And so they continued—a generous, indulgent, spendthrift mother; an unambitious, unlettered father without a trade; and an energetic, pampered, yearning son. A family with strong clan feelings toward other Presleys, Smiths, and Mansells: It was an unbeatable combination for economic disaster. The Presleys were not able to put aside enough money to keep up the payments to Orville Bean for the house.

It seemed a case of "water, water, everywhere—but not a drop to drink." Surrounded by postwar prosperity, by peace and plenty, the Presleys could no more take advantage of this prosperity than they had been able, back in 1936, to take advantage of the electricity wired to their house.

To return to the $3,000 question: What did happen to it when Vernon sold the house on Berry Street to his friend Aaron Kennedy? Put simply, Vernon saw no money from the transaction. The transfer of the house from Vernon to the Kennedys was in lieu of foreclosure, Orville Bean having held a lien on the property all the time the Presleys lived there.

Immediately after Vernon deeded the property to Aaron Kennedy and his wife, the Kennedys gave Bean a deed of trust, which is the same thing as a mortgage. This is a step that is sometimes still used to avoid foreclosure proceedings. It benefits both parties. In this case it saved Bean the legal step of kicking out the Presleys and therefore probably also saved him a little money. And, of course, it did give the Presleys an opportunity to get out without going through foreclosure and eviction.

The Kennedys then moved to Berry Street owing Bean $2,240, having paid him $760 down.

And that accounts for the $3,000 "paid" to Vernon.

Do these figures merely reflect how far behind the "improvident" Presleys were in their mortgage payments—or is Bean just making money for himself from these transactions?

Aaron Kennedy has this to say: "Orville Bean was a politician. He made his money by taking advantage of people and keeping them indebted— quite a few other people besides Vernon." Without doubt he is including himself.

There is no other conclusion about the Presleys than the one that Elvis had come to himself, long ago: they could not make ends meet. They would never be able to. If the family was going to survive it would only be through him.

It would be very wrong to think that the eleven-year-old Elvis saw the family move from the new four-room house on Berry Street to the old shack on Mulberry Alley as a move merely from one section of the wrong side of the tracks to another, and that he would not feel this deeply. Living Above The Highway might be living eastward in Eden but it was the Presleys' Eden and their expulsion from it was a kind of expulsion from paradise. They were not only losing their house and their neighborhood and their community but also, for Vernon, his sense of purpose and his hopes.

Just how strongly the Presleys felt about this exodus, about Orville Bean and the foreclosed house on Berry Street, is proven by the Lee County Courthouse records. There it comes to light that eleven years later, *before* Elvis directs city officials to purchase the land behind his birthplace for the Elvis Presley Youth Center, Orville Bean on December 14, 1957, has been made to sell that same house, or rather the lots on which it stood, back to the city for the price of a mere $500. Soon after the house was condemned and destroyed.

NINE

The Singer and the Song

Nowadays Mulberry Alley faces the Downtown Mall shopping center. Then, this narrow alley was near—too near—the city dump which, to add an historical note, was Gum Pond filled in.

Ernest Bowen, home from the war, had gone to work as a salesman at L. P. McCarty's wholesale groceries company and it was in his father's carpentry shop where Vernon worked from time to time at his true trade, eliciting Bowen, Sr.'s admiring comment that Vernon could do anything with wood. Anything, it would seem, except make money.

Eventually Vernon was able to get himself a job driving a truck for L. P. McCarty delivering the wholesale goods, a job he would hold with varying degrees of tenacity for some three years. It meant driving two hundred miles, sometimes daily, on a route that included the towns of Sturgis and Starkville, and brought on a strain on his back that would recur disastrously in Memphis later on. But the pay was better than he'd ever received in Tupelo—twenty-two dollars a week. And Vernon liked it. It was his form of escape. In any case, putting his best foot forward, he saw to it that he got along with his fellow workers (for instance, personally loading the goods on Bill Mitchell's truck for him during the latter's first weeks on the job so that Bill was able to unload them in the proper order en route) and generally going out of his way to make himself so helpful that in return the salesmen gave him food samples for his ever needful family, now consisting of Minnie Mae as well as Elvis and Gladys. While it is true these food samples would not have struck most people as exactly appetizing, being "slightly damaged," it was also true that if they had not been in that condition they would not have been offered to the Presleys in the first place. For which the Presleys, as always, were duly grateful.

L. P. McCarty himself was pleased enough with Vernon's show of industry at first to allow the Presleys to use the truck on Sundays—Elvis behind the wheel even then—to get to their church in East Tupelo. That Vernon retain his deaconship was vital to the Presleys; it was their sole toe-hold on respectability.

Moving into Tupelo proper meant, however, that Elvis would no longer be able to attend his old school on Lake Street, the school upon whose consciousness he had somewhat impressed himself not only as a singer and "ladies'" man but also as an enterprising youngster who would organize singing groups to perform in school assemblies and churches and cafeterias.

Instead he walked from Mulberry Alley barefoot and in overalls to begin sixth grade at his new school, Milam, a big brick building right in the center of town on the corner of Jefferson and Gloster. This "long mile" as Corene Smith called it, from East Tupelo to Tupelo and from East Tupelo Consolidated School to Milam School was Elvis' biggest cultural shock, not only because it was his first one but because the majority of his schoolmates would make him feel it. There were over twice as many pupils in the school. Instead of thirty children per homeroom, there were over forty, and three homerooms instead of two. That might not have bothered Elvis too much; he might see these pupils merely as a larger potential audience. But there was also a very rigid and, to him, entirely new social system to adjust to.

A child does not rock with the full impact of the realization that he is from the wrong side of the tracks until he hears it from a child living on the right side. It was Elvis' particular bad luck to have to absorb this shock alone without the fellowship of other East Tupelo schoolmates who, two years later, would transfer to Milam to have their collective eyes opened to this same fact of life.

Kenneth Holdritch, originally from Tupelo, now a professor of English at the University of New Orleans, wryly sums up how the Establishment pupils at Milam School regarded the infiltration of poor students from East Tupelo:

"We who were already in the school were not kind to them, I suppose. They were outsiders and such is the nature of the human beast—especially at twelve, thirteen, and fourteen—that an outsider is a convenient target for whatever animosities may have developed or are developing."

As for Elvis, he is remembered by Professor Holdritch as "a sad, shy, not especially attractive boy, a bit clumsy... standing on the stage of the Emma Edmonds Auditorium playing his guitar as part of a talent contest and *not* winning."

What Elvis felt towards his new schoolmates can easily be surmised. Certainly he would smart with feelings of resentment and humiliation as he sat there in his overalls while the other boys wore pants, shirts, sweaters, and jackets. Who wouldn't? Nor would it need special sensibility for him to become very quickly aware of his classmates' hostility.

But in his innocence—that remarkable, indestructible, that almost *inhuman* innocence, that self-perpetuating, self-regenerating innocence that would remain with him all his life, an innocence for which there has as yet been no archetype, so that one has to call it Elvis-innocence— he would never quite understand what their hostility was all about. And he would puzzle over his peers then as he would for the rest of his life, inquiring, it would seem, both of God and the world, "Why don't they like me? Can't they see I'm just like them?"

For the secret of this remarkable child was that he *was* just like them. Had not his family—the Presleys, the Mansells, and the Smiths—always been there, always been interwoven into the fabric of Lee County? Yes, they were poor, that cannot be said too often—but at least they were not something much worse: they were not immigrants, foreigners, itinerants, scalawags, or carpetbaggers. They had been Americans for generations; they had a history. They belonged and they knew it. Elvis would always have that sense of belonging to the whole American scheme of things. Elvis was almost unique in the field of entertainment in that he knew who he was. The generations of sharecroppers had a pride of place similar to that of generations of Welsh coal miners. Besides, was not Elvis' uncle Noah mayor of East Tupelo?

From the back row in a new school, the poor boy could still flash that lopsided grin, the silly grin that Eloise Bedford spoke of that said "I know something you don't." And it would also be a grave mistake to see his sitting back there as an indication that he was dropping out—or dropping off, for, was it not really all the better to survey the terrain from that vantage point?

Elvis was then what he would be for the rest of his life: impossibly shy and impossibly above himself. He was awaiting his opportunity. It would only take two weeks for it to come.

"Don't any of you children have any talent in here?" Mrs. Camp, his homeroom teacher, asked them that day by way of getting to know her new students. She was going to hold a talent show in the English class that coming Friday.

The new boy in the back row raised his hand.

"What can you do?" Mrs. Camp wanted to know.

"I can play guitar and sing," Elvis said.

"Well, bring the thing tomorrow and sing for us," said Mrs. Camp.

Elvis brought his guitar along with him to the school the next day and he sang. And just as in Mrs. Grimes' memorable fifth-grade class the year before, he sang at devotions. Undoubtedly he sang "Old Shep." Obviously, from the reaction which followed, it is clear that Elvis did not give a halfhearted rendition of it, but that he flung himself into the song as he always had and always would—as if his very life depended on it. He was, in a word, good.

"He was so *good*," recalls Mrs. Camp, "and the children—they just got so *quiet* and pleased with him—and I just got so overjoyed I carried him down to Miss Virginia Plumb's sixth-grade class and I said, 'Miss Virginia, I hate to break up your arithmetic class, but this little boy's *good* and I want you to hear him,' and her class just applauded and Miss Virginia said, 'Take him over there to the other room.' This was years ago," explains Mrs. Camp, "and teachers weren't allowed to leave their rooms but I took him to another sixth-grade room and then we sneaked back to my home-room before the principal could catch us.... It was a shock that he was so talented."

Even taking into consideration how hindsight encourages hyperbole, the ring of proof remains: Mrs. Camp was so astonished by Elvis' talent that she obeyed her impulse, which was to spread the news.

After that, Elvis came to school with his guitar over his shoulder every day unless it looked like rain. He was to do this for the entire time he attended Milam, in sixth and seventh and part of eighth grade. Yes, Elvis was determined to tote that guitar of his to school every day. But then, guitar players—as everyone knows who has ever come across one—are like that.

"I never met a guitar player worth a damn," a statement attributed to Vernon is, in fact, an old southern expression. Over and over again in southern imagery is the figure of a man sitting on his front porch with his guitar, pickin' and singin' while the crops go to ruin; an image not unlike that of Nero fiddling while Rome burned.

Mrs. Camp, obviously an Elvis aficionado from the minute she heard his voice, as so many of his teachers would be, continues her breathless reminiscence: "Elvis played guitar at recess and different times and the children would *swarm* around him and they just *loved* him... and he played out there by the bicycle shed and all the children were his dear friends...."

It is at this point that one has to interrupt Mrs. Camp in full flood with a firm '*No*, Mrs. Camp!' That is not what happened. That is only what *should* have happened.

For the children did not love Elvis. They would hear him sing and their hearts would fill with emotion; they might even, some of them, be moved to tears—but only for the duration of the song. It was the song they loved, not the singer. His schoolmates would no more love Elvis than they would love the blind man on the corner singing "Beale Street Blues." But how they would listen to them both with their hearts and their minds and their bodies; and how they would love and understand the songs.

The element of ridicule that surrounded Elvis all his life had begun early: Elvis' cousin Maxine Williams remembers in 1956 driving with her friend Evelyn Helms past her now famous relative's ranch-style house on Audubon Drive, a wealthy section of Memphis, and Evelyn suddenly bursting into laughter. "We used to laugh at Elvis in sixth grade," explained Evelyn, "because he didn't have a front porch on his house— and he *still* doesn't!"

Young Milamites on the whole regarded Elvis, no doubt because of Vernon's shady past (in that small town where everyone knew everything about everyone) but also because of the Presleys' specific present circumstances, *not* as "polite poor white" (the deserving poor) but, outspokenly, as "poor white trash" (the undeserving). The expression was in popular usage at the time—very much, incidentally, as "rich white trash" is retaliatively used nowadays.

To add to his troubles, the fact that Elvis could sing and did sing at every opportunity was a mark against him. As everyone knows who has been in that position, the new kid is not supposed to be good at anything. He has no right to be good at anything. He hasn't earned it. Getting down to what his schoolmates actually did make of Elvis, we see that their reactions fall into two predictable categories: those of the "in" group and those of the "out"—the rich and the poor. Mostly the "in" group remember him not at all. To use a direct quote from Shirley Lumpkin, whose father in 1947 ran for lieutenant governor of Mississippi: "The nicest thing I can say about him was that he was a loner." Or from Shirley Threldkeld: "I just don't remember him. He was that type—forgettable."

Or from Mary Jo Godfrey: "He was not outstanding." But Mary Jo goes on, "There was the money clique and the nonmoney clique. Elvis and I were both in the nonmoney clique. We sat across from each other in math class and swapped papers each day to grade. He was average—at any rate better than me. Yes, he wore overalls."

Or from Evelyn Riley: "Then, as now, if you weren't *in* the clique you were out. We did enjoy listening to him sing. But Elvis was not popular."

In the winter when Elvis was twelve the children would go to the basement during recess where the boys would play on one side and the girls on the other. There, according to classmate Roland Tindall, Elvis entertained them almost daily, sometimes singing duets with Billy Walsh, another poor boy who along with Roland and Elvis, "wasn't socially up there, lived in the wrong neighborhood and didn't wear the smart clothes the other kids had. Elvis," Roland continued, "never turned down an opportunity to sing in the weekly homeroom activity period and on more than one occasion suddenly announced to the class that he was going to sing at the Grand Ole Opry."

The climactic effect that all this singing and boasting would have on what Leroy Green calls "the rougher-type boys—the criminal element if you like" is sadly predictable. In the first month of eighth grade they stole Elvis' guitar and cut its strings. What is not so predictable is that this would cause another faction, the pro-Elvis boys, to get together and buy him another set. In other words Elvis was very early possessed of that disturbing power to stir up violent opinion both for and against himself.

One Christmas when, as custom dictated, schoolmates drew names to exchange Christmas gifts, Elvis drew Roland's name and gave Roland a blue toy truck. Roland saw immediately that the truck was an old one and realized that Elvis had not been able to afford to buy a gift but, his pride not permitting him to admit it, had given Roland one of his own toys.

Elvis sang not only "Old Shep" but the old Scottish ballad "Barbara Allen," remembers Maude Dean Christian, and it was, in fact, ballads that he favored rather than fast songs. When she heard his first record on the radio she reacted with disappointment, thinking that he sounded so much better back in class. Then later when he "calmed down and did the slower tunes," she recalls recognizing *that* as the Elvis she remembered. At the same time as the other kids "snurled up" their noses at him, says Maude Dean, they would beg the teacher to let Elvis sing in Activity once a week. In perhaps the most revealing testimony of Elvis' early siren powers, Maude Dean recalls that the teacher would have to *close the door and all the windows during the hot months whenever Elvis sang so that the kids from the other classes would not hear him.* Because when they did, they all wanted to come and listen to him, too.

Finally, throughout his stay at Milam, Elvis continued his indefatigable pursuit of girls.

In light of the fact that most boys between eleven and thirteen in those days were content to leave girls alone and that the girls themselves considered Elvis not only goofy and crazy but a perfect pest, his perseverance to charm them seems truly astonishing; that is, until it is taken into account not only how adored he was by his mother but by his ordinarily brisk no-nonsense grandmama as well, and conclude that these satisfactions spurred him on to conquer the rest of the female world.

In this he was singularly ineffectual. Indeed, from their testimony, it would seem that one of the heaviest crosses the little girls at Milam bore in common was Elvis. It got to the point where some of them started leaving home early for school in order to avoid meeting him on the street because he plagued them so.

"Miz' Camp, make this little ole boy quit flirting with me!" one little girl exploded.

"Elvis," Mrs. Camp admonished him, "when you get married you be sure to send me an invitation."

"And he just grinned," adds Mrs. Camp. "And those little dimples just shined out back there and he just got down to work."

Kitty Brewer recalls her younger sister Carolyn coming home from school "all fussed" because *that* Elvis Presley dared to nominate her for the Most Beautiful in one of those "most" contests which were such a feature of American schools in that day.[7] In fact, anyone wishing to provoke a little girl to tears of rage had only to chalk "Elvis loves—" and then the girl's name on the blackboard when the teacher was out of the room. The very idea that this goof, this clodhopper, would single you out for his affection was intolerable. Yet Elvis persevered in the face of all rejection, continually pressing his point though surely the snubs would have stung. How did he manage to keep going?

He *must* have known something they did not. Actually he knew quite a few things they did not know. He knew if he was going to get anywhere as a singer he would *have* to make them love him as well as the song. He knew that he was powerful only when he sang. Moreover, he knew that not only was *he* powerless but—by extension—so were his mother and father when he did not sing. It was the extraordinary intensity with which he felt the pain of this dilemma and was able to communicate it to others that gave to his singing its soul.

During Elvis' stay at Milam it comes as no surprise that his closest

---

[7] These beauty contests would leave an indelible mark on Elvis: Linda Thompson, his girlfriend from 1972–76, was Miss Tennessee and his last girlfriend, Ginger Alden, was Miss Traffic Safety. It was not only important that Elvis have beautiful girls but that they had won a contest, *proving* that they were beautiful. This weakness made Elvis an easy mark for ambitious young girls eager to give their all to get ahead—eager to compromise him for their own aims.

friend was the already mentioned James Ausborn (a classmate though not in his homeroom), the younger brother of Mississippi Slim whom Elvis regarded increasingly as a lifeline to his professional future.

More to the point, Gladys, always so careful of the company Elvis kept, not only approved of her son's friend James, but encouraged their friend-ship.

"I think Elvis' mother liked me," says James today, "because I was quiet, like Elvis, and if she wanted us to stay in the house instead of running off, I obliged, and perhaps this built a trust in her."

Certainly Gladys was delighted that Elvis had found a well-behaved playmate rather than joining up with the rough, tough bunch who would lead him astray. But this is only half the story. Her house, her neighbor-hood, her community lost, Gladys as always in the face of adversity relied on her strong primitive instincts for survival. For all her palpitating in-ternal fears, her attitude toward life was that of an adventurer, though now a frustrated adventurer with a husband who was removing himself not only physically but emotionally from her by entering into the mystique of the road.

It is interesting to speculate on why Vernon, that extraordinarily hand-some but thoroughly discouraged young trucker, with all the opportu-nities and temptations for erotic encounters that presented themselves at the roadhouses along his route, did not one day just take off for good like thousands of other men in similar situations in that day. According to Lillian, he certainly liked flirting and was not above making Gladys jealous by doing it in her presence. Yet he always came home. Was it simply because it was the path of least resistance? Or was it because he and his old buddy Travis Smith, his brother-in-law and brother-out-of-law in that long-ago, impulsive, ridiculous, and disastrous "crime" (and who had served a longer sentence than Vernon in Parchman), so much enjoyed loafing about together—fishing, drinking beer, playing tricks on each other, and just jellybeaning around? One theory has it that in staying around, Vernon was responding to Elvis' need rather than to Gladys'.

One is forced to ponder whether Elvis would not have profited by a little good old-fashioned neglect. Undoubtedly he would have. But then Elvis would also have had to have been the kind of child who allows himself to be neglected, and this he was not. There were physical reasons for him giving his family concern. His body temperature was always higher than normal and though his frail skinny body moved like a coiled spring and he never walked but dashed from one place to another, he always arrived out of breath. He was highly susceptible to colds and suffered from loss of appetite.

Encouraging Mississippi Slim's brother James' friendship with Elvis was a small indication of how Gladys was reassembling and reconcentrating her ambitions ever more intensely on Elvis as the beauty and power of his voice kept developing. Often—and instructively—she sang him her favorite Jimmie Rodgers songs. They both agreed that Gladys had the musical ability but sadly not the opportunity herself to gain riches and fame.

At last they could be totally open with each other about their ambitions for Elvis. They dreamt high, bright, grandiose dreams of Elvis becoming another Jimmie Rodgers... or Roy Acuff... Gene Austin... Eddy Arnold. Another? No, far greater. They dreamt of inhabiting their palaces in Texas and Nashville.

The quickest way out of the tyranny of poverty always involves the highest risk. For the blacks in the forties and fifties it meant becoming prizefighters, in Spain in meant becoming bullfighters, and for the poor whites in southwest America, becoming country singers. Sure you could fail—or you could make it and end up drunk, doped, riddled with TB and dead; Gladys and Elvis and everyone in the South knew all about that. But that was something that happened to other people.

The widespread notion that Gladys dreamt no higher for her son than that he become a preacher collapses in the face of all evidence. No preacher she knew ever made any money. Like Brother Frank and Uncle Gains, they were forced to support themselves with lowly jobs in the daytime. The evidence indicates that Elvis was trained, rehearsed, and coached by Gladys—all her frustrated desires mixing with her dramatic flair—as thoroughly and as seriously as any other potential professional singer is coached.

Around the beginning of 1947 Gladys went back to work at the Mid-South Laundry, improving the Presley fortunes to the extent that they could move to Dr. Jim Green's fairly decent two-family house (sharing it with some other Presley relatives) at 1010 North Green Street. Now a photograph reveals a keen, smooth-faced, determined-eyed Elvis, his dishwater-colored hair slicked and sleeked, wearing a neat jacket, his shirt pressed knife-sharp as if fresh from the laundry.

James Ausborn remembers that Gladys was perfectly agreeable to Elvis going off with him to the picture shows—though never without first delivering long cautionary lectures on dos and don'ts before they went. Of the two movie houses, the Lyric and the Strand, the Strand got most of their patronage because it was cheaper. The Strand played reruns and had rats as big as elephants running around inside in the dark but it was there that they spent many of their happiest hours. Though they both

liked Roy Rogers, Gene Autry, and Tarzan, Elvis was particularly en-
thralled by musicals, the dancing of Fred and Ginger, and the singing of
Bing.

If in seeing movies Elvis was going against the teachings of the First
Assembly of God which, as Annie Presley says, "taught us it was a sin
to go to the picture shows," they could not stop him from sinning, nor
his mother from allowing him to. As strong as the church is in southerners' lives, stronger at times perhaps is something all are familiar with.
Today it stands at the altar as the pleasure principle.

In an interview in *McCall's* (February 1981), Dolly Parton, who was
also brought up in the Church of God, gives a splendid lesson in how to
doublethink your way through the duality of nature. She explains that
she has taken "the great and good things" from her church "and left
behind the stuff that don't work for me—strictness about make-up and
hair and sex and stuff." Though sometimes, she says, she tried to live by
all that preaching—she used to get renewed at every revival meeting—
she soon found herself "just as freespirited as ever." God, she concludes,
"must have a sense of humor, because I have, and He's in me. I know
the energy in my soul is God and I express it through love."

James Ausborn tells of Elvis often taking him to the Priceville Cemetery
to visit his twin. Elvis would say to him, "I want to see my brother." "He
would go," says James, "burdened and low. Elvis would look at the grave
and talk a little to Jesse and after the visit, he was always jolly and lifted
in spirits."

On all their Sunday fishing expeditions Gladys would impose a strict
curfew. "We would leave at noon but she would insist on us being back
at 2 P.M. After thirty minutes to an hour of fishing or whatever, Elvis
would become restless, neither of us having a watch, every few minutes
asking, 'What time is it do you reckon?' This made Elvis a nervous wreck,
so rather than worry about the time we would just pack it up and go in
early. Much to the delight of his mama, Elvis was never late for one of
these curfews."

This is the kind of information that has led biographers to underline
Elvis' well-known overobedience to and overconcern for his mother. But
a more rational interpretation—what danger, after all, could either of
them have encountered at two in the afternoon—reveals merely an Elvis
eager to get home, change his clothes and go off to the courthouse for
the WELO Saturday afternoon "Jamboree Hour", or stay home and listen
to the Saturday afternoon radio programs of country-western singing. Of
course Gladys was delighted.

James states firmly that never once did Elvis reveal to him his intention of becoming a singer. James, however, was not in Elvis' homeroom and therefore missed those sudden announcements that popped out of Elvis willy-nilly, that he was going to the Grand Ole Opry. With James, it would seem, Elvis always tried to remain Freddy Freeman, the poor newsboy, rather than Captain Marvel, Jr.

How did Elvis reconcile himself to these bouts of power and power-lessness he kept being prey to? He had turned to his comic books for his inspirational reading. There at the age of twelve, reading *The Sivana Family Strikes Again* in the Captain Marvel series, he had found his answer. The key to power was secrecy. Captain Marvel, his twin sister Mary, and Captain Marvel, Jr., had each embarked on their finest hour. They were taking on "the wickedest family in the world" whose head, Dr. Sivana, was popularly know as the Big Red Cheese and whose children—Georgia and Sivana, Jr.—were the wickedest children in the world. While Captain Marvel took on Dr. Sivana and Mary Marvel, Georgia, Captain Marvel, Jr., took on Sivana, Jr.

In Marvel, Jr.'s futuristic adventure *Atlantis Rises Again*, which takes place in the thirteenth-thousandth-century A.D., the secret of his super-human power does escape and we see the result.

"Far in the future," begins the story, a young scientist, Chass Passon, whose ancestor was Chal Patzun, an original inhabitant of Atlantis, has managed to raise the continent from its watery grave by, it turns out, stoking a thirteenth-thousandth-century boiler—which resembles a twentieth-century one with knobs on—called an "electrium." Chass looks exactly like Marvel, Jr., except that he wears glasses. Twinship again.

Now enters the evil young Sivana, Jr., got up in natty plus fours and checkered socks. He greets Chass Passon's emergence on dry land with a mighty crack on the head. But just when young Sivana is about to steal the electrium, Captain Marvel, Jr.—"the most powerful boy in the world"—swoops down and settles *his* hash with an explosive right to the jaw. When Chass comes around, naturally the grateful young scientist wants to know his benefactor's name.

Marvel, Jr., begins, "Why, I'm Captain Mar...er...uh..." And then he halts.

Why?

On the last panel on the page is the explanation: "Captain Marvel, Jr., alone of the Marvel family, always has a peculiar problem when people ask his name for..." And then Marvel, Jr., explains it to his readers in a thought balloon: The words "Captain Marvel" make him change back into poor *Freddy Freeman!* So he hesitates. However, as he is so far in the future, he then decides why not disclose his true powerful identity? What has he to lose?

"I'm Captain Marvel, Jr., of the twentieth century," he says.

Boom! More lightning zigzags with the uttering of the two key words. For with the telling of his name, he is transformed back into Freddy Freeman, the poor crippled newsboy.

Thirteen-thousandth-century Chass is astonished. "What... wh-what! There are *two* of you?" "Yes," says Freddy, "You see, we change back and forth by magic lightning. It's safe to tell you because this is far from the twentieth century: *Nobody knows my secret back there.*"

In short, Elvis must constantly be on guard against declaring himself to anyone, for if his outrageous secret were known he would no longer be the most powerful boy in the world.

So far, the one-quarter of the population of Tupelo that was black has not entered our story. Now it does. Living in Mulberry Alley and then moving to 1010 North Green Street, the Presleys were living on the edge of Tupelo's black section, Shakerag. This was a community of house servants, cooks, and nurses—as well, if not better, off than the Presleys— who worked for Tupelo's wealthier families. A self-contained, well-mannered community, they had their own stores and their own Sanctified Church, which was a tent with one side rolled up.

It was commonplace, says Ernest Bowen, for young white boys interested in music to sit in the back and listen to the Sanctified Church services. The tambourine, guitar, and piano sounded like a full orchestra, the voices like a full choir, and 1010 North Green Street (on Tupelo's map today as Elvis Presley Circle) was right near the church. Did Elvis listen to the singing? Elvis, like Ulysses' sailors, would have had to have his ears filled with wax *not* to have heard their shamanic song.

By being so close to the black population, young Elvis met the black truck driver, John Allen Cooke. Some afternoons after school was over Elvis would go to Brown's Store on Gloster Street next to Milam and there he would catch John Allen Cooke and Curtis Johnson in their pick-up truck delivering groceries for the black grocer, D. L. Andrews. Elvis sat in the back of the truck, says John Allen Cooke, and would run out and deliver the groceries in exchange for which services they would give him money or food. Says John Allen Cooke: "The Presleys always liked the blacks and were always on our side." "They'd better have been," says a white Tupeloan. "They would've starved without them."

On the afternoon before Valentine's Day, Friday, February 13, 1948,

Gladys gave Elvis a valentine of great significance to them both. Dressed in their best clothes they walked into the Lee County Library on Madison Street where Elvis made out an application for a library card. This would have been an unusual step for any thirteen-year-old in Tupelo to have taken, let alone a Presley. A survey shows that until 1940 less than 1 percent of the children ever used the library at all. It was in order to correct this state of affairs that Mary Moore Mitchell, the librarian, had in 1947 initiated a series of activities which included a family night once a month in which book reviews were read aloud to stimulate the interest of parents, while teenagers were offered special film and music programs along with two separate radio programs consisting of dramatized readings of books for and by the youngsters.

What would that momentary attack of embarrassment matter to Gladys as she painfully affixed her signature under Elvis' on the application card to make it valid? As for Elvis, whatever stab of dismay he might have experienced looking at her poor, blotted, badly formed letters would have been quickly healed by the rush of tenderness and pride he felt for her as he smiled at her and she bravely smiled back.

Leaving the library that dark winter afternoon, their transient uneasiness quickly turned to joy and satisfaction as they walked home talking over the new opportunities that would now be open for Elvis—for free.

Gladys, by her support of Elvis on that important day, was no longer just dreaming along with him that he was as good as anyone else; she had actively involved herself in helping him to become better. Joining the library and using its facilities through that winter and all the next summer pointed Elvis in a new direction. He would become a doer, a self-developer rather than a dreamer. By instinct a joiner, he wanted only the chance to join.

But while the boy and his mother were thinking along what their faith and optimism told them were the straight, right lines, the father seemed to have slipped back into old winding paths. By September bad luck had struck the Presleys again.

Vernon, for some time, had been using the McCarty truck for purposes other than delivering groceries and attending church. "Vernon was the delivery boy of my bootlegger," at least two members of the upper echelon in Tupelo will tell you today with amusement, adding that "bootlegging was then a way of life."

So why would a delivery boy, that low-but-essential man on the totem pole, suddenly have the whistle blown on him? There seemed to have been an accumulation of things. Vernon was involved in selling a hog here and there whose original ownership was in doubt, and there is one recorded instance in which a horse he sold turned out to be dead on delivery. For whatever reason or reasons, Vernon was certainly let go by L. P. McCarty. And one day either in late September or early October (accounts vary), the Presleys headed for Memphis and a new start.

"Dad packed all our belongings in boxes and put them on top and in the trunk of a 1939 Plymouth. We left Tupelo overnight. We were broke, man, broke," was the way Elvis remembered it in later years, giving to their exodus the aspect of a moonlight flit.

Actually, the Presleys left in good enough order to arrange for Travis and his family (his wife Lorene and their two small children, Bobby and Billy) to join them in the migration; for Lillian and her family to move from the country into the rooms vacated on Green Street (there was still a housing shortage); and for Leroy Green to remember that on Elvis' last day in school, at the children's request, the teacher gave him thirty minutes to perform before the class. The last song he sang for them was the traditional tune, "A Leaf on a Tree" ("the leaf on the branch, the branch on the tree, the tree in a hole, the hole in the ground, and the green grass grew all around, all around, etc.").

Since plain old practical experienced schoolteachers, as well as fancy psychologists, call the ages from one to thirteen the crucial as well as the formative years, it is right and fitting to conclude Elvis' Tupelo days with a statment from Mrs. Camp:

Elvis was always one of my main characters in homeroom and chapel programs. He would talk, sing, and play anything you wanted him to. I don't think I did very much. I'm sorry I didn't do more.... But you know, I had forty-two students and that means forty-two papas and mamas as well. I wish I had done lots more. If I could go back now I would do more for these talented children, now that I recognize it.

Around that time in another town in Mississippi, when it was discovered that a poor young black girl had an extraordinary singing voice, Leontyne Price was guided and trained for a triumphant career in opera.

Should Mrs. Camp's conscience trouble her? Milam was not, after all, the High School of Performing Arts or Juilliard. And the serious question one is left with is whether or not we should add—"thank God." Looking ahead, we might never have come to May 4, 1982, when Priscilla Presley opened Graceland to the public as a memorial to Elvis Presley with the following words: "When we went to the Smithsonian to discuss the opening of Graceland, they felt that the appearance of Elvis Presley on the American music scene was possibly the most significant single influence in the entire two hundred-year history of American music."

As for L. P. McCarty who, by firing Vernon, sent him and his family to

Memphis and Elvis to immortality, the wheels of fate ground slow but they ground exceeding fine. After Elvis' death, the architect chosen to design the Elvis Presley Memorial Chapel, which was opened in East Tupelo on May 18, 1979, was none other than L. P. "Buddy" McCarty, Jr.—L. P. McCarty's son.

TEN

Memphis Blues

It took the Presleys a while to get their bearings in the city which, except for visits to the zoo in Uncle Noah's school bus, Elvis had never seen before. In the first year, after a brief stopover at a boardinghouse on Washington Avenue, the Smiths and the Presleys, with Minnie Mae, moved one block over to 572 Poplar Avenue, near the downtown commercial section in North Memphis that was, not to put too fine a point on it, in the slums. And there they would stay for the next four years.

Outside, the house on Poplar Avenue was large, a once-elegant four-storey dwelling set back from the wide boulevard by a big front yard. Inside, it was roach-infested (southern cockroaches fly) and in need of major repairs. Its sixteen high-ceilinged rooms had been converted into one-family flats with inadequate bathroom facilities and no kitchen facilities at all. Most of the families living there had several children; this meant a total of some sixty souls pressing together. That they were able to rub along in daily harmony required from them the strictest enforcement of those cardinal southern virtues—exquisite manners, ritualized politeness, sly humor, and the unlimited capacity for concerning themselves with each other's business while at the same time steering clear of each other's tempers.

The next year, when the Presleys finally made it past the housing authorities into the federal housing project of Lauderdale Courts on Winchester Avenue (which, compared with the highrise horrors of today, make them seem models of cozy domestic architecture), even though they were occupying vastly more spacious quarters—a living room, two bedrooms, kitchen, and bath—they were nevertheless surrounded by four hundred families in the same project and the same rules of southern etiquette applied; rules that for his own good Gladys made sure her growing son obeyed.

Though it is commonly thought that Elvis entered Humes High directly on arriving in Memphis, no one seems to have any recollection of him there that first year. The reason is simple. According to Lillian, his first year was spent not at Humes but at the smaller Christine School on Third Street.

That still nobody remembered the fourteen-year-old when he began ninth grade at Humes High could be accounted for by the fact that he was going through a very alarming period in his life—his voice was changing. When he opened his mouth to sing he didn't know what would be coming out, and he had the singer's fear that after it changed perhaps he would not be able to sing at all.

Humes High on Manassas Street, where Elvis spent the next four years and from where he graduated with a good-conduct certificate, is generally described as an overpopulated, understaffed, ill-equipped slum school. In fact, its big red-brick building was located so as to draw its sixteen hundred pupils from a fairly wide spectrum of income brackets, which meant the comfortably-off white-collar class as well as the blue-collar and "overall" classes were represented. Like the majority of large high schools in medium-sized American towns in those days, it offered a program fairly bursting with both academic and athletic activities, calculated to urge its students onwards and mobilize them upwards.

As Elvis' generation was perhaps the last generation of school children to operate wholeheartedly on the premise that education was an advantage and a preparation for life, a goal to be mastered or at any rate grasped at (the age of achievement was now drawing to a close as the Beat Generation began hitting the road), the image of Elvis would be so successfully distorted as to become a public monument to the closing down of the old era. It must nevertheless be emphasized that young Elvis began as one of its most fervent participants.

One glance at the Humes High yearbook, Class of 1953, which lists his majors as history, English, and shop, and his activities as ROTC, Biology Club, English Club, Speech Club, and History Club—and shows him in a group photograph as one of the library workers as well—confirms that his optimistic self sought after physical skills, practical skills, scientific knowledge, and academic learning. In other words, whatever the free American school system was offering at the time, Elvis was determined to take full advantage.

Why was he not presented, after his initial notoriety, in his true light of a high school graduate who had striven over exceptionally high odds to *learn*, rather than as a rebellious, ignorant young punk interested only in fancy clothes and cars—the image that was early imposed on him?

Much of the blame for this is rightly placed on the Dogcatcher from Tampa, "Colonel" Tom Parker, but another clue of enormous significance as to why the silly, shallow, selfish superficial image of Elvis was being pushed so enthusiastically on to the public can be found in an influential magazine called *Motivation* (February 1957 issue) in an article which dealt with the big moral and moneymaking issue of the day: teenage revolt. In this article, *Motivation* is striving to reassure America that the Presley rage can be dismissed as a *non*destructive aspect of the revolt because "the only reason that Presley is a teenage hero is simply because he has succeeded with little formal schooling and without any of the adult graces and polish." In other words, not to worry, he's harmless. If, on the other hand, the article seems to imply he *did* have masses of formal schooling and heaps of adult graces and polish—watch out: The boy could be *dangerous*!

But as long as the false image of this real person could be projected in this way, that is, as silly, shallow, selfish, superficial; in a word, *dumb*, an image which was later to fossilize throughout Elvis' life—his part in the teenage rebellion, which despite the famous James Dean movie title, had in fact *many* causes—would present no threat to the nation. The parents could all relax and better still, the kids could all rush out, buy his records, and "resonate" with him.

This is thinking along rather peculiar lines. But as will be seen, there were some rather peculiar people doing Elvis' thinking both for and about him. In any case, what is never called attention to in Elvis' high school days is the one thing that should be—that what he began in Tupelo by joining the Lee County Library—he would continue as best he could throughout his high school years.

It should also be emphasized that while Humes High was offering a free education for poor boys like Elvis, as he and his family were well aware, nothing is "free." That time is money is equally true for the poor as for the rich. And for an able-bodied youngster of sixteen years of age, time spent in the Biology Club dissecting frogs was money lost by not being able to take a regular paying job. Sixteen, in fact, was time to quit. And many of the poor boys at Humes High who lived in the Lauderdale Courts Housing Project did just that. Gladys' determination alone spared Elvis this fate.

The first of the Presleys to land a job in Memphis was Gladys. She immediately went to work as a seamstress at Fashion Curtains. There Lorene, Travis' wife, followed a couple of weeks later.

After many weary, discouraging months of "pounding the pavements all over town and having to put cardboard in our only pair of shoes to cover the holes [a nice, if dated, Depression touch] in our soles," to hear Vernon's version of it to his friends, he and Travis at last found jobs, *mirabile dictu*, not a stone's throw from their own front door. The United Paint Company, where Vernon went to work in 1949 loading paint cans, was located on the corner of Concord and Winchester Avenue, the very street on which they lived.

Vernon was paid 83¢ an hour, which meant that if he could put in five hours of overtime, he could earn $38.50 per week. As the monthly rent for their apartment was only $35, if he could have just brought in this top pay regularly week after week all might have been smooth sailing and—who knows?—the Presleys might have spent the rest of their lives in Lauderdale Courts instead of only three years. As it was, they were in trouble. Vernon was soon assailed with that most vague, mysterious, unsympathetic, yet nevertheless most specifically painful of all ailments: a bad back. It meant that he worked less. It meant that the Presleys fell behind in their rent and were in danger of being evicted. It meant that in the first year, Elvis was supplementing their income by mowing lawns and that Gladys would help by working first at Fashion Curtains and then by being a waitress at a cafeteria. Luckily, as they were both paid in cash, these extra funds did not turn up on the Home Service reports.

In June 1951 they were again on their merry-go-round of not making ends meet. The Home Service report showed Vernon had received a $10 raise and the rent was, of course, bumped up accordingly. And how do you feed Vernon, Gladys, Elvis, *and* Minnie Mae on that?

In the fall of 1950 Elvis had taken a part-time job as an usher at Loews State Theater from 5 P.M. to 10 P.M., but quit on Gladys' insistence when he began falling asleep in class. The following summer was bad enough to make it necessary for both Elvis and Gladys to take jobs that unfortunately did turn up on the Home Service reports. Elvis worked again, now full-time, as an usher at Loews State Theater. His favorite actor then was a dead ringer for Captain Marvel, Jr.—glistening black hairstyle and all—the handsome young Tony Curtis, who was making a series of wonderfully funny junior swashbuckling epics with titles like *The Prince Who Was a Thief* and brandishing his Bronx accent as triumphantly as his sword.

And Gladys went to work at the nearby St. Joseph's Hospital as a nurse's aide. Unexpectedly, this menial job provided her with moments of supreme satisfaction; for in these moments it was her own glory she was basking in, not her son's. Wearing the becoming nurse's aide uniform of aqua green, she scrubbed floors, helped in the kitchen, emptied bedpans, and changed sheets. But she also served the patients their food trays, propped them up comfortably on their pillows, helped them dress and undress, and—above all—chatted with them, listened to their troubles, and kept their spirits up.

When the patients were ready to leave they often presented her with their leftover chocolates, cookies, eau de cologne, and, noticing her feet, bedroom slippers they assured her they couldn't be bothered to pack. And one elderly patient who stayed there a long time became so fond of Gladys that upon leaving she gave her a little box saying, "It's just a little something for you because you were always so nice to me when the other nurses just shoved me around and didn't even remember my name." Inside the little box was a silver-plated filigree brooch.

It was there, outside the St. Joseph's Hospital, that Gladys first laid eyes on the pink Cadillac from which she saw a patient emerging and then later being picked up. Everything in her imagination went out to that pink Cadillac. She talked to Elvis about it all the time, describing it down to its smallest detail; she just could not get it out of her mind. If you had asked her there and then what was the thing that she most desired in the whole world, she would have unhesitatingly said: "A pink Cad." To which Elvis would have replied with the promise, indeed *did* reply with the promise, "Don't you worry, mama. I'm going to buy you one one of these days, you'll see." And sure enough, when that time came, Elvis—instead of dismissing it as the sort of silly, shallow promise of a silly, shallow adolescent with little formal schooling and without any of the adult graces and polish—did keep his promise and was able to revel in the vulgar thrill of watching Gladys and Vernon proudly tooling around Memphis in a pink Cad.

Gladys' choice of the ultimate was not as unsophisticated as it seems. For in America at the time, the pink Cadillac, with its combination of utility and luxury, safety and frivolity, was the flashiest symbol of conspicuous consumption this side of the English yellow Rolls Royce.

As for the patients, so positively did they respond to "that nice country woman with the gentle hands" and so often did they ask for her, that the staff began to take notice. One day at the end of that summer, Gladys was summoned by the head nurse to her office. To her astonishment she was asked if she had ever thought of taking up nursing as a profession. If so, she was told, the hospital would be delighted to recommend her for the regular course.

In that moment Gladys fully understood that in offering this opportunity to a woman no longer in her twenties, her nursing skills had been recognized as special.

She left the office in a flutter, promising to think it over. There was, of course, nothing to think over. Apart from her financial situation, her lack of elementary schooling made the offer impossible to accept. But it made her proud to tell Elvis what had happened, and it made him proud that the hospital had also seen how special she was. And together she and Elvis shared a moment of bittersweet triumph.

But in truth it was more bitter than sweet and in reality no triumph, for it meant that due to circumstances, the injustice of which Elvis keenly felt, Gladys was condemned to drudge on with her job at the hospital with no chance of advancement.

It was not long after that that Elvis was fired by the manager of Loews State Theater. The girl at the candy counter was reported to be sneaking Elvis candy and when Elvis found out that another usher had tattled on him, he sought him out and knocked him down. It was the kind of incident not uncommon in cinemas employing a lot of high school kids of both sexes, and one that could have been avoided by all concerned sitting down and talking the thing over. But in this particular case Elvis' indignation over what he felt to be the unfairness of Gladys' lost opportunity caused his anger to spill over. And his punching the usher can be seen as a puzzled substitute for not being able to confront his real enemy directly at just that moment. And the enemy, though he might have thought it to be the world in general, was surely his father with his inconvenient lumbosacral troubles.

It is well worth noticing Elvis' misdirected rage in this early example, for it would continue all his life, causing this essentially gentle-natured and tenderhearted man to explode with increasing frequency and violence at objects that were not his main target. It was at the very heart of his tragedy, his fatal flaw, that he was virtually—one might almost say constitutionally—incapable of confronting his real enemies head on. He would later take out his frustrations either in karate or on those around him, some of whom just happened to be standing in the way.

In his twenty-ninth year, in desperation, Elvis became interested in a discipline of yoga called Kriya Yoga and determined to master it because, as he explained to his teacher, "I read that one who practices this technique is gradually no longer subject to the conditions of cause and effect and I wish to be freed of them." Which is rather like saying, "I would like to be free of the laws that govern human nature."

That Elvis did not do much singing in his first year at Humes High was understandable with the onslaught of puberty and voice change. But at sixteen, when his voice had steadied, it had returned in fact better than before, eventually to have a range of three octaves; although he began to be known after a fashion as a singer, there were still many examples of his backing away from performing, forgetting to bring his guitar to a party, or waiting to be persuaded to sing until just before the school bell rang and the class dismissed. This was perhaps another indication that his academic activities were absorbing him at least to the point of confusing his priorities.

As if in sympathetic agony, his face burst into a bloom of acne. Adolescent dismay at this requires a series of tactics to divert the eye from the erupting skin and it is then that hairstyles and clothes begin to assume importance for young males. One notices very few crew cuts among adolescents with bad skin. As for the way Elvis wore his hair in high school—parted on the side, one lock quiffed forward over his forehead and doused in plenty of brilliantine—a quick leaf through his high school yearbook reveals that nine-tenths of the other boys wore theirs in a similar fashion. Either people have badly misremembered crew cuts in the early fifties, or they are unaware that the crew cut was then an American *class* symbol of eastern prep schools and Ivy League colleges. It went with button-down collars, red or black knit ties, single-breasted gray flannel suits with thin lapels, cashmere and seersucker jackets. It would be an odd thing to find someone with a crew cut in a middle- to lower-class southern public high school.

This is not to say that Elvis, in wearing his hair just that much longer than the other boys and growing sideburns, was not trying to get noticed. Short of standing in the middle of Manassas Street and being run over by a car, he began to do everything within his means to get noticed. For being unnoticed meant being powerless—a condition Elvis was unable to tolerate for any length of time. As his Aunt Lillian put it, "Elvis was curious about his clothes." If he could have found a store that sold Captain Marvel, Jr., outfits, he no doubt would have purchased one instantly. In the event, he had to make do with what Beale Street could supply in the way of "powerful" clothes. Its clothing store, Lansky's, catered to what made *its* clients feel powerful: bright colors, zoot suits, pegged trousers, and "flat hats with rare flairs."

But the whole mystique of dandyism is far too full of complexities, perplexities, contradictions, and subtleties to be dismissed as merely being the urge to show off. Tom Wolfe, author, dandy, and southerner, has always ascribed magical properties to his clothes. "If that shirt and that shirt were running a race," he once said, pointing to what appeared to be two identical shirts, "*that* shirt would win." Yet he also bitterly complained, after taking a new coat of his out for its first airing, "What's the matter with people, don't they realize that *everything*'s wrong with my coat? Too-wide lapels, too much shoulder padding, and more buttons than a policeman's uniform. Why don't they mention it to me?"

It would seem that the dandy plans his wardrobe for quite contradictory reasons: to look good and feel powerful in, while simultaneously giving offense to his viewers—"to shake 'em up," was the way Wolfe put it, a phrase that seemed to harmonize exactly with Elvis' motives. Additionally, it is also possible that Elvis' choice of pink in his famous early wardrobe schemes was influenced by Gladys' preference for that color of her dream car.

The ridicule that he was attracting now at Humes High in his sixteenth year was on a more serious level than at Milam. At Milam some of the boys just wanted to break his guitar strings; now they wanted to break *him.* His clothes helped, though most of the time he only wore two-tone western shirts at school and saved his fancy pink and black outfit for First Assembly of God Church on Sundays and singing engagements at the Odd Fellows Club. But these were only the superficial reasons that encouraged Elvis-baiting, and no doubt another boy with an easier personality could have got away with funny clothes quite happily. It can be seen from a class photograph of the time that the majority of the boys were self-expressing in shirts of such wild and riotous florals, geometric, and abstract patterns as to blind any onlooker to what Elvis might have been wearing.

But something in Elvis' personality found it hard to endure the frustrations of the gifted. His impatience to fulfill himself, his impatience for recognition, no doubt aided in making him, in the eyes of his fellow students, both precocious and obnoxious and too slyly well-behaved to be true. As at Milam these anti-Elvis feelings were often paradoxically stirred up by the small pro-Elvis faction. Who were they? One answer can be found in the class will of his yearbook, which among its bequests, has: "Donald Williams, Raymond McCraig, and Elvis Presley leave hoping there will be someone to take their place as *teacher's pet.*"

Like his mama before him, Elvis had cultivated, or rather developed, his natural gift for getting favors without asking for them and accepting them with grace; for getting people interested in him and concerned about him for which he repaid them by his eagerness, humility, politeness, and willingness to learn. But Gladys canonized all of Elvis' weaknesses— his fears and anxieties, his diffidence, his insecurity, his timidity—under the heading of good manners, not only because she felt his obedience to her and to his elders a safety measure against destruction but also because she felt it presented him, coming from the lowest rank of poverty, in the best possible light. To her it was his way of standing out from the rest of the slum children; of getting more for free; of attracting, in short, the sympathy and notice of the teachers. To the other pupils, of course, Elvis' oily behavior was apple-polishing and sucking up and, as such, was deeply resented. Summed up neatly by his ex-friend Red West about a teacher: "I think she always had a soft spot for Elvis because he was so polite to her." The teacher's natural pet is invariably the other pupils' natural enemy.

And it was not just the women teachers whose pet he became. His class before lunch was shop, and the shop teacher noticed one day that Elvis lingered behind during lunch hour. Discovering that it was because he didn't have money for lunch, he gave him some, a practice he continued from time to time. Shop promptly became one of Elvis' majors. "There were times," said Vernon later, "when I never had more than twenty-five cents to give Elvis for lunch money, but he never fussed about it." There were also times when he had less.

It was in the beginning of his last year at high school that the explosions of Elvis-baiting began in earnest. As Elvis later was to see it, it was the other kids' way of saying, "Hey, look at that squirrel up there in the trees—let's *get* him!" One day the bullies, all set to beat him up, closed in on him in the washroom where he had gone to comb his hair. It was to Red West's eternal credit that he stepped in, risking his own skin to defend Elvis against these unsporting odds—and to his eternal discredit that he never let Elvis forget it.

Was it simply a heroic deed? Or was Red's action caused by a moment of blind empathy and identification when Elvis' naked fear communicated itself to another slum boy living in another slum housing project? The feelings of fanatical love and protection that the person of Elvis inspired in boys and girls alike have to be looked at as steadily as the hate, disgust, and ridicule he also inspired.

In his late teens, the blue-eyed Elvis' features were taking on more and more of Vernon's handsome cast. He had grown into a beautiful boy. Like all beautiful boys, he was sending out disturbing sexual vibrations and not only to the opposite sex. Of all the inequalities of childhood, the inequality of beauty is perhaps the most unfair and the one least able to be dealt with. Some children are more beautiful than others and everyone knows it, and it sets up a tension that works both for and against them. The English public schools do not have the exclusive story on the love and loyalties adolescent boys bear for their own sex—they just go on about it more.

So, though Elvis was making enemies in school, he was also making friends, some of whom he would keep for most of his life. Two schoolmates in particular were destined to become close friends. On the surface they are very different, though it is important to note that, like Elvis, they were also "achievers": Red West, after graduation from Humes, went on to Jones Junior College on a football scholarship. The school won the state championship and he played the Junior Rosebowl in Pasadena. George Klein, the president of Elvis' class, "the most likely to succeed," the editor of the school yearbook, and the president of practically every extracurricular activity in Humes High, became a leading disk jockey and lecturer at a university in Memphis. What all three had in common, besides being ambitious, was that they were also very, very poor.

Important as it was to Elvis to have these two on his side, their friendship would have been far less valuable to him at that moment than the new one he was forming with a bass player, some ten years his senior, whom he had met up with in his own front yard at Lauderdale Courts.

It was one of the most propitious meetings in Elvis' life, his meeting with Bill "Blackie" Black—one which immeasurably hastened his progress along the yellow brick road to fame, as crucial a meeting in realistic terms as his imaginary meeting was with Captain Marvel, Jr. Without this meeting there would most certainly have been an Elvis story, but it might have been a different one. It is essential to pinpoint when exactly this friendship began.

Here again, one is confronted with the useful addenda to Parkinson's law which has it that the accuracy with which an event in Elvis' life is remembered varies inversely with its importance. For not one person in the cast of leading characters around Elvis' early success in 1954—not Marion Keisker, Sam Phillips, Blackie, Scotty Moore, or even Elvis himself, when embarking on the fairy tale of how Elvis' professional career came into being—gets it straight. Though the story is repeated ad nauseam of Sam Phillips introducing Bill Black and Scotty Moore to Elvis and telling them to go off and rehearse for (always allow for variation here) two days—two weeks—two months, in not one of their versions is the truth ever remembered: which is simply that Scotty and Blackie *already* knew Elvis, and that Blackie knew him very well and long before Sam Phillips in 1954.

The date of their meeting has now been established by Bill's son Louis Black as being 1951, when Elvis was sixteen. Blackie was at the time with a country band called Doug Poindexter's Starlite Wranglers, Doug Poindexter being the leader and sometime singer and the other members being Millard Yeo, fiddle; Clyde Rush, guitar; Tommy Seals, steel guitar, and Scotty Moore, lead guitar. Not only were they a professional band playing in Memphis clubs but they had already worked for Sam Phillips who had started up his famous Memphis Recording Service in 1950.

For Elvis it all began a good three years before what should be called the official or "Sam Phillips" story. Blackie was at Lauderdale Courts to visit his widowed mother, Ruby Black (soon to become a good friend of Gladys), who lived there with Blackie's two younger brothers, Johnny and Kenny, both of whom went to Humes with Elvis and were around his age. "But it needn't have happened that way," Louis Black assures me, "for a good musician is always looking for a good musician and they will always find each other and get together."

Bill Black was a jolly, kind, friendly soul, and being the first-rate musician he was, after listening to Elvis sing for him in the courtyard—shy Elvis being no more backward with Blackie than he had been with Mississippi Slim—took an immediate interest in the boy.

It has been remarked with much truth that one is either a mama's boy or a daddy's boy. Louis Black was certainly most beloved of his father (later on, the Bill Black Combo would record under the Louis label), constantly in his company from childhood on, and some of his most vivid recollections of the trio go back to pre-fame, to before it all happened, when he would sit by his father in Lauderdale Courts on summer nights and listen to Elvis and Blackie (with other musicians, possibly Scotty) singing and playing together. He remembers specifically an old geezer who used to throw water out the window at them trying to shut them up. It stays in Louis' mind that they rehearsed one song for four hours. In fact he recalls this period so strongly that when he heard "That's All Right, Mama" played over the radio in July 1954, his reaction was, "But that's just what they've been doing in the front yard."

Blackie, says Louis, was urging Elvis as early as 1952 to go over to Sam Phillips' recording service, put down four dollars, and cut himself a record. That way Elvis could hear himself, and so could Sam. Further, Blackie was aware—as was everyone connected with the Sam Phillips operation—of his famous dictum, "If I could find a white man who had the Negro sound and feel, I could make a million dollars." Blackie must have thought that Elvis might just fit the bill. Also, as these informal Lauderdale Courts sessions progressed, so did the excitement these musicians were generating in each other and out of which came the spring, the beat, the bounce, the drive of the fast numbers and the deep lyric feeling, the almost unbearable tension and release in the ballads. Surely Blackie would have found himself thinking that Sam had better hear this kid (but "casual-like," with no advance build-up) with the possibility of forming a group; something that neither Blackie (nor Scotty for that matter) at this point would want the other Starlite Wranglers to know about. But it could also mean that they were merely looking for a new lead singer for the Starlite Wranglers. In 1952 the talented rockabilly singer, Johnny Burnette—slightly older than Elvis and already graduated from high school—had sung occasionally with the Wranglers but he had left them to form his own trio with his brother, Dorsey, and Paul Burlison.

The seventeen-year-old Elvis, however, was still refusing to take that step—partly through shyness and diffidence but also because in cutting a record with Sun, he was in essence auditioning for Sam who would be in the control room. And he wanted to be good and ready before not only wasting four dollars but having Sam Phillips chalk up a black mark against him.

Christmas of 1951 had been a particularly bad one for the Presleys. The income from Vernon's United Paint job, together with Gladys' job at St. Joseph's Hospital, showed that they had gone over the stipulated amount per year for income in the Project. They were threatened with eviction. Vernon tried in vain to explain the situation to the authorities in a letter dictated by Elvis:

"Have had illness in family, wife is working to help pay out of debt. Bills pressing—and don't want to be sued."

The invalid was Vernon, the illness was his back which was now bad enough to require medical care and some hospitalization. But that didn't matter. They were still down on record as being over their earning limit. Gladys had to quit her job.

Then in the spring there came another notice from the housing authorities informing them they had now fallen behind in rent. The amount due was $43.74, and a fine of one dollar a day was being imposed, effective immediately. Interestingly enough, it is at this point that Elvis was seen so often driving the old family Lincoln coupe, a piece of cardboard standing in for one of its windows, that his fellow students assumed it belonged entirely to him. No, the Presleys were really not good housing project material.

There is no record of what job or jobs Elvis took that summer of his seventeenth year because he was paid in cash, and also because he would have liked to have forgotten them. Sweeping and cleaning up a nightclub or honky-tonk dive was one way of picking up cash, with the possibility, if lucky, of getting on the stand and singing. Waiting on tables or behind the bar was another way, with the possibility of tips; so was parking cars; and being a carhop at a diner yet one more. A carhop uniform, in fact, was one of the outrageous getups Elvis' fellow students saw him in in his last year of high school. Like his other wild clothes, they seemed primarily to have been his working clothes.

For this was not a summer to be idled through like the one before, as an usher in a movie house dreaming of becoming a movie star; this was the summer Elvis forced himself to give up what he realized were the childish pursuits of history, English, biology, and all that higher-learning stuff and address himself to the grown-up prospect of supporting himself and his family.

In deciding to confront life straight on, he did what every other young boy without money or connections does who wants to be a singer or an actor or what Elvis would always refer to himself as, "an entertainer"— he went to where the action was.

It becomes important now to keep an eye on Johnny Burnette, because that is exactly what Elvis would be doing from now on—Johnny's daytime job that summer was driving the same Crown Electric truck that Elvis would be driving the next year—and also because Johnny was keeping his eye on Elvis as well.

This is the way the late Johnny Burnette remembered Elvis then:

Wherever he went he'd have his guitar slung across his back—never did bother with a case like the rest of us boys. Sometimes he used to go down to the fire station and sing to the boys there—they were the only ones around Memphis who seemed to have a lot of listening time. And every now and then, he'd go into one of the cafés and bars and slouch across a chair. He never sat up straight, he'd just sort of lie there with that mean look on his face. Then some folks would say: "Let's hear you sing, boy," and old El would stroll up to the most convenient spot, looking at the ground all the time. Then all of a sudden he'd slide that guitar round to his front and he'd near raise the roof with that real rocking sound of his.

Obviously Burnette had not come across old El in certain other honky-tonk cafés and bars patronized by the more boisterous clientele, who would not urge old El to let them hear him sing, but to get his guitar, his mean look, and his butt off that chair and just keep right on walking out the door, son.

The only photographic record that exists of Elvis that summer is a series of snapshots taken of the still blond seventeen-year-old in the Eagle's Nest nightclub on Highway 78. One photograph shows him in the act of his lifelong habit of biting his nails, wearing a light-colored 1952 version of a polyester windbreaker. Already his collar is turned up for the unglamorous reason, Elvis later confided to his friend Sterling Hofman, that he thought his neck was too long. If he did get to sing at that nightclub, there is no record of his reception. One can be sure that it was rarely by singing that he got any money and that the pains, indignities, and frustrations he awakened to face every morning that summer were from trying to break into the entertainment world and ending up instead running errands, sweeping, cleaning, washing up, and just generally doing whatever struck his bosses' fancy at the time. It was in part these memories that would inspire him to tell *Newsweek* in 1956: "English was what I liked best in high school. Some day I want to write a book about what it's like to be an entertainer. It's tough, man, tough!"

But so it was for everyone. Marlon Brando once ran an elevator; Burt Lancaster worked in the lingerie department of a big store; James Cagney was a female impersonator. What it boils down to is how keenly are these mortifications felt? While some seventeen-year-old would say to themselves, "What the hell—I'll look back at this some day and laugh"; others would decide that this brush with reality was a little too sleazy for them and perhaps they'd better think of another way of life. Elvis both minded badly the humiliations he was exposed to, but didn't quit. He did something else. At the time, the great gospel singers—the Blackwoods and their younger members, the Songfellows—held all-night sings at Ellis Auditorium. There Elvis would go to wash his soul clean. He went for relief and inspiration on his nights off, to immerse himself in long hours of his beloved music with its reiterated message of God loves you, God forgives you, God looks after you. His love of singing songs both sacred and profane, supposed to expose the sinister Jekyll-and-Hyde aspect of Elvis, was in effect simple obedience to the laws of cause and effect. And as the music flowed through him Elvis was able to shift from the powerless, the pushed around, kicked around, ridiculed, secular Freddy Freeman, to the powerful, magic Captain Marvel, Jr. This shift from secular woes to sacred joys, from mundane existence to a glimpse of the eternal, was what the blacks had been doing since they had been brought as slaves to America. But it is not what your ordinary everyday young white punk is likely to do, and the spiritual satisfaction Elvis received from these experiences was probably of the same sort as his visits to Jesse's grave.

Well, at least he was growing older. Too old, he felt, to go through yet one more year at school. That his birthday came in the middle of a school year so that he was always a year older than the rest of the kids at the end of it, had always made him self-conscious; he would be eighteen when he graduated while all the others would be only seventeen.

Altogether, that summer had been a transitional one for the Presleys— not just because it was Elvis' first active attempt to break into the tough competitive world of entertainment, but because Gladys was changing. That April, the month when they had fallen behind in their rent and were paying out the extra dollar a day to make up for it, Gladys was facing her own private crisis: she had turned forty. Though publicly she kept up the fiction that she and Vernon were about the same age—he was thirty-six—inwardly it was a severe jolt to her. Like all women she found this landmark of midlife beset with difficulties. Like many women, her way of coping with these difficulties was by trying to hide them.

Vernon and Elvis were making enough money that summer to free Gladys from the necessity of working. She was able to fill her idle hours brooding about herself and her life. Inevitably nature had taken control and the most astonishing of the changes wrought was that her anxious grip on Elvis had mysteriously loosened. It was as if, quite suddenly, her interest in him had dropped, leaving only preoccupation with herself to fill the void. She was unused to introspection; it made her feel both uneasy and unreal. Eggville... Tupelo... Memphis... she found herself going back over her life again and again; sometimes it seemed to have happened to someone else; sometimes she wondered if it had happened at all.

Yet while her thoughts, roaming over the past, made her feel a hundred years old, she began cultivating a manner that was consciously youthful. She found herself dwelling on her dead child Jesse with surprising intensity. He at least seemed real to her. But when she looked at the seventeen-year-old Elvis it was his six-year-old image she saw instead.

Turning forty weighed so much on her mind that she knew it must show on her face. She began concentrating on her appearance to disguise the years. Her black hair had to be touched up more often than before. Fervently she tried out new cosmetics: another foundation base, a different color lipstick, eye shadow, and even a touch of mascara to call attention to her dark eyes. She was determined to lose weight. When she went to a doctor he prescribed diet pills. She had been enjoying going out with Vernon to the movies and then to the nearby beer hall for a beer or two; she now found the beer having an even more pleasurable and harmonious effect on her. Did she know what she was doing? Probably not. We are talking about 1952 when almost no one did—much less the doctors who were prescribing these pills. Traditionally, drinking was frowned upon for women in her walk of life during their childbearing years, although a nip or two after those years was considered not unbeneficial. But Gladys began looking forward to her visits to the beer hall with Vernon, to the jukebox, the company, the fun, the dancing and the singing, with perhaps too much relish.

Elvis, too, was confused by his mother's metamorphosis. He was used to having her listen to his daily experiences, used to her being the one person he could always turn to for support, used to her always being on hand whenever he was troubled or upset. That summer marked for him the transition from adolescence to manhood. It had been late in coming. Often when he came home at night, he would find her in funny moods—sometimes giddy, giggly, and overexcited; sometimes tearful as she reminisced about all the things he used to do and say when he was a child.

At these times Elvis fell back into his early pattern of calming her down, of cheering her up, hugging and petting her, calling her his baby, and talking to her in their old vocabulary. But in a way, for Elvis, Gladys' self-absorption was not unwelcome. There were things Elvis was doing that summer he would not want her to know about and he was glad that she did not inquire of them too closely. It was this summer, however, that Elvis began his habit of going and paying the grocery bills—$25, $30. "We didn't ask him to do it," Gladys said later. "He'd just do it himself."

Another strange thing about that summer was that their mutual dream, which by now they might have expected to have become to some degree palpable, was in fact blearing. And it was that dream, that bright, clear dream Gladys wanted back—the dream they had spent so many happy hours weaving together. In Tupelo dreaming of Elvis as a star had made them feel very special, very out of the ordinary. But to hold on to that dream in as important a center of contemporary music as Memphis, where it seemed every boy in town who owned a guitar also owned the same dream, had by that very token made the dream less possible.

It was with great reluctance that Elvis returned to school for his senior year. It was not even a matter of wanting to do something else. It was just a matter of no longer seeing any point to it, dragging himself through one more year of classrooms and being made fun of.

He wanted a real job, any job that would earn him some money. He wanted money, freedom, escape. He wanted out from the eternal struggle of their economic situation and caught himself dreaming disloyally of running away from home forever. Almost a grown man, he immersed himself nightly in the adventures of Captain Marvel, Jr., flying off with him into heroic deeds.

The "downs," known as the sophomore slump and the junior jitters, that most youths do not experience until college, he had already experienced in high school. When Gladys found out he was skipping school and objected, Elvis argued that he didn't need a high school certificate to drive a truck or dig a ditch or especially to be a singer; not that he was at all sure, after the disillusionments of the summer, that that was what he wanted to be.

Any way you looked at it, he insisted, this last year of school was not just time wasted—it was going to be time lost. When Gladys objected even more vehemently Elvis turned to his father for manly support. Vernon backed him to the hilt. Never had these two been in such complete accord. "Anything you want for yourself is all right with me, son—you know you can always count on that," was the way Vernon put it before going off to his wife to enlighten her on the masculine point of view. Surely their son was old enough to know his own mind about quitting school; why when he was Elvis' age—

He got no further than that. All of Gladys' pent-up fury and frustration exploded and she let him have it—a résumé of his life. Making sure they were out of Elvis' hearing, she didn't spare him the highlights: Parchman, Como, Tupelo and the city dump, Tupelo and bootlegging—Memphis and still loading cans for the United Paint Company at his age and with his back. Sure he was as smart as the next fellow, hadn't Aaron Kennedy always told him that? But hadn't Aaron Kennedy always tried to get him to sit down and study to read more easily so he'd be able to learn something from his Bible? Lack of education—that's what had caused all the bad things that had happened to them. What could be clearer than that? Was that what he really wanted for his son, too? When he knew that a high school certificate would make all the difference at the employment agencies?

Vernon backed off. Elvis sulked in his room and continued skipping school.

One of the ways country women who lived in Memphis could make seasonal money was by picking cotton. For two weeks in September trucks daily crossed the state line over the Memphis–Arkansas bridge into the city to collect these workers and carry them to the Arkansas cotton fields. It was hard work but if, like Lillian, who had also now moved to Memphis, you enjoyed being in the open air rather than shut up in a laundry or garment mill and—as she still proudly remembers— you could pick 150 pounds a day, the money was good.

Gladys didn't talk it over; she didn't say anything about it to anyone, but the day she went out and joined Lillian and the rest of the workers in the truck over the bridge, she had that look on her face that Elvis knew meant nothing would stop her.

Elvis went back to school. Briefly he took an evening-shift job at Marl

Metal Products from 3 P.M. to 11:30 P.M., and when he started to fall asleep in class again Gladys made him quit and resumed her old job at the St. Joseph's Hospital.

Money may be said to inflict its own psychological pattern of behavior. While many middle-class mothers in their midlife crisis will put off returning to work because they feel their teenage child is not yet ready to give them up and still needs their support, Gladys returned to work for the same reason: to give Elvis one more year of adolescence.

Elvis no more liked her having to work at the hospital again than he had liked her having to work those few days in the fields. It distressed him deeply; yet paradoxically, in doing what upset him, she was doing what was best for her. Returning again to a source that gave her, this supreme nurturer, a natural outlet for her care-giving, she was provoked into getting back her grip on herself, thereby almost certainly averting a nervous breakdown.

But by having her salary added back on the Home Service report along with Vernon's, she had also provoked the inevitable Christmas eviction notice. Again they were over their income limit. This year, however, it was Elvis who made the decision about their dilemma. As he told Mrs. Ruby Black, he was just plain tired of seeing his mother on her knees scrubbing the wooden floors for the monthly housing authority inspection after working so hard all day at the hospital. So that Christmas, instead of getting into the same old arguments with the authorities over whether Vernon was really earning the $53.22 a week the United Paint Company claimed he was, Elvis said, "OK. That's it. We're getting out of here."

On January 7, 1953, the day before Elvis' eighteenth birthday, they left the housing project forever.

Their next move—a brief one—was to Cypress Street. That it was in a part of the city well off their beaten track meant they were being put up by relatives. All the Smiths and Presleys, nearest to them in blood, had also by then migrated from Tupelo to Memphis.

By April the Presleys had left Cypress and were back in their old neighborhood—a first-floor apartment on 462 Alabama Avenue right across the street from Lauderdale Courts, but no longer under the wing of welfare. They were on their own.

The big theatrical event of the school year at Humes was its annual variety show held at the beginning of the second semester. Its purpose was to raise money to supply the poorer kids with something special they might need, from football gear to money to go to a school dance.

It was an event the students had always looked forward to, but for some reason this year the enthusiasm had peaked, not only in attendance but in participation. No less than thirty acts had declared themselves ready, willing, and eager to stun their peers with their talents. Two extra teachers had to be recruited to organize the show besides Miss Scrivener, Elvis' homeroom and history teacher, who was its producer. No, it was not the High School of Performing Arts, though by the tension generated backstage by the kids bumping into each other, revving themselves up, or calming themselves down for the ordeal, you might have been excused for thinking so. Whatever the variety show meant to the other twenty-nine acts, to Elvis it meant that for the first time since his successful appearance at the Mississippi-Alabama Fair eight years before, he was getting another chance to sing to an audience of a comparable size. Sixteen hundred pupils and the teaching staff had jammed themselves into the auditorium. Because of the large number of participants Miss Scrivener had decreed that only one act would be allowed the honor of an encore—the one that got the most applause, and who would, by that token, be declared the winner.

At the end of the show Miss Scrivener turned to Elvis who was still standing on the edge of the stage hidden by the curtain. "It's you, Elvis," she said, "Get out there and sing another song." But, as we can see from where he'd placed himself, he already knew. How could he not? The torrential applause had picked him out an easy winner.

Elvis had prepared himself for the variety show by rehearsing his songs on anyone who would listen. (The Presleys' old friend from Tupelo, Mrs. Marshall Brown, up visiting in Memphis at the time, remembers Elvis singing love songs to a girlfriend over the telephone, balancing the receiver between his ear and shoulder so as to leave his hands free to play the guitar.) He also paid special attention to the way he would look for the occasion. Details like this separate the serious from the trifler. Determined that this time it was going to be the *singer* as well as the song they would love, he not only carefully combed his hair into its most eye-catching Captain Marvel, Jr., swirls, but carefully chose for the color of his shirt, red—the color that universally cries out, "Stop, look, and listen." That he did not own a shirt of this color and could not afford to buy one, simply meant he borrowed one from his friend Buzzy Forbes.

One wonders what thoughts went fleetingly through the minds of those fellow students who knew him as an insignificant, not-much liked, odd-ball senior, as Elvis came slouching out on stage, eyes on the ground, only his glistening hair and red shirt vibrating off the stage lights as he propped a foot on a chair and suddenly slid his guitar round to his front prior to raising the roof. How much initial resistance did he have to overcome? How many Elvis-baiters would be sitting there hoping he'd make a fool of himself? How long did it take the scoffing to switch to surrender, for thought to be conquered by feeling? Perhaps midway into his first number, "Cold, Cold, Icy Fingers." Perhaps earlier than that this born performer again established the dominance of his eery twinship, his magical mutuality with a large audience.

And since many in the crowd were seen crying during his performance, one can be sure he had not forgotten to rely on dependable "Old Shep." According to Martha Wallace, a classmate of hers in eighth grade actually fainted during the song.

After the encore which was received with even more tumultuous applause, Elvis took his bow and returned to the wings. Says Miss Scrivener: "I'll never forget the look on his face when he came off stage then—'They really liked me, Miss Scrivener. They really liked me.'"

It is at such moments that we do not censor our thoughts. Out of our surprised reaction, whatever first pops out of our mouth is the truest expression of our feelings, and for that reason should be regarded as both enlightening and justifiable. It would have been entirely justifiable, for instance, if Elvis had said instead, "I guess I showed 'em—that'll fix 'em" or "I wasn't at my best—I wish I could do it over." Bombast or resistance are both legitimate reactions to such success and both perfectly reveal that the true drives behind achievement can be either aggression or self-torment. But for a simple, pleased, thankful recognition, how better could satisfaction and enjoyment be expressed, how better his realization that the singer had at last become the song than in those four words: *They really liked me.*

Now at last the signs were good. And whatever had happened to him in the past year that had made him hide and halt and despair had suddenly and marvelously turned a corner where he could see before him the clearing in the wood.

That evening he had "boocups" to tell Gladys who, of course, would pass it all on to the neighbors and especially to her friend Ruby Black, who had already heard about it from her sons Johnny and Kenny, who had told Blackie who, in turn, again urged Elvis to go down to Sam Phillips' studio and cut a record. Yet even now, with applause still fresh in his ears, Elvis demurred. The closeness of graduation was his excuse to Blackie. He reckoned he'd better just concentrate on that, you know, better keep his eye on the ball, not slide off the track at this late date. Another way of saying perhaps, not yet, not yet—I'm not ready yet. Yet during his last months at Humes, Elvis returned to his old Milam ways of arriving every day with his guitar slung over his shoulder and as summer and the warm weather came around, he took to sitting under a tree on the school grounds at recess and singing—softly at first as if in self-communication, until invariably he collected his attentive audience. Now he was in great demand at his fellow students' parties. Accompanying himself either on guitar or piano, he always made sure the stage was properly set, first by his having to be coaxed and then by insisting all the lights be turned out for the proper atmosphere. Just as during the cold months, recalls Lillian, if the room the party was going on in had a fireplace Elvis always insisted on it being lit. It was the performer he was working on now—the role which he was becoming more confident in and comfortable with.

The months that at the beginning of his senior year he had envisaged as dragging endlessly on had, in fact, flown. Now there were only three months to go. Then two. And then one. Suddenly there were only two weeks left.

On the Tuesday of the last week—May 26 to be exact—Elvis was not in Memphis. He had hitched some 240 miles by himself to Meridian, Mississippi, where he arrived with ten cents in his pocket.

ELEVEN

Meridian and Onward

On May 26, 1953, Meridian was holding its first Jimmie Rodgers "The Father of Country Music" Festival. It was to become an annual memorial to Gladys' beloved singing brakeman who had died at thirty-six of tuberculosis.

The program was to include 120 country singers at the fairgrounds and—for native sons only—a Mississippi talent show organized by Meridian's leading newspaper, the *Meridian Star*, to be held at the Lamar Hotel. Curtis Robinson, a reporter on that newspaper, still vividly recalls his encounter with Elvis:

There was this kid, Elvis Presley, wandering around with his guitar looking lost. I was with my colleague Dick Smith and the kid told us he was from Tupelo and had hitched all the way here to get into the contest. That's right—Tupelo. Of course, if he'd said where he was really from at the time, not living in Mississippi would have disqualified him. He was flat broke. It turned out he only had ten cents on him. Dick took pity on him and paid for his room and board. He entered the contest and won second prize. I can't remember what he sang but I remember the prize. It was a guitar. Dick and I always remember this because Elvis never paid him back.

Although documentation of this event—of this daring breaking out of Elvis from his daily routine, this unfunded dash to Meridian only one week before graduation wafted on the wings of nothing but a Captain Marvel, Jr.-like crazy optimistic belief that the journey would end in triumph—although its documentation is impeccable, you will look in

155

vain in all the hundreds of books written about Elvis for even a mention of it.

Curtis Robinson suggests that this escapade has remained unchronicled because Elvis himself wanted it buried. What happened, thinks Robinson, was something like this:

Three years later, Elvis returned to Meridian on the same day for the third Jimmie Rodgers memorial. He was on the main program with Hank Snow and Roy Acuff. First he sang "I'm Left, You're Right, She's Gone," a country-type number, and then he let loose with his rocking version of "Baby, Let's Play House." That was a mistake. The audience, hillbilly purists to a man, had come to hear country music, not rock, and they booed and laughed him off the stage. Elvis was so mad he swore he would never come back to Meridian—never mention it again—and that I guess included wiping off his slate any mention of the fact that the first time he had come here he'd gone and gotten himself second prize in the talent show.

There is undoubtedly some truth to this supposition. There was a plethora of artistic stresses at work in Elvis' temperament. He was not able to shrug off failure with the ease less sensitive people are blessed with. He allowed rebuffs to get under his skin and erupt into feelings of resentment—these feelings being infinitely preferable to him than the ones of insecurity he was constantly plagued by. And so it may be that his anger at his reception in 1955 had spilled over to sour the triumph of 1953.

The only trouble with this theory is that whether Elvis liked it or not, many other early failures—such as his failure to pass the important audition for the Arthur Godfrey Talent Show—have always been recorded in great detail.

So we are still left with the sturdy, substantial fact of Elvis hitching 240 miles to Meridian which, like the fact of Elvis' hitching from East Tupelo to Tupelo when he was eight, seems to have been, well—what, exactly? Missed? Dismissed? Abandoned? Suppressed?

Not only in thrillers but in biographies, one of the cardinal rules must be observed: If a verifiable fact does not fit into a theory, it is the theory, *not the fact*, that must be thrown out.

Theories which present the energetic, growing Elvis, while living in a downtown area alive with children's recreation centers, poolhalls, the Ellis Auditorium, the Odd Fellows Lodge, drugstores with jukeboxes and so on, tied to his mother's apron by hoops of steel, docile and obediently sequestered in their tiny stuffy apartment through the long hot nights of the long hot Memphis summers, his ears glued to the black station WDIA whence (and whence only) sprang all his knowledge of music—

such theories as in Albert Goldman's *Elvis*—must be thrown out once and for all.

Facts are dangerous things. One dismisses them at one's peril. The unwieldy, jagged, recalcitrant facts about Elvis will keep popping up and they are impossible to jam into the theory of Gladys as the all-restricting, all-constricting mother. Take for instance the following sentences from Goldman's biography of Elvis: "As for the notion that the adolescent Elvis spent a lot of time hanging around blues joints on Beale Street, all one has to do to test the truth of that theory is to imagine how Gladys would react to such a pastime. Why, every weekend people got killed on Beale Street. No, it is unthinkable..."

Although we all know from the song that on Beale Street "the business never ceases till somebody gets killed," the last person who was going to be killed on Beale Street was a polite, white, fourteen-year-old boy listening raptly to their music. More likely he would become their mascot. Nor, of course, would he be the only white person there. In the forties and fifties, white music-lovers from all over the world, as well as Memphis, went often and safely to Beale Street to listen to the music. A recently published book, *Beale Black and Blue*, is sprinkled throughout with appearances of Elvis in his early teens. To support his theory Goldman footnotes Nat D. Williams, a black teacher at Booker T. Washington High who was also a radio man and writer of a humor column in Memphis at the time, as proof that Elvis' contact with Beale Street was minimal. The irony of the whole sentence cannot be perceived by quoting only these words from Williams' column on a goodwill show in Beale Street sponsored by a local black radio station: "Why Elvis came and how he got in the middle of such a concentrated kodachrome we may never know." It is simply Nat D. Williams' elaborate wink at his black readers; of *course* they know why Elvis is there; he is there because he *always* had been there—listening, learning, and imitating. Williams' comment, and the perhaps justifiable attitude behind it, has always been of such common knowledge it is hardly worth repeating. However, Williams does not stop there. He continues and the point he makes is certainly worth noting:

... But [Elvis] was there. He tried to stay backstage. But somebody spotted him and asked him to come out and take a bow. Well, he did. And that did it. A thousand black, brown and beige teenage girls in the audience blended their alto and soprano voices in one wild crescendo of sound that rent the rafters... and took off like scalded cats in the direction of Elvis.

It took some time and several white cops to quell the melee and protect Elvis. The teenage charge left Beale Streeters wondering: "How come cullud girls would take on so over a Memphis white boy... when they hardly let out a squeak over B. B. King, a Memphis cullud boy?"

Both the boys have made names for themselves. And some folk feel that Elvis might just barely have borrowed something from B. B.

But further, Beale Streeters are wondering if these teenager girls' demonstration over Presley doesn't reflect a basic integration in attitude and aspiration which has been festering in the minds of most of your folks' womenfolk all along.

Williams is either placing Elvis historically as one of the early accelerators of the process of integration or simply remarking on the topsy-turvy situation in which the black man resented Elvis being "one of them" but their teenage girls loved it. Or did they just agree with Minnie Mae, who when people said to her that Elvis sings like a black man, replied, "Fiddlesticks! My boy sings better."

To throw away, dismiss, ignore, or bypass the actuality of Elvis in Meridian at that talent contest is to perpetuate a complete misunderstanding of who Elvis was and what singing meant to him.

Elvis was a poor American southern boy who had about as much chance of becoming a star entertainer as El Cordobes, a poor Spanish country boy, had of becoming a star matador. El Cordobes began his career in the ring as an *espontáneo*. An *espontáneo* is that skinny kid at a bullfight who, suddenly overcome with emotion, leaps into the ring in the middle of a *corrida*, pulls out from under his shirt a stick and a red rag tacked together to make a *muleta* and then, with insane courage and to the pity and terror and amusement of the astonished spectators, cites the bull and attempts a series of passes until he is either carried out of the ring by the police or, if good enough, pardoned by the crowd's uproarious cheers. In just such a spirit of an outsider leaping into the thick of it would Elvis have stood out among the many at the Lamar Hotel in his red shirt with his guitar as he began to sing and shake.

Since the first golden age of Elvis—1954–58—coincided with the golden age of several young bullfighters called *phenomenos* who were looked up to as pop stars in the same way as Elvis—their personalities, characteristics, and lifestyles bore such a striking similarity to Elvis' that it is worth pursuing the comparison a little further.

The first similarity was that they were never alone; the bullfighters were always surrounded by their *cuadrillas* (their squadrons) as Elvis by his hangers-on and bodyguards. The second was that the bullfighters, like Elvis, drank only Pepsi or Coke. The third was their predilection for pastel-colored Cadillacs—the bullfighters favoring lavender, Elvis pink. Both bullfighters and Elvis were mother-worshipping and medallion-laden, enjoyed playing pool and simple card games with their pals, and were often seen scowling intently at American comic books. As with Elvis, as their celebrity grew, introductions to girls subsequently arranged for them were at the bullfighters' instigation but only carried out through the offices of a member of their *cuadrilla*. As with Elvis, the approach was never made by the bullfighters themselves.

Kenneth Tynan wrote in 1954 of one young bullfighter: "What we were seeing is something which is seldom made public: An instinctive artist had stumbled upon a classic form and made it so intimately his own that one would have thought he had invented it; the stresses of his temperament had led him irrevocably toward the form that was waiting to express them." One can only note how perfectly that comment could be applied to the Elvis of 1954 who had also taken a classic form—blues—and made it so intimately his own.

Elvis returned from his first Meridian encounter in triumph to lay his trophy, his guitar, at his mother's feet. He finished his last days of school and graduated the next week with a testimonial of good conduct.

The death of two of Elvis' heroes the previous winter might be seen as the passing of the old order making way for the new. The great country singer Hank Williams had been found dead in the back of his Cadillac as a result of his long, drawn-out, and losing battle with drugs and alcohol. And the Captain Marvel/Captain Marvel, Jr., comic books had folded as a result of a long, drawn-out, and losing battle over a lawsuit with Superman and were no longer on the newsstands. As these departures coincide with a new determined Elvis, it is almost as if he began incorporating their magical qualities into himself as he had done with his twin Jesse's in the past.

The world looked very different to Elvis that June from the previous one. He had forced the new challenge upon himself, had accepted it, had conquered it and had found best of all that what he was conquering was in fact something he was already lovingly familiar with—was returning to—something all mixed up with his mother's musical roots as expressed by Jimmie Rodgers: in what has been described, to be technical, as a melding of Anglo-Saxon-Scottish folk tradition with the gut-essence and heartbeat rhythm of Delta blues burnished with jazz phrasings.

The success of the high school variety show had been a good go-ahead signal, but he had needed another one of larger dimensions and significance. If, up to Meridian, Elvis could use the excuse of the continual precariousness of the Presley finances to shrivel his dream (which at its most inflated included not only the Grand Ole Opry but being right up there, ten feet high, on the silver screen) to the size of a hobby—"Yeah, I play some," that sort of thing—after Meridian he knew he could never again fall back on the old excuses. No matter what the obstacles in his path—shyness, stagefright, money, the exact knowledge of who he was and how far down he was on the American social scale—he knew he could never again relegate his singing to the status of a hobby.

Graduating from Humes he lost no time in contributing to the support of his family by taking a full-time job on the assembly line at the Precision Tool Company. Elvis left it three weeks later when the job he really wanted fell vacant—driving a truck for Crown Electric Company, run by Jim and Gladys Tipler at 353 Poplar Avenue, close to where he lived. The pay was less than at the Precision Tool Company, about forty-one dollars a week after taxes, but Elvis knew precisely what he was doing and held on to the Crown job for fourteen and a half months until the fall of 1954. Crown Electric wired churches, schools, industrial plants, shops, and residences. Elvis was one of the two truck drivers who delivered materials to where they were needed and sometimes helped keep stock in the warehouse.

What may not have looked like anything special was, in fact, the job that ideally suited his needs. Just a year before, Johnny Burnette and his brother Dorsey had driven those two Crown Electric trucks in the day-time, while at night they offered the services of their band to all takers. And now this year they were professional musicians who could get paying engagements at high schools, halls, and on radio.

Doubtless one of the reasons Elvis chose to go the same route as Johnny was the hope that the same truck so loaded with electrical provisions would attract the same lightning to strike again in the same place. Also, with his guitar always beside him on the passenger seat, he was using the job as a sort of postgraduate course in getting known around town as a singer; for wherever he went he was always ready to oblige with a song to lighten the labors of the workers he delivered the materials to. At the same time he was getting some on-the-spot training in the watts and ohms and three-wire circuits for a possible future job as an electrician.

Perhaps Elvis' luckiest strike in following the Burnettes to Crown was that, in working for Jim and Gladys (even the name boded well) Tipler, he was working not only for a really nice couple, but one already broken in, so to speak, and used to the ways of hopeful young musicians; patrons, one might say, who could be relied upon to take an interest in their careers, give a valued opinion on a new haircut, a new jacket, a new shirt, or a new song.

Yes, the long hair and the sideburns took a little getting used to, but the more Gladys Tipler got to know and like this naive, polite young man who so good-naturedly let himself be the butt of the older electricians' jokes, the more amused and intrigued she became at the sight of Elvis returning from a run in the truck and dashing straight to the mirror to comb his hair until it was just so. There is a curious double standard at work here: The portrait of the young Laurence Olivier, carefully studying his reflection in the mirror for hours and from all angles, wins our approval as a young artist preparing for greatness, while the portrait of Elvis studying himself in the same manner wins our scorn as the preening of an insecure narcissist. Yet no less than Olivier was Elvis intending to be seen as well as heard.

In one more way was the Crown Electric job ideal for Elvis. The Ford pickup he drove daily was in far better shape than any of the Presleys' cars he had had to contend with, and the sheer pleasure of driving a vehicle with all its parts in working order was considerable.

Even more than most American men, Elvis metamorphosed his cars into the mules and horses of his ancestors and valued them as necessities, luxuries, possessions, and objects of pride and love, as highly as his forebears did their animals of work and locomotion. Elvis' lifelong love affair with everything on wheels—cars, trucks, motorcycles, jeeps, trailers, tractors, even golf carts—has been well publicized, as have his gifts of cars to both friends and strangers; in other words, he gave away that which he himself prized most highly. Cars were such an integral part of his nature that at times it seemed impossible to say where he left off and they began; at times indeed he seemed like a contemporary centaur with wheels for extremities instead of hooves. It is inconceivable that Elvis would ever have settled down to a job that did not involve driving.

This was for Elvis a very happy period in his life. The job had its contentment and its freedom. All day long he drove the truck around Memphis while at night he touched his musical bases: Beale Street, Ellis Auditorium, making music with Blackie and Scotty and others at Lauderdale Courts when they were available, hanging out and sometimes singing with both the Blackwoods and the Songfellows. Elvis also became a very familiar face around TV studios—though only in the audience— for shows such as Wink Martindale's and country singers Slim and Mary Rhodes', and at Bob Neal's radio show, "High Noon Roundup," which featured country artists on the first half of the hour-long program and the Blackwood Brothers and the Gospels on the second half.

It happened every day when he first started working for the Tiplers. Every lunch hour of every day he seemed to find himself in his truck driving in the neighborhood of 706 Union Avenue—the Memphis Recording Service was only seven blocks from where he worked—and then driving past. No matter that after Meridian, Blackie kept urging, "Well, what are you waiting for now? Go *on*, Elvis, cut that disk, I *want* Sam to hear you"—to which Gladys would inevitably agree, "Blackie's right, son. You do like he tells you to." But Elvis kept hanging back.

It was one thing to sing to people, a sea of faces, a gathering of twenty, a gathering of fifty, a gathering of two hundred—it made no difference; that was something he could gear himself up to, galvanize his fear into electric excitement. That was like going back to childhood and singing to the highly responsive First Assembly of God congregation. As a live entertainer he could feel an audience and like a tuning fork send vibrations shivering endlessly through them. But standing alone in a small studio in front of a microphone separated by a glass partition from the control room—wherein sat a couple of sensationally uninterested engineers fiddling with knobs and not even looking at you, plus the guy in charge who, if he did happen to glance in your direction, let you read anything into that glance that you wanted to while at the same time stopped you from wanting to—that was something else; something that did not bring out the best in Elvis; something that could downright intimidate him.

The day in July that Elvis finally forced himself inside the Memphis Recording Service was a Saturday, not a weekday, which should dispel any notion that he was taking off a couple of minutes from his lunch hour to shell out four dollars, one-tenth of his salary, to make a record on mere impulse. Sam Phillips, whom he expected to be faced with, was not there. Instead, behind the desk in charge of the office was an attractive woman in her early thirties with red-gold hair and a look of Ann Sheridan about her. She was Marion Keisker, who had been, in her time, a well-known radio personality. For years she had one of the earliest women's talk shows and had built up a very good name for herself doing a variety of shows which included news broadcasts. She had been named "Miss Radio of Memphis." An intelligent woman, highly knowledgeable about music and a devotee of drama, she was and still is an active member of a local theater group now called Theater Memphis. She had left radio in the early fifties to take on the new challenge of going to work for Sam Phillips as his indispensable girl Friday.

Elvis found himself in a waiting room full of young guitarists. "They *all* had their guitars in those days," said Marion to Jerry Hopkins. "All waiting to make personal records. All waiting to be discovered by Sam as well."

Something must have struck her immediately about Elvis, as no doubt he meant it to—the long sideburns he had now grown and his clothes for a start. But there seems to be no question that he was also communicating something else—that young and special charm that a much-beloved son subliminally communicates to women—which Marion Keisker, herself a mother, received and returned.

Elvis chose a seat near her, and she found herself striking up a conversation with this new arrival, a conversation that she says she was never able to forget because she had to tell the story so often in the years after. When she asked him about himself he told her he was a singer and that he was making a record for his mother. What kind of singer was he? she wanted to know, and he said, "I sing all kinds."

"Who do you sound like?" asked Marion.

"I don't sound like nobody," was the fabled answer.

"Hillbilly?" she made a guess.

"Yeah, I sing hillbilly."

"Who do you sound like in hillbilly?"

"I don't sound like nobody."

When they went back to make the record which he had told Marion was to be the present for his mother—a ten-inch acetate—Elvis sang two of his favorite Ink Spots numbers, "My Happiness" and "That's When Your Heartaches Begin." The latter song begins as a weepy ballad but, if he sang it then the way he later would in 1957, about halfway through he switches from the melancholy mood into one of humorous, self-mocking, philosophical acceptance—a technique that lends that unique color to black blues and which always keeps them this side of sentimentality.

About halfway through the first side, Marion thought, I want to tape this. It was something they never did but she wanted Sam to hear it. "I got maybe the last third of the first song and all of the second. I don't even know if Elvis knew then that I was taping it." And then comes her famous quote about the reason she taped it: "Over and over I remember Sam saying, 'If I could find a white man who had the Negro sound and the Negro feel, I could make a billion dollars.' This is what I heard in Elvis, this... what I guess they now call soul, this Negro sound. So I taped it. I wanted Sam to know."[8]

It is interesting that what Marion said was, "I wanted Sam to *know*" rather than, "I wanted Sam to *listen*." Unmistakably, whether consciously or unconsciously, it was not only what she was hearing that was sending out such strong signals to her, but what she was seeing as she watched the young boy sing.

For if Sam had only wanted a black sound in a white body, how many dozens of older, more experienced white musicians could have gotten that to perfection? Marion, reacting to the whole image of Elvis, and also being theatrically astute, must have realized that it was not only a black

---

8. *Elvis: A Biography*, by Jerry Hopkins (New York: Simon & Schuster, 1971).

sound Sam needed but that sound coming from *that* particular teenage face.

It was more than a decade since Sinatra had had the teenagers screaming, and since then there had only been that comet Johnny Ray, brilliant but brief—and in 1953 Ray was twenty-seven.

With the postwar era the whole star image had drastically changed. With people hardly realizing it, stars had dropped in age by at least two decades. Clark Gable, Spencer Tracy, Cary Grant, Errol Flynn, Humphrey Bogart, James Cagney—those were for grownups, and they struck teenagers as definitely over the hill. It was the youth embodied in the new ones—Marlon Brando, Montgomery Clift, Tony Curtis, Robert Wagner, Paul Newman—a wave that would work itself up to James Dean. They were not only young in age, they embodied the confusion, the vulnerability, and the unformed question marks of youth in their faces. Elvis' face and age fitted right in. They were all beautiful boys—not handsome men.

Sam Phillips had got one word wrong in that oft-quoted sentence about what he was looking for to make a billion dollars. What he was looking for was a white *boy*—not a white man—with the Negro sound and the Negro feel.

Let us suppose, however, that it had not been Marion in charge of that busy waiting room on that day in July, not Marion the attractive and receptive woman Elvis had sung to through the glass partition of the studio, but Sam Phillips. What would Sam have heard and seen? Probably a lot more of Freddy Freeman than Captain Marvel, Jr.

Any way you looked at it, by 1953 Sam Phillips was a formidable figure on the Memphis music scene, a man whose inner contradictions sprang from his background. Brought up with his two brothers on his father's place in Florence, Alabama, and exposed from birth to all the civilizing intellectual paraphernalia that went with it—including being dangled on the knee of old black Uncle Silas who sang him the blues—all of which had suddenly gone with the wind with the death of his father, forcing Sam to drop out of high school to help support his widowed mother and spinster aunt. These circumstances had left him short on ready cash but long on paternalistic southern aristocratic attitudes and with a genuine love of music, especially black blues.

It was these blues that led him to work as a disk jockey on radio, first in Alabama and then in Nashville and finally, in 1946, for WREC in Memphis. Later he had become a sound engineer as well, coordinating the broadcasting of bands from the Peabody Hotel. In 1950 he had saved up enough money to form the Memphis Recording Service, the small studio on Union Avenue. He began by recording the finest black artists in Memphis such as B. B. King, Bobby Bland, Willie Nixon and Junior Parker, at a time when there were no other facilities for cutting their records. These master tapes he leased to such companies as RPM Modern in Los Angeles, run by the Bihari Brothers, and Chess in Chicago, run by the Chess Brothers, who would pay him so many cents per side sold. In no time Sam was in trouble with RPM Modern for giving Chess the master of Jackie Brenston's "Rocket 88" (an ode to the new Oldsmobile) and when it really hit big and he had another success with an artist named Howlin' Wolf there was more contention between Sam, Chess, and Modern.[9] It soon became clear to Sam that becoming an independent record producer meant exchanging the mores and manners of life on a plantation for those of a jungle. He coped with difficulty, refusing ever to give up the one for the other.

He was also prey to swift changes of mind. A good example of Sam's early chopping and changing at the very beginning of his career can be seen when in July 1950, following a session with black singer Joe Hill Louis, Sam sent the dubs to Modern and then recalled them because of what he felt was a more attractive proposition. A namesake but nonrelative of Sam's, Dewey Phillips (who will soon turn up again to play an important role in Elvis' story) had approached Sam to go into the record business with him. Dewey, one of Memphis' most prominent disk jockeys, himself a singer of the type called screamer-and-yeller who also had a penchant for black music, would find blues singers without record deals. Sam would record them and Dewey would run the label. It would be called the Phillips label, subtitled "the Hottest Thing in the Country" (out of which would seem to have come Sam's own label Sun two years later). Sam agreed to a trial run with the two Joe Hill Louis dubs he had recalled from Modern: "Boogie in the Park" and "Gotta Let You Go." They released the Phillips record in August, and when it didn't do well Sam dropped the whole idea of the label and went back to Modern to negotiate a contract for Joe Hill Louis.[10]

This way of operating justifiably made Sam extremely cautious, not to say downright unwilling, to take a chance on anything until *after* it was proven, and which in the end, in many people's opinion, was why Sun never became the major label it should have. In the early stages, however, it was difficult to know whether with Sam one was dealing with a faint heart or merely a realistic man on a tight budget with a wife and children

[9] *Sun Records*, by Colin Escott and Martin Hawkins (London: Omnibus Press, 1980).
[10] Ibid.

to support. He had the same kind of philosophy as certain stagnant publishing houses, which goes: "Nobody ever went broke *not* publishing a book."

Further, Sam was that oddity, a perfectionist who seriously wanted to make a million dollars—in other words he wanted to make that million by recording the music he most loved the best way he could and with the best artists he could find. So, while the black sound was kept firmly in his heart, his eye was just as firmly kept on the commercial market, looking for ways of exploiting that sound to make it sell to the largest possible audience.

Sam was no scholarly Alan Lomax, tirelessly roaming the Southland with his sound equipment in the service of the Library of Congress, searching out America's folk music roots and turning up folk geniuses like Muddy Waters (and frightening Muddy out of a year's growth because he initially assumed Lomax was a revenue man trying to nail him for making moonshine); Phillips was on no musical mission but, from the very beginning, he was on what he hoped would be a commercial venture. That he liked what he was doing enhanced the product. His boast was that he recorded the finest artists, both black and white, before anyone else did. His autocratic nature led him to be the kind of impresario obsessed with discovering and developing unknowns.

In March 1952 when he began his Sun Label, his releases were only those of black musicians. The following March he came up with a potential hit in an answer-back record to Big Mama Thornton's "Hound Dog" called "You Ain't Nothin' But a Bearcat," sung by Rufus Thomas, Jr., which promptly landed him in trouble again, because Thomas was singing it to the tune of "Hound Dog." Litigation ensued and was solved by releasing it and splitting the royalties with Peacock, which was the "Hound Dog" label. This success was followed by Joe Hill Louis' wild, bouncing "Tigerman."

By then Sam was pretty sure that the sound that was selling and going to sell bigger and bigger was slick, urban, jump blues. This was a conclusion he reached firsthand while doing a great deal of record distributing at ground level, which meant getting into his car and peddling Sun records personally to distributors and records shops in neighboring states.

But there was a problem. As his brother Judd puts it in *Sun Records*, "Everyone dug the black r & b records of the fifties, the music the black people were putting down, but there was so much prejudice and division they couldn't idolize the artist that was singing the song." In fact, no black singer would really be idolized as a heartthrob until Harry Belafonte.

Though Sam continued recording black artists he started in 1953 to get white country singers and their bands interested in incorporating the "new" blues sound. Whether rockabilly was as Carl Perkins said, "taking country music and giving it a colored beat," or whether it was as some other white musicians still insist—a fusion of white honky tonk (heavy piano and a drum beat) and country boogie—or whether it was all a revival of a beat that stemmed back from 1938 when Joe Turner and Peter Johnson, two New Orleans rhythm and blues singers, took boogie-woogie to the famous Café Society nightclub in New York and started a craze that went nationwide, it is something that can be argued forever without profit or conclusion.

When Elvis walked into the Memphis Recording Service that Saturday afternoon to cut his first record, he might or might not have known through Blackie about the black and white fusion Sam had in mind, though he would not have been able to guess it from the current Sun catalogue, which featured only black artists. But he certainly knew what every aspiring musician in Memphis knew; Sam and his Sun Records were the only game in town.

While presenting himself publicly as a mild, absentminded gentleman, Sam had a private view of blacks and poor whites and their proper place in the scheme of things—a view, one might say, powerful enough to be felt by Elvis and the black musicians—that his role was that of their ole massa and they were his little children—little children whom he was going to raise. What Sam Phillips' many statements also made clear was that his patronage would brook no insubordination. All things considered, had Sam been there that first day at the studio, the plantation aura of Bossman Phillips might have produced a far more subdued performance from Elvis than Marion Keisker witnessed.

Call it luck, fate or a miracle—Marion was there and Sam was not. And she saw Elvis as well as heard him. And so she taped him, and asked him for his name—which she spelled 'Pressley'—and address and telephone number, and added to his file: "good ballad singer—hold." And something about Elvis stayed with her. She even found herself telling her mother about him that evening and her mother said, "Oh, I've seen that kid on the streetcars. The kid with sideburns." Already he had a face people remembered.

As for Elvis, he could not wait to tell Blackie his news and give his mother his present. There are two reasons, it is usually claimed, why the record could not have been a present for his mother: First, her birthday was back in April, and second, it is supposed that the Presleys did not have a phonograph. In fact as his relatives and friends at the time will tell you, Elvis had had a phonograph for several years—it would have been one of the essential things he would have spent money on; a phonograph and records would have been as essential as clothes. And it didn't need to be Gladys' birthday for Elvis to want to give her a present of him singing.

But if an occasion *were* needed for him to give her a record, there was one not too far past—one very important to them both. June 17, 1953, was Gladys' and Vernon's twentieth wedding anniversary. And without their marriage Elvis would not have been born.

TWELVE

"That's All Right, Mama"

Marion played Elvis' tape for Sam. And Sam said that he was impressed but that the boy needed a lot of work. Nevertheless Elvis' tape and his card went into the files, and here the Sun story usually stops dead in its tracks, not to be resumed for six long months. But in a town the size of Memphis, where everything that happened in music happened in the small downtown area where the Presleys lived—the area that included the radio and television studios, Beale Street, and Union Avenue—would it have been like Elvis, knowing he had at least gotten a foot in Sun's door, to leave it at that? There is one story which has Elvis continuing to turn up at the Sun studios, and Sam typically greeting him with remarks like, "Here's old Pres come to see what sort of a star I can make out of him." But that would be out of character for them both. If there was one thing everyone including Elvis knew about Sam, it was that he could not and would not be hustled.

However, there was a restaurant called Taylor's Café where all the musicians hung out. The multitalented Jack Clement, a native Memphian who had been in turns and simultaneously a singer, a bandleader (Elvis once appeared with his band at the Eagle's Nest), and a songwriter, and who contributed most importantly to the Sun sound as a producer of many of its Johnny Cash, Carl Perkins, and Jerry Lee Lewis recordings, has gone on record as saying the real secret of Sun was the popularity of Taylor's Café. He was not joking. "That's where all the guys did their writing and talking, and that's where the Sun sound was really born." It is a truism that every particular branch of the performing arts in whatever size city in whatever country in the world has a special restaurant which functions as a clearinghouse of information as well as furnishing food, drink, and companionship to those particular artists and would-be artists. These places are invariably described by outsiders as "full of atmosphere," which translated means they are the best places for these artists to see and be seen. One could say that as the Russian Tea Room is to Carnegie Hall, so Taylor's Café was to the Sun studios. Right next door.

For Elvis it would only require getting Marion's timetable right in order to hang out at Taylor's when she was most liable to be there. Having found favor with so specially placed a person as the attractive lady with the red-gold hair at the court of the Sun king, it is unthinkable that Elvis would not have strived to keep in some kind of touch with her and develop their initial meeting into a friendship. Taylor's was the right way to do it. There, southern manners would dictate an exchange of pleasantries between these two in the course of which Elvis would let on that as it happened, in a couple of days, he would be singing at the aforementioned Eagle's Nest or with Johnny Burnette (which he did on at least two occasions), or whatever. Although later Sam was to claim that he and only he discovered Elvis—putting forward the unlikely story that Marion, a woman of wide experience in broadcasting and its technicalities, didn't know how to work a tape machine—we have about Elvis' debt to Marion and his early knowledge of this debt Red West's irrefutable statement in *Elvis: What Happened*: "Whenever Elvis came across magazines and newspapers saying how he got started and all the stories with Sam Phillips as being the man who discovered Elvis, well, Elvis told me I don't know how many times that Marion Keisker was the one who really did the job. She was the one who kept his telephone number and she was the one who knew that Sam was looking for a black sound inside a white body. Now Elvis had respect for Sam, but he would say to me, 'If it wasn't for that lady, I would never have got a start. That woman, she was the one who had faith, she was the one who pushed me. Sure, Sam had the studio but it was Marion who did it for me.'"

From this distance it seems clear that the upward swing in Elvis' morale stemmed from his decision at the very beginning of 1953·for the family to leave the housing project. What set it off may well have been, as he said, no longer being able to watch his mother on her knees scrubbing floors. The truth was that on the eve of turning eighteen the government housing, with its welfare aspects, could no longer contain Elvis' pride, ambition, and developing sense of himself.

Something else—or rather *someone* else—was also contributing to Elvis' buoyancy during this period. Elvis had fallen in love with a girl who had actually responded by falling in love with him. After Elvis' death Vernon briefly chronicled this love affair for *Good Housekeeping*: "In high school Elvis met a girl named Dixie Locke. Gladys and I thought maybe they would get married because Dixie was a mighty likable girl and Elvis thought the world of her. It didn't work out, but I still hear from Dixie to this day." For all its compression, Vernon's words radiate with feeling, and the same might be said for Elvis himself on the subject. In an interview for *New Musical Express* some six years after the event, when he was in the army in Germany, he is described as listening to a record of "Smoke Gets in Your Eyes" as he talks about Dixie. "She was kind of small with long, dark hair that came down to her shoulders and the biggest smile I've ever seen anywhere. She was always laughing, always enjoying herself. She dropped her books once and I picked them up and we began laughing and she said why didn't I do it more often. We were a big thing. I gave her my high school ring. She loved me to pour letters of sand down her back. For two years we had a ball."

Dixie Locke was fifteen when they fell in love. She did not go to Humes but to Southside High, and they met at the First Assembly of God Church in Memphis that they both attended. Their relationship did not ripen until summer when Elvis was driving around in the Crown Electric truck and Dixie was on school vacation—and then it burst into full bloom.

Was it a coincidence that all during that summer and the following fall Elvis seemed less in a hurry to hustle his career as a solo singer, that instead he took even more of an interest in the gospel quartets which Dixie also loved, turned up more at the all-night sings because she enjoyed them so much? The cold facts show that the hot summer of his content made glorious by this daughter of the South so aptly named Dixie saw very few signs of career activity on Elvis' part and brings up the question: If love conquers all, does that not include ambition as well?

Dixie was by all accounts one of the most popular girls in her class. She was one of those straightforward girls, comfortable in herself and of an outgoing disposition, who looked forward with both eagerness and sureness to attaining the two goals she desired in life: love and marriage. Though her background was simple working-class (her father worked at the railway express terminal), coming from a far more ordered non-welfare-type home than Elvis', some people may have considered her one step up the social ladder from the Presleys, but his being three years older and having a steady job would seem to redress the balance.

A first glance took in Dixie's bright, far-set dark eyes and soft dimples.

Only a second glance took in the firmness of her chin and the determination of her jaw. Both glances told one she was unimpeachably respectable. Pretty and smiling, Dixie was no doubt many other things as well. But one thing she was definitely not: she was not like—if she has to be "like" anyone—Gladys. To begin with, her childhood and adolescence had been comparatively untroubled; and to continue listing their dissimilarities, Gladys' nurturing instincts had led her to marry someone younger than she, while Dixie, in responding to someone three years older—and three years to a teenager is double that in their eyes—was responding to an older man who would take care of her. But this is all so much psychological musing, when really the one she was most like in aspect, age, and levelheadedness, was none other than the lively Mary Batson, or rather Mary Marvel, Captain Marvel's twin sister who, when not done up in her Marvel gear, wears simple blue school dresses, bobby sox, or knee socks, and whose long dark hair was worn like Dixie's, shoulder-length with a short swirled off-the-forehead lock.

For the first time in his life Elvis felt easy enough in the company of a girl to confess all his anxieties and hesitancies and his family's continuous financial struggles. For the very first time Elvis, steering his course along the mainstream of young love, felt normal; and this step away from always feeling odd, inspired him for the moment to feel that her continuing presence would free him forever from the giveaway signs of his country boy awkwardness. In fact, with Dixie he felt so at ease he hardly noticed that he was still biting his nails, running the motor with his left leg, constantly tapping his fingers, and going right on being shy and ambitious.

Knowing Dixie would understand and sympathize, he told her all the things about himself he thought he would never be able to tell any girl—except his ambition to become a professional singer. As with James Ausborn and all his subsequent close friends, in this there was still the element of Freddy Freeman guarding his Captain Marvel secret, but more because with Dixie he was content in being plain, ordinary, everyday Elvis Presley, truck driver. The pangs of ambition almost subsided when he was with her, so content was he then no longer to be this oddball, this joke, this freak in sideburns and crazy stage clothes who happened also to have a glorious voice and a mission to use it to change his family's situation in the world. Nor, since they talked much about marriage, would he want to risk losing her by confessing a desire to devote his life to a profession rife with risk and unemployment. Dixie was a prize Elvis had no intention of losing. Says Lillian, "I think Dixie was the one girl he loved most in his life." She was certainly the first girl he had known who hadn't left him the minute something better came along, or who was only flirting with him, teasing him, and making fun of him behind his back.

They were happy in each other's company—happy in the Crown Electric pickup truck driving around the tree-lined boulevards of Memphis, strolling hand-in-hand through the steamy summer heat and dust, through the glass doors of a southern drugstore, along the parqueted linoleum floor, into a sparkling, clean-aired world, the air-conditioned breezes fluttering colored paper streamers. It was a cosmetic-scented world, the bouquet of a million bars of pink soap, pyramids of amber perfume and green eau-de-cologne, huge dazzling displays of plastic pink hair curlers, of incredible brand-new bargains of cheap celluloid toys, brand-new greeting cards, brand-new postcards, brand-new magazines, brand-new toothbrushes (in all sizes), brand-new toothpaste tubes (in all sizes), rows of Johnson's Baby Powder (in all sizes). Posters on the long mirror behind the soda counter boasted that the ice cream was Borden's, and little cards balanced on the clean formica counters pressed customers to try their tuna-fish salad sandwiches on toast.

Daily that summer Elvis and Dixie sat at the soda counter and exchanged glances in the mirror behind it, as side by side they drank a sweet, freezing, melting ice cream soda. Or slid into one of the nearby unoccupied red leatherette booths. The other gardens of their youthful delights were equally ordinary and commonplace: the local movie houses they frequented; the gymnasium done up for Dixie's high school prom— Elvis in a white summer tuxedo, Dixie in a strapless, full-skirted ankle-length white evening gown. Things that other teenagers all over America had already been doing for many summers, Elvis was doing for the first time: lying in the sun after swimming and spilling warm grains of sand on Dixie's back that spelled "I love you," or "Kiss me quick or a snake's going to bite you," spending hours in the evening on a park bench where they embraced under the Tennessee moon overlooking the shining brown-black Mississippi River, opaque with mud.

That Gladys who, in her sister's words, "was always too big a fool about Elvis," would produce a classic mother's darling—highly strung, over-sensitive, overemotional, overexcitable, and quick-tempered: "He's a little high-tempered," is the way she put it, "but then who isn't?"—is the standard conclusion that can comfortably be settled into. Traditional psychology also demands that Gladys must look at Dixie not only as a threat to her domain, and her serious rival, but also as an evil that must be expunged by ways subtle or unsubtle.

But the expected rejection of Dixie by Gladys must be balanced against

Gladys' southern tradition. It was a way of life that decreed marriage at the earliest urge, with children to follow quickly, and which resulted in an attitude toward sex more relaxed in its acceptance of the way things were for teenagers in the sultry South. A relative of Gladys in Tupelo comments casually about her grandson, "He's fifteen and still hasn't got a girlfriend—I don't know, he must be backward or something." One of the most popular jokes in Tupelo was the one which has the young girl saying, "We never do it standing up in case mama might catch us and think we're dancing."

Gladys, a country woman as well as a mother, would have been more worried if Elvis did not have a serious girlfriend at this age than if he did, especially a respectable and "mighty likeable" one. If all of this did not preclude Gladys looking at Dixie and going back on her diet, having her hair restyled and adding a bow or collar to a dress that needed brightening, neither did it preclude Gladys liking Dixie and approving of her. Moreover, the feeling seemed mutual. Later, when Elvis was away so much, Dixie would always come over to keep Gladys company. So that it would seem that Gladys' desire to live through her son extended to her determination to share in every aspect of his life. "Even when he gets married," said Gladys serenely three years later in an interview for the *New York Daily Mirror*, "part of him will always be here."

It is rare to enter the house of a young couple in Tupelo that does not contain the presence of a grandmother or a grandfather sitting quietly through dinner, helping with the dishes, contributing to the conversation only occasionally, mostly playing with their grandchildren. Gladys' attitude toward what was later Elvis' endless supply of girlfriends, toward all his friends in fact, was benign to the point of appropriation. And as their living space grew larger the presence not only of Minnie Mae but Uncle Travis, Aunt Lorene, and their two sons, Billy and Bobby, became permanent fixtures.

But in the small quarters at 462 Alabama Street, things were tight as usual. Vernon was working some: Gladys herself, though still working some, occasionally "gave out"—her legs were hurting badly and, as when pregnant with Elvis, had begun to swell. Only Elvis was working steadily. Minnie Mae (that extra mouth to feed and that extra body to clothe) was, as always, making herself useful doing grandmotherly things but, though she might go for two weeks or even a month to help out a daughter in West Point, Mississippi, her base was as ever firmly with her son Vernon's family. That was the situation at the beginning of 1954. On January 8, Elvis was going to be nineteen and what—a truck driver for the rest of his life? The truth was that all through that period of outward calm and contentment he was sharing with Dixie, there was inside of him an arsenal of fireworks that would finally explode. Though Elvis still thought the world of Dixie, that other world again began to impinge on his thoughts.

No doubt prompted once more by Blackie who, though still with Poindexter's Starlite Wranglers, had on the side with Scotty "tried backing so many different people for a combo we couldn't even remember their names"—or perhaps by a tip picked up at Taylor's Café that the time might be ripe for him to audition again for Sam—Elvis, four days before his birthday and on a Monday, which suggests he had given himself plenty of time to rehearse over the weekend, returned to the Memphis Recording Service with another four dollars to make his own record and this time, as he had expected, he was confronting Sam himself.

Trying for the thin end of the wedge, Elvis asked Sam if Marion had by any chance mentioned him. Sam, giving nothing away, conceded that she had. End of conversation. So Elvis took his place in the small, eighteen-by-thirty-foot studio and Sam, his, in the control room. The session lasted no longer than the time it took Elvis to make his record. Nevertheless, it is interesting to note that the first time round Elvis had chosen to sing two black recordings and that this time he chose two country songs, "Casual Love Affair" and "I'll Never Stand in Your Way." This would seem to indicate a knowledge of Sun's changing catalog and Sam's changing mind. As we have seen, in 1953 the catalog consisted entirely of black singers but now some white singers and country bands were turning up in it, and the word was out that Sam was looking for a fresh white country sound as well as rhythm and blues. "I can do black and I can do country" seems to be the message Elvis was conveying in his selections. The message was received in Sam's own way and in his own time. Like Marion he noted down Elvis' address and phone number and even where he could be reached at work. Then with something that either could or could not be interpreted as a smile, Sam told Elvis he would call him if anything came up—and with that, Elvis was dismissed.

Well, not much to go on there, as Elvis reported back to Blackie. So he turned to the Songfellows, the younger group connected with the Blackwoods, and through his friend, Cecil Blackwood, redoubled his efforts to join them as there was now an opening. As he loved gospel singing more than anything, and at the same time loved Dixie very much indeed, it could have presented the perfect solution: steady job and steady girl. Whether he would still have felt this way a year later we will never know because he flunked the audition. "They told me I couldn't sing," was the way he put it to Vernon. Since these same Songfellows asked Elvis to join the quartet some months later, one wonders if those extremely harsh words were not what Elvis actually heard but the way Elvis reacted to the rejection, the typical trick his sort of temperament played on his mind. What they actually told him, according to the Reverend James Hamill of the First Assembly of God Church in Memphis who was present at the time, was that his voice was fine but that as it was not yet a baritone, it would not fit in with the other three. When the Songfellows asked him again, the opening was for a tenor.

Not until May was Elvis finally sent for by Sam, who had received a dub made in Nashville of a song called "Without You" but couldn't locate the black singer to get permission to release it. It was while looking for another singer to do the song so that it could be released that Marion (for the how-many-thousandth time?) suggested the "kid with the sideburns." Absentminded Sam professed to have forgotten his name.

Marion then said, "I just have the card right here." She called Elvis at work and, according to her, was still standing there holding the phone when Elvis arrived panting, having run all the way.

Some accounts have it that Elvis' attempt at "Without You" was disastrous and though he tried it again and again, there was little improvement. But according to Elvis—whose word we may take, knowing how critical he was of himself—it was simply that he "couldn't get it right to perfection." In any case, it could not have been too bad, for what followed was that the not-easily-impressed Sam then asked him to do everything he could. At last, a proper audition! For hours Elvis sang snatches of everything he knew—blues, gospel, country, and, Marion noted, "really heavy on the Dean Martin stuff."

The three of them stayed there late into the night. When it transpired that Elvis was looking for a band, Sam, we are told, said maybe he could help him, he wasn't sure. So far so good. But here now comes the part of the official story that seems curious to say the least: Sams gets on to Scotty, who, we are told, had never seen nor heard of Elvis up to that point, and tells him to make a date with him for a rehearsal.

One of Sam's strongly held convictions, as strong as his other conviction that he was going to make a million dollars, was that the talent to produce the sound he wanted would be found no further away than the streets of Memphis or the nearby farms and towns, and for this reason he employed two main talent scouts, Bill Cantrell and Scotty Moore. If Scotty truly had no knowledge of the by-now-fairly-visible kid with flashy clothes and sideburns, he would seem to have been falling down rather badly on his job.

Be that as it may Elvis turned up on the next Sunday as arranged at Scotty's apartment in his most powerful outfit: pink shirt, pink slacks, and white buck shoes. Elvis and Scotty began playing their guitars, with Elvis singing Eddy Arnold, Hank Snow, and as Scotty remembers, a black favorite of his—Billy Eckstine. At this point, too miraculously on cue one might say to be accidental, a musician, a bass player named Bill Black, just happened to wander over to Scotty's place. He listened for a short time, wandered out again, and returned after Elvis had left. Then followed the really unbelievable bit of dialogue with Scotty asking Blackie what he thought of Elvis:

"Well, he didn't impress me too damn much," our old friend Blackie is supposed to have said.

Upon which they both agreed they didn't think much of the "snotty kid with the wild clothes who had come in."

And when Scotty called Sam to report on the session, their mutual verdict, so the official version goes, was that "the boy had a good voice but didn't do the songs better than the originals did."

Yet in spite of what would seem to be a thoroughly discouraging prognosis of the kid's future as a Sun artist, everyone began behaving as if the verdict were the opposite. Sam got the three of them together at the studio, listened to some of their music, and then gave what can only be seen as one of his rare stamps of approval: He told them to start rehearsing until they got themselves a style. Moreover, Sam let them use his studio, when it was available, to rehearse. What exactly was going on? Was Sam getting more impressed by the kid's voice and personality that he might initially and instinctively, like so many men, have had a strong resistance to? And it must not be overlooked that Sam, in "giving" Blackie and Scotty to Elvis, was giving him what he felt were two of the finest white musicians he had found so far.

If anything about Sam was consistent through the years, it was his habit of cutting disks and then deciding not to release them; until the late seventies the Sun vaults were full of such records. Johnny Burnette and his trio were among the many recorded and unreleased by Sam, as were those fine artists the Kirby Sisters, Luke McDaniel, and dozens of others. Before Elvis' famous "That's All Right [Mama]," Sam had only released seven records by white artists. One was a record by Doug Poindexter and his Starlite Wranglers in May of '54, the same month that Sam called Elvis. Sam must have not only harbored commercial hopes for the record, but liked it very much indeed to accord it so signal an honor. Listening to the A side, "My Kind of Carryin' On," it is immediately apparent why. This up-tempo number is the nearest thing Sam produced till then to what was to be called rockabilly. There are no drums, nor is there rock 'n' roll backbeat, but clearer than anything one hears the riffling rhythms of Blackie's driving bass and Scotty's hot guitar. These then are the two musicians that Sam was matching with Elvis.

And from Blackie and Scotty's point of view, it is essential to remember that they had little time to waste on dud ventures. Why was it that with their already overloaded schedules—Blackie working at a tire company during the day, Scotty at his brother's dry-cleaners, and both playing with the Doug Poindexter band at night—would they have taken the time, something like two months, to rehearse late at night at Sam's studio, unless they all felt (not only Marion, Scotty, and Blackie, but Sam as well) that something very extraordinary, very remarkable was happening?

One must trace these details of the discovery of Elvis in order to make sense of what happened not only during Elvis', Scotty's, and Blackie's first recording session on July 5, the day after the explosive Fourth of July celebrations, which yielded up Elvis' winning version of an Arthur Crudup forties blues song, but also to make sense of the incredible swiftness of events that followed and the efficiency with which these events were put into action.

A glance at Elvis' subsequent cyclonic calendar shows that he was indeed "made overnight." Yet behind this victory we can catch more than a glimpse of the dreams that Sam and Co. had harbored for it—dreams that began at least two months before "overnight...." Or was it even before that? The star treatment Elvis was to receive throughout his life began right at the start of his career with Sam. And nicely parallels the star treatment he always received from his mother.

On Monday night of July 5, while fooling around during a break in the recording session, Sam's search for his elusive sound finally came to fruition with Elvis singing "That's All Right [Mama]" which inspired the following verdict from *The New Yorker*: "Elvis' voice is like a high sharp shiver. There isn't any part of the song not covered by a thrilling energy. This is a significant American song, sung by a significant man." It is also significant that these words of praise did not appear in that magazine until twenty-three years after the release of the record, in August, 1977. By way of obituary.

Just two days after, on Wednesday, Sam's old friend and ex-partner Dewey Phillips played "That's All Right [Mama]" on his popular evening WHBQ radio program, "Red Hot and Blue," and played it fourteen times in a row (translated into theatrical terms: thirteen curtain calls and at least a year's run), the switchboard lighting up for some forty-seven phone calls. On the same program he held an interview with Elvis mainly to establish that this new sensation had attended Humes High School and therefore was a white boy.

The votes had come in: seven thousand requests for a record that was not yet in existence, for Sam in his excitement—and caution—had given Dewey a dub; the master had still to be cut and the record still did not have its flipside, an error corrected three or four nights later, according to Scotty, when this time Blackie, playing the fool, came up with the old country standard "Blue Moon of Kentucky," which they then proceeded to metamorphose into their very own thing.

Three nights later this song got its big play on WHHM by another popular disk jockey, Sleepy-eyed John Lepley. On July 12, following Sam's orders, Scotty Moore signed Elvis to a year's contract as part of their trio—fifty percent for Elvis, twenty-five percent for Blackie and Scotty. How else can this be seen except as a swift gambit on Sam's part to prevent other groups from stealing him?

The following Monday, July 19, those two songs, under catalog from number Sun 209, were released, and by the end of the month the black blues song, "That's All Right [Mama]" was number three in the Memphis country-and-western chart, of all places.

Eight days after that, on July 27, Edwin Howard, a leading entertainment reporter for the *Memphis Press–Scimitar*, received a phone call from Marion Keisker whom he certainly knew by name if not personally, and agreed to interview "the promising young Sun artist." Howard remembers:

They would have to come in on the boy's lunch hour, Marion said, because he was still driving a truck for Crown Electric Company. I said I'd be glad to see them, and shortly after noon they got off the elevator on the fifth floor of the *Press–Scimitar* and came over to my desk. The boy's hair looked as if it had been cut by a lawn mower, but the trademarks were already there—flattop, ducktail, and sideburns. He was shy and, except for "yes sir" and "no sir," let Marion do all the talking.

Here is the item that ran the next day in "The Front Row"—the first interview ever done with Elvis Presley:

In a spin, Elvis Presley can be forgiven for going round and round in more ways than one these days. A nineteen-year-old Humes High graduate, he just signed a recording contract with Sun Record Co. of Memphis, and already has a disk out that promises to be the biggest hit that Sun ever pressed....

Just now reaching dealer's shelves, the record is getting an amazing number of plays on all Memphis radio stations. "The odd thing about it," says Marion Keisker of the Sun Office, "is that both sides seem to be equally popular on pop, folk, and race record programs. This boy has something that seems to appeal to everybody.

"We've just gotten the sample records out to the disk jockeys and distributors in other cities," she said, "but we got big orders yesterday from Dallas and Atlanta."

Sun, started by Sam Phillips, former WREC engineer, several years ago, has forty distributors from coast to coast, so there's a good chance of a big national sale.

Elvis, son of Mr. and Mrs. Vernon Presley, 462 Alabama, is a truck driver for Crown Electric Co. He has been singing and playing the guitar since he was about thirteen—just picked it up himself. The home folks who have been hearing him on records so often during the past weeks can see Elvis in person when he's presented by disk jockey Bob Neal in a hillbilly show at Overton Park Shell Friday night along with veteran entertainers from the Louisiana Hayride.

On July 30 Elvis performed at his very first concert. The main attraction at Overton Park Shell was the well-known country singer Slim Whitman, but from the ad Sam had put in the Memphis newspapers you would have thought Elvis—who had not yet even had time to join the Musician's Union—was the star.

On August 10 he turned up again at the Overton Shell. And all summer long he was doing gigs either with Doug Poindexter and his Starlite Wranglers, but mostly with the Malcolm Yelvington band.

On September 9 Elvis, Blackie, and Scotty—now the Hillbilly Cat and the Blue Moon Boys, as they were briefly called—performed on a flatbed truck for the grand opening of Katz Drugstore, which yielded Elvis $32.50 and a lifelong fan and prominent member of the Elvis Presley Fan Club, Gae Macrae. September also saw Marion efficiently organizing a Memphis fan club to answer the growing need.

On September 23 Elvis cut his second record, "Good Rockin' Tonight"/ "I Don't Care if the Sun Don't Shine," which Sam released straightaway.

On September 25, two quick months after Elvis had turned professional, Sam arranged for Elvis, Scotty, and Blackie to be booked into the Grand Ole Opry where, if you listen to Scotty about their reception, "the applause was light," and if you listen to most other people it was a disaster. It was Elvis' first professional snub which, characteristically, he took hard.

October 16 was his first appearance on the *Louisiana Hayride*, where he would be singing regularly Saturday nights until December 17, 1955.

But back to the evening when Dewey Phillips first played "That's All Right [Mama]" on radio: Much has been said about Elvis sitting in the Suzore 2 movie house nervously biting his nails, knowing that Dewey Phillips would be playing it and trying to pretend that it didn't really matter or that anything was riding on it. Yet nothing has been said about Gladys and her reaction. Later she was to tell friends that the one thing that really took her by surprise was "hearing them say his name over the radio just before they put on that record. That shook me so it stayed with me right through the whole song—Elvis Presley—just my son's name.

I couldn't rightly hear the record the first time round." But then, of course, she had thirteen other chances to hear it. What could she have felt but a thrill—a pure, sharp, simple, physical thrill. Elvis was on a real live radio station in Memphis! He wasn't singing in church or high school or some old talent contest or used car lot or in between sets at the Eagle's Nest, but on a record put out by a big radio station. It was this, of course, that made all the difference. It meant that Elvis had got what he wanted, and she had got what they wanted all their lives.

It would also mean that Gladys could now organize her dreams into delightful practicalities—debts paid off, a nice house away from this old neighborhood; a good house in a good neighborhood, and plenty of good food, a good car, electrical appliances with proper wiring, a big bright kitchen filled with labor-saving devices. And good company too—new friends to add to her old ones. She always loved meeting new people. Life would be possible now on a different level. Clothes—clothes for Vernon especially; his shirts were all threadbare.... Then in the middle of her thoughts there was Vernon, telling her the radio station wanted to inter- view Elvis right away, and they had better go down and get him.

"What's happened, Mama?" Elvis asked anxiously when they found him at the Suzore.

Gladys began laughing, "Nothing but good, son. They want you over at the station."

Afterwards she and Elvis had talked till the early hours of the morning, going over and over again what had happened and all the things that now might happen, and just before Gladys fell asleep a wave of pure complacency, made up of self-satisfaction and self-justification, bore her aloft. And her last thought must have been "I raised him right," a thought that would be echoed and reiterated by Elvis through all his days, "My mama raised me right."

Part Two

THIRTEEN

The Dogcatcher of Tampa

What sort of a world had Gladys raised her son right for? However much they might have dreamt together about a better one for them it was no fairytale world she had prepared him for.

In their world of social barriers, of economic and class distinctions and injustices, she had impressed upon him that shirking work and a lack of education would seriously handicap him. Especially she had impressed on him respect for authority and the terrible consequences of breaking the law, no matter how small the infraction, for always before them was the example of Vernon. For them honesty was not just the best policy, it was the only one. In short, Gladys had raised Elvis, quite consciously, to be as different from Vernon as possible. But being Gladys meant that she raised him to be not only hardworking, but openhanded, and though these two things do not always go together, in this she succeeded.

Mickey Knox, who played one of Elvis' army buddies in *G.I. Blues*, observed Elvis jumping up every time a woman came on the set—whether he knew her or not—to give her his seat. Remarking on this to Elvis, he received the answer, "My mama raised me to have good manners and be a good Christian."

It was understood that the good manners Gladys insisted on were useful not only in making Elvis liked and helping him get ahead, but also as a way of distancing himself, creating an impenetrable wall behind which he could with dignity withdraw when attacked. To disarm with good manners was one of the traditional ways people like the Presleys had of dealing with their superiors; but on another deeper level in raising her son right, Gladys also passed on to him the idealistic, utopian teaching of their church, which urged its followers to separate themselves from the world in order to rise above its corrupting influences. Unfortunately, the world of entertainment—of all worlds possibly the worldliest—was the battleground on which Elvis had to struggle throughout his life to preserve the spiritual side of himself.

And also—being Gladys—she did her best to impress on him that it was a world fraught with physical danger, especially in all manner of ordinary boys' sports. From this he would soon rebel violently, welcoming the physical dangers of fast cars and motorcycles and later his karate. Her whole attitude towards his physical safety stirred up a rage in him that he continually had to suppress. Yet, as if she were the child and he the father who could not bear to frighten his baby, he would give in to her irrational fears. Both Vernon and Gladys unwittingly reveal a perfect example of this in an interview in the *New York Daily Mirror* in 1956:

"At fifteen, after school the white boys would team up against the colored boys and play football," said Vernon, "and they would come with their clothes torn and their hides, too. Elvis being all we had, we didn't want him to get hurt but he wouldn't stop. Gladys was working in the hospital and then one day a boy was brought from one of these football games and he died of a blood clot. That scared both of us and we made Elvis quit."

"Know what he told me?" Mrs. Presley asked. "He said, 'I'll stop because I don't want to worry you.'"

"I guess we overprotected him," was the way Gladys put it, never for a moment noticing that it was Elvis who was overprotecting her. That weakness—that tendency in his nature to give in gracefully, to placate, to reconcile, which produced such ineffable dimensions of tenderness and surrender, particularly in his gospel singing, that was to prove fatal later on—surely began with his feeling compelled to give in to Gladys' anxieties.

And yet, given that he had "nothing to start out in the world with" as Elvis said, "and nothing but a hard way to go," can one still conclude that Gladys, with all the old-fashioned virtues she had instilled in him, had indeed "raised him right"? At least one person thought so. "Elvis was the finest human being I ever met," categorically states Jean Aberbach, whose music company Hill and Range was associated with Elvis for twenty-two years, "very religious, very loyal, and *not* bigoted." Other people, however, might point out with some justification that the world Gladys had raised him for was forty years out of date—the world of 1914 rather than 1954.

Looking back from the point of view of the fifties, it seemed to the ordinary citizens of the United States that no four decades of any century since their country's birth had demanded so much of them, or had put them through so much.

No sooner was World War I over than Prohibition began, and with it the installment of gangsters and lawbreaking as a way of life; the shaky recovery from the Great Depression ended only with the next tragedy, World War II, whose victory led them directly into another war, the Korean one, which produced the dismaying side effects of American children drilled from kindergarten to lie down on the dirt and cover their heads with their hands as protection against the atom bomb that the Russians were going to drop on us.

Having dealt with this series of killing events by seeing them as plagues, acts of God, or at any rate as acts instigated from outside, Americans in the '50s now felt themselves impelled to turn back to their own country, to look inside it and see who had been minding the store all this while. In came the series of congressional investigations: the House Committee on Un-American Activities, Kefauver's investigation on organized crime, and the juvenile delinquency hearings.

History has chosen to name the '50s, those 'dull Eisenhower years,' the McCarthy Era. McCarthy himself had nothing to do with the Hollywood witch hunt—the House Un-American Committee being responsible for that—but he did instigate State Department and army witch hunts. Somehow all three merged together in the public's mind under the senator's name, and McCarthyism was what people learned to call the subpoenaing of the glamorous galaxy of Hollywood names—stars, directors, and screenwriters—before the congressional hearings as witness to the "extent of Communist infiltration of the motion picture industry." That got the first of the world series going while his various other Red exposés insured that it would last through and beyond the decade.

It was a totally effective piece of drama. The hearings ranged from comedy to tragedy. The witch hunts succeeded spectacularly in causing people to betray their own consciences and each other. They succeeded in landing some people in jail and exiling others, blacklisting many more, and were the direct cause of several suicides.

It was wonderfully clear-cut: There was the crime—Communist infiltration, and never mind that it revealed itself for the most part as celebrities signing "left-wing" petitions that could then be labeled "prematurely anti-Fascist"and "prematurely anti-Nazi"—and there were the punishments. It even incorporated a satisfactory epilogue in which McCarthy, during the army hearings, stood revealed as the true villain and got what was coming to him. It also effectively split the nation—one half looking upon it as a national disgrace, the other as a national necessity. But who really remembers the other congressional investigation in 1950–51—the Special Committee to Investigate Crime in Interstate Commerce that became known as the Kefauver Committee? Who in fact remembers much about the senator from Tennessee except that on occasion he campaigned in a coonskin cap? And yet it could be argued that the Kefauver Committee was trying to do the really serious work of the fifties, i.e., to establish that there was such a thing as organized crime in America and that it was run by an organization called the Mafia whose roots and ties were with Sicily.

In city after city the Kefauver Committee exposed nationwide organized crime syndicates whose existence depended on the support or tolerance of public officials. That was pretty strong stuff to dump on the majority of genuinely unsuspecting citizens of America. Why did this crusade fail? It certainly had its moment in the sun, and television could be said to have come of age when the hearings began to be televised and three million Americans sat glued to their sets watching a parade of hoodlums testifying... or were those public officials testifying? Which was which? Children begged to be told by their parents who were the bad guys and who were the good guys.

Public and congressional interest in the crime hearings proved as ephemeral as the television programs. For here was crime without punishment, with the ensuing years finding most of the lawbreakers—both criminals and colluding politicians—back at the old stand mostly doing what they were doing before the fun started. The recurrence of a few twenties-style gangland shootings did not really count—it was all so déjà vu, as were the in-again, out-again jail sentences on the old income-tax dodge of some of the most notorious miscreants. The most depressing proof of this fact was Congress' failure to approve any of the nineteen bills which grew directly out of the investigations.

No, you could not call the fifties the Kefauver Era, for his book *Crime in America* proves as relevant today as it was thirty years ago when, as he put it, the Mafia emanating from Sicily had scarred the face of America with almost every conceivable type of criminal violence including murder-for-hire and narcotics, smuggling and extortion, and underlined that crime had shifted now to become big business; that, while its heads were still willing and eager to use hit men or what they called "muscle," "brains" were now the dominant factor in mob leadership as it successfully infil-trated more than seventy types of formerly legitimate businesses. Taking into account when *Crime in America* was written, is it not wonderful that this list is applicable today? And though only a few of the businesses will be discussed as having any bearing on Elvis' story, it is, I think, worth printing them all alphabetically from "advertising" to "washing machines" as Kefauver did. And to wonder if, in fact, *any* type of business in America has been left untouched by the Mafia:

Advertising, amusement industry, boxing, candy, construction, dress manufac-
turing, drug manufacturers, florists, foods of all types (meat, groceries, and fruit,
etc., both wholesale and retail), furniture, gambling casinos (legal in Nevada),
garages, hardware, hotels, ice, jams and jellies, jukeboxes, liquor (wholesale and
retail), loans, olive oil importing and wholesaling, publications [Kefauver makes
a special note of "scandal sheets," which posed as legitimate but whose operations
verged on blackmail], racing, real estate, restaurants, shipping, slot machines,
trucking, transportation, and unions.

However, in spite of *Crime in America*'s general interest, there is one chapter that is of specific interest here and which is entitled "Tampa" and subtitled "The Strange Domain of a Sheriff called Melon-head."

Why a whole chapter devoted to Tampa? New York, Chicago, Kansas City, Miami, and Los Angeles had certainly earned such special treat-ment: Attention had been called for years to the continual political cor-ruption and crime eruption of these cities. But Tampa? This barely known port in Florida? Why, you could live your whole life in America without finding an occasion for the name of that city to pass your lips unless you were a connoisseur of cigars. Yet here was Tampa exposed by the Kefauver Committee as tainted and tarnished a trouble spot as ever deserved to have a chapter and some hearings all of its own.

"Human life in Tampa," reported the Committee dramatically, "was almost as cheap as the sands of the beach...." The city stood revealed as an important subcapital of the nationwide Mafia-backed narcotics ring in interstate crime. On a national scale the Committee also found links between Tampa, Miami, New Orleans, Kansas City, Chicago, Cleveland, New York, and even Havana, not only in narcotics but gambling and murder-for-hire traffic.

On the local level, law enforcement was so thoroughly corrupted that the Cuban gamblers who ran the illegal *boleta* (lottery ticket) racket referred contemptuously to the sheriff of Hillsborough County as *Cabeza de Melón*—"Melon-head." During the sheriff's nineteen-year reign, Tam-pa's numerous murders and assassination attempts had resulted in only one conviction. According to the investigation, the reason for this "high ferment of violence was the longstanding rivalry between the two gang factions: the Mafia-backed clique composed of criminals of Sicilian or

Italian extraction and the numerically larger Cuban faction... mixed in with these was a leavening of racketeers native to the section."

"The situation is not helped by the seeming willingness of some law-enforcement officials—and the apathy of others—to go along with the underworld," wryly concluded Kefauver.

When Sheriff "Melon-head" Culbreath took the stand and had the usual trouble that most other witnesses had in explaining why he was in possession of amounts of money so incommensurate with his yearly salary, the usual good time was had by all at the expense of this not-at-all-funny and not-so-small-time crook. But the results were interesting because they were so archetypal. In March 1951 after the hearings, a county grand jury indicted Melon-head on a series of proven lawbreaking activities and he was suspended from office. Two months later, after a series of legal maneuvers, a local jury acquitted him, the Governor of Florida reinstated him, and Culbreath was "the law" again in Hillsborough County.

Of all the people in America who were becoming hooked on the crime investigations and their media revelations, we can be sure that one, "Colonel" Tom Parker, would be following the Tampa hearings with particular interest. For he had made his home there for sixteen years, which included the very period in which the Committee was so specially interested.

In fact it was at the beginning of World War II, when Melon-head had started, that Tampa chose to bestow upon Tom Parker the honor of appointing him its dogcatcher, a position of patronage which enabled him to enjoy not only a free apartment over the dog pound but also special allotments of rationed items, such as paint, furnishings, meat, sugar, tires, and gasoline. Although only thirty-two years old and with only a wife and one grown stepson to support, Parker's draft qualification was 3-A—"registrant deferred by reason of extreme hardship to dependents." This, no doubt, referred to all the stray dogs that were now dependent on him.

There would have been many reasons why the Dogcatcher of Tampa—to give Parker his only official title, since "colonel" was an honorary one first bestowed in 1948 by Governor Jimmy "Pappy" Davis of Louisiana—would feel comfortable enough in Tampa to settle down there; for the world Parker had been raised for—or, to put it more accurately, had raised himself for—was very different from the world Gladys had raised Elvis. The early background of the man known as Colonel Thomas A. Parker is the source of great speculation. It is widely believed (and there is some evidence for the fact) that he was actually born Andreas Cornelius van Kuijk in Breda, Holland, on June 26, 1909. He entered the United States, perhaps illegally, in 1929, by which time,[11] though the bootleggers had reduced rum-running to a riskless science, the Department of Immigration and Naturalization was seeing to it that jumping ship had become a very risky art. If this is the case, it is possible that Parker remains a Dutch national, never having become an American citizen.[12]

When Parker's life is considered from this point of view we can look back and see how the necessity of preventing this secret from becoming known may have colored all his deeds and actions and in fact painted the red, white, and blue colors of his whole personality. For it is obvious that Parker always strove to be almost *plus américain que les Américains*. And it does not need hindsight to see that he went at it with the zeal of a convert.[13]

The answers to the continual whirl of personal questions about himself that constantly pecked away at him throughout his career like so many sparrows—indeed like those very sparrows he so loved to boast of painting yellow and selling as canaries—turned out to be very different from the red, white, and blue answers he glibly produced, by which he strove to present Colonel Parker of Dixieland as a certain traditional type of American folk hero celebrated in fact and fiction: the real fake, the unabashed con man, the Great American Medicine Man eager to explain how he never gave a sucker an even break and expecting to be admired for it.

[11.] Letter to the biographer dated October 9, 1983, from Wilhelmina Enterprises, P.O. Box 195H, Great Kills, Staten Island, N.Y. (a firm specializing in tracing immigrants), produced the following information: "Made the search, per your instructions, for mention of: Andreas Cornelius van Kuijk, and found: No mention of Andreas' arrival in the compiled lists of passenger arrivals by Filby and Meyers. No mention of Andreas' arrival at Federal Archives, card file index of arrivees. No mention of Andreas' arrival at Immigration and Naturalization Service. No mention of Andreas' arrival at State Department's records of passenger arrivals which have now been opened to the public and are housed in N.Y.C. No mention of Andreas at the Holland Consulate General's Office." They added a postscript: "The folks at the Dutch Consulate General's Office felt that he might have been a worker on a Dutch ship and 'jumped' ship in order to stay in the U.S."

Variety, June 8, 1983, has an item headlined "Parker Admits He Never Was American Citizen," which goes on as follows: "Tom Parker, manager of the late Elvis Presley, has confirmed published reports that he was born in Holland and never became an American citizen. Parker, whose original name was Andreas Cornelius van Kuijk, revealed his origin in court papers seeking dismissal of a lawsuit filed against him by the Presley estate in Manhattan Federal Court. Declaring 'I am a man without a country,' Parker claimed he cannot be sued under Federal laws."

[12.] *Variety*, June 28, 1983, re the terms of the *Presley* v. *Parker* out-of-court settlement had this to say: "Parker's illegal entry into this country in 1929 was one of the major factors in the out-of-court settlement, according to unimpeachable sources. Parker, whose real name is Andreas Cornelius van Kuijk, was born in Holland and never became an American citizen."

[13.] See *Elvis*, by Albert Goldman (New York: McGraw-Hill, 1981), chap. 10, pp. 153–179.

Instead of the cocksure blusterer of old, we must now comtemplate the psychology and behavior of this extremely vulnerable man.

Parker's first move towards becoming all-American was to enlist in the Army. What could be more patriotic than that? and what could be more *out* of character for such a wily, individualistic, opportunistic, ambitious, energetic young man than to spend two years in an organization that offered less chance of advancement than any other? Nevertheless, the army unwittingly provided something far more important for him than advancement. It offered him a foothold in American society.

If he were indeed a native-born Dutchman, he could have had no greater fortune than that which stationed him at Fort Barrancas, Pensacola Harbor, Florida, in the South. No one who has ever had any dealings with Parker has ever detected a trace of give-away foreign pronunciation in his speech—his *"good ole boy"* accent was reknowned.

His particular American accent—that famous southern accent—has such an insidiously persuasive way with it that few are the strangers returning from two weeks below the Mason–Dixon Line who are not told by their friends to "Come off it!" Into no other mode of speech does one slide into unconscious mimickry with such ease and out of it with such difficulty. It is amazing how many native New Jerseyites, after a couple of years in Tennessee, are talking pure Memphis.

After his hitch in the armed services Parker chose to cast his lot with a series of carnivals including one of the biggest, the Royal American Show, which toured the United States and Canada and wintered in Tampa, the largest city near Fort Barrancas, and where presumably he met his wife-to-be, the former Mrs. Marie Ross *née* Mott—whom he charmingly calls Miz' Rie ("misery"?). Consistent all through his many manifestations is his enjoyment of a good joke. On the other guy, of course.

It was during his carnival period in this environment of dupery and spoofery and hokum and hoopla that Parker was supposed to have flowered and "found himself." The carnival scene also, it might be said, offered him the unique opportunity to devote some eight or nine years toward perfecting his lovable American rogue act. But, here too, it is important to note that while nothing could be more American than traveling carnivals, nothing could be less American than their personnel which was, by tradition and fact, cosmopolitan. Most of the people were foreign-born, or if not, would be likely to transform their dubious backgrounds into whatever they sublimely chose them to be. For an individual involved in an organization whose group effort is to fool the public will invariably extend this habit to fooling his colleagues and even, in the end, to fooling himself. Hence it is likely that Parker acted his role so vigorously he often took himself in.

Now is probably as good a place as any to pause and behold the Dogcatcher in action in the good old days and observe the way he served up his own version of his life story so as to make the world swallow it whole.

A typical example of the kind of brew he stewed—ham and gravy—and the way he dished it up to the media can be found in a May 16, 1960, article about him in *Time*, May 16, 1960, headed "Impresario," published just after Elvis got out of the army, and when the Dogcatcher was riding high.

So *Time*, with its battery of highly trained journalists and researchers, was presuming to pry the truth out of this mystery man whose legend, said the magazine, had "grown to proportions that might well reduce P. T. Barnum to the size of Tom Thumb." Was it? Parker was ready for them—he was more than ready for them. In fact there were several powerful reasons for him to be eager at that juncture of his career to be interviewed and written up by a magazine of international repute, celebrated for both its accuracy and acerbity.

Where better to establish once and for all the following points he found increasingly necessary to make clear:

First, that he was an American carny man, born, bred and evermore to remain so. Secondly, that he and he only was responsible for the discovery and development of Elvis. Third, that not only did Parker completely own Elvis but that Elvis must be publicly *seen* to be owned by Parker. And fourth, that Elvis must always have his nose rubbed into this fact.

To achieve his first point, one can imagine the colorful Colonel setting the stage by receiving his *Time* interviews colorfully dressed for the part. And—just as he intended them to—they carefully noted down all the detail of his costume. How could they not, confronted with a fat, balding, cigar-smoking, fifty-one-year-old man got up in fawn-colored pants, white shoes, pink satin shirt with ELVIS embroidered on the back, and a small Presley hat decorated with an Elvis picture adorning his head as he sat in his four-room executive suite on the Paramount lot in Hollywood? And how could they not see through this act and add—also just as he intended them to—that he was "trying very hard to look every inch a rube"? Seeing through his act, he knew, would only make it more opaque.

And quickly following up the sight-gag of this colorful, flamboyant, unabashed carny man, came the colorful, flamboyant, unabashed anecdotes furnished by him and a group of his carefully selected stooges of the variety of how-he-beat-the-foot-long-hot-dog-fad by using footlong buns, sticking a bit of meat into each and filling the middle with onions. Then followed colorful, etc., anecdotes of his selling "Elvis photos" on the spot at Elvis concerts at huge profits along with doing a lucrative trade of renting army surplus binoculars for an overpriced two bucks, followed by equally colorful ideas of promoting Elvis with rented elephants and the Elvis Presley Midget Fan Club. After enough of this, what choice had any magazine but to write of Parker's origins as *Time* did:

"*The least surprising fact of Tom Parker's life is that it began in a traveling carnival which his parents worked.*" (my italics) Just as he intended it to do. Note with what swiftness and simplicity he disposes of his American childhood: "Orphaned as a child," wrote *Time*, "he worked for his uncle's Great Parker Pony Circus and had his own pony-and-monkey act in his teens."

"Barker, merry-go-round operator, candied-apple dipper, ice-shaver for snow cones and general man-about-the-midway," *Time* continues, he once took a job as a dogcatcher in Tampa, Fla...." And so the years sped by until "as a carny press agent" he worked his way to the attention of country singers and "profitably managed Gene Austin, Hank Snow, and Eddy Arnold before he found the boy with the coin in the groin."

But where, one wonders, does Parker come from? Sometimes he varied the orphan theme: sometimes he had no parents at all but was a poor foundling adopted by that Uncle Parker of the Great Pony Circus. Often Huntington, West Virginia, was claimed by him as his birthplace. What made him take Huntington as his point of departure, or rather of no return? It should be noted that the town is situated right slap on three state lines—Kentucky, Ohio, and West Virginia. A good location. If anyone tried to check up on the Parker family in that town there were plenty of that-a-ways for them to have gone. Needless to say, the least surprising fact in Parker's life is that recent investigations by a Huntington newspaper were unable to trace the existence of Parker or his family.

Did he simply invent an uncle from whom he took his name? An alternative possibility can be found in Partridge's *Dictionary of the Underworld*, one which seems altogether too much of a coincidence not to mention. There the word *parker* is defined as "to talk; parlyaree: the language of circusmen, showmen, itinerant and/or low actors.... It often merges with the language of tramps." This opens the conjecture that the name Parker was not one he selected but one he had bestowed upon him, as in Nosey Parker.

As for the second point Parker wished to put over—that the discovery and development of Elvis was *entirely* of his making—he simply relied on the shortness of people's memories, or their ignorance. Few readers of *Time* had ever heard of the nineteen-year-old Elvis whose voice, personality, and fully developed style had made him a local hero before the Colonel lassoed him. But that's neither here nor there. The really big bucks only came rolling in with Parker and, as he makes sure that the gravy boat never strays far from the ham in any of his pronouncements, the nice fat six-figure contract he negotiated with RCA for his client gets slipped in here.

But it is in his desire to establish the final two points on his agenda— that he owns Elvis and must be publicly seen to own him, and that Elvis must constantly have his nose rubbed in the fact ("Presley depends completely on Parker, never talks to the press unless the Colonel nods...")— that old Parlyaree finally whips off the velvet glove and gives us a good look at the iron fist beneath. Then at last we get the true measure of the man "with eyes as soft as ball bearings."

Consider this (again from the same article in *Time*): "[Parker] also refused to let Elvis go into Special Services and spend two years entertaining troops. 'A sure way to debase your merchandise,' he said, 'is to give it away.'"

What can be said about such cynicism and contempt displayed for both the U.S. Army and Elvis? What can be said about a remark which so clearly places Parker above the Army and Elvis below humanity? One thing that can be said is that the surest way to debase a human being is to refer to him as merchandise.

On the simplest level then, this infamous utterance could be called perfectly lousy public relations. And it is this aspect of it which raises the interesting question of what lawyers term "good faith." As a personal manager Parker stood in an accepted fiduciary relationship with the client he was handling exclusively, which translated from legalese means that their whole relationship (including all their contractual agreements) was based on Elvis' trust in Parker to act for him "in good faith." Surely this should not only extend to his advising his client what was in his best interests artistically and financially, but also to seeing that his client's image was presented at all times to the public in the most positive and attractive way.

What more damaging way of presenting your client—an artist—than as a piece of merchandise? Furthermore, what more damaging way of presenting your client to the world at that *particular* time than with a statement which flatly contradicted everything your client had patriotically affirmed prior, during, and after this army service: that he had purposefully not asked to go into Special Services because he "wished to be treated no differently from anyone else"?

By serving two years in the army without fuss, Elvis had returned an American hero. Was Parker acting in good faith then? Was he serving his client's best interest in his constant determination to turn Elvis back into an American joke? For the Parker remark was only one of many similar disparaging, tasteless, and hurtful "jokes" Parker made to the media in his twenty-two years of managing Elvis, such as: "I'm going to get a wiggle machine to time the wiggles. When Elvis stops singing, we'll put him on stage and just let him wiggle," to the *New York World-Telegram* in June 1956.

Serious directors in Hollywood like Nicholas Ray and George Cukor had always been seriously interested in working with Elvis—not only for what they had caught glimpses of in his pre-army films: his electric presence, his great rhythmic and sexual charge, his gift for comedy and the very appealing good-humored quality he exuded—these are all star qualities, but also for that extra quality that is as rare as it is impossible to define. Elvis was a true original—the very real right thing, as Henry James might have put it. Would not these directors think twice and then change their minds (several did) about working with an actor who no matter how popular is a *joke*, and whose appearance in their film might turn the whole film, particularly as viewed by the critics, into a joke? It has been known to happen.

This conflict of interest on Parker's part had become the very basis of the Parker-Presley relationship—or more accurately the Parker *versus* Presley relationship as it was finally exposed to the public in a lawsuit between the Presley Estate and Parker, though not till five years after Elvis' death. The guardian *ad litem* report found that Parker was not seeking his client's best interests, but his own, and that he could not be described as acting in good faith.[14]

Down the years Parker's main problem, as he saw it, was how to keep Elvis a viable commercial product while at the same time never allowing him to be taken seriously. One doesn't have to be a brilliant logician to arrive at the same conclusion Parker had early on, that the more Elvis might grow in artistic achievement and confidence the more he would realize that the Dogcatcher, in holding onto him, was holding him back. Would Elvis then have done what he should have done early on in dealing

[14] Guardian *ad litem*; first report filed, September 29, 1980, in Probate Court of Shelby County, Tenn.; Second report filed July 31, 1981.

with Parker—put himself in the hands of a couple of expert show business lawyers and dump him?

What a falling off for the Colonel that might have been! How quickly the naked truth would have emerged that Parker was the most powerful man in the entertainment world only because he owned the most powerful boy! What a swift, not to say violent, reversal of his financial and social status might have undergone!

"You don't have to be nice to people on the way up if you're not coming down," was one of Parker's more attractive mottos. But surely van Kuijk's possible transformation into Parker had not been accomplished altogether unseen. Certainly there were one or two people around who knew him from his military or carny days and to whom he had not been nice on his way up. And there was, for instance, that strange organization, the American Snowmen's League, of which he was "proud" to be its Imperial Potentate. It was a club about whose meetings he would plant items in the papers regularly from the fifties on. Its purposes remained murky or jokey or just a lot of double Dutch to outsiders, as he intended them to be—some elaborate rag about "snowing" (conning) its members into doing favors for him. But there was nothing jokey about its membership, which "according to the Colonel's friends included top television and motion picture personalities, the executives and businessmen who control the networks, the important radio people, as well as dozens of the country's top executives and *two, perhaps three U.S. Presidents*"[15] (italics mine). Now what the devil were *they* doing in that *galère*? When we further learn that "according to members of the Snowmen's League— who say they would be 'unsnowed' if it were known they talked—it cost nothing to get into the league, a thousand dollars to get out," the joke stops abruptly. In this context, what other interpretation can be put on the threat of being "unsnowed" other than that of undue moral pressure.

And yet here we have this blusterer whose wind is apparently strong enough to blow the army down, this blusterer who can sweep two or three presidents into his capacious pockets, who can control the very weather of showbiz by snowing and unsnowing at will, still apparently reluctant to confront the Immigration and Naturalization Service. Wouldn't it have been the work of a moment for this powerful, well-connected, wealthy man to get it all straightened out once and for all?

It has never been the policy of the Land of the Free to deport well-to-do entrants if they can prove they have lived peaceably in the United

15. *Elvis: A Biography,* by Jerry Hopkins.

States for any length of time, have been regularly employed, have regularly and fully paid their taxes, and have no criminal record.

America in fact offers these aliens the choice of three amnesties by which to legalize their status: *a legislative amnesty* created by the passage of private laws which make an exception in the immigration law for a specific individual or family; a *judicial amnesty* brought about on behalf of a person or persons who have retained legal counsel to appeal to the courts to legalize their presence; or an *administrative amnesty* worked through the Immigration and Naturalization Service processes. For years the most common rationale for granting this last form of amnesty was the alien's ability to prove his continuous presence in the country since June 30, 1948,[16] which Parker certainly could have.

Perhaps one should ask first why not? Dutch people have always been high on the list of acceptable American immigrants, though the actual numbers of their immigration have always been low. Even in the twenties when the law was passed limiting immigration to two percent of that nationality residing in America, although the Dutch quota might have been low, it was not filled.[17] Why would a twenty-year-old be in such an all-fired hurry to get out of Holland that he couldn't wait for proper papers? In taking out naturalization papers he would have had to reveal his real name. Would any inquiries then made in Holland reveal some interesting scuffle between him and the law over there that he would not care to have brought to light? Or in America—was there something in his behavior there, something that left a black mark on him with his various business dealings and managerial contracts? Then there was that Hadacol scandal, of which more later.

Perhaps the Kefauver crime investigation was a watershed in Parker's life. For it resulted, among other things, in strong recommendations to Congress to amend immigration laws by tightening them up and facilitating the deportation of undesirable aliens. That Congress would fail to approve these recommendations, Parker was not to know of course—but the very attention focused on aliens could have thrown a scare in him for good and made him forever stay that Dutch chicken dancing on a hot plate to American music.

Time ends its article asking him: "What if, after all, Old Soldier Elvis fades away?" To which Parker, giving a carny man's shrug, replies, "He could go back to drivin' a truck. And I could always go back to being a

---

[16] *Migration for Employment Project,* David S. North, International Labour Office, Geneva, October 1979.

[17] Annual Report, Commission of Immigration, 1930 edition, U.S. Dept. of Immigration.

dogcatcher. Head dogcatcher, that is." This paragraph is captioned "Head Dogcatcher" in case we failed to get the point: It is not an impresario and a star *Time* has been writing about, but some kind of a circus act.

Let us return then to the Head Dogcatcher that was in Tampa when his world consisted only of dozens of stray dogs, and cats too. Assisted by a youth of eighteen called Bevo Bevis, who idolized him and his long-suffering wife Miz' Rie (for many years his bookkeeper), Parker's fertile mind soon began to fill with ideas of how to turn dogcatching into people-catching and the dog pound into a profit-making scheme—for himself of course.[18]

But first he needed hard cash. Now Parker can think complicatedly, but he can also think simply. In this case when it was a simple matter of exploiting an already existing situation—people's built-in emotionalism over animals—a simple direct appeal for money was the gambit most likely to work. Therefore he simply placed a brightly painted barrel in the center of the pound's entrance hall, indicating by a large sign that donations were urgently needed for the animals. To his delight the daily take was good—on some days excellent; in fact a real moneymaker for him. It encouraged his promotion-conscious mind to think bigger about the possibilities for his stray animal kingdom.

Knowing that people equate uniforms with authority, Parker and Bevo were now seen wearing long white laboratory coats (which turned out to be dentists' smocks) while out on their rounds catching dogs with nets or climbing trees for cats. This official-looking gear connecting them vaguely with some branch of the medical profession laid the ground for his next people-catching scheme.

It, too, started simply—in the pound's own backyard. Cleared by Bevo of weeds and broken bottles and debris and with the insertion of one chiseled marker commemorating a mythical dog called Spot, our magician transformed it into an animal cemetery. Gradually bringing into play all the paraphernalia that accompanies humans to their resting place (Bevo-constructed caskets, Parker-conducted funerals, flowers courtesy of florists' end-of-the-day throwaways, ever more elaborate gravestones replacing the original fifteen-dollar chiseled markers), Tampans acting under Parker's guidance, advice, and good faith now found themselves burying their pets for one hundred dollars per interment.

In no time he was the darling of the local pet-lovers and, for no other

---

[18.] *Up and Down with Elvis Presley,* by Marge Crumbaker and Gabe Tucker (New York: Putnam, 1981).

reason than the ecstatic charge he got every time he put something over on his public, he was into such pranks as selling people desirous of lap dogs, animals which in three months would end up as big as ponies. He also kept six ponies outside his house, charging kids for rides on them, while talking other kids into looking after them by giving the ponies their names.[19]

In later years, he got a great deal of pleasure in bragging about his dogcatcher days. He was never one to hide his neon under a bushel but perhaps his true nostalgia for this enterprise lay in the fact that it was his first *successful* one, not only for obvious reasons but for deeper ones. For the first time he was in a position to satisfy the needs of a tyrannical nature. He did not grow to love tyranny because he became a personal manager; he became the sort of personal manager he was because he loved tyranny.

Prior to dogcatching he had promoted several concerts for the singer Gene Austin before each went his separate way—Austin back to his home in California and Parker back to his Tampa base. In the circumstances, so brief an association could hardly have given Parker the status of manager he was later to claim. Nor was this association an overwhelming success. The blame for its failure has always been placed at Austin's feet: He was by then too far into his declining years for anyone to revive him, is the way it is always presented. In fact Austin was no more than forty at the time. And he did not die until he was seventy-two. This popular singer with many hit records that were standard, steady bestsellers, his most famous being "My Blue Heaven" (which until Bing Crosby's "White Christmas" was the bestseller of all time), enjoyed, as most of these singers did, a large segment of loyal middle-aged fans. If he were indeed then declining he might be considered to have had one of the longest, most comfortable declines in the history of popular music.

I think we must assume that Austin was less than taken with young Parker and that Parker saw this association with Austin as his big chance and its failure as a big blow. Parker early on would have had to face the fact that his appearance was against him. Even in his early thirties he was gross and round-shouldered with an overflowing potbelly. His balding head narrowed as it rose, like an egg, to its peak. His first chin rolled into his second, his mouth seemed to slide all over the place in a fat smile, and his eyes were set too close together. Yet it was more than his physical appearance that would make people instinctively and intuitively suspicious of him. He would also encounter the deep suspicion always

[19] *Up and Down with Elvis Presley,* by Marge Crumbaker with Gabe Tucker.

aroused in people when confronted with someone who has too strenuously invented his own personality. In order to overcome this serious setback, he had begun practicing hypnosis, though just when is not clear. Perhaps it was back in his carny days when, it has been said, he sometimes ran a mit camp, i.e., a fortuneteller's booth, that he first discovered his considerable natural psychological and psychic gifts. Somewhere early in his career he must have been convinced of the wider use he could put these gifts to. If he could exercise some hypnotic control over people, he could overcome the first bad impression that always put them on their guard.

Any carnival uses hypnosis as part of its method of training animals. Hypnotizing animals was also a feature of the carny sideshow, the most common demonstration of it being with a rooster: A line is chalked on the floor, the cock's beak put on it, the cock believes he is tied there and remains immobile, a condition which could last from ten minutes to three hours. Similarly, returning again to those sparrows Parker painted yellow, he would have hypnotized them in much the same way to keep them inert during the refurbishing process.

A dog is man's best friend—obedient, loyal, responsive, receptive—in short, trainable. And at the pound Parker had dozens at this disposal. Any man who, as Parker did, put chickens on a hot plate and had them dancing to *Turkey in the Straw* for a gag would not hesitate to have dogs salivating like Pavlov's. Or, if controlled experiments sound too intellectually scientific, there is always the simpler method of softening up dogs for hypnotic experiments: It is called fear. If credulity balks at the idea of Parker in a dentist's smock obsessively hypnotizing a bunch of stray dogs, it may be helped over this hurdle by the documented evidence of this obsession progressing from Parker hypnotizing dogs to Parker hypnotizing some *men* into behaving like dogs.

"He would make us all get down on all fours and tell us that we were dogs," recalls Sonny West, Elvis' bodyguard in *Elvis: What Happened*, and he would have us barking and yelping like dogs and snapping at each other. The people who saw this performance were convinced all the Memphis boys were insane. Then on a command, he would tell us to attack one dog and that dog would be Lamar and we would be all over him biting and yelping."

It is hard to believe that Parker had not first exercised mind control over the hapless Sonny in order for him to agree to take part in these bizarre public displays. But then the whole subject of mind control and hypnosis is hard for the resolutely rational to believe.

One witness to such an occasion, John O'Grady, head of a private detective agency, could not *quite* believe it. Perhaps Elvis' friends were merely playing up to Parker? "'I remember once in one of the dressing rooms Parker told Charlie Hodge to get down on all fours and bark like a dog and poor, dumb Charlie did it. I looked at Parker and told him, 'If you ever said something like that to me, I'd push your damned head through the wall.'"

Although the flamboyant Phil Spector is often quoted as saying, "The Colonel hypnotizes Elvis, I *swear* he does!" Steve Binder, who produced Elvis' NBC–TV '68 special, provides a more feet-on-the-ground and therefore more chilling assessment of the Colonel's hypnotic powers. "The Colonel," he recalled talking to Albert Goldman, "used to sit at a meeting with those cold steel-blue eyes staring at me like he was trying to get a subliminal message into my brain. I'd stare back, knowing that there was nothing he could do. Yet, he did convince me that there is such a thing as *mind control*. That strange hypnotic way he had of exercising total control and power over Elvis. That kind of hold is totally unexplained in terms either of deals or loyalties between people."

Biographers of Elvis spend a lot of time on Parker's elephant obsession: his early use of them to advertise his shows and singers, his elephant-headed cane, his office festooned with stools made of elephants' feet, statues and figurines of elephants in ivory and wood. None of them seems to have noticed his obsession with dogs and the symbolic use he makes of them. Take Nipper, for instance, the original lovable little mongrel with the head on the side and the ear cocked to hear his master's voice—the trademark of RCA as far back as 1929. As the papier-mâché RCA dog who often turned up on stage in Elvis concerts and photographs, he undergoes a decided personality change. Now his expression is grim, dour, if not unpleasant. Although his markings are the same as Nipper's— white body and black ears—he is no longer a mongrel but more of a Jack Russell, a temperamental breed of hunting dog threatening to anyone but his master, with a tendency to bite both other dogs and people. In connection with this subject there is a much-printed photograph circa 1957 of Elvis and the Colonel taken in the Colonel's office. The Colonel, dressed in glasses, pipe, and shirtsleeves, is seated by a typewriter as though about to write some press release about his client. Elvis himself is seated next to him wearing a checkered jacket and an unhappy grin on his face. The print of this photograph is sometimes cropped in such a way as to hide a most interesting framed photo hanging on the wall above Elvis' shoulder. This portrays a clearly defined RCA Nipper looming large over a basset hound in a ridiculous top hat—the same basset hound that Elvis was made to sing "Hound Dog" to on the Steve Allen Show. The basset hound looks timidly up at the inscrutable Nipper. The message: Tom Parker and his performing dogs.

By 1944 Parker had left his pound full of live animals and his cemetery full of dead ones to have another go at people-catching.

He secured himself a job as front man for the Grand Ole Opry traveling tent show which starred the singer Eddy Arnold. The job involved traveling ahead in his rusty old International truck, putting up posters, spreading the word, and making sure the show ran smoothly when it hit town. It was in this capacity that Parker met Gabe Tucker, who was also working the show. Gabe was one of those ubiquitous characters always found around the country music scene, valuable because they are able to turn their hand to any number of things. In this case Gabe was not only playing trumpet and bass with the band but helping out with the show's publicity at the same time.

Gabe became a very close crony of Parker's and remained so down the passage of time, even working for him on and off during the Elvis years. He has, with Marge Crumbaker, published a book which, although it bears the title *Up and Down with Elvis Presley*, should really be called *The Way Up and the Lowdown on Colonel Parker*, for it is on him that the book concentrates.

Gabe's firsthand accounts of Parker in action are eye-openers. Though at first glance he seems to be admiring his boss with something close to idolatry, ole buddy Gabe nevertheless blows the whistle on ole pal Parker at every stop. And the whistle often has the ring of solid gold truth to it as he describes Parker doublecrossing and freeloading, posing and imposing, as he wends his way through life. A lot of Parker's behavior is crystal-clear to Gabe but some of the great man's eccentricities, idiosyncrasies and sleights of hand are not—or he pretends they are not. Nevertheless he writes them all down for us and leaves these unexplained bits to stand out like clues in an Agatha Christie novel waiting for Hercule Poirot to come along and tidy up the whole thing. Sometimes they are only tiny insignificant pieces towards the solving of the puzzle.

As a member of the Eddy Arnold show, Gabe was able to watch Parker moving in on Arnold and finally becoming his manager.

Parker's personal style of managing Arnold foreshadowed his style with Elvis more as a revelation of his intention than its successful completion. For Eddy was an altogether different proposition from Elvis. He was twenty-five for one thing, not nineteen, and married and settled down in a comfortable four-bedroomed house in Madison, just outside Nashville. Although still at the beginning of his career, he was already in the accepted mold of a country singer in the Grand Ole Opry tradition dear to the hearts of the fierce hillbilly purists. And he was backed by a solid RCA contract as well as a music publishing contract with Hill and Range—and he also had a good head for business.

Nevertheless, "moving in on Arnold" is the correct phrase to use in describing Parker's idea of how he was going to manage his artist and very soon, to quote Gabe, Arnold and Parker were dissipating much of their energies ironing out differences in their personalities and private lives. In a word, Eddy's wife Sally strongly objected to Parker's constant presence in their home. While she became unofficial cook and maid to the uninvited guests, Parker—often accompanied by Miz' Rie—sometimes stayed on for days, for weeks, even for months, at the Arnold home supervising Arnold's business. A desperate way out was sought by Arnold. He opened an office in Madison from which to do business. Parker promptly moved into his office space the better to keep an eye on his client.

With Tom Parker, Eddy was learning you took the rough with the smooth. The smooth was the deals he brilliantly organized involving commercial products which promoted Eddy who in turn promoted the products; the contracts he shrewdly negotiated; and the national publicity for his client he tirelessly pursued. The rough was Parker. Parker, Parker everywhere—breathing down your neck and into your soup.

Arnold's growing success meant that he was spending more time in radio stations and recording studios and less time on the road with Parker dogging his every footstep. When Arnold expressed himself somewhat tactlessly on this happy side-effect and it got back to Parker, it was a deeply wounded and not a little shaken dogcatcher who mulled over this turn of events. Spare a kind thought for Parker: Had he not feelings, too? Had he not by prodigious feats of energy, imagination, and cunning raised Arnold to the top? And by doing so, had he not also put himself in the dangerous position of decreasing his power over Arnold—of reducing himself in fact to a more menial status, to be sent for when needed and dismissed when not?

In fact, by October 1948 Parker had done his job so well there was little else to do for Arnold for the rest of that year.

Lonely, frustrated, and at loose ends, he decided to tour the country looking for action. (It should be mentioned that although Arnold's arrangement with Parker at the time was exclusive, Parker also booked and therefore managed other acts in connection with Arnold's touring shows.) He hired Gabe, paying him expenses and five dollars a day, to keep him company. But in order to insure that Gabe did just that, Parker would suggest each payday that it would only be polite for Gabe to take his boss out to dinner that night. This invariably left Gabe flat broke for the following week.

"If the thought would ever cross my mind to leave," said Gabe after several weeks of this, "well, hell, I couldn't pay my way to the edge of town."

"That's exactly right," Parker replied.

In this way the Dogcatcher and his captive audience of one progressed down to Baton Rouge, the capital of Louisiana, where Gabe witnessed the further Americanization of his boss.

Through an old carny connection who worked on Governor Jimmy ("You Are My Sunshine") Davis' staff, Tom Parker became an honorary Colonel of Louisiana. But wait a minute—no! Successful Americans, be they businessman or politicians, cannot feel properly dressed in public without a middle name. So Colonel Tom Andrew Parker it was to be. Military style, he barked out the order for Sergeant Gabe to "See to it from now on that everyone addresses me as the Colonel."

At this time, not many miles from Baton Rouge in Lafayette, a state senator by the name of Dudley J. Le Blanc was stirring and brewing in large wooden barrels a new scientific formula, adding a little of this and a little of that, until he was entirely satisfied as to its perfection. Soon this potion would become known all over the United States as the new wonder patent medicine which promised to cure mankind of all its trifling ills such as the common cold, and further guaranteed "to make old people feel young." This medicine he would name Hadacol.

Through amazingly lavish use of practically all known advertising media, Senator Le Blanc, now known affectionately as Uncle Dud, in a short span of years built the sales of his tonics into a multimillion-dollar business. He hired top-drawer entertainers and celebrities from Hollywood and New York, such as Mickey Rooney, Jack Dempsey, Connie Boswell, Ernest Tubb, Minnie Pearl, as well as a chorus line of beauties in French bathing suits, a Dixieland band, and a twenty-piece orchestra to tour the country with expensive caravans that required only Hadacol box tops as the price of admission. This by the way was the same gimmick the Colonel had formerly employed with his monkey-and-pony act on the "cherry soda circuit," where the price of admission was cherry soda and bottle tops.

By March 1951 Hadacol was being banned in various states. Its alcoholic content was discovered to be between twelve and twenty-four percent per bottle (depending, no doubt, on which barrel it came from).

In the face of the erupting scandal, Le Blanc announced he had sold his medicine business to the Maltz Cancer Foundation in New York. Medical sources in New York said they had no knowledge of such an organization, nor was it listed in the telephone directory. Le Blanc then changed his statement, saying his "dietary supplement" has been sold to a group of eastern financiers. And Hadacol vanished as suddenly as it had appeared. But not quite. Six years later Uncle Dud was in the news again when an item in the *New York Times* of May 3, 1957, announced that he had been indicted by a federal grand jury for evading payment of $58,000 in taxes due from the Hadacol Company in 1950.

How involved was Parker in Hadacol? Though his name was often linked with it and, in character, it seemed to be the sort of carny joke slipped over on the suckers that he would have gloried in in the past, it was quickly made clear to anyone who wished to remain on good terms with him that he had *no* connection with Hadacol. *None whatever.* Yet the charge turned up to haunt, annoy, and embarrass him in the press throughout the years. In 1957, when Hadacol was news again with Uncle Dud's back taxes, newspaper columnists slyly took to referring to Parker as Colonel Tom (Hadacol) Parker—especially those like Louella Parsons, famous for knowing where the bodies were buried. And in 1962 the newspapers let him in for another impish round of "Colonel Tom (Hadacol) Parkers" whenever his name was mentioned. Somebody out there didn't like him. Probably quite a few. Finally we have this reference by Hal Wallis in his autobiography *Starmaker* to the Hadacol association: "Parker traveled around the country hawking cough medicine so successfully that he became famous in his own right."

As Eddy Arnold became America's most popular country singer, he began overtly to bridle under Parker's "ownership" style of management; yet the bigger he became and the more he knew himself capable of calling all the shots on what he was going to do—and how and when—the harder it was to get away from the heavy hand and the heavier physical presence of Parker. True he had gotten Parker out of his home but it was also true that by now the Parkers had left Tampa and moved to Arnold's town, Madison. Also, the more established Arnold became, the more actively he disliked Parker's carny-flamboyant ideas of publicity schemes. In relation to this, it is entirely possible that he would not wish to be connected in any way with anyone who was widely rumored to be involved with the Hadacol scandal.

According to the late Oscar Davis—another manager and more importantly in this connection, one who had been known to serve as front man for Parker when down on his luck—matters came to a head in 1953 in Las Vegas when Eddy, finally fed up, visited Parker's room at their hotel unexpectedly and confronted the manager. Angry words followed and, shortly after, Parker was fired.

How much did Eddy Arnold's dismissal of Parker affect him? When a moneymaking artist leaves his manager there is no two-week notice, no severance payments or gold watches for nine years' faithful service over and beyond the call of duty. Therefore the first thing that was affected, and abruptly so, was his pocketbook. It is entirely possible, in fact, that his pocketbook was affected more than his reputation, for both parties were wise enough to know that in these situations bad-mouthing invariably backfires on the bad-mouther. There was talk of course, but then it wasn't the first time an artist had left a manager. Eddy had simply outgrown old Tom—or Tommy, as he was still known in those days, in spite of his insistence on his grand new title.

Yet, without doubt, what caused Parker the most suffering over the break, down to the depths of his possessive nature, was that his prey had gotten away. "Poor old Tommy! How will he ever get back on the gravy train?" his enemies must have been speculating through crocodile tears.

As an independent promoter, managing work was not easy to find, for most of the acts were booked by the Artists' Service Bureau run by Jim Dunny, the same man who ran the Grand Ole Opry, thereby effectively closing the charmed circle.

The first thing old Tommy seems to have done was to wrangle another one of those colonelships so necessary to his *amour propre*, this time from Governor Frank C. Clement in Parker's new home state, Tennessee. Armed again, the Colonel went straight back to Nashville to look around for his next big star.

For many months he was reduced to scrambling around with the rest of the independent promoters using the free telephone in the lobby of the Grand Ole Opry radio station WSM to book those other acts that he had always handled on the side and to look for the new big one.

If his heart were broken and his wrath inflamed by Arnold's betrayal, you would not have known it standing in that lobby where old Parlyaree daily held forth. And to look on the bright side of things, his removal from Arnold's association had not removed him from the strong RCA and Hill and Range contacts he had assiduously cultivated in the past nine years. These two giant musical organizations had always liked doing business with him and their faith in his genius for spotting and exploiting talent would seem to have remained unshaken by his break with Arnold.

When the free phone was finally removed from the WSM lobby, Parker, forced back home, operated from his one-storey, eleven-room flagstone house on Gallatin Road in Madison. There he assembled the nucleus of his small staff which would remain with him forever. It consisted of a man called Tom Diskin, whom Parker had come across in Chicago with Eddy Arnold. Diskin at the time had been managing his two sisters, who called themselves the Dickens Sisters and were on several of Arnold's shows. When he joined Parker it was as his right-hand man, at first doing office work and then as leg man personally taking over the management of the tours. Along with Jim O'Brien, Parker's personal secretary, both these bachelors remained with him permanently.

By the fall of 1954 Parker was managing another country singer, Hank Snow. This forty-year-old, angular-featured, wiry, little Canadian hardly had the appeal of the good-looking Eddy Arnold, but what he lacked in looks he made up for in exuberance, determination, a fine singing voice, and repertoire of great songs. On his own since fourteen when his father kicked him out of his home in Nova Scotia, Snow had been singing in Canada all his life. With his growing popularity there, he had acquired an RCA contract, and when his records began to sell in the United States he and his wife Minnie and his son Jimmie Rodgers Snow moved to Nashville. His debut at the Grand Ole Opry in 1949 was greeted with the same "light applause" as Elvis in 1954—possibly due to the reluctance of the Opry's audience to accept a Canadian hillbilly at the bastion of American country music. But he stuck it out, overcame their prejudice, or their memory, and five years later he was a regular there; in 1954 his record "I Don't Hurt Anymore" was number one on the country and western charts.

But Snow still felt something of an outsider with a lot to learn about his newly adopted country, and it is a nice paradox that it was to that archetypal American, Parker, that he turned for guidance, advice, and good faith.

Initially he was delighted with the "Colonel"—the title only really began to stick with his management of Hank Snow—and together they developed "Hank Snow Jamboree Attractions," a touring show with such staples as Jimmie Rodgers Snow, Mother Maybelle and the Carter Family, Minnie Pearl, Faren Young, the Wilburn Brothers, Slim Whitman, Martha Carson, the Davis Sisters, Onie Wheeler, Ferlin Husky, and occasionally Webb Pierce, into one of the major booking agencies in the south.

It is almost too tempting at this point, simply by following Elvis' connection with "Hank Snow Jamboree Attractions"—four or five months after the Parker-Snow partnership—and the Colonel's subsequent finessing of Snow out of his half-share of the management of Elvis, to interpret the whole enterprise as being formed by Parker solely to give Elvis a year to break in his act throughout the South and Southwest before going national—and global.

But, to the facts. Who first called Elvis to the Colonel's attention? Why, everybody, just everybody it would seem who ever knew Parker, from Gabe Tucker to Oscar Davis to the young singer Tommy Sands to Steve Sholes, the artist and repertory man for RCA who "saw Elvis tearing them up at the 'Louisiana Hayride'"— to Hank Snow himself, who later repeated his claim in the form of a lawsuit. The *Journal American* reported on 26 September 1961: 'Hank Snow, the nation's number-one western singer is suing Tom Parker for 'a taste' of the Presley earnings. Snow and Parker were once partners in Nashville and Snow claims he was the one who really discovered Elvis and brought him to the attention of Victor Records. Lawyers for both sides are trying to settle the case out of court." Again we are faced with an event in Elvis' life where the accuracy with which it is remembered varies inversely with its importance. Surely with "That's All Right [Mama]" third on the Memphis charts in August at the same time that Snow's "I Don't Hurt Anymore" was number one there; and with Hank Snow himself introducing Elvis, Scotty, and Blackie at the Grand Ole Opry a month later in September; and with Elvis being chosen as the eighth most promising country artist at the disk jockey convention in Nashville in November; and the quality of "sensation" that surrounded Elvis from his debut, Parker would have had to have been deaf, dumb, and blind not to have made the discovery all by himself.

The opportunities for Parker to have heard Elvis' first record—if not seen him in the flesh performing in 1954—were immense.

But since this important event needs some springboard, the story that most often gets told is the story that will now be retold —if only for its faint aroma of an attempted double-cross—which proves how hot Elvis was by November and December that year.

It seems that during one or the other of those months Oscar Davis, working again as the Colonel's advance agent, came to Memphis a week before his boss to promote a show the Colonel was handling at one of Memphis' auditoriums. While Oscar was at the radio station WMPS doing his promotional spots for the upcoming show, he ran into Bob Neal who had done a lot of bookings for Elvis and nurtured plans to take over from Scotty and become Elvis' agent. Oscar asked Bob, also a disk jockey at the station, if he had any records of this new kid he was hearing so much about and if he'd play him some. Bob had and did, adding afterwards, "I can't play them on this station because they're barred here—too raucous." Notwithstanding, Oscar must have liked what he heard, for when Bob told him Elvis was playing at the Airport Inn that night, they both went off together to hear him. What he saw of Elvis—and the effect he had on the audience, mostly women and screaming their heads off—was enough to make Oscar's managerial glands begin to salivate. He wanted to meet Elvis then and there. Bob, however, suddenly having his consciousness raised by all this enthusiasm, saw that Oscar had slipped off his metaphorical booking-promoter hat and was now wearing his agent one, and firmly demurred. From Bob's view, that would have made one agent too many. "I can't introduce him," he explained. "He hates my guts because I can't play his records."

Oscar, undeterred, waited it out until Bob left and then had Elvis, along with his "manager" Scotty, brought over to his table. Oscar Davis, the man who had managed Elvis' idol, the late Hank Williams (Elvis and Scotty might be brand new to the music scene but they knew *that* much), promptly offered the two boys the moon in the form of a tentative deal to be discussed over a cup of coffee the following Sunday when he returned to Memphis. They would wait for him at eleven o'clock at the auditorium and then go to the coffee shop opposite. "They were somewhat excited about getting me in the picture with them," was the way Oscar put it. Scotty and Elvis would have put it far more strongly. Not only Gatsby believed in the green light.

But when Oscar showed up that much-anticipated Sunday, something had gone tactically wrong, for by the time they were all—Elvis, Judd Phillips (Sam's brother), Blackie, and Scotty—at the coffee shop waiting for Oscar to come in and make a deal, who should waddle in closely following Davis but the Colonel who had in that way of his caught the scent.

The very first thing he said not only revealed how much he already knew but effectively set the cast among the pigeons. "Well, the guy will get nowhere on Sun Records." To which Judd replied that Elvis was not going off Sun Records and that was for sure. Then Oscar had to reveal that in fact the Colonel was his boss and whatever he said went, whereupon the deal fell apart. At least *Oscar's* deal did.

Assuming this was the first time the two protagonists had sat down face to face, what did Elvis see when he looked at our old friend?

The Colonel, attired in his informal working clothes, was not the most pleasant of sights. In those days, summer and winter, he favored a tee shirt under his jacket; never can there have been a tee shirt on a man so wrinkled and creased in so many different directions—the wrinkles beginning well above his protruding fatman's breasts and continuing down over his vast paunch. And his droopy pants were always unpressed.

But, being Sunday, perhaps the Colonel was dressed up—which could well have been an even worse sight. All his suits were under a tremendous strain at the seams, constraining the armpits, constraining the elbows, buttons strained across his huge circumference, trousers strained over the belly to reach his ankles. The Colonel's advice to one of the series of mailroom boys from the William Morris office he was later to employ: "Never," he said solemnly, "never dress better than your client"—a splendid example of the way he was able to turn a necessity into a virtue. Yet photographs of him through the years show how he tried to find a style for himself. Ten-gallon hats, coconut-straw hats, boaters, even a bowler, may have covered his baldness but could do nothing to enhance his features. He looked liked Humpty Dumpty with those bow ties he affected.

And what did the forty-five-year-old Colonel see when he looked at the nineteen-year-old Elvis? He saw at once, of course, that Elvis was everything he had ever wanted to be and never was or would be. He was young, innocent, handsome, slender, shining with talent... and American through and through.

Whatever it was, in spite of his seeming nonreaction to this first meeting with Elvis, Parker moved fast. One month after Elvis was being officially managed by Bob Neal, which was December, the Colonel began booking Elvis on many of the "Hank Snow Jamboree Attractions" shows, and watched him closely as, in a very short time, he became the main attraction.

And seven months later, on August 15, 1955—mark the day well for Gladys will die on the fourteenth of that same month in 1958 and Elvis on the sixteenth in 1977—Parker signed him up to a most extraordinary contract, the first of many that would bind Elvis to him for life.

Thus the man of low cunning effectively acquired mastery of the boy of high simplicity. Can such things really happen? Dickens thought so. "That they are achieved is an everyday experience," he wrote. "How long such conquests last, is another matter...."

And how complete such a conquest could ever have become when the boy of high simplicity was also a musical genius who went on to develop into one of the world's supreme solo performers is yet *another* matter.

For in one vital way which must never be overlooked, to call Parker's hold on Elvis Svengali-like is totally false. Svengali, whatever his serious defects of character, had a love of music as intense as his knowledge of it was complete. And Parker? Had Parker died before his protégé as Svengali did before Trilby—had he dropped dead in fact the day after he signed Elvis to his first binding contract—unlike Trilby, Elvis would have gone right on singing.

FOURTEEN

When Elvis Sang

What was the world hearing when Elvis sang?

Critics have several ways of explaining why certain popular singers have, above all others, held us so completely in their thrall. One way is to explain them away. By bearing heavily and learnedly on their "influences" and using them to uncover the highway robberies of every swiped note, the little thieves are left at the end with nothing of their own but a pair of (probably stolen) vocal chords.

Back in 1955 an anonymous critic in *Time* magazine explained away Sinatra: "From Bing, of course, Frank borrowed the intense care for the lyrics and a few of those bathtub sonorities the microphone likes so well. From Tommy Dorsey's trombone, he learned to bend and smear his notes a little and to slush-pump his rhythms in the long, dull, level places. From Billie Holiday he caught the trick of scooping his attacks and of working the 'hot acciaccaitura'—the 'N-Awlins' gracenote that most white singers flub...." Of his rhythmic approach: "He never let go of the old Balaban and Katz beat." And his way of breathing in the middle of a note without breaking it was "an old trick of the American Indian singers."

Nor did Bing escape at least one sleuthing critic in the early days of his career. Bing's style and, it turned out, intense care for lyrics, bathtub sonorities, and all, was simply lifted from our old friend Gene Austin.

By the time Elvis' voice had been worked over there was no singer, black or white, he had not and was not stealing from simultaneously, consecutively, alternately, and constantly, as the masses of contraband black rhythm and blues, white country, black and white gospel, rock, and Dean Martin poured out of his mouth. In addition this same school went to work on his body: his flailing arms belonged rightfully to Johnnie Ray, his writhing torso to Bo Diddley, and his stomping legs to Little Richard. Thus have certain critics attempted to reduce Elvis to a veritable lost-property office, from which even the long-dead could put in some direct claim. Was Elvis in the heat of performance wont to break a guitar string? Back to Paganini—he'd thought up that gag with his violin strings a century ago. Even worse—far from inventing rock 'n' roll, Elvis didn't even invent juvenile delinquency—it had been going on long before him.

It is not by looking at singers' influences but at their fluencies that we find the answer to the power they wield over us.

In the twenties Robert Benchley, fanning his muse to fire, renders just such a service in describing Al Jolson in *Big Boy*, who in those days invariably appeared on stage in blackface, whether in plays, revues, or as a solo performer:

To sit in on Jolson's performance in *Big Boy* is to know what the coiners of the word personality mean; though the word personality isn't quite strong enough for the thing that Jolson has. Unimpressive as the comparison may be to Mr. Jolson, we should say that John the Baptist was the last man to have such a power. There is something supernatural at the back of it, or we miss our guess. When Jolson enters, it is as if an electric current has been run along the wires under the seats where the hats are stuck. The house comes to a tumultuous attention. He speaks, rolls his eyes, compresses his lips, and it is all over. You are a member of the Al Jolson Association. He trembles his under lip, and your heart breaks with a loud snap. He sings a banal song and you totter out to send a nightletter to your mother. Such a giving-off of vitality, personality, charm, and whatever all those words are, results from a Jolson performance. We got enough vitamins out of being present that night to enable us to ride our bicycles at top speed all the way to Scarsdale, and we had enough left over to shingle the roof before going to bed.

Remaining on Jolson a moment longer, there is a passage by Hemingway in *A Moveable Feast* worthy of attention:

Zelda [Fitzgerald] was very beautiful and was tanned a lovely gold color and her hair was a beautiful dark gold and she was very friendly. Her hawk's eyes were clear and calm. I knew everything was all right and was going to turn out well in the end when she leaned forward and said to me, telling me her great secret, "Ernest, don't you think Al Jolson is greater than Jesus?"

By the elaborately ironic way—"I knew everything was all right and was going to turn out well in the end..."—Hemingway introduces Zelda's "great secret," he leaves us in no doubt that with this outrageous suggestion she has irredeemably unmasked herself to him as nuts. For Papa, with his literal-minded density and his distrust of the very kind of bold imaginative flights with which Zelda might be said to have inspired Scott's writing, was unable to grasp the importance of the discovery she was trying to call his attention to (one not unconnected with John Lennon's "we're more famous than Jesus" episode): the shatteringly spiritual effect certain singers have on people—in which category I would include Edith Piaf, Judy Garland, and especially Elvis as well as Jolson—so that listening to them becomes more of a religious experience than listening to the words of Jesus. Blasphemy it may have been but insanity it wasn't; for doesn't the eminently sane Benchley find himself comparing Jolson with John the Baptist?

"Strange how potent cheap music is" is one of Noel Coward's most quoted remarks. But we have only to see where he places it in *Private Lives*—the music referred to is his own haunting little classic, "Some Day I'll Find You," and hearing it played by the hotel orchestra draws the two lovers irresistibly back together—to realize the Master is having his little joke. Not for a moment does he think the music is "cheap," nor that its potency is "strange."

What *is* strange is that snatches of songs are in continual occupancy in the recesses of our minds. And what is even stranger is that although many of us are unable to sing the simplest melody aloud without going off key, we are all capable of reproducing accurately in these recesses of our minds the unique voice that lodged those songs in our brains in the first place.

One of the most adroit descriptions of this universal phenomenon—which he calls "a kind of melodic malady" and "an unconscious musical cerebration"—is found in George du Maurier's *Peter Ibbetson*:

I am never without some tune running in my head—never for a moment; not that I am always aware of it; existence would be insupportable if I were. What part of my brain sings it, or rather in what part of my brain it sings itself, I cannot imagine—probably in some useless corner full of cobwebs and lumber that is fit for nothing else.

But it never leaves off; now it is one tune, now another; now a song *without* words, now *with*; sometimes it is near the surface, so to speak, and I am vaguely conscious of it as I read or work, or talk or think; sometimes to make sure it is there I have to dive for it deep into myself, and I never fail to find it after a while, and bring it up to the top. It is the "Carnival of Venice," let us say; then I let it sink again, and it changes without my knowing; so that when I take another dive the "Carnival of Venice" has become "Il Mio Tesoro" or "La Marseillaise" or

"Pretty Little Polly Perkins of Paddington Green." And heaven knows what tunes, unheard and unperceived, this internal barrel-organ has been grinding meanwhile.

Finding I myself suffer from this same melodic malady concerning dozens of Elvis' songs which seem to lodge in only semiretirement in the same corner of my brain as "Pretty Little Polly Perkins of Paddington Green" and "La Marseillaise" lodged in du Maurier's, I am grateful for his further revelation that these cerebrations are caused by "the organized vibrations of a *certain* larynx's invisible, impalpable, incomprehensible little airwaves in mathematical combinations" and "the laws that govern them have existed for ever, before Moses, before Pan, long before a larynx had been evolved."

The only true survey that would register the extent of Elvis' godhood both during and after his life is, unfortunately, one it is not possible to carry out. It would not be a survey that shows the number of people who bought his records, saw his movies, or attended his concerts, but one that registers the dictatorial takeover his voice effected day after day, year after year, consciously and unconsciously, all over the world on the billions of minds that have nothing else in common but that Elvis is singing away inside them. They also have the largest repertoire to choose from than any other popular artist; from itchy, hot bewitchment to a wailing despair that yet derives comfort in the act of expression, to a soothing lullaby; whether melancholic, lonesome, happy, singing to a loved one about a loved one or to God, Elvis sings as if people were reachable by only that form of communication.

What is now left to say about Elvis's fluencies? It isn't as if they were not immediately obvious, available and accessible to all. One doesn't have to sandpaper one's mind in the manner of a safecracker sandpapering his fingertips to unlock the combination before getting to the secret of this voice that synchronizes with the heartbeat, assimilates into the bloodstream and then goes straight to that part of the brain that remembers without rationalizing or analyzing; one only has to watch people listening to a record of Elvis—watch the unawareness of the smiles on their faces, the tapping of their hands and feet, the wigglings in their seat.

Gospel, it is known, was the foundation stone of his singing. And he reserved for it a most perfect voice for the celebration of God—a voice so effortless, egoless, simple, supple, and pure that for the most unbelieving of us, for that space of time that we are listening to his hymns, we believe in his belief, in the same way that the metaphysical poets of the seventeenth century were able to make us believe in theirs.

As is also well known, Elvis' first great fluency sprang from the fact that he was a southerner and that singing in a native southern accent— that melodic, mesmeric manner of speech with its seductive elisions and diphthongs that naturally make two syllables even out of the word "own"— is the closest you can get to singing in Italian, the language made for song. Nor is there any notable difference between black and white accents in the South—as, for instance, there is between Cockney and Mayfair or Brooklyn and Boston.

Here it is perhaps relevant to note one specialist on southern speech, Professor Cleanth Brooks' opinion that although "a Southern pronun- ciation—lumping it all together, despite the fact that in the South there are many different ways of speaking—is usually thought to have originated from the negro... many of the pronunciations which are usually regarded as specifically Negro represent nothing more than older native English forms. In both black and white pronunciations, for instance, 'seven' is frequently heard in the South as 'sebn,' 'heaven' as 'hebn.' The same form occurs in a number of dialects in southwest England." [20]

Therefore, although the southern Negroes composed the melodies of the blues that made Elvis famous singing "like" them, their joint inspi- ration was derived from some even earlier dialect.

Professional opera singers have to be taught to weaken their consonants (they constrict the breath channel) and to watch out for their sibilants (they are mostly toneless and interrupt the flow of the melody). Another of Elvis' fluencies is that his southern accent led him to do them instinc- tively yet consciously. Hence, until it was understood why he was doing it, his diction was charged with being incomprehensible to the unini- tiated. Al Jolson and Bing were certainly aware of this, but from Elvis on, the singing of Bob Dylan, the Beatles, the Rolling Stones, and so forth, consciously aped the accents of the South.

The phrase "mass hysteria" became so quickly associated with Elvis in the media that the truth has somehow been hidden. However simul- taneous his discovery appeared to every one in the fifties, without that initial sense of *Eureka!* he roused in each separate individual upon first registering him, the second satisfaction—that of being proved right by millions—would not have followed.

People describing the first impact Elvis' voice made on them describe it either in a situation like that of the mother in her kitchen: "At six

[20.] *A Southern Treasury of Life and Literature*, edited by Stark Young (New York: Charles Scribner, 1937).

o'clock every night the radio would play 'Love Me Tender' and I got so I was saying to my children, 'Quiet, children, this man is singing to *me*'"—or as if whoever was with them had completely faded from their minds. "We had one of those radios built into the wall of our sitting room at the time," remembers the actress Irene Handl (honorary president of the major Elvis Presley fan club in England), "and suddenly I heard this *magician's* voice coming out of it. The effect was completely magical—as if there were a genie sitting there inside the wall." Or a man remembers: "I was walking by a record store and I heard a voice coming out of it. The sound was so different from anything I'd ever heard in my life—so fresh and full of vitality I went into the store and asked the clerk who it was. He said it was Elvis Presley and for the longest time after, I felt *I'd* discovered him."

What the world was hearing in what would become one of the most famous voices of the century was the sound of *strings*. Until Elvis, the sound underlying, intertwining, and blending with all popular vocalists, especially in the Big Band era, was of course the sound of horns. Bing Crosby's voice reproduced Paul Whiteman's horns; many of the best black horn players backed Billie Holiday; Louis Armstrong back-and-forthed himself on his own horn; and Sinatra's voice was the sound of Tommy Dorsey's trombone: it had to be—that's why he was hired.

Elvis' voice backed by Scotty's guitar and Blackie's bass created a sound of strings totally different in rhythm, tempo, phrasing and "decay"—the technical term for the dying vibrations of strings after they have been struck—from the echolalia of the big bands' massed horns. And the sounds were also produced differently—not through the mouth as in horns but through the fingers. When purists complained of Miles Davis adding guitars to his band to drive on the rhythm, he replied, "Guitar players don't have to breathe." The way a guitar is held vibrating against the gut must also be taken into account as giving the musician an entirely different feeling.

But to repeat—what is there now left to say about Elvis' fluencies?

What Elvis conveyed to millions was the ecstatic experience of singing itself—whether bouncing joyously along on the notes or hitting one with a power that makes it explode like a shattering of diamonds; like the game Elvis was fond of playing, shooting light bulbs bobbing in his swimming pool. This ecstasy he never lost and over the years, as his voice grew richer and more technically accomplished and as he experimented with larger and more innovative orchestral textures, it took on a greater splendor and grandeur.

Throughout it all pervaded a tenderness that flowed both outwards to the subject of his song and inwards to the song's sufferer. Whatever wisdom he was lacking in his everyday life he never lacked for it in his best work.

One of the latest of his "compilation" albums, which consists of recordings he made in 1973–75, has been released under the title *I Can Help*. He does.

FIFTEEN

The Yellow Brick Road

To return to Elvis and what happened to him after the release of his first record "That's All Right [Mama]" and "Blue Moon of Kentucky" in July 1954, it is customary, if not mandatory at this juncture, to say that he could never have foreseen how completely it would alter his life. But looking at the way he flung himself into what turned out to be virtually nonstop touring for the next fifteen months—Elvis, Scotty, and Blackie once calculated they had covered 100,000 miles in the first year—one is forced to quite the opposite conclusion. Elvis not only foresaw that the success of the record would alter his life but *insured* that it did by his every subsequent action and decision—including what later turned out to be the fatal one.

From childhood on, his aim in using his talent had been to change his own and his family's circumstances. If the dreamlike quality of the degree to which he was succeeding swept over him often, his continuous confrontation with live audiences, with fans screaming their adoration, was always right there in front of him to reinforce his sense of reality that his ever-growing popularity was actual (that important distinction between live performers and film stars who, once-removed from their public, have difficulty in believing it is *they* who are the cause of *that* effect) and that what was happening was the extension of his long-laid plans.

From the age of eight he had inhabited two homes: his family's in East Tupelo with its proscribed world of poverty, and the other, not a mile away, the world of WELO in East Tupelo, the world of infinite possibilities for fame and fortune. He had now found this other home again in Sun

Studios, this home which naturally led him onto the road: that world to which Elvis was attracted as to a magnetic field.

From his very first appearance at the Overton Shell in July, which Sam Phillips had arranged for him through Bob Neal, it became obvious to both Sam and Bob that Elvis *in person* had not just the possibility of being a hit but the probability of being a smash; for Sam had been finding some difficulty in getting Elvis' record accepted by radio stations that considered his sound too "race." Dewey Phillips who was there that day remembered how it happened. At the afternoon show, Elvis sang country ballads to—again quoting Scotty—"light applause." For the evening performance Dewey and Sam told him to forget country stuff and sing his yet-to-be recorded "Good Rockin' Tonight." That night Elvis went out and put everything he had into it. This included what was later to become the famous "shake of his mean left leg." These half-conscious leg shakings when laying down a beat is something many musicians do without any noticeable reaction from the audience. But Elvis' leg shakings were such as to receive a more than hearty response. Besides, the shakes didn't stop with his left leg but ran up his whole body, causing it not only to shake but rattle and roll, as the song had it. That turned the trick. The place came apart and from there on his corybantic moves became an integral part of Elvis' act. For more reasons than one this was a happy solution. Initially it solved the question of stage fright by externalizing the internal shook-up state his nerves were in before going on. It also produced an important sidelight. The more he developed these moves, incorporating them into little dances during the instrumental passages, the more eminently describable he became and the more journalists bashed their typewriters into metaphors in the attempt to describe him. "Like watching a striptease and a malted milk machine at the same time," was a memorable one. Wrote John Lardner in *Newsweek*, "There is nothing to be said against Elvis—and many people have said it—except that when placed in front of a microphone he behaves like an outboard motor," which he then corrected to "a *lovesick* outboard motor." Further pointing out that since there had been no movement to stabilize or deaden the "rabbit ball" in baseball, Lardner continued that offhand there would seem to be no clear need to stabilize the "rabbit vocalist"—as he redubbed Elvis.

From the very beginning Scotty and Blackie went on record in Memphis papers as saying "when Elvis cuts out the movement he loses the drive in his voice." While later, against charges of vulgarity and obscenity (the charges mainly gathered momentum up north; in the beginning the southern epithet for Elvis was "wild"), Elvis would tirelessly explain, "I don't do no dirty body movements. When I sing I just start jumping. If I stand still I'm dead. I ain't got no definition of rock 'n' roll. I just feel it very strongly, that's all, because there's some very beautiful ballads in it, if people would only listen. Ma'am, I'm not trying to be sexy. I didn't have no idea of trying to sell sex. It's just my way of expressing how I feel when I move around. *My movements are all leg movements. I don't do nothing with my body.*" (my italics.) What he seemed to have neglected to take into account is that the knee bone is connected to the thigh bone. And the thigh bone to the hip bone. So what about that? He had his answer ready: "You gotta put on a show, you know? Otherwise they could just as well sit home and listen to their records."

Elvis, who had barely spent a night away from his family home in all his nineteen years, now took to the road with the same exhilaration that in his mind as Captain Marvel, Jr., he had taken to flying—seeking to conquer the road, it may be remarked, with the same wild glee as his literary contemporaries, the Beat Generation. In point of fact, the fifties were seeing the almost simultaneous explosion of the new social cult of the hippies, which grew out of the Beats, as well as the new musical cult of rock 'n' roll,[21] without understanding what permanent inroads these counterculture movements would make into the fabric of society in the Western world.

Though the arc described by Jack Kerouac in *On The Road*, back and forth from New York, Chicago, Denver, San Francisco, Los Angeles, might be called the northern route—and Elvis, Scotty, and Blackie's arc the southern route through Tennesee, Mississippi, Alabama, Louisiana, Arkansas, and Texas—it was undertaken with no less sense of dedication. From the first time he was introduced on the "Louisiana Hayride" as the nineteen-year-old who was forging a new style, Elvis had a sense of mission about the trio's music: They were there to convert the natives and the fact that the natives were his own people made him feel the cause all the more passionately.

Although Elvis was paid only eighteen dollars a show once a week and had to travel four hundred miles from Memphis to appear on it, the "Louisiana Hayride" broadcast at Shreveport Municipal Auditorium, which seated 3,500 (never an empty seat when Elvis played there), turned out to be the starting point of Elvis' spreading fame and his love affair with the road. The "Louisiana Hayride"'s eyes and ears for the new and exciting were as open as those of the conservative bastion, the Grand Ole Opry,

[21.]The Beats, musically, were a beat behind rock—panegyrizing bop and cool jazz; the only "Pres" they dug was tenor saxman Lester Young, coincidentally also born in Mississippi.

were closed. His shows were also broadcast by KWKH, a powerful station that went over much of the mid-South and was cycled on to the southwest. Once Elvis was heard on it, the bookings began to pour in.

Originally they traveled in Scotty's wife's Chevrolet, and when that gave out Elvis began to buy a series of cars. A study of their one-night stands during this fifteen-month period shows that they seem to have accepted every engagement offered them in every hamlet, town, and city in Mississippi, Alabama, Arkansas, Louisiana, Texas, and Florida, no matter how big or small. It shows them playing not only in schoolhouses, roadhouses, clubs, movie houses, radio stations, and stadiums, but for police benefits, at airforce bases, and lodge picnics as well.

The road was also the beginning of Elvis turning his clock upside-down. Night was now day, spent driving from one town to another. And day began often after only two hours' sleep with breakfast at six in the evening. However, this still-growing youth, in spite of the killing schedule, managed in this time to add on thirty pounds to his weight and at least another inch to his height. Reversal of day and night suited him then, and would for the rest of his life.

Two months into all this hyperactivity, it became obvious to Scotty, as a nonstop performer with the trio, that it was impossible to remain Elvis' manager in anything but name. At first, unofficially and then finally in late December of 1954, to everyone's relief, Bob Neal became Elvis' manager. It would not have been possible for anyone then living in Memphis not to come across Neal in one way or another. If you did not happen to be up between five and eight every morning to catch his "Farm Show" for WMPS, you could always switch on his "High Noon Roundup" at midday. He also ran a record shop. And a management agency. All these activities would have left his afternoons and evenings unbearably empty, it would seem, were it not for the fact that he used them to organize little musical shows within a 150-mile radius of Memphis. It was basically a schoolhouse circuit which he ran with his wife, Helen, and the eldest of his five children: admission was fifty cents for kids and one dollar for adults. The answer to how he got through this overpacked day was that one activity fed into the other. Soon after the Overton Shell show, he began not only booking Elvis but promoting him enthusiastically by ads in the trade papers as "the freshest, newest voice in country music." As Elvis grew more popular with each appearance Neal spread his net wider, booking the Hillbilly Cat (also briefly "King of Western Bop") and the Blue Moon Boys deeper into the territories, and as Sam Phillips too began sending them on Sun package tours, their price rose.

At first the money didn't come rolling in—dribbling in would be a more accurate way to describe it—but it did come in regularly and steadily and on an ever-increasing scale. And as Elvis refused no demand except those that required him to be in different places at precisely the same time, one can see him rising in nine months from earning five dollars or ten dollars a show, to $200 by the late spring of 1955. Charlie Boren, who may be recollected as the Card and who worked first on WELO in Tupelo and now worked in Amory, Mississippi, is the authority on this. It was Charlie himself who organized what has come to be known as the "historic" Amory Concert. "I had not only Elvis that night," Charlie says, "but Johnny Cash, Carl Perkins, and Gene Simmons (also originally from Tupelo), and the total cost for the artists was $600. Elvis was the star— even with that bunch—and took $200. Less than nine months later, with all those TV appearances and the movie contract and all, his price was up to $1,700. Me, I just kept on using Cash and Perkins and Simmons." That night was also supposed to be the night Carl Perkins wrote "Blue Suede Shoes" on the back of a paper bag while waiting to go on.

Elvis' first car was a second-hand 1951 Lincoln Continental which Bob Neal helped purchase. Blackie wrecked that one. Then Elvis himself bought his first Cadillac, a secondhand model he'd had painted pink. That one burned up near Texarkana—the next day he phoned Gladys to discover she had seen it all vividly happening in a nightmare at the actual time of the event—but not before Becky Martin, one of Elvis' favorite fifth-grade classmates at East Tupelo Consolidated, had gotten an electrifying eyeful of it one day.

Becky was walking home from work on Lake Street, having stopped to pick up one of her little sisters from school when all of a sudden a pink Cadillac stopped on the curb right in front of her. Its pink door opened and before her dazzled eyes out sprang a vision clad in bright Kelly green. Before she could take in anything but those colors blazing in the sun, the Kelly-green suit wrapped itself around her in a great big hug and then plucked her little sister clear off the sidewalk with another big hug.

"Elvis!"

"Becky! Come on, hop in you both."

They rode in style for about ten yards to Becky's father's café next to his grocery store. Once there Elvis freely ordered them the sodas of their choice and all the candy the youngest Miss Martin could consume on the spot and store up for later. Then, casually, Elvis wandered over to the jukebox, ran his eyes over the titles, and put in a couple of nickels. He strolled back to their table, sat down and began chewing his nails.

The jukebox came to life and made that funny lurching noise it always does before the record clicks into place. Then came the amplified whooshing sound of the needle spinning for a couple of silent groove revolutions and then at last—music. Through the five crisp fast bars of rhythmic strings, Elvis sat silent except for his fingers drumming on the table—and then unexpectedly cutting in somewhere, somehow at the end of the fifth, or was it the beginning of the sixth bar, like silk tearing across the taut strings, came that clear, piercing, unearthly voice, pure and pleading, that voice unlike any ever heard before, "Well, that's all right, mama...."

Elvis, grinning from ear to ear, couldn't sit still. Back and forth he slid around in his seat, turning from Becky to her sister and back again asking, "Who's that? Huh? Who's that?"

The record played once round and then it played for the second time. Becky looked at Elvis in amazement. There they were sitting in the same café they had sat in when they were kids of ten, when Elvis used to sing in Mrs. Grimes' class.

As for Elvis, in his eyes his old friend Becky remained unchanged; East Tupelo was unchanged and he himself was unchanged—except for the fact that it was undeniably his voice singing to them over the jukebox. It would be hard to imagine by what more satisfactory yardstick Elvis could have measured what he had accomplished than by the expression on Becky's face at that moment.

Elvis looked at his watch and saw that he had to leave. He was on his way up to Corinth to appear on WMCA on Buddy Bain's show that evening, he explained, and he just happened to find himself passing through Tupelo—but here he broke off to confess it wasn't like that at all. The truth was he'd suddenly felt the need that day to get in his car and come down to see Tupelo alone. He didn't know why, really. Didn't know what he expected to find. ... Then Elvis was kissing Becky goodbye and making her promise to come and see him whenever she came to Memphis. She promised she would and she meant it. Her mother and father had recently divorced; her father was living with his new wife in Memphis and thereafter, whenever Becky went to visit her father, she stopped in to see Elvis. And often afterwards, whenever Becky recalled their meeting, his Kelly-green suit, his pink car, and his record on the jukebox, she thought whatever it was he was looking for that day, he'd found it.

Elvis arrived in Corinth, met up with Scotty and Blackie and was greeted by Buddy Bain who said he'd put him up for the night if he didn't mind sleeping on the sofa. Elvis didn't mind at all.

Buddy Bain, who with his wife now has an early-morning TV show in

Tupelo, remembers, "Bob Neal was managing him then and had paid a couple of girls to come along and scream. That wasn't too unusual by the way. You have a couple of girls start up and the others pick it up and it warms up the audience some. The kids stop pretty quick after they figure they've given their money's worth. But from the minute Elvis walked on, just stood in front of them with that stance and that lopsided grin—or sneer, if you thought of it that way—and struck a couple of chords on his guitar, they started screaming and they didn't stop. And neither did the rest of the audience. It was pandemonium backstage afterwards; it was pouring girls. 'What're you going to do with them all, Elvis?' I asked him. 'I don't know about the rest,' he said, 'but I know one thing. I'm going to pick me the prettiest and get out of here.' Which he did. I was fast asleep by the time he came in. I was living with my mama at the time. She'd broken her hip and was confined to her wheelchair, but she was just as feisty and outspoken as ever. She made him breakfast the next morning and Elvis was real appreciative—he kept thanking her over and over again for the breakfast and the sofa and finished off his goodbye with a hug and a big kiss planted smack on her lips. I hope he was out the door when she rubbed her mouth with the back of her hand and said, 'Huh! What's that young fella want to go slobbering all over me for?' Outside our house, it was like backstage the night before—pandemonium. The girls had spotted Elvis' car there and they came charging in—we couldn't stop 'em—they saw by the bedclothes he'd been sleeping in on our sofa and I couldn't believe my eyes but they ripped that sofa to pieces—it was nothing but a wooden frame by the time they were finished."

There is a photograph of Gladys and Vernon which Lillian has identified as having been taken during the summer of 1954 soon after Elvis' first success when they were still living on Alabama Street, which is so astonishingly different from every subsequent photograph of them that it fairly cries out to be captioned "At the Beginning." It is a studio portrait, such as would be at home in a silver frame on top of a piano. It shows a young couple in their thirties, their faces radiant with happiness. Vernon is at the height of his good looks. He is impeccably groomed from the top of his wavy fair hair to his easy flashing smile to his nattily double-knotted tie setting off his sparkling white collar and good black suit. Indeed, he seems positively to glisten with well-being.

But it is to Gladys, whom the camera has caught at that perfect moment which revealed both the depth and the unself-consciousness of her affectionate nature, that the eye keeps returning. While the same glinting highlights shine on her jet-black hair as shine on Vernon's blond head and her apparel is equally new and smart—a simple black dress with short cape sleeves slit at the shoulder and a V neckline which reveals a gold locket—it is the glowing expression in her wide-set eyes, black and round as coals, and the curve of her cheeks as her lips half part, childlike, with excitement and anticipation of the future, that rivets us.

The reason for the studio portrait was celebratory. Elvis had surprised his parents with gifts of new clothes and now they in turn were surprising Elvis with a photograph of themselves wearing them. If one had never laid eyes on the people before and were asked to place them on the social scale by this photograph, one would be unable to because of the totally unexpected aura of showbiz that comes through loud and clear.

But is it so unexpected when one remembers the family in its early days as a popular singing trio at churches and revival meetings in Tupelo? Vernon and Gladys, in now presenting themselves as they wished to be seen, had opted for the glamour associated with performers. Gladys was profoundly stage-struck—or more accurately movie-struck and per-former-struck—since her early days, and so might have been Vernon despite his oft-quoted "I never met a guitar player worth a damn." How-ever little we know of Vernon's private dreams of glory, it would not be inconsistent with his good looks and his singing voice if he, too, had longed to get into the profession. Judging by the high standards of semi-professional groups around Tupelo who sang mostly in churches and who often made records, it seems inconceivable that Elvis, Gladys, and Vernon never thought of making a record together. It may just be possible that somewhere stashed in the attic of Graceland where Elvis never threw anything away there might turn up an old record of this family trio circa 1954, cut at the Memphis Recording Service—unreleased, of course.

The first service the sudden acquisition of money renders people who have been very poor for a long time is the ability to gratify their desire for life's essential luxuries rather than its inessential necessities. Flash, per se, plays a pivotal part. The suddenly monied man must not only have it, he must be seen to have it. Hence the first things Elvis used his money for were new clothes for the family—and this included Minnie Mae—as well as himself; rings, lockets, and trinkets for Gladys and of course a car for them—as well as himself. The first car he could afford to buy Gladys, it is true, was not the promised pink Cadillac (that will come later) but, although it was only a Ford, it was pink. How much more pleasure and satisfaction can be gotten from showing off a pink car than from showing off a paid debt! Not that those debts—the cause of so many agonizing family discussions in the past—did not eventually have to be paid, but it is important to get the newly affluent Elvis' priorities right. For Elvis, after the first luxury of flash, came the glorious second one— the freedom to eat favorite foods at fancied hours, breaking loose from the constricting regime of only three (and in his case sometimes only two) meals a day. For Elvis, this meant as much as eight cheeseburgers and three milkshakes at a sitting on the road and at home, sandwich after sandwich of his favorite—peanut butter, sliced bananas, and crisp bacon.

The next goal for Elvis was to secure Gladys' comfort. And of all the rooms in the house, she cared most for the kitchen—which meant gadgets. Washing machines for clothes and dishes would have to wait, but one of the early purchases Elvis made was a Mixmaster. A week later, having earned some more money, he was back at the hardware store. The storekeeper looked at him curiously when he made known his request. "See here, sonny," he said, "ain't you the same young man as come in last week and bought yourself one?" "I want my mama to have two Mixmasters so we can put them at each end of the kitchen counter and it'll cut down on all the walking she has to do," Elvis carefully explained.

About six months into his burgeoning career Elvis was able to demonstrate in another way that he and his family were, in the words of Ben Franklin, "emerging from poverty and obscurity to a state of affluence and some degree of reputation in the world." They moved out of their old neighborhood. They rented a little four-room house on the vast Lamar Avenue in an area totally devoid of any atmosphere of "neighborhood." Now converted into the Tiny Tot Nursery School, 2414 Lamar Avenue seems to have been set down in the middle of a highway for no discernible reason except too serve the Presleys as a sort of halfway—or more accurately one-fourth-of-the-way—house. Six months later, around June 1955, the Presleys were ready to move up again. This time they rented a far more substantial house on Getwell Street—1414 Getwell Street is a three-storey, solid, brown-brick house in a lower middle-class neighborhood set back from the road with a front and back lawn. Although it has been stated that both these houses were bought by Elvis, a search through the deed purchase records in the Memphis court building, which lists such transactions, proves this statement false.

To imagine that Elvis would actually consider buying, with all its implications of "settling for," either a dinky four-room cottage smack on a busy thoroughfare or even the larger, more comfortable but still ordinary house on Getwell Street, is seriously to misread his character, his situation, and his ambitions.

Elvis' story, it must be emphasized, is not a Horatio Alger story, however much it is mistakenly given that name. "From rags to riches" in Alger's *œuvre* did not have the hero going from rags to the millionaire class but from rags to respectability—that is, from the working class to the affluent middle class with the horizons of further mobility implicitly narrowed by an emphasis on respectability. The Alger bootblack is invariably transformed into a solid, responsible citizen. In contrast, the quality of Elvis' upward visions would in no way be able to cope with the strains and restraints of respectability. And though at the beginning of his career all this was below the threshold of his perception, his every instinct would have warned him not to buy a house that would so publicly, privately, and permanently reflect the idea of his and his family's status until he found the house that satisfactorily marked the distance he had traveled. It was not until March 1956 that he finally found one.

The first house Elvis actually bought was on Audubon Drive in one of Memphis' most socially select areas. Elvis paid $40,000 in cash, a huge sum in those days, for 1034 Audubon Drive, a brand-new, ranch-type, one-storey house with pastel green board-and-batten sliding, slate-gray tiled roof, red-brick trim, white windows decorated with black shutters, and a black ranch-style front door but—as one may recall Elvis' old classmate from Milam remarking—without a front porch. Instead, the Presleys now sat around in the privacy of their large patio in *back*. They had come up in the world. However, like certain of the most expensive parts of Beverly Hills, Audubon's wide curving drive is jammed with luxurious and elegant houses each separated by no more than ten yards of manicured lawn. It is easy to foretell, in this rich, peaceful neighborhood where the very houses seem to breathe in well-bred unison unrestrained by the demarcation of fences, the disrupting effect the Presleys' moving in would have with its inrush of cars, motorcycles, and round-the-clock fans, to say nothing of the infernal din made by the construction of a swimming pool and new two-car garage. Later would come the final outrage: the brick and iron fence surrounding it.

The social and geographical disadvantages of Audubon Drive are so immediately obvious one wonders what, besides a sense of elevation, drew the Presleys there. But it is safe to guess that their prime consideration was Gladys. That the house was new and of wood was sure to be a reminder—though on a much larger scale—of that other new wooden house on Berry Street, the one Orville Bean had sold to them long ago in East Tupelo, the house they had not been able to hang onto. Also, that it was all on one floor made it easier on Gladys' legs. And the very fact that all the houses were so close together was a psychological plus: Close neighbors always made Gladys feel safer.

What did the Presleys make their neighbors feel? In fact how did Memphis society react to this phenomenon, Elvis, now in their midst? A former Memphian with a long, distinguished career, and the scion of an old Memphis family, has written me the following candid communication which includes his reasons for wishing to remain anonymous:

I have only one overall impression about Mr. Presley's position and acceptance in Memphis. And that is naturally from the point of view of the world I was born and raised in, the world of the country club, etc. He was referred to by them as an embarrassment to the community, as his art was vulgar and common, tacky and lower class.

As the years passed and Presley's wealth as well as his fame began to benefit the Memphis charities, a transition occurred. He became known as "a fine young man." Of course, he was still secretly mocked as being tasteless and vulgar—all those many-colored Cadillacs, etc. And in the typical fashion of the hypocrisy of people of that class and its culture, or should I say lack of culture, Presley was admired but you really wouldn't want him to marry "our daughters" or sit down at "our table," or belong to "our club." But it would be nice to have him present at some social event to add some "kickness" to the occasion. Or some fund-raising event where he could be valuable.

His early death was mourned even by the country club set. After all, it marked the loss of income to the community's charities. But he was of course after all in their eyes one of those common people who naturally get mixed up in the un-respectable evils of the high life and drugs. Poor Elvis. He just wasn't 'to the manor born.'

I suspect in a classic and tragic sense he yearned to be accepted and became a self-destructive recluse when he realized he wasn't. Perhaps he would have been accepted if he made his home somewhere else, but he stuck to his roots and I think that was a part of his downfall. This is an opinion and a very un-documented impression. If you want to quote anything I have said, I would be most grateful if you did not use my name as I have labored now for many years to protect my dear parents from any aspect of my opinions, particularly of the world in which they have lived all their lives. They have been most generous and kind to me and I do not want to hurt them in any way.

... Echoes of the active committee woman in Tupelo who had explained with great delicacy: "If the Presleys came to my house today I'd be just as friendly as could be. But I wouldn't ask them to tea at the country club."

Most famous people have felt themselves cursed in childhood by par-ents who neglected them by early death, disappearance, indifference, or by subjecting them to active disapproval—the disapproval the famous-person-to-be feels the need to keep provoking by constant rebellion until the battle is resolved by his leaving home. Once on his own the shrewd-ness and suspicion he has developed in surviving the early years of combat may be said to make him tough—if not lovable. And by the same token, the parents' feelings about the success of what was once their troublesome brat who, it seems, by his very act of defying them, has succeeded, will remain ambivalent.

Needless to say, ambivalence of this kind could never possibly have diminished Gladys' joy at her loved and loving son's success.

In the beginning Elvis' meteoric rise was her greatest source of unalloyed happiness and pride, for one is talking about a genuinely nice boy whom, it seemed, everyone who had ever had anything to do with, suddenly loved. And they went out of their way to tell Gladys that it could not have happened to a nicer boy, sweeter, more thoughtful or better behaved. Not just Sam and Marion and Blackie and Dewey Phillips praised him to her in these terms, but Bernie Lansky of the Lansky Brothers Clothing Store on Beale Street came to her full of stories about how he used to see Elvis in the past with his face pressed longingly against his store window and what a pleasure it was now that he could buy all the clothes that he had yearned for. "Know what that means to that shopowner, that Elvis still buys his clothes where he did when he was driving a truck?" Vernon once asked an interviewer. "He's just had to push his walls out and double the store!"

The friends Gladys still sought out most were, just as in Elvis' childhood, those in some way related to his career. Bob Neal's wife Helen became a particular friend and comfort to her. They visited with each other when Elvis and Bob were away. But of all her new friends probably Slim and Mary Rhodes, who took her under their wing, performed the most needed service. Not only were they her contemporaries in age but Slim and Mary and his band had been in show business for years. The Rhodes family was one of the most influential in Memphis country music; Slim's show was in fact the longest running on WMC. Beginning in 1944 it went out regularly until the sixties. Slim and Mary also had a TV show which Gladys and Elvis regularly attended. They were therefore in a position to advise, explain, and enlighten Gladys on every aspect of Elvis' new involvement in the country music scene.

Mary Rhodes often talked to her friend Buddy Bain about Gladys. There was no halo around Gladys as far as Mary was concerned—Gladys was a kindhearted country woman who liked her beer and her movies, who was made anxious and not a little confused by what was expected of her in her new role. But she was someone who stubbornly resisted attempting to be anything she wasn't. Though she knew she would have to deal with their changing status, it was difficult to get her to realize the extent to which it would change, and more difficult for her to realize that, besides giving up her privacy, an even higher price she would have to pay was watching Elvis becoming involved with people who would remain complete strangers to her—and that among those she did grow to know, there would be at least one she didn't like.

As the auspicious day was nearing for the Presleys to take that giant step from Getwell Street to Audubon Drive, Mary realized with astonishment that Gladys simply intended to move all her old furniture in. It took all of Mary's eloquence to explain to Gladys why this just wouldn't do. Now, as homeowners, they should appreciate that a new house wasn't complete without new furniture as well; besides, those new neighbors were going to be watching like hawks as each piece was unloaded.

Under her guidance she headed Gladys and Elvis to a reputable furniture store. But Gladys and Elvis, once turned loose, quickly developed their own ideas. How they filled the nine rooms of Audubon Drive has been described at length, down to the red plastic phone studded with rhinestones; the yellow wallpaper in his bedroom, speckled with blue and orange and hung with leaping ceramic minstrels on oval plaques which overflowed through the rest of the house; the white quilted bedspreads printed with pink and blue flowers on the twin beds in his room, blue puppies resting against the headboards; there was an abundance of sofas and chairs covered in some pebbly material; a preponderance of lamps in every shape and size; standing ashtrays; a good hi-fi set, and the walls, when not papered, were panelled in dark mahogany.

To the more esthetically minded, it might look, as someone once remarked, like "all the furniture in a store you *wouldn't* buy"; but in fact as the photographs show, there is much to be said for its undeniably having its own voice while appearing extremely comfortable, with all the nubby chairs and sofas available for the clan of Presley and Smith cousins and uncles and aunts who had in the traditional way staked out their claim there. And there was also, for Elvis' special enjoyment, an organ, and later on there would be a piano.

Gladys, however, had intransigently refused to throw her own furniture away. It was piled into the den, not moved until it made its final resting place in the attic of Graceland.

For the first months Gladys attended Elvis' concerts in and around Memphis whenever possible; he wanted her there. The girls in the audiences screamed and applauded but they stayed put so Gladys was able to enjoy their enthusiasm; and it especially thrilled this musically knowledgeable woman to see Elvis growing with each performance; getting better each time. However, with the "double eye-string" contact that existed between them she saw how much it was taking out of him and it began to take a lot out of her, too.

Then one day she and Vernon went with Elvis to listen to him sing at a high school dance being held, as Lillian remembers, at a high school gym in Mississippi. This was the first time Gladys had ever seen Elvis and the boys playing at a dance. The kids were on their feet now, reacting to Elvis with increasingly wild flights of passion on which he, in turn, soared. The temperature in the gym was set for "riot" and a riot was exactly what took place. One minute the boys and girls were more or less dancing and the next the dancing stopped as the girls, discarding their partners, rushed to the bandstand with but one thought—to fling themselves at Elvis. Gladys reacted as if she had never left East Tupelo, as if Elvis were still eight years old and she was on her front porch watching the Hand boys ganging up on him. Then she had jumped off the porch wielding her dogwood broom; now she threw herself into the mob of girls, and grabbing the one nearest to Elvis, whirled her around and hung onto her hard.

"Why are you trying to kill my boy?" she demanded angrily.

"I'm not trying to kill him. I just love him so, I want to touch him," the girl protested.

This did nothing to lessen Gladys' determination. Flinging the girl aside, this tall, husky woman with the help of her tall, husky husband lifted Elvis bodily off the platform and, cleaving through the crowd, bore him off in the primitive security of her arms to safety.

This marked in her the beginning of a dilemma she could not solve: Her pride in her son, her understanding and support of him, always got mixed up in the dread she had not felt since the first four years of his life—that atavistic dread of what would happen to him when out of her sight.

"Mom and Dad still haven't gotten over all this hoopla about me," Elvis told an interviewer in 1956. "Mama was down in Florida once when the girls mobbed me and she was afraid they were hurting me. Shucks, they were only tearing my clothes. I didn't mind a bit. I told her, 'Mama, if you're going to feel that way, you'd better not come along to my shows because that stuff is going to keep right on happening'—I hope."

The concert Elvis was referring to was the one at the Gator Bowl in Jacksonville, Florida, on May 13, 1955. Now known officially as the "first Presley riot," it was the one where not just dozens but hundreds of screaming teenage girls leapt from the stands, slipped through the unprepared police guards, and cornered Elvis in his dressing room. As they ripped his clothes off him and tore them to shreds in the battle for possession of these sacred relics, there is no doubt that had he panicked he would have been in real danger before the police had a chance to rescue him. That he didn't, that he laughed off not only the close encounter but the sight of his pink Cadillac now completely covered with girls' names scratched or lipsticked all over it, indicates in this extraordinary boy a unique, even unnatural, willingness to accept what equally great idols from Chaplin to Brando have instinctively hated, feared, and hidden from— the unacceptable face of naked mob worship. This rare feeling Elvis had, of genuine trust in his mobbing fans, was based not only on his expectation of idolatry but his sure knowledge that his power protected him. However frightening it may have looked to those watching, Elvis felt safe in the knowledge that this was a demonstration of adulation. The fans were simply returning the love—sacred or profane—that he had lavished on them during his performance. "They don't mean any harm," he would insist. "They just want a piece of you."

As difficult as it may be to understand Elvis' nonchalance in the eye of the hurricane, it is not difficult to understand even a normal mother's feelings about the way that night ended.

And in the light of this, Elvis' subsequent laying it on the line for Gladys—if that sort of thing upset her then she'd better not come to the shows, because (the implication is clear) he was going to see to it that it kept right on happening—can only be viewed as Elvis' long-deferred Declaration of Independence to her. Take it or leave it, Elvis was saying in essence, from here on in, fame is my first home. "But I'm doing all this for you, baby," was how he tried to soften that message and to placate Gladys. He no longer called her "mama" or the mysterious "Sattening" (smooth as satin?) but instead reverted to words of his earliest days when he was the man of the family. "There, there, my little baby," were now for real. He had a job to do and he had to go out into the world away from her to do it.

Given the ultimatum, Gladys outwardly tried to accept the situation. And so did Dixie Locke. All through her last school year in 1955 Dixie was still Elvis' sweetheart, still the girl of all the others he loved the most. School, decorum, or the Colonel's orders, however, decreed that she not accompany Elvis on his tours. In the early days Elvis would come back to Memphis and see her once every two weeks, then once every three weeks, and then when he was gone for almost a month the inevitable happened. It was around August. She had graduated from high school that June and had barely seen Elvis all summer. She had been going with him for eighteen months and her contact with him had largely been on the phone when he would call his "babies," as he now referred to both Vernon and Gladys, and afterwards would talk to Dixie for a while. For the most part she was kept informed about the blatant behavior of his fans from what she read in the newspapers. Dixie was not only a level-headed and determined young girl, she was a popular one. That particular evening when she came to the Presleys she took Gladys aside to tell her she was going to be married—to someone else. She asked Gladys to tell Elvis. She couldn't bear to tell him herself, she said. Perhaps it was because she was afraid he might talk her out of it; he was so persuasive and she wasn't going to take the chance. It may seem odd that one's fiancée (even one's unofficial fiancée) would ask one's mother not only to break off the engagement but announce her coming marriage. But Dixie unquestionably accepted that only Gladys would be able to make Elvis understand. For perhaps the last time, someone was acting as if Gladys and Elvis were one.

First love comes and first love goes and we all get over it, especially a young man whose attention has been so violently distracted from it. But Elvis did not get over it. Dixie's defection cut deeply into the illusion he carried around with him in the quiet moments by himself on the road when he thought about his family and about Dixie as very much a part of it. The hurt he suffered by losing her surfaced later at the same time he was first suffering the loss of the one he loved most. The double loss of Gladys and Dixie became entwined.

It is ironic that three months after his Declaration of Independence to Gladys, Elvis signed his first imprisoning contract with the Colonel.

SIXTEEN

Under Contract

From the beginning of 1955 Parker's interest in Elvis was active and productive and obvious. As the booking agent for his partner Hank Snow, his first move was to "help" Neal book Elvis into Carlsbad, New Mexico, a town near the Texas border where the reaction was enthusiastic enough for Parker to book him immediately on a Hank Snow ten-day tour of one-nighters beginning in Texas. Texas loved Elvis from the word go—it was Texas that first christened him "Elvis the Pelvis." The crowds he drew were bigger and noisier and more varied in age than in any other state.

"Good Rockin' Tonight" and "I Don't Care If the Sun Don't Shine" had been released the previous fall and on January 8, Elvis' twentieth birthday, Sam released "Milk Cow Boogie" and "You're a Heartbreaker," none of which, in spite of Elvis catching on like wildfire when he made personal appearances, ever made the charts. He also recorded in January "I'll Never Let You Go, L'il Darlin'," the first four phrases being among the most exquisite Elvis ever sang but which Sam, for his own mysterious reasons, did not release, and it wasn't heard until RCA released it in 1956.

In February, however, Elvis recorded "Baby, Let's Play House" and, on its flip side, what has gone down through the decades mislabeled as "I'm Left, You're Right, She's Gone" (it is actually "You're Right, I'm Left, She's Gone"). Perhaps the mislabeling was the result of Sam being in-decisive again. The record first went out to the disk jockeys with "My Baby's Gone" on the flip side, but Sam felt that the action was sluggish, so he had them send it back and substituted another song; the hurry of getting it out must have caused the mislabeling. In any case it was released April 1, and by July Elvis was for the first time on the national charts. The votes were coming in. Well, they had always come in, but now the ballot boxes themselves were mushrooming.

As early as March 1955, just after Elvis' first Hank Snow tour, in pop-musically advanced Cleveland, Bill Randle, the pop-musically advanced DJ (he also had a show on CBS in New York and commuted between Cleveland and New York weekly and was the first DJ outside the South to play Elvis' records regularly) got Cleveland's Circle Theater interested in booking Elvis for its "Country Music Jamboree." On the same show were Pat Boone and Bill Haley. A film was being shot at the time about Randle to be called _The Pied Piper of Cleveland: A Day in the Life of a Famous Disk Jockey_ and when they saw the rushes, Elvis had obviously swept all before him (before it was released, Parker paid to have his appearance cut). Bill Randle's reaction to Elvis at the Circle Theater was to telephone Freddy Bienstock (who later as manager of Elvis' music publishing company collected all the material for which Elvis would select his records) and say, "I've seen a great singer. He wants a manager. Why don't you manage him?"

Bill Randle had discovered Johnnie Ray among others, said Bienstock, "and when he said something you listened. But I turned down the chance. I wasn't interested in going on the road. The next person who talked to me about Elvis was Hank Snow," continued Bienstock. "We [Hill and Range Music Publishers] had a contract with Hank and he called to say Elvis was great and he strongly recommended we sign him up quickly. Hank said, 'I started him at the opening of the show and it was impossible because everyone was saying, "when is he coming on again?" So I had to move him to the last part of the show.'" Adds Bienstock, "Hank also pushed me to get out an Elvis Presley folio which didn't sell anywhere except in Memphis and in Texas, where it sold out. And it was Hank Snow who first talked about Elvis to RCA. Not the Colonel."

But more and more the Colonel was seeing to it that Elvis was aware that he was the solid presence behind the bigger bookings he was getting.

What should never be forgotten in any gullible pop singer's story is how many more singers than managers there are and the proportion of red-hot singers to straight managers is, alas, far higher; which is one reason why lawsuits brought by pop singers against their managers, involving huge rip-offs, are regularly reported in the newspapers—and these are only the tip of the iceberg. In no other client-manager relationship is the first more needful of the second. Need blunts suspicion.

So should we be surprised on May 1, when Parker had booked Elvis again for an important three-week tour with the Hank Snow show, to find Elvis eager as a puppy, seeking out the Colonel to thank him for all he'd done for him, and to underline the point, even asking him if the clothes he had on—a snappy combination of black and lavender—which he intended to wear on the show, were "all right?"

This sort of humility was cat's meat, or rather dog's meat, to the Colonel. He was not the first to notice the difference between the dynamic, uninhibited, all-powerful Elvis on stage and the shy, powerless young man off, but he was the first to see how this contrast might be exploited for his own use. Everything about Elvis, his extreme youth, his impoverished background, his single status, along with his desire for a proper manager, was playing into the Colonel's hands. Parker had also done his homework. He knew that, simple as it would be to talk Elvis into accepting him as his manager—"All you've got now is a million dollars' worth of talent. but by the time we're through you'll have a million dollars"—unbudgeable was the fact that Elvis was still a minor. His real job was going to be convincing Gladys and Vernon that he was the right man.

Elvis was as eager for this to come about as Parker was, and when Elvis mentioned that he would like the Colonel to meet his mother and father, Parker's courtship of them began.

Gladys, of course, had been hearing a lot about the Colonel and asked Slim and Mary Rhodes about him. Who was this man? What could they tell her except the obvious—that, like him or not, he was a mighty powerful man in a mighty powerful position. Parker began meeting the Presleys at various concerts, always careful first to have an artist in the company who would sing his praises to them. He visited them at their modest home on Getwell Street where during his daylong stay he alternated between his admiration of Elvis and his million dollars' worth of talent and projections of the actual million dollars Elvis would have in hand under his management. According to Gabe Tucker, the Presleys were "cordial but uncomfortable with the formidable Colonel."

Vernon was immediately sold on Parker and his lucrative plans for Elvis, but Gladys instinctively distrusted him and made it clear to both Vernon and Elvis that she did. Parker, sensing he had failed to sway her, thought Hank Snow could do so and urged him, not only as one of the most famous country stars but as his partner, to go and visit them. Hank Snow emphasized to the Presleys what he himself believed to be the case— Elvis wasn't signing up only with Parker, but with Snow too; with Hank Snow Jamboree Attractions, the best in the country.

No doubt Snow's wholesome family image, as well as the rewards to be gained being more permanently connected with his outfit, put things in more reassuring light for Gladys, though it did not relieve her initial uncomfortable feeling about the Colonel. Indeed, not until Bob Neal's insistence that even though Elvis had an existing contract with him, she need not feel it morally wrong for Elvis to sign what would amount to an additional and extremely beneficial agreement with Parker/Hank Snow Attractions and one that Neal himself approved of, did her last line of resistance fall. Back in his high school days when Elvis had wanted to quit school Vernon had supported him but Gladys had prevailed and won. Now, again, Vernon was supporting Elvis. And this time Gladys gave in. It turned out to be a grave surrender.

The result of her acquiescence was the very first contract Elvis ever signed with Parker. (Not until the guardian *ad litem's* report[22] in September 1980 prior to the *Presley* v. *Parker* case, did this contract come to light; nor was its existence known except to the parties concerned.) Since then it has been printed in one book about Elvis, but no book which seeks to understand how completely Parker went about dominating Elvis is complete without it. The date was August 15, 1955.

AGREEMENT

SPECIAL AGREEMENT between ELVIS PRESLEY, known as artist, his guardians, Mr. and/or Mrs. Presley, and his manager, MR. BOB NEAL, of Memphis, Tennessee, hereinafter referred to as the Party of the First Part, and COL. THOMAS A. PARKER and/or HANK SNOW ATTRACTIONS of Madison, Tennessee, hereinafter known as the Party of the Second Part, this date, August 15, 1955.

COL. PARKER is to act as special adviser to ELVIS PRESLEY and BOB NEAL for the period of one year and two one-year options for the sum of two thousand five hundred dollars (2,500.00) per year, payable in five payments of five hundred dollars ($500.00) each, to negotiate and assist in any way possible the build-up of ELVIS PRESLEY as an artist. Col. Parker will be reimbursed for any out-of-

[22]The appointment of a guardian *ad litem* or temporary guardian for Elvis' daughter, Lisa Marie did not come about until five years after her father's death, when on Vernon's death his share of the estate devolved on her. The executors presented a petition to the court for the approval of all arrangements made between the estate and Parker, but when this request went before the judge he, disturbed by Parker's claim on the estate, ruled that somebody be appointed to represent Lisa Marie. That person was Attorney Blanchard E. Tual, who for two years diligently and meticulously investigated the whole business of Elvis' estate and its management and whose findings are summed up in the two lengthy reports I refer to and quote from in this book. The first was filed on September 29, 1980, in the probate court of Shelby County, Tennessee, and the second on July 31, 1981, in the same place.

The attorney consulted gave the following view of the reports. "From the documentation, there can be no shadow of doubt per adventure that the Colonel did not respect his fiduciary role with Elvis Presley and the several agreements he entered into with RCA and others certainly, on the face of the documents produced by the guardian *ad litem*, could not— ever—have been in Elvis' best interests. In particular, the "buy-out [in 1973 all of Elvis' previous tapes were sold outright to RCA] with its collateral agreement cannot be viewed other than with the gravest doubt as to the Colonel's probity."

pocket expenses for traveling, promotion, advertising as approved by ELVIS PRESLEY and his manager.

As a special concession to Col. Parker, ELVIS PRESLEY is to play 100 personal appearances within one year for the special sum of $200.00 (Two hundred dollars) including his musicians.

In the event that negotiations come to a complete standstill and ELVIS PRESLEY and his manager and associates decide to freelance, it is understood that Col. Parker will be reimbursed for the time and expenses involved in trying to negotiate the association of these parties and that he will have first call on a number of cities, as follows, at the special rate of one hundred seventy-five dollars ($175.00) per day for the first appearance and two hundred fifty dollars ($250.00) for the second appearance and three hundred fifty dollars ($350.00). San Antonio, El Paso, Phoenix, Tucson, Albuquerque, Oklahoma City, Denver, Wichita Falls, Wichita, New Orleans, Mobile, Jacksonville, Pensacola, Tampa, Miami, Orlando, Charleston, Greenville, Spartanburg, Asheville, Knoxville, Roanoke, Richmond, Norfolk, Washington, D.C., Philadelphia, Newark, New York, Pittsburgh, Chicago, Omaha, Milwaukee, Minneapolis, St. Paul, Des Moines, Los Angeles, Amarillo, Lubbock, Houston, Galveston, Corpus Christi, Las Vegas, Reno, Cleveland, Dayton, Akron, and Columbus.

Col. Parker is to negotiate all renewals on existing contracts.

The contract is signed by Elvis, Vernon, Parker (for Hank Snow Jamboree Attractions), and witnessed by Tom Diskin.

The obvious reaction to this short document is that the tone is as outrageous as the demands: "Col. Parker *is to* act," "As a *special concession* to Col. Parker Elvis *is to* play," "It is understood that Col. Parker *will* be reimbursed," "Col. Parker *is to* negotiate." Was this a contract or a series of barked orders? With just such an imperious manner might Captain Bligh have signed up his crew.

As for the content, items of interest to note are:

Item 1 Parker is no more than three lines into the contract before young Elvis already owes him $2,500.

Item 2 Parker's obligations to Elvis are left vague and general, while Elvis' duties to Parker are precise and specific.

Item 3 By distributing Elvis' pounds of flesh throughout forty-seven cities, should he have any second thoughts about this Faustian contract Parker turns it into a Shylockian one as well.

Item 4 By empowering himself to negotiate all renewals on existing contracts—thus making this contract open-ended—the Colonel gives himself total mastery over Elvis' career.

Item 5 The Colonel's signing the contract for Hank Snow Attractions will be dealt with later.

Item 6 Although the contract, looked at superficially, seems devoid of double Dutch, it will nevertheless earn the accusation in at least one instance of being "inartfully drawn"—legalese for unclear. In the "100 personal appearances," it doesn't make clear whether each appearance is counted singly or whether a number of appearances on one day constitute one appearance. This is something over which any number of legal hairs could be split. But the big question that needs to be asked is why the not-inexperienced Bob Neal allowed Elvis to sign this open-ended contract. It is answered in future contracts between Parker and Neal which make clear that Neal did not suffer financially. Up until March 1956, Neal as well as Parker would still be taking a piece of Elvis.

Why did Elvis sign this contract which one lawyer with considerable show business experience calls *"out of the ordinary, extraordinary, and not in any way a recognizable form of contract"*? Was Elvis just plain stupid—or what?

It is often said that very few people are stupid; they *all* know something you don't. What Elvis knew then was that, strong as the external pressures from Bob Neal and Vernon were for him to sign the contract (and his own internal desire to thrust upon a manager the burden of his bookings and business dealings was stronger still), it was his ambition and the turmoil and impatience he felt that tipped the scales, that made him eager to sign with the Colonel no matter *what* it cost—including his mother's misgivings. Plainly, he regarded Parker as his patron. That he would be supporting his patron rather than the other way round did not seem to matter just then. That it was a naive, shy, green, gullible twenty-year-old who signed the contract with the firm conviction that he was not "selling out" but "buying in," invokes, if not our awe then our stunned attention. This foolhardy act, by the laws of Aristotelian tragedy, made Elvis—if not a better man—a heroic one.

It was the sense of hurry, the not-to-be-denied urgency of the contract, with its implied penalties for stalling, the immediate nowness of it that made Elvis all the more eager to rush in. For both Parker and Elvis had one important thing in common. They were both in hot haste.

From then on, to Gladys' confusion, there seemed to exist two Elvises: her own son whose every thought and hope and fear she had shared with him and whom she understood so well, and this other, almost unreal creature whom she hardly ever saw but who jumped out at her with increasing frequency from newspapers and magazines, and whose separate existence belonged not only to the public, which she was forced to accept, but to the Colonel—which she couldn't.

Not a month after the contract was signed, the first article on Elvis appeared in a magazine called *Country Song Roundup* and was followed by others in which references could be found to herself and Vernon as

Corinne Richards snaps Gladys' relatives (*left to right*) Shelby Jean Tate, Leona Richards, Curtis Tate, Gladys and Vernon in the back yard of Audubon Drive 1956. (*Corinne Tate*)

This photograph is reproduced here for the first time. Elvis at Graceland with cousins Shelby Jean Tate, Corinne (Richards) Tate and Curtis Tate. Summer 1957. (*Corinne Tate*)

Mississippi – Alabama Fair of 1956. Gladys, briefly happy, at Elvis' side. (*Private Collection*)

LEFT Elvis as he appeared in *Love Me Tender* in 1956. (*Aquarius, London*)

By late 1956 the strain begins to tell on Gladys. (*Elvis Presley Fan Club, Leicester*)

LEFT Elvis and Gladys outside the house on Audubon Drive in 1956. (*Robert Williams*)

Jailhouse Rock (1957), Elvis with Mickey O'Shaunessy. Note 'twin' bassett hounds setting up resonances of Elvis-the-twin on the TV show in which he was ingloriously made to sing to a top-hatted bassett. A few months before in his night-club act Mickey had relentlessly parodied Elvis. (*National Film Archives*)

The Colonel and his lady have a night out. (*Private Collection*)

lvis inducted into the army, Memphis,
March 24, 1958. (*A.P. Wide World Photos*)

Elvis confronts his father outside the hospital room where Gladys died, August 14, 1958. (*Gilloon, Aquarius, London*)

LEFT According to Lillian, at this point the only thing that Gladys cared about other than Elvis was this little dog. (1958) (*Syndication International*)

Several years after Gladys' death Elvis added to her memorial stone the Star of David as well as the Cross. (*A.P. Wide World Photos*)

SUNSHINE OF OUR HOME
GLADYS LOVE PRESLEY
APR. 25, 1912 — AUG. 14, 1958

NOT MINE
BUT THY WILL BE DONE

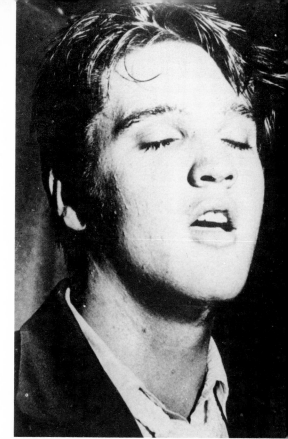

RIGHT Gospel (*Aquarius, London*)
BELOW Lullaby (*National Film Archives*) . . .

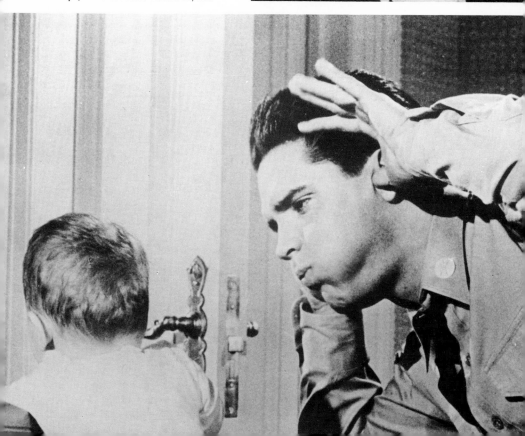

Rock 'n' Roll (*Elvis Presley Fan Club, Leicester*)

well as Elvis. These references upset far more than pleased her. They were an unexpected shock. She hadn't had time to get used to their lives suddenly being exposed. Vernon, on the other hand, revelled in it to the hilt. He was, at least, a somebody.

When Parker arranged for RCA to buy Elvis' contract from Sun Records. Gladys knew it only meant more separations from him. For now even his recording sessions, which until then could be counted on to return him to Memphis fairly regularly, were taking him not just to Nashville but farther and farther away—to New York—to California.

In 1956, two days after he celebrated his twenty-first birthday at home, he was gone again, this time to the RCA studio in Nashville to record for them for the first time. Along with Scotty and Blackie and the drummer, D. J. Fontana, who had joined the trio during "Louisiana Hayride," there were added the musicians Chet Atkins on guitar and Floyd Cramer on piano. The second record they cut was called "Heartbreak Hotel" which Sam Phillips told an interviewer in the *New York Post*, with his usual disarming candor, "was so bad that Colonel Parker and the owners were thinking of withdrawing it." The record, he announced, "was a morbid mess."

Elvis, in fact, almost didn't get to sing it on "The Stage Show," his first national TV appearance. This was the ailing series with Tommy and Jimmy Dorsey, produced by Jackie Gleason, for which Elvis had been hired in the hopes of widening its appeal. RCA had sent "Heartbreak Hotel" to the producers thinking that the flip side "I Was the One," would be the one for Elvis to sing, but Jack Philbin, the executive producer, decided otherwise. Elvis sang "Heartbreak Hotel" on three different appearances on "The Stage Show." In May a national magazine had the headline, "Young Elvis Presley's Complaint Becomes Nation's Top Tune."

What surely is most worth mentioning about this doom-filled ballad (but never is) is that young Elvis should have chosen to sing it at all— for what he is describing in the song is nothing less than a hell of lost souls—and that millions of teenagers all over the world would so instinctively respond to it. Sam was half right at any rate: It was morbid. Would any other teenage idol have been able to put over the dark side with such stunning self-revelation? For the song's immense success said a great deal about the universal condition of adolescence: that the thoughts of youth were deep enough to encompass not only the daydreams of dating, puppy love, high school dances, and the wedding ring, but the nightmares of rejection, of utter despair, of loneliness that could envisage suicide in a claustrophobic flophouse.

It was in 1956 that Elvis went national and global. He did six "Stage

Shows," two "Milton Berle Shows," one "Steve Allen Show," and two "Ed Sullivan Shows" (the third "Sullivan Show" was aired at the beginning of 1957). He signed a movie contract with Hal Wallis, made an appearance in Las Vegas, and starred in his first movie, *Love Me Tender*. Already rumors of his being drafted into the army, now that he was twenty-one, were keeping pace with his rise. It was also in 1956 that the attacks on Elvis' performing style became a national pastime. Those gyrations! Such wigglings and wrigglings had not been seen since the serpent caused man's expulsion from paradise. Youth burst into flame for perhaps the millionth time.

Jolson had gone down on one knee; Johnnie Ray had unbent a lot more, leaping about the stage as if dodging a process server and being the first man to break down and cry in public as part of his act. That was pretty bad. But what upset grownups of both sexes about Elvis' performance was that he had broken the deepest taboo of all. He used his body as rhythmically and erotically and seductively as a *woman*—that was the forbidden territory he had entered. It was not only repulsive and offensive—it was *nauseating*—the word most used. It was an attack on male dignity.

The kids, however, not yet grown into the stereotypes of gender, saw in him an exhilarating physical freedom.

Gladys only saw Elvis as her exhausted son, whose skin had taken on a deathly pallor from overwork and lack of sleep and daylight. Moreover, during that whole year she saw him briefly, five or six times at the most, and then he was off again into a kind of life where his airplanes made forced landings (this happened twice); where, besides the danger of being mobbed by the girls, there was the added danger of being beaten up by their irate boyfriends; where police protection was standard; and where most of the time her only connection with him was a telephone that sometimes didn't ring.

By September Gladys was telling an interviewer that of over a thousand letters Elvis received a week at Audubon Drive, half of them were addressed directly to her and Vernon, a good sprinkling came from parents certain Elvis was rousing juvenile delinquency to new and horrifying heights. The mildest charge hurled against him was that he was obscene. "Those things hurt," was the way Gladys understated it. But she had a deeper anxiety. "Although he's grown better all the time, everything he undertakes he keeps at it. That frightens me because he burns himself up."

Gladys' feelings were becoming not unlike those of the young bullfighter's mother whose classic response to her son's profession is that what is applause and excitement for the public, is for her nothing but grief and sorrow. And however much the young bullfighter tries to re-assure her that there is nothing to worry about and that she must keep calm (Elvis' precise words to Gladys), the mother knows there is nothing to do but stay at home and wait for news.

A further worry for Gladys was that Elvis' sleepwalking had started up again, requiring that Elvis be protected privately as well as publicly. Gladys' sister Levalle's children, Junior and Gene Smith, now accompanied Elvis everywhere, along with Elvis' high school friend Red West and rockabilly singer Cliff Gleaves. These formed the beginning of an entourage that would grow and change and which included Lamar Fike, Sonny West, and Dave Hebler, some of whom would later betray him, performing their tasks, to paraphrase Oscar Wilde, with all the added bitterness of old friends. It was to these buddies and relatives—and to Parker—that Gladys never quite entrusted her son.

In August, as we have seen Parker's first contract with Elvis Presley clearly included Hank Snow as a partner. But in November, when Parker bought Elvis' contract from Sam Phillips for $30,000—plus $5,000 for Elvis' back royalties with money provided by Hill and Range who, with $15,000 out of that sum, would have all the publishing rights to Elvis' songs—Parker alone negotiated the contract (with a percentage to Neal to whom Elvis was still under contract). And when Parker then sold that contract to RCA, there was no mention of Hank Snow or his "Jamboree Attractions" in the deal. How did Snow, who had boosted Elvis so actively to both RCA and Hill and Range, get finessed out of his expected fifty-fifty share in Elvis?

According to Gabe Tucker, Parker used the following approach: After the Jacksonville riot he suggested to Snow that they both put everything they earned, *including Snow's RCA royalties*, towards buying Elvis' con-tract from Sam. As Parker predicted, Snow flatly refused to let go of his royalties. And although for Snow this changed nothing in his declared willingness to join Parker in the buying of Elvis, Parker was able, after the deal had been concluded, to answer Hank's "Well, Colonel! I hear we've signed the kid!" with, "Uh, no, that isn't exactly the way it hap-pened. You didn't seem to want any part of it from the beginning" (basing that remark on Hank's refusal to put up his RCA royalties). "I have signed him. You don't figure in it at all." So Sam had the money, Parker had the contract, Hill and Range had publishing rights, and Hank had nothing.

Parker's so-called Snowmen's League must have had an especially dis-agreeable meaning for Hank, having been so thoroughly snowed under by it himself.

After November 15, when Elvis was signed to record for RCA, Parker signed two contracts. One was with Bob Neal, which designated that he would still co-act as Elvis' manager with Parker until March 15, 1956. This contract is full of complicated percentage swappings, but at the end of the day what is clear is that for the next five months Elvis was paying Neal fifteen percent of his earnings as per his original contract with him, as well as twenty-five percent of his earnings to Parker. The other one was with Elvis on November 21, 1955.

"When Elvis became twenty-one years of age, he signed another agreement with Parker on March 26, 1956. In that agreement Elvis and Parker ratified their agreement of November 21, 1955, and Elvis hired Parker for twenty-five percent of his earnings as his sole and exclusive advisor, personal representative, and manager."

"This agreement did not have a terminate date," adds the guardian *ad litem* report which is quoted in the above paragraph. Sometimes what is *not* in a contract can be as important as what is. And what was omitted from this contract would prevent any artist who has taken sound legal advice from ever signing it. An agreement without a terminating date can, of course go on. And on. And on.

It is impossible to get anyone who has ever worked with Parker to assess how much he actually *enjoyed* Elvis' music—if at all. And it is downright amazing how these close co-workers seem to assume they are answering the question by launching into some anecdote which proves how cleverly Parker promoted his client. Freddy Bienstock said: "The Colonel was very sharp. The schemes he would dream up, right down to the last detail. Like booking Elvis into a very small theater or moviehouse and then keeping the box office closed until he could photograph the lines of people waiting to get in. He was full of those ideas." This forces one to deduce for oneself that Parker's attitude towards Elvis' songs must have been like his stated attitude towards Elvis' films, "All they're good for is to make money." If this is true, can we begrudge him the sums of cash he piled up against these assaults to his sensitivity?

According to Hal Wallis the contract he arranged with Parker for Elvis' film services in April 1956 was a nonexclusive three-picture deal—$100,000 for the first, $150,000 for the second, and $200,000 for the third. According to most newspapers, it was a seven-year, one-picture-a-year, nonexclusive contract. Take your choice. In any case Elvis, "this genius—and genius he was," as Wallis emphatically refers to him in his autobiography *Starmaker*, was to do nine films of him. Viewing most of these soggy travelogues that Wallis chose for his "genius," films so far below the standard of most of Wallis' other ventures, one longs to grip him by the lapels, shake him, and snarl, "So *this* is the way you treat your geniuses!" But to what purpose? The old Starmaker has already come up with his answer: "[Elvis] very much needed the balance and strength of his practical straight-thinking mentor. He [the Colonel] is a shrewd, clever businessman and a supersalesman. I admire and respect him very much. We are good friends to this day." But of Elvis, says the Starmaker, "We didn't mix socially. I was not invited to his home, nor did he come to mine." This sounds like Elvis' way of saying he would work for Wallis, make money for Wallis—but he would not break bread with him.

The screen test Elvis made for Wallis in April was a scene opposite the actor Frank Faylen with Elvis as a young man just starting out in life and Faylen his father holding him back. This was a primal scene all right, and a very clever one for Wallis to have chosen. If a strong reaction was what he wanted to get out of Elvis, he had hit on just the right psychological element to bring it out. Wallis was also about to film *The Rainmaker* with Burt Lancaster and Katharine Hepburn. There was a part in it for a young boy in opposition to his family, and there seemed to be some confusion as to whether this would or would not be Elvis' first movie. People have often speculated about how it might have changed his life to have experienced actors like Hepburn and Lancaster take an interest in him at the beginning of his movie making, showing him the unwisdom of the Colonel and his carny approach to his film career. Had he done that film, it is speculated, the Colonel might have ended as only an amusing footnote in Elvis' biography.

Realistically, one wonders if this would have happened. How likely would Lancaster have been to agree to appear in a film "supported" by a teenage idol who regularly turned this public into screaming maenads? Besides—*don't teach your grandmother to suck eggs!*—Wallis was one of the old-school producers who had been around a long time. He would have been quick to realize that audiences who came to see Hepburn and Lancaster would not be the ones who came to see Elvis, and vice versa. Elvis instead made his debut at Fox in a film originally called *The Reno Brothers*, a Civil War story. Interestingly, his leading lady was Debra Paget who was already associated with Elvis in the public's mind because they had recently appeared on the same "Milton Berle Show." They even had a little gag together in which Debra hurled herself at Elvis like any teenage fan. This short had provoked the noisiest press attacks on Elvis to date. Countered Elvis: "They can talk about me but they don't say anything about Debra Paget in the same show getting up there half-dressed shaking her tail feathers all over the stage." Seen in this light, Elvis and Debra made a lot of dollars and sense in box-office terms. It also makes nonsense of the idea that Wallis would allow his hottest and most expensive new property to turn up in any old film that happened to be ready to shoot at the time. It is obvious that a very great deal of thought and money had gone into exactly how and with whom Elvis should first be presented to the moviegoing public.

In the beginning of August, 1956, at a Fox sound studio in a room full of aspirants waiting to do their screen tests, Maureen Stapleton, in Holly-wood for the first time and for the same reason, was waiting with her four-year-old son, Danny. "Elvis was there, too," she recalls. "He must have been going to record 'Love Me Tender': It was around that date. Anyway, he had his guitar. I was doubled over, gripping my stomach with an attack of nerves. Suddenly there he was bending over me asking, 'Is there anything wrong, ma'am?' I said I was going to take a screen test and couldn't get my stomach to stop churning. And if I wasn't surprised enough already, he said, 'I feel that way every day of my life, ma'am.' Then they called him in to do his song. My turn was next. When he came out, instead of leaving he came up to me and said, 'Don't worry about your kid, ma'am, I'll sit with him and look after him. Go on now. Don't worry. He'll be all right with me, ma'am.' I couldn't believe it: There had to be dozens of other people in the room still waiting who could have looked after Danny. When I came out of my test, there they were, the two of them. Danny was totally absorbed. Elvis was showing him how to play his guitar." When Maureen thanked Elvis, he said, "That's all right, ma'am, and good luck, ma'am." Then he went to the door and opened it. The roar from the fans outside came rolling into the room, shaking the rafters. Elvis turned to Maureen, smiled and said again, "Good luck, ma'am." And went out into the din.

Love Me Tender—always referred to as a "low-budget hoss-opera"—was nothing of the sort. It had a budget of $1,500,000—no small amount in those days. The settings, buildings, landscapes, and costumes, down to the last torn Confederate uniform, reek of the kind of research that costs money.

Elvis must have gotten a certain amount of quiet amusement from the *Love Me Tender* sets: the pretty farm-house they lived in, so nicely and authentically done up with period frills and period wallpaper and good early American furniture and good early American brass beds and fertile early American lands to plough. Home had never been like that, even back in the 1860s.

The situation begins briskly enough when the older Reno brothers, Vance, Brett, and Ray, first having robbed a Union depot, return home after the Civil War to discover that Cathy (Debra Paget), whom Vance had hoped to marry, has married his younger brother Clint (Elvis) who thought Vance was dead. After this promising beginning, it all becomes increasingly confused. Clint attempts to kill Vance but is himself killed. End of picture—or so the studio thought....

The picture's shooting schedule began late in August. It was to be called *The Reno Brothers* but then Elvis' song "Love Me Tender"—the melody taken from an old Civil War song "Aura Lee"—had been released and was so popular that it became the film's title.

The filming was due to be completed by September 26, when Elvis was to return with Gladys and Vernon to Tupelo for a special Elvis Presley Day and to sing, eleven years after his previous appearance, at the Mississippi-Alabama Fair. This time he would be accompanied by the Tupelo *Daily Journal*'s headline: 20,000 PERSONS, MOSTLY SCREAMING TEENAGERS, WELCOME PRESLEY HOME. NATIONAL GUARDS JOIN 40 HIGHWAY PATROLMEN AND LOCAL OFFICERS IN HOLDING BACK HYSTERICAL GIRLS. MANY FAINT IN THRONG. The article read:

For twenty thousand screaming fans it was Heartbreak Hotel all over again Wednesday, when Elvis Presley came home to the Fair. And this time he didn't have to climb a fence to get in.

National Guardsmen called out for the night performance had their hands full of hysterical teenage girls who fought the cordon of men thrown around the stage. Dozens scratched, pulled hair, and shoved for a desperate chance to touch the hip-slinging Presley, who managed to stay out of reach.

The native-son rock and roll idol arrived amid wailing sirens in a white Lincoln Continental and turned an already gaudy fair into shrieking pandemonium....

After clearing welcome facilities for the local boy who made good, gyrating Elvis and his guitar launched into his matinee performance before a roaring mob of some five thousand. More than 40 highway patrolmen and city police circled the five-foot stage, built to keep eager fans at a safe distance.

Once Elvis got too close to his tearful, hysterical admirers and they tore the silver buttons from a blue velvet shirt sleeve. Reporters and photographers had to scramble up on the stage to safety when Elvis first opened his mouth and a yelling wave of teenage girls broke for the guitar king.

One young blonde, a fourteen-year-old Adams, Tenn. girl in black toreador pants, scaled the platform and threw her arms about Elvis in the middle of one of his numbers. She was dragged screaming from the stage.

"Elvis! Elvis!" the girls shrieked, tearing their hair and sobbing hysterically. "Please! Elvis!"

Footlights were torn from their sockets as girls tried desperately to touch their idol. Several fans fainted and were nearly trampled in the melee.

Presley picked up $5,000 plus a sixty percent gate guarantee for his two performances. A long parade in his honor went on without him Wednesday morning. The risk was too great, his manager said.

Elvis' parents, the Vernon Presleys, said they thought the homecoming celebration was real nice. "We really appreciate it."

"It's all great," said Elvis. "These people are really great, and all that."

Backstage Elvis ran into his old friend Ernest Bowen of WELO.

"Well," said Elvis, "it's been a long way from where I was then to where I am now. And you're *finally* letting me on radio."

"That was the truth," Bowen now admits. "I would get all the Elvis records but I didn't play them for a long time. They were race music— *and then some.* Tupelo was a very conservative town. It wouldn't have stood for it. Not till they had reached such popularity through the rest of the States did I play them."

Although Elvis thought he had finished *Love Me Tender*, he had to make a special trip on October 28 to a sound studio at 157 East 69th Street in New York, where he was to shoot a new ending. Word had traveled like wildfire across the country that in the original version of the movie, which was to have its premiere in November, Elvis... died! Not since Dickens was preparing Little Nell for a similar fate had fans' protests been so strenuous. "For all that's known," reported a newspaper in a gentle attempt to forewarn fans of the worst, "Elvis' emoting for a 'live' ending may still come to naught since a spokesman for the studio would only say, 'The new scene will be studied before a decision is made if Elvis lives or dies at the end.' As it turned out, he died, but his ghostly apparition reappeared in the upper right-hand corner of the last frame singing "Love Me Tender." The teenagers cried. And so did Gladys.

If Elvis as an actor seems more at home with the rural surroundings of *Love Me Tender* than with the other actors, and if the technique of reaction shots and integrating himself into a scene with more than two people had obviously yet to be mastered, the truthful eye of the camera revealed an extremely appealing, extremely willing young boy with an inner and outer radiance. In short, to use the Spanish term, he was *muy simpático*.

That was Elvis the actor. Elvis the singer was something else. In his musical numbers—when he gets hold of a good song—a curious thing happens. The whole tempo of the film changes. It is as if an entire new technical staff steps in along with a different cameraman; as if they had gotten rid of the stand-in and turned the real Elvis loose. The engagingly accessible amateur vanishes: The incomparable professional presents his awesome credentials. One is totally under the spell of a royal fluency. This magical switch is most obvious in his barn-raising song, the tear-up "Poor Boy." At the end of that number anyone who had not already seen how inseparable his driving body language was from the rhythm and melody he poured out of it would now at last know what all the fuss was about.

It was during this first stay in Hollywood that Parker must have realized fully the difficulties he might have in hanging on to Elvis. A whole set of real dangers not found on the road or in recording or television studios suddenly presented itself. Up till now Elvis had worked with his musicians, played with his entourage, made love with willing fans who crossed his path, and all was well. But in Hollywood Elvis was making *other* friends—his peers. They were the "young rebel" actors who saw themselves as carrying aloft the torch James Dean had dropped a year before when he died—Nick Adams, Natalie Wood, Russ Tamblyn, and his then-wife Venetia Stevenson, Dennis Hopper, Sal Mineo. These were Method-influenced youngsters intent on bucking the system and doing what would later be called "their own thing," which always included motor-cycles. More mature actresses, like Jean Simmons (who later named one of her horses after Elvis) and Shelley Winters, were immediately struck by his sense of humor as well as his beauty. Of the Natalie Wood/Elvis romance, which looked like the usual press/agent hype, Shelley has these insistent, if unexpected, words to say: "I knew them both very well at the time. Natalie and Elvis were *deeply* in love." She concludes no less assertively, "And if they had been allowed to marry, *none* of the rest of it would have happened!" Shelley Winters, as is known from her recent book about her long career in Hollywood, has not missed much. So perhaps one should pause to consider these two young people, dead before their time. If Elvis and Natalie had gone ahead and married, the course of Elvis' life would certainly have been altered.

When writer meets writer, having dispensed with pleasantries and flatteries, they quickly get down to shop talk: agents and percentages and publishers—briefly, those staples upon which their continuing careers depend. When actor meets actor it is no different. The sophisticated youngsters befriending Elvis would be holding similar discussions. Questions would be asked, like "How much does your agent or manager get?"— and comparisons made. Elvis would soon learn that twenty-five percent was not the norm, especially since it was *in addition* to the ten percent the William Morris office was getting as his agent; that neither was a too-flamboyant manager the norm—he detracted from his client—and, worst of all, that Parker's whole carny approach was downright old-fashioned and demeaning. In this way were the seeds of doubt being planted in Elvis' mind.

Parker's solution to these threatening outside influences was clever. Of all Elvis' new friends, Nick Adams, by background and temperament the most insecure, was also his closest. By 1963 Adams was an impressive enough actor to earn an Oscar nomination and star in the popular TV series "The Rebel;" but back in the fifties, he was a brash struggling young actor with a background of poverty equal to Elvis'. His main scheme to further his career was to hitch his wagon to a star, the first being James Dean, about whose friendship he was noisily boastful but who did help him to get several parts. This made it easy for Parker to suggest that Nick be invited to join Elvis' growing entourage of paid companions, and for Nick to accept. Nick, as a paid companion, would, of course, have been readily accessible to Parker (following Adams' hiring, there appeared a newspaper item stating that Nick and Parker were writing a book on Elvis together). As master manipulator, Parker was in a position to use Nick to counteract subversion. And keep a check on Elvis' movements. For the rest, Parker continued to make sure that Elvis' original entourage—composed of cousins, former Humes High or Memphis contemporaries, and his (Parker's) own brother-in-law Bitsy Mott—vigilantly kept their ranks closed and actively discouraged newcomers.

But Parker had another problem at least as pressing. And for that, May Mann's *The Private Elvis* has the following interesting information:

The Mafia, alert to moneymaking record kings, decided to dip into the country music field. They decided to dip into a piece of "the Presley action." They'd had no trouble buying percentages of new singers. With their controls in the pop-music world and jukeboxes they could make or break young singers. "How about this new freak Elvis?"

Colonel Parker wasn't selling Elvis in any percentages. "Cut up my boy? I should say not!" He ignored the Mafia's offers and later on their warnings. No one was going to muscle in on his boy. Elvis was becoming so sensationally big worldwide, "the dark-suit boys" decided not to press the action. The powerful Mafia, for once, was forced by the sheer spotlight of Elvis' popularity to lay off!

While Elvis was filming *Love Me Tender*, another picture was also getting under way at the same studio, called *The Girl Can't Help It*. It was a slick, expensively mounted comedy that would be billed as "the first rock movie in color." It starred Tom Ewell as an agent on the skids, Edmond O'Brien as a "comic" gangster, Jayne Mansfield as a grotesque parody of Marilyn Monroe, and as guest artists the newest and best rock stars: Fats Domino, Little Richard, Eddie Cochran, and Gene Vincent. Parker turned down the enormous sum they were offering for Elvis to do a guest slot in it. In this case he was absolutely right. It would have reduced Elvis' status to one of the many instead of the only. He had, after all, already been dubbed "The King."

Another good reason for turning it down was the film itself, which exposed to everyone, for the price of admission, how the rackets had taken over the jukeboxes and were infiltrating the record industry. The film opens with a clip from an old newsreel—Fiorello La Guardia, New York's famous crime-busting mayor of the thirties and forties, is seen, ax in hand, smashing the illegal, mob-controlled slot machines.

The main thrust of the story showed how these same gangsters— thwarted, jailed, and deported—returned after the war to America and moved from slots to jukes into the music racket. In one scene the jukebox war reaches its peak. Now we see the muscle men smashing the old jukeboxes in drugstores, eateries, and saloons and replacing them with their own new ones. While this is taking place, the films' background music changes from swing (legit) to rock (Mafia). There is another scene where Ewell, as an agent peddling a song, pushes his way into a music publisher's office to find it run by his boss's hood rival. Throughout the picture, rock's close association with the old Mafiosi is constantly being reiterated—it even ends with O'Brien in prison stripes singing his own comic rock song, a plaint about doing hard labor breaking rocks in jail.

The Girl Can't Help It began as a short story by Garson Kanin, which he then expanded into the Broadway musical *Do Re Mi*, from which this film was an adaptation. As in *Born Yesterday*, whose basic plot dealt with corruption in Washington, Kanin's technique was to deal with the serious theme of large-scale corruption in a comic way, but the message was always there. *The Girl Can't Help It* offers as good an answer as any to what has baffled a whole generation of older popular-music buffs, namely how rock 'n' roll became associated with violence and crime while the equally vigorous dance beats of boogie-woogie and the jitterbug had been looked upon in their time as harmless teenage outlets. To most of the older dance fans it must have seemed that musicians had simply taken either of two turns at Glenn Miller's *Tuxedo Junction*: the wrong one to undanceable bebop and cool jazz, or the right one to danceable rock 'n' roll.

No one has hesitated to pin the spread of petty crime and hard drugs on the Mafia. But for the Mafia to succeed, must not the ground first be made fertile? If the "new" teenage music—their very own music—could be presented as enticingly violent and crime-oriented, it could be counted on to widen the generation gap and to pit children against parents with more ferocity at every level.

The Mafia may have given out to their syndicate that "in union there is strength," but "divide and conquer" was their strategy in setting generation against generation. That way you sold a hell of a lot more records. Division had already started with the proliferation and popularity of the dirty comics and crime comics. For a brief moment "Reds under the bed" moved over for "porn under the pillows," and a Senate investigation on juvenile delinquency was kicked off by the publication of *Seduction of the Innocent*, psychiatrist Frederic Wertham's polemic against these comics.

When the crime comics themselves were actually examined by the Senate subcommittee, like today's scrutiny of video nasties, they gave the committeemen a considerable jolt. Blood, gore, kinky sex, and violence gloated out of every shocking page with particular emphasis on a vast variety of human torture methods vividly pictured—such as the adolescent girl being held down while a needle-sharp chisel begins gouging out her tear-filled eyeball.

Although all attempts to tie up organized crime with these comics on their publication and distribution, as well as their subject matter, met with no success, Dr. Wertham's book did go so far as to prove that some distributors were not above using strong-arm tactics on certain newsdealers:

Actually these small dealers [who objected to selling crime or dirty comics] live in fear and do not want their names revealed. For example, I received a petition signed by six people, sent to me in the mistaken belief that I had some influence. "We are taking the liberty of writing to you, as my friends and I have a problem which we do not know how to attack. The subject matter of the problem is such that we cannot take it to our ministers, as it is a delicate subject and one which we know has to be corrected at its source.... Our druggist says that he is dictated to in the matter of buying magazines for the reading public. He wished to dispose of some comic books, the tone of which he did not like, but was told that unless he bought all that the publishers offer he could not buy the magazines he wished. In a free country why does this have to be? Who is doing the dictating?... I would like to ask, What is happening?... We cannot stand by and see this happen. ... Please don't use our names...."

To quote an old Mafia phrase, "Sounds like the old-time action, all right." And later on in his book Dr. Wertham comes right out with another equally interesting piece of information—his sources being the children he himself interviewed: "... when unscrupulous adults seduce and use children for sexual and criminal activities, they... shower the child with the ordinary crime comic books. In this way children have been softened up by adults for the numbers game, the protection racket, drug addiction, child prostitution (female and male)...."

Though the senatorial investigation of these comics did not result in the government imposing any censorship, it did alert the mothers of America to what their kids were reading. This resulted in what might be called the first feminist postwar stand—only then it was known as purse string power. Bridge clubs turned overnight into vigilante committees and took to the streets pressuring newsdealers not to sell what they found offensive. This caused the major publishers of the comic book industry to band together quickly and create (rather like the Hays Office and the Motion Picture Production Code in films) a Comic Code Authority and a seal of approval without which no comic could be sold. Their goal was simply to protect the crime comic industry but many companies ceased publication shortly after the code came into effect.

This, according to crime comic lovers, was because the survivors now ground under the oppressive heel of the Comic Code Authority simply lost their enthusiasm and with it, the wild free soaring imagination which had given this medium some pretty stunning moments. Though Dr. Wertham was rewarded for his prying into a matter dear to the hearts of so many children by being mercilessly scapegoated and satirized in *Mad* magazine as "Dr. Worthless," he was not the only writer on this subject. In his book Dr. Wertham refers to an essay by Richard B. Gehman, "From Deadwood Dick to Superman," which dealt with the cynicism of the editors behind these crime comics. This same writer, Gehman, in *Elvis Presley: Hero or Heel*, refers to the December 1956 issue of the magazine *Tip-Off*—an article titled "How Racketeers Tried to Silence Elvis Presley"—and states that the article contained "information on how the Mob threatened to reveal Elvis Presley as a $100-a-day dope-user."

The fact that no other mention of the above can be found in any other publication during this touchy time, when the anti-Elvis groundswell was gathering strength in lengthy newspaper editorials, indicate that no amount of further investigation could produce any truth behind the Mafia smear and that the Mafia was indeed bent on harassing Elvis with a view to cutting themselves in on him.

SEVENTEEN

The Decline of Gladys

Ask any of Gladys' acquaintances—the ones originally from East Tupelo who continued to see her from time to time and who noted her rapid decline, while they watched her son become the most famous boy in the world—the short pertinent question, "What killed Gladys?" And the answer, equally short and made no less shocking for being delivered with the same flatness of tone, will be, "Elvis, of course."

Lillian, from a much closer vantage point, concurs. "After Elvis became famous," she says, "Gladys was never happy another day. Only when he'd come back, the little he could, to be with her in Memphis, then she'd be all right for a spell. But the further along he got, the more she worried. And after he went to Hollywood and then was on the road all the time in between doing pictures and she didn't hardly get to see him at all because he never got to come home much, you know—she never had peace no more. That's right, girl. She *never* had peace no more."

It is only when it is all spread out in front of one—the events leading up to Gladys' death, those events occurring not month by month, but week by week, often day after day from August 1956 to August 1958, that the pieces of the puzzle begin to fit together. It becomes possible to see the reasons for the strange but rapid deterioration of a mother to whom her son would have fervently hoped to have supplied only one happy occupation: that of thinking up ever more delightful new prayers to be answered now that the old ones had been so astonishingly fulfilled.

Gladys' situation was not entirely unique: The surprised mother of the *enfant terrible* who is adored and abhorred by the public in equal parts—

254

that has happened before. A good many other mothers of sons, who overnight have gained a notoriety along with their fame, have been made confused and uncomfortable by having the spotlight spilling over onto them—though none, it might be argued, with such a blindingly bright glare. What other world figure over twenty-one can one imagine finding himself engaged in the following exchange with a journalist that took place in Vancouver as late as 1957:

Q. How are your mum and dad? Where are they now?
A. They're in Memphis. They're at home. I talked to them this afternoon.
Q. Well, how do they feel about you being on the road all that time? I mean, doesn't it bother them you being away all the time? Wouldn't they like to see their son once in a while?
A. Well, it's my life, you know, and they don't say too much about it.
Q. They accept it, in other words?
A. Yes.

The fans had bought the whole package; father and mother (especially) as well as son. To lay siege to the Presley home, to somehow climb over the iron gates and get inside it, to be in Gladys' presence and be shown around his house by her, to have her fill the cups, bought especially for the occasion, with water from Elvis' bathroom taps or be given Kleenex by her to collect the golden dust from one of his cars was, for the idolators, the next best thing to being with Elvis himself. That summer of 1956 it really made no difference that he was not at home. Gladys was kept busy day and night answering the doorbell, sometimes as late as three in the morning.

It is difficult to abandon the theory that Gladys' strength of character which had done so much to shape Elvis' destiny should, now that its mission was accomplished, find its disciplines and resources disappearing. For along with the disappearance of all those battles against the old familiar kinds of adversity came the disappearance of her positive side, laying her open to all her weaknesses and allowing her relentless absorption in the physical safety of her grown son to take possession of her so much so that her health suffered.

Was she reacting body and soul to a fathomless hurt now that Elvis no longer needed her in the old and necessary way? Or now that her son was spectacularly launched, had implacable nature deemed her life's worth over? Certainly that wide-eyed, childlike look of excitement and anticipation in the portrait she and Vernon had given Elvis will not be seen again, and from now on the photographs will catch her as she clearly feels: fed up, put upon, even disapproving, and with a look in her eye as if seeing beyond...to what? That baby smile peeks out rarely, and only when Elvis' arm is reassuringly about her or when he is holding her hand.

But there was still that other side of her character: the pink Cadillacs, fresh-cut flowers, pretty trinkets, sybaritic side of the woman who always yearned for the good things in life and who at the very beginning of Elvis' career had been thrilled with them. And yet, though she could now buy all the clothes she had ever dreamed of having to make herself as attractive as she had ever dreamed of being (and proudly showed off all the new things she had to Lillian), she was often seen in public wearing the same dress over and over again.

To turn from these considerations of the enemy within Gladys and concentrate on the enemy without: What *was* actually happening to her son out there in the real world? Those events that came tumbling down on his head in such rapid succession—would not even the most level-headed mother in the world have had trouble dealing with them, much less being able to assess whether they would turn out good or bad?

In the beginning Gladys would judge events as good or bad merely by whether they meant Elvis would be home afterwards. But now his home-comings merely meant the stepping up of the fans' activities around their house, with Elvis interminably bargaining with them that if they'd just be patient and hold on he'd come out again, sign autographs, and kiss them. His homecomings, of course, were always *supposed* to be secret, but somehow the Colonel managed to tip off the fans and the press as to his whereabouts so that any chance of privacy was rendered non-existent.

The son Gladys saw so briefly was even more exhausted and pale than before. He was overexcited, his nerves were stretched thin. He slept all day and could only go out late at night after hours to hire the amusement park or the moviehouse to entertain himself and his growing number of friends, hangers-on and the handpicked assortment of young girls. The nights he spent at home he spent talking feverishly till dawn with Gladys about this other world—which she would never be part of, never understand—while ceaselessly wolfing down the mashed bananas, peanut butter, and bacon sandwiches she made him. What upset her most in these long exchanges was how ignorant she felt. How could she begin to advise him on things about which she knew nothing? Her role had been so totally usurped by the strange Colonel. It was he who had created this gulf between her and her son. It was he who was keeping Elvis away from her and putting him on this killing schedule. Over and over Gladys would beg Elvis to slow down. Who was this Colonel, who wasn't really a Colonel, anyway?

"Gladys didn't like the Colonel one bit," says Lillian, "didn't like the way he looked, his manner, or anything about him. She was polite when he came to the house but that was all. We used to wonder about that Colonel. He didn't look like our kind of people: Sometimes when he'd come round he'd wear that hat, you know the one with the big curly brim, but it didn't look right somehow. He didn't act like our kind of people neither. He'd come busting into the house and never had a smile for anyone, never made a joke or passed the time of day. Never so much as nodded at any of us who was there. He was all business, always in a hurry—dashing, dashing all over the place, making money, dashing like he was going to grab it right out of the air. I don't know how much Gladys ever said to Elvis about what she felt about the Colonel. I think he pretty much knew. No one could have done for Elvis what the Colonel did, no one in the world, but it didn't make her like him any better."

Nevertheless, it is not unlikely that what Elvis publicly allowed himself to quote Gladys as saying—"if you don't slow down you won't live to thirty"—concealed her much more direct protests in him in private. These hurried visits home that Elvis paid to Gladys left them both unhappy at each other's unhappiness and frustration. Whereas before the two had been in complete accord, loving, admiring, and desiring the same things, she was now beginning to feel a hatred for them and a hatred even for his success. And that, most of all, was what she had to keep hidden from him and caused her mental confusion and the resurgence of her never very deeply hidden morbidity.

About all his good news, all the big things about to happen that Elvis announced to her on the telephone, she would experience a familiar stab of fear. Then, for his sake trying to swallow it, she would try to express her pleasure. Certainly in many cases she was right about events that came tumbling down upon Elvis' head singly or in battalions—those events that had a way of beginning well and ending in disaster. Often, and this made for more confusion, they would be at the same time both triumphs and disasters.

Those events in August 1956, for instance. Already Elvis had been away from home so long, had only stopped over for a brief few days on July the Fourth to do a concert in Memphis and then he was gone again, this time for preproduction plans on his first film and to record his first song for it, "Love Me Tender."

Then came his Florida concerts. The ones in Tampa provoked only a mini-riot which focused specifically on his new Lincoln Continental. The kids had broken into the garage, stolen his gas cap, and some of his cigarette lighters. But as a tolerant Elvis explained to interviewer Bob

Hopper, the fault really lay with the garage, and not with his fans.

However, when he was in Jacksonville again, the scene of the riots of the previous year, he found the civic leaders waiting for him. A juvenile court judge had warrants prepared that he threatened to sign if Elvis repeated the "spectacle" of his earlier visit. Though still protesting, "I don't do no dirty body movements," Elvis, the humorist, chose his own way of communicating with his audience that night. Whenever he knew they felt the wiggle or whirl demanded of him by the music, he indicated it by merely whirling his index finger. The kids caught on and promptly went as wild as if it were the real thing and the concert ended in a triumph. Though Elvis was actually rushed to the hospital after his last performance, said to be suffering from nervous exhaustion, he was back at the hotel the next morning at 6 A.M., telling his cousin Gene Smith how the nurses were pawing and puckering at him so much he couldn't get any sleep.

Then came Sunday. It seems that a Baptist minister in the area had got the bright idea of calling in the press and its photographers to attend a meeting he was holding in which, after denouncing Elvis from the pulpit as having "achieved a new low in spiritual degeneracy," he ordered the teenagers of his parish "to pray for Elvis' soul and his recovery to good." *Life* magazine came out soon after with a picture of the minister, Bible in one hand, Elvis poster in the other, accompanied by a large photographic spread of rows of teenage girls in various postures in abandonment to prayer which, in fact, strikingly resembled photographs of their postures while listening to Elvis in concert. The only difference lay in their faces. When watching Elvis they smiled seraphically, when praying they frowned with gloom. It was funny, really—if one was able to look at it that way. Gladys could not. She was a genuinely religious woman. She had gone often in the past to her own church for help and sustenance and had received it. And now some Baptist preacher in Florida was telling his flock, telling the whole world really, to pray for her son's soul as if he had sold it to the Devil. Every time she went out shopping there was that copy of *Life* with that awful picture in it, staring from every rack in every drugstore she passed.

The extent to which this event hurt not only Gladys but also Elvis was apparent in the way it turned up months afterwards in an interview he gave to Louella Parsons on the *Life* spread. It is obvious it was still rankling when he said, "I feel the preacher was just looking for publicity because I'm on top now. I belong to the First Assembly of God Church and have gone to church since I could walk. My mother was very upset about this article because it hit at my religion and I had to telephone her not to worry about it."

To digress for a moment—1956 was an election year and throughout that summer it is interesting to note in various interviews Elvis making it clear that he was against the draft; it was news to him that Uncle Sam had already sent him a greeting; he hoped whoever was elected would cut out the draft law; and that he was a Democrat for Adlai Stevenson. The pro-Stevenson quote the *New York Daily News* attributed to him that September reads as follows: "I'm strictly for Stevenson. I don't dig the intellectual bit but I'm telling you, man, he knows the most." Does this sound like our Elvis? Or did he pick it up in Beale Street?

After the dismaying repercussions of that concert in Jacksonsville, Elvis returned directly to Hollywood to shoot *Love Me Tender* and appear on his first "Ed Sullivan show," hosted by Charles Laughton, on September 9. It was the first of the three "Ed Sullivan Shows" he was to do, and he sang "Love Me Tender" as he was to do on the other two shows, but never again would he sing it like this. He sings the first bar, the audience screams, and he stares—first the impact of the ever-fresh surprise and delight (they *like* me) at their pleasure and then a smile of such radiance, of such unalloyed happiness that your instinct is to reach out for some device that will freeze the frame. Then the thought seems to come through so clearly that you are reading it: Shall I rock it, or shall I sing it straight?— a man in total control not only of his audience but also of his musicians. And then he sings it straight, subdued and tender, making the audience come to *him*—a very different Elvis from the one on the "Steve Allen Show" three months before in the harness of white tie and tails and the humiliation of having Steve Allen smirkingly present him with a roll that looks exactly like a large roll of toilet paper with, says Allen, the "signatures of eight thousand fans." With the audience on his side Elvis simply looks at Steve as if to say, "It's all right, I've been made a worse fool of in my life," and after he patted the basset hound he is about to sing "Hound Dog" to, he wiped his hands on his trousers as if to wipe away Steve Allen, the dog, and the whole show.

Then he was calling up his mama excitedly with good news: Tupelo's hero was to return in style. Elvis was to sing again at the Mississippi-Alabama Fair on September 26, but this time it was to be Elvis Presley Day. And there would be a special parade down Main Street and the mayor and even the Mississippi governor would be present. Gladys herself made the blue velvet blouse with puffed sleeves and rhinestone buttons he wore for the occasion and for herself chose a round-necked brocade dress. Around her neck she wore a locket with a photograph of Elvis. From then on, this dress became a mainstay of her wardrobe, turning up again and again on dressy occasions. With the fairground stands overflowing, with girls fighting the police cordon to leap on stage, with Elvis' friend Nick Adams suddenly grabbing the microphone to announce, "I was a friend of James Dean," and with the jostling crowds who had traveled to Tupelo overnight for the occasion, Gladys, on the whole, did not look too happy. In only one photograph, with Elvis' arms round both his parents, is she relaxed into a smile. And she had one curiously grim reaction to the event, which she told a friend from Memphis about: "It made me feel bad," she said, "to go back there like that and remember how poor we was." Seeing that in the future all her remembrances of how poor they were would be phrased by the wish that they could just go back to being poor again, one wonders if their return to Tupelo that day did not revive in her the darkest and most difficult patch in the Presley lives.

Vernon's reaction was quite different—tie loosened, hat on the back of his head, good ole boy and glad-hander—he was having the time of his life. But what stunned his old buddy, James Cannon, was watching him dip into his pocket at the gate and pull out, instead of his entrance tickets, two one-hundred-dollar bills for admission. Cannon was probably watching the first and last example of such impetuous extravagance on the part of Elvis' father.

When Elvis received his check for his performance he endorsed it and gave it back to the city. This was to become the beginning of a fund that Elvis would donate to the building of an Elvis Presley Youth Center to be constructed on the fourteen acres of hills just behind his birthplace. When Elvis returned to the fair to sing again a year later it was for a benefit, with the box-office proceedings going toward the realization of this project.

It was an undertaking dear not only to Elvis' but also to Vernon's heart. Vernon even had stationery specially printed for correspondence relating to it—and this he would not see as an extravagance but a necessity. Its logo, on both the envelopes and the writing paper, features a guitar-shaped swimming pool over the flowingly scripted words, "Gratefully yours, Elvis." Its list of sponsors included James Savery, president of the Mississippi-Alabama Fair, Hal Wallis and Colonel Parker, as well as Elvis and Vernon. The conditions according to which the Center was to be financed, already touched on in an earlier chapter, are interesting enough to elaborate on. None of the money Elvis made in Tupelo for his two benefit performances in 1956 and 1957 would go toward the *purchase* of the actual land. The city itself would buy this land from its owners, one of whom was Orville Bean. Only then would the rest of the money Elvis had raised go to the development of the center. Not to be forgotten was the rider to the city's special purchase of the lot on Berry Street which the Presleys had lost due to Orville Bean's foreclosing: Vernon's revenge.

Unquestionably a demonstration of the "Elvis touch" was the grandiosity of the original plans for the center. They included, besides the guitar-shaped swimming pool with the diving board on the bridge of the guitar, a day-camp area, a picnic area, a comfort station, two horseshoe pitching courts, a croquet ground, a shuffleboard area, a preschool-age wading pool and swings, a badminton court, football field, tennis courts, and bathhouse. What was actually built in the sixties was far more modest: a baseball field, tennis courts, a comfort station, and a youth center building. But forever unpardonable to Elvis was what he envisioned as its special glory, the guitar-shaped swimming pool which emerged as a plain old everyday *rectangular* one. The money had run out—so said the officials. Vernon felt otherwise. "Every time he came to Tupelo," says James Cannon, "he'd start in about the pool. He was sure the funds for the center were being used for some other purpose by the city. You couldn't argue about the difficulty of building on that site or rising cost—he stayed unconvinced."

After the first Elvis Presley Day in Tupelo was over and the Presleys returned to Memphis, Gladys looked forward to having Elvis back home for the promised few weeks of peace. It was not to be. Some four days later, they learned through both the newspapers and a lawyer that a suit was being slapped on Elvis for having a photographer snap him playfully putting his head on a girl's shoulder in an all-night restaurant. To assuage the affronted girl's embarrassment was going to cost Elvis $42,500, the lawyer informed him. Elvis settled for $5,500 to keep the peace.

October 18 proved to be another publicly eventful day in Elvis' life. Elvis had walloped a Memphis gas-station attendant, one Ed Hopper, in the eye. A week later when both parties landed in court (and in the newspapers) the story came out: Elvis had stopped at a gas station to fill up his car, got stuck signing autographs and, according to witnesses, didn't start swinging at Hopper until he had hit Elvis on the back of his head and ordered him to keep moving. The judge cleared Elvis of the charge. The gas station fired Hopper. Elvis urged the manager to give Hopper his job back.

On October 19, the very day after the fracas, Elvis was some four hundred miles away, giving his all at the Cotton Bowl in Dallas for thirty-two thousand fans. And the day after that he appeared in Waco.

On October 24 *Variety* ran a front-page banner headline: ELVIS A MIL-LIONAIRE IN ONE YEAR, over the following paragraph:

Controversy has always meant cash in show business and the latest proof is Elvis Presley, whose jet-propelled career will reach stratospheric heights in his first full year in the big-time with an indicated gross income of at least $1,000,000. Tally is an underestimation, based on what he has done in the first nine months of 1956....

It went on to give a breakdown of how the figure was arrived at: income from record sales, royalties, picture deals, personal appearances, and the merchandising of a line of Elvis items which included cosmetics and all manner of apparel. This information was picked up now by papers all over the world, some of which (only half-humorously) would vote him Businessman of the Year.

As one of the foreseeable results of this newly disclosed affluence, Elvis was flooded with benevolent financial requests from public charities. Would there not also have been financial demands from certain malevolent private individuals?

The next bombshell exploded three days later. The front page of *Billboard* magazine carried an item about Elvis, dateline Fort Dix, New Jersey, which purported to come straight from the army itself. It announced startlingly that Elvis would report there early that December as an army inductee. He would have his famous sideburns shaved off, it went on, and after a short basic training period was slated to join Special Services for an entertainment tour. It contained, among other bits of misinformation, one very odd sentence that has struck aficionados of Mafia codewords as useful for possible study: "High on Presley's agenda," goes the article, "is extensive dental and periodontal (gum) work." Why? Elvis' dentist in Memphis, Dr. Lester Hofman, is at a loss to explain the "gum work." He says Elvis paid great attention to having his teeth professionally cleaned, sometimes as often as once a month. He needed no gum work; was in no danger of infections. But, say informants, when the Mafia speaks of people needing gum work, it is as a warning to keep their mouths shut, do what they are told, or they will get gum "poisoning." The article stated that Elvis would be allowed to continue his TV and recording dates, probably granted an early six-week furlough to make a second film for Paramount Pictures and, before his induction, would be making a New York debut on the Paramount stage and singing on the "Ed Sullivan Show," and that the exact time of his arrival at Fort Dix would be as secret as possible, known only to a "handful of his business staff and army officials." It ends by saying that even a deliberate last-minute switch would place Private Presley in another training camp to ensure a minimum of disturbance and publicity.

What was *that* all about? In the first place the army categorically denied making this statement; it was entirely untrue. The Memphis Draft Board assured Elvis they'd had nothing to do with the article. It was true that they'd sent him a questionnaire, merely to bring his change of address and marital status up to date. Should Elvis be 1-A, there were still several hundred 1-As ahead of him. So who was the villian who had leaked the misinformation? It has been suggested that it sounded like Parker, now afraid of losing Elvis, trying to maneuver him into the army, the better to keep his hold on him. The article's facts were denied, along with the implication that he was going to get special treatment. It received enormous publicity and was followed by noisily outraged pronouncements from veterans' associations and, indeed, every other organization waiting for the chance to jump on the anti-Elvis bandwagon. But could we not detect just as easily the Mafia's fine hand at harassment in it? Or is it too fanciful to suspect the current "heavies"—the late J. Edgar Hoover and his FBI band—of planting the piece with the idea of cutting down juvenile delinquency? Elvis finally went to the Draft Board, on January 4, 1957, for a pre-induction physical to clarify his status. He was classified 1-A, and told the call would probably not come for six months to a year and that during that time he could enlist at any branch he chose.

With the appearance of the *Billboard* article, "that war thing" as Gladys called the strong possibility of Elvis being thrown into the army in two months' time, became one of her major and most incessantly growing worries. With no knowledge of world affairs or the international situation, the fact that the United States happened not to be at war in 1956 was no consolation to her. How did she know another "war thing" would not suddenly break out with Elvis in the front line? Her only reference to the danger of her son's position was what had happened to his first cousin, Junior Smith, in the Korean War. There he had gone berserk, been invalided out of the army, and hospitalized for a while in Germany, suffering a massive nervous breakdown.

October was not over yet. Their Audubon Drive neighbors, for several months now, had been making it known that they were not going to suffer silently the vexation of the strange cars and strange idolators of this "embarrassment to the community" blocking their road and wrecking havoc with their respectable lives. They brought a public nuisance suit against Elvis. Again, a judge ruled in his favor: The fans' behavior was not Elvis' responsibility. There was nothing to indicate that he was not a good householder. When it further emerged that his house was the only one on the street paid for in full, an angry Elvis proposed to buy up the rest of the houses. Neighborhood relations, understandably, remained strained.

On Sunday, October 28, Elvis was in New York for his second "Ed Sullivan Show." At 2:15 P.M., while rehearsing in the TV studio, the New York Health Commissioner arrived in person to inoculate him with the revolutionary new Salk vaccine against polio, thereby encouraging other young people to get their shots at once. Then on he went to sing "Love Me Tender" for the second time. He remained in New York to shoot the possible new ending of the movie *Love Me Tender*, taking time out on the sidewalk to sing two bars of the song into a couple of secretaries' thrilled ears.

Two more days of October for Gladys to get through. Elvis seems to have spent one of them having his hair dyed Captain Marvel Jr.–black— or Gladys-black, or Indian-black. In any case, on Halloween a jet-black-haired Elvis arrived back in Memphis in time to greet his new love, Natalie Wood, for her visit to meet his parents. Gladys to Lillian on the subject of Natalie: "I think she is a bit too fond of the boys. She didn't even finish her meal when Nick Adams and the others came over—just got up from the table and went to the next room to be with them."

Gladys was left at the end of that busy month washing the dishes of the hurriedly eaten meal she had been at such pains to prepare; her son out on the town with Natalie and his friends; herself surrounded by hostile neighbors.

EIGHTEEN

Inside Paradise

Natalie Wood stayed on till November 8, during which time there were rumors of an elopement. Then she returned to Los Angeles saying, "The romance isn't serious—not yet anyway." But it was not to be.

In contrast with hectic October (one observer noted that the Colonel seemed to be handling "his boy" on the old racetrack principle of taking a good horse and running it to death), the last months of 1956 were fairly uneventful. For the greater part of November and December, Gladys was experiencing the ineffable joy and relief of having Elvis safely back under her roof again for the longest period since it all began.

The reason for these quiet months had nothing to do with Parker. *Love Me Tender* was to have its premiere on November 15 at the Paramount Theater on Broadway with a thirty-foot cutout of Elvis and guitar above the marquee dominating Times Square. It would then open the last week of November in six hundred movie theaters across the country. Twentieth Century–Fox had insisted Elvis stay under wraps until the opening and as much as possible during its run. In those days, with moviegoing on the decline and the major studios in disarray, television was viewed as the archrival stealing their audience. Fox had already expressed its disapproval of Elvis going on the "Ed Sullivan Show" in October and would try, unsuccessfully, to stop him from appearing on it again in January. For much the same reason they were also averse to his touring. The almost ritualized riots that now seemed obligatory after an Elvis concert would, as one studio spokesman put it, simply "lessen the curiosity on the part of the saner audience sector" to seeing the film. In this connection it is notable that although the popularity of *Love Me Tender* was everything that could be desired in Middle America and the South, New York told another story. Only twelve days after its opening there, the teenagers presumably having had their fill, box office business was reported to be "uppish and downish." New York sophisticates clearly could leave him alone. This marked the beginning of the policy that would be adhered to for the rest of his film career: Elvis films were not to open in major first-run New York cinemas. Elvis was not for the carriage trade.

Being back with Gladys for this unusually long period gave Elvis time to observe her more closely. And the change he saw in her alarmed him as much as the change she had been seeing in him. He saw how easily she tired and what an effort it cost her to get around. He saw that her feet and legs were giving her even more trouble, and she had put on weight so fast she seemed to have swollen up overnight. He noticed her massaging her lower left side. She was not well. She was not at all well. Of course she had been seeing the doctor, she would reply to his urgings. He had said something about water-retention and given her some diet pills—not that they were doing any good, she noted wryly. In fact her doctor's assessment of her ailments was far less superficial than she ever let on to her son.

"Dr. Evans was looking after her at the time," says Lillian. "He wanted her to go right into the hospital for a complete check-up. But she refused to do it while Elvis was at home. He gave her rows and rows of medicine to tide her over but she never did take any."

How did Gladys keep going? If Elvis had cast his mind back to his seventeenth year, he might have recognized in Gladys symptoms similar to the ones he was seeing now in her extreme mood changes. He might have recognized them, coming home after his evening pleasures, in the sometimes giddy, giggly, excited Gladys who would burst into one of his songs (and sing it pretty near as well as Elvis himself, plenty of her friends will vigorously attest); and equally in the sometimes tearful Gladys desolately reminiscing over the high points of his childhood and the young boy all grown up and gone from her forever. Certainly for over two years now, Elvis had seen enough of drinking and drunken behavior from various fellow musicians during his tours to recognize the signs.

That he did not recognize them can be ascribed to the strong denial factor operating within him. That his mother, who had lectured him so stringently against the pitfalls of alcohol, would herself succumb to it was unthinkable: Her secret nips must have been so controlled as not to register on him.

Oddly enough, what distressed Elvis most was that Gladys had ceased to *want* things. It was that which finally made Elvis fully conscious of the depth of her unhappiness. What she had said was not entirely untrue: Some part of him had grown up and had gone away from her forever. But surely he could make it up to her. Surely he could revive her interest in life if he could only find out what to buy her that she wanted most.

And something similar was also happening to Elvis during those two months at home with his parents.

Along with his youth and his energy, a momentum fed into his system by adrenalin had kept him on the go continuously for two and a half years, but on its stopping, a fatigue and with it a sense of glut had temporarily taken its place. He began to ask himself why did he keep buying all those cars? Because nobody drove them, they just set there and got stale and their tires went down. It was great being able to get Gladys the pink Cad in September but he had no need for most of the rest of them. He'd just gone crazy.... What profiteth a man if he gain the world...? He began to feel sharply his neglect of his mother. Now when she talked to him about his health and what "they" were doing to him by burning him out, he was ready to listen. Perhaps in the signs of her mortality he saw his own.

Back in Gladys' sphere of influence they finally had a family pow-wow. What did she want? She was more able to tell him what she didn't want. She didn't want him working so hard. There was no more reason to. He was making more money than they had ever known existed, than they could ever spend in their lifetimes. Hadn't he just signed a contract with RCA for $1,000 a *week* for the next twenty years? (Though this would be instead of his five percent royalties, galloping inflation being unheard of at the time, it was seen as a lifetime's security as well as a tax relief.) And there was all that other money coming in, too, from his merchandise—the cosmetics and the clothes. And—she looked around the house crammed with furniture—and of the lamps he'd kept sending to her from every town he played in, "Why don't you just get married and settle down and open a furniture shop?" she joked. "I don't want no more of them lamps, son!" Well, what else didn't she want? She didn't want the clamoring fans on her doorstep day and night, nor the uptown neighbors who thought they were better than them. And most of all she didn't want that Colonel who, no matter what he said, was controlling all their lives—not just Elvis' career. Back in the old climate of family pow-wows, a lot of things finally got talked out; and finally got decided.

It had tickled Elvis to see the picturesque farmhouse surrounded by acres of fertile land that was supposed to be his family homestead in *Love Me Tender*. But during the month he had spent on the movie lot, both its interiors and exteriors had seemed strangely real to him. They had in fact kindled an image in his mind that found a corresponding spark in his parents'. Was not the ultimate in happiness, especially for Gladys the country girl—the ancestral dream that had driven folk like the Mansells, the Smiths, the Hoods, and the Presleys to America six generations before—a farm? A big farmhouse with acres of rolling lands surrounded by barns, house dogs, chickens, and hogs (we can assume there was nothing Vernon had not learned in his past about hogs), maybe later cattle and horses. But the barn would house Cadillacs and the house would contain every luxurious modern convenience that had ever lightened women's work and eased their comfort.

As far back as September 23, with the completion of his role in *Love Me Tender*, Elvis had called his parents especially to spring on them this idea of buying a big farm. To Vernon he even mentioned the precise sum he was in the market for—$100,000.

When they talked it over again Elvis was quick to see the positive effect it had on Gladys. A farm on the outskirts of Memphis. A farm she herself would choose for them. Yes, that was what she wanted above everything—a place in the country so beautiful and so full of things to do and see that Elvis could not help but spend most of his time there. Gladys, floating off in her dreams, saw it all; he would do the movies once or twice a year, and his recordings along with them, and the rest of the time he'd be home. That was the only right way for their kind of people to live. And so it was decided. A place big enough—tradition was rigid about this—so their kinfolk, the Presley and Smith uncles, aunts and cousins, could find refuge—provided, Vernon was quick to point out, they were willing to carry out such tasks for the farm and the family's maintenance as they arose. Just as thrilling to her was that the decision had been reached without first having to ask permission of the Colonel.

Elvis confessed to his parents that his Hollywood friends had been far from complimentary about the Colonel—not only them but people like Dewey Phillips were always kidding him about his "keeper"—and Elvis himself had come to resent reading in the papers all the time about the old man (as Elvis saw Parker from the very beginning) taking credit for discovering him, for creating him. It irked him to read of Parker as his "handler" and being "largely owned" by him. Sure he owed him a lot but that didn't give him the right to own him.

This started Vernon wondering if Elvis, with his agent Abe Lastfogel of William Morris—who everyone knew was the best—taking ten percent of his earnings, and being under contract to Hal Wallis who with his reputation as a starmaker could be trusted to steer his career right, had not outgrown the carny Parker. Shouldn't the Colonel be relegated to handling only the concert tours? Any way you looked at it, that twenty-five percent he was taking regularly from Elvis was just too big a piece of the pie.

Vernon, as business manager of Elvis' personal fortune, was now a man of consequence, a man whose custom was sought by bank managers, tax accountants, investors, and tradesmen of every sort—and, of course, legal advisers. Had one of them at some time put a word in his ear about the Colonel's contracts, pointing out that they might be able to prove his percentage was unusually high? It might, they all agreed, be worth looking into.

Meanwhile the date for Elvis' first film with Hal Wallis whose title, *Lonesome Cowboy*, had been shifted to *Something for the Girls* before ending up as *Loving You*, had been scheduled to start shooting on January 21, 1957. This time the Presleys decided that Vernon and Gladys would come out to Hollywood and watch him make the picture. Beneath the highly publicized nature of a treat in store for Elvis' small-town parents to see their son in the heady, glamorous surroundings of Hollywood would lie a more serious purpose, for Gladys especially. She was confident that in the month spent in Hollywood she would be able to familiarize herself with his problems there and, once more, be able to offer him useful advice.

Yet during all the hopeful and optimistic conversations they held together, individually their moods fluctuated. They tried not to let each other see their recurring doubts, but in their hearts there were always moments of foreboding that the rollercoaster Elvis was on—for however long a ride—might always be controlled by the Colonel at the switch.

A week or so before Christmas a visitor from Hollywood called upon Elvis. He was the screenwriter Hal Kanter. Hal Wallis had bought *Lonesome Cowboy*, a story in *Good Housekeeping* by Mary Agnes Thompson, in August and had commissioned Kanter to adapt the screenplay, from which little finally remained of the original story other than a song with that title. Although the script had already been roughed out, Wallis felt Kanter needed to get to know the real thing and see him in action. The fact that Kanter was a southerner too, from Savannah, Georgia, would be a plus. The visit, therefore, was carefully planned to coincide with Elvis' one public appearance that month: a "Louisiana Hayride" concert held at Shreveport's Youth Center.

What Kanter discovered about Elvis during his stay, talking to him, driving to Shreveport with him, watching him at the concert, above all, skillfully drawing him out about his life, was not at all, one senses, what he had been prepared for. What he discovered was neither a callow young show-off made arrogant and cocky by success nor an ignorant hillbilly unexpectedly swept to the crest by some silly new music fad.

Some of what he discovered about Elvis inspired the article he wrote for *Variety*, and the rest went into the revised script of *Loving You*.

That article, dated January 9, 1957, began "The young man with the ancient eyes and the child's mouth, a body as loose and unadorned and as unpredictable as a whip...." This description, incidentally, was thought sufficient identification: Elvis is never once mentioned by name. Though Kanter has him waking from the nightmare of poverty to find the brilliant sun of fame suddenly burst in his eyes, a tristful and melancholic note is nevertheless soon established. For the first time in print the thorns are to be seen in the bed of roses. More than just reporting a happening, Kanter had picked up Elvis' mood that December:

In the eye of the hurricane the young man took it all with unnatural good grace and humility. Certainly he was enjoying himself: He was enjoying the himself he read about, the himself people stormed to see, the glamorous, exciting, romantic, soul-stirring himself that evoked a strange magic on audiences, whipping them into a frenzy of appreciation no entertainer in his time had been able to match.

But after a year, there were no more clothes to buy; there was no more good food to be wanted; there was no room for more Cadillacs or motorcycles; the home appliances were all bought and paid for; the future was assured; Mom and Dad had nothing left to desire, for they had all they could ever use....

After giving the exhibition of public mass hysteria and the tidal wave of adoration caused by Elvis' performance at the "Louisiana Hayride" their due, Kanter ends by recounting an event, small, quiet and banal, but which under the circumstances lands with a shock and leaves a taste of irony and pathos:

The rear door of the auditorium flies open and the young man, dripping wet, dives headlong into the back seat of the patrol car. The door slams.

Back in the alley, more cops whisk the young man through the kitchen, into the service elevator, and up to his floor. En route along the hall, other police join the entourage to form a bodyguard. Not a moment too soon.

Inside the room, the young man falls exhausted on his bed.

Slowly he peels off his shirt, wipes his back with a towel. He stares at the ceiling in silence.

Now he has a decision to make. He'll take his time about making it, because it's the only thing left he has to do tonight; the only thing left he can do. He can't go out for a walk. He can't go drop dimes in a jukebox and drum his fingers on an oilclothed tabletop. He can't press his nose against the windows of haberdasheries. He can't take the top down on any of the Cadillacs and cruise in the moonlight. He can't ask a girl to dance or share a Coke with him. He can't do any of the things he'd really like to do. He has to stay in that hotel room, a prisoner until early morning when he can escape again.

The night stretches ahead, long and bleak. There is only one decision to make: What will he order for dinner?

The title of the article is "Inside Paradise."

Christmas at Audubon Drive was the Presleys' first really bountiful one. Together, Elvis and Gladys carefully selected the tree and made sure it was the very last word in such things: branches of white nylon pine needles hung with bright red ornaments made brilliant with strings of fairy lights. And banked high around it, exquisitely wrapped presents, and presents, and presents, for all. Especially, of course, for Elvis. Well, it beat those Christmases on welfare not so many years ago. Gladys even donned a little Santa Claus cap for the fun of it and wore her dressy brocade frock.

Finally, on January 4, as already noted, Elvis reported in a blaze of publicity to Kennedy Veterans Hospital in Memphis for a pre-induction physical. The Army had not asked him to—he went apparently for his own sake, wanting to clear up his status, which was 1-A. The only new thing to say about this is that as long as the draft was compulsory, which it would be for a very long time, nothing and no one could have kept him out. As Elvis could not help but know with the spotlight on him since he'd turned twenty-one, it was only a matter of time. The most significant remark he made on the subject was after he had just gotten out of the army. He was glad to get it over with, he said, and not have it hanging over him for the rest of his life, as, he might have added, it had hung over Frank Sinatra's and Errol Flynn's lives.

As far as the army was concerned, far from being eager to snatch him up, it regarded the whole thing as a big headache—especially if he were assigned to Special Services. The *New York World-Telegram* on February 12, 1957, said:

An army spokesman said today it would let Elvis keep on singing only if it decided that would help recruiting.

Our studies indicate that his basic appeal is to young girls. Our interest in that field is somewhat limited. We have not been able to obtain affirmative evidence that he has a similar appeal to young males, particularly in the age groups we seek to reach.

The theory is that the Colonel had as many worries over Elvis being drafted as Elvis himself. Not just because it meant Elvis' career being cut off at a crucial point, but because it most certainly meant being stationed for two whole years out of the States and in a foreign country where the Colonel, without a passport, could not follow. God knows what could happen to their relationship during that time. No, the army was not Parker's answer to keeping his grip on Elvis, though, as was his genius, he would exploit it for all it was worth. He would have to think up something of a far more permanent nature.

Those two months at the end of 1956, which Parker had spent practically without sight of "his boy" caused him plenty of concern. It was curious that one of the things that upset him the most—curious unless you study his background and psychology—was that Elvis was suddenly being taken seriously as an artist.

The doyen of music critics, John C. Wilson of the *New York Times*, pronounced: "The overwhelming nature of the arrival of Elvis Presley as a national figure has tended to overshadow what should be the heart of the matter—his music." He then went on to praise it as a "valid aspect of American folk music" and concluded that Elvis "actually has an incisive if somewhat distinct talent."

Burl Ives, doyen of folk singers, was less stately in his enthusiasm: "I think he's the greatest. I bought his latest records long before he was popular. This boy's got a lot of voltage."

Louis Armstrong, doyen of jazz musicians, announced both his and Elvis' desire to cut a record together: "Elvis has said, 'I want to make one with Satch.' You'd be surprised," added Armstrong, "what we could do together."

And Dr. Frederic Wertham, doyen of crime comic killers, astonished everyone by declaring himself pro-Presley. "They [teenagers] always have to have some kind of hero. That is a good thing and they certainly could have worse heroes than Presley."

While Fred Sparks of the *New York World-Telegram* delivered this appreciation of him: "He is of the soil himself, like Will Rogers or Carl Sandburg." He expressed a wish that Elvis, who he pointed out was very competent in such matters, would punch a few of his more vicious critics on the nose and suggested he might also sue several for eight or ten million dollars. "Most of the songs he has singlehandedly rocketed to the hit parade stratosphere are also the happy hollerings of Americana."

If things went on that way, Parker reasoned, and the curiosity of the "saner audience sector" was not lessened but in fact stimulated and they accepted Elvis not as the Great American Freak or the Great American Joke but—as Al Lomax, musicologist-folklore expert said—the man historians would look upon as the first to liberate American music from European tradition; Elvis would slip right through his claws, fly away like Captain Marvel, Jr., and land in areas which could show Parker up badly. In the future, refusing to allow Elvis to sing for the president, to sing with the Boston Pops Orchestra, to sing at Carnegie Hall—to keep him as a low cultural taste—was not based on an outrageous originality but on the plain old fear of losing him.

"Do you consider the Colonel deliberately isolated Elvis?" was one of the questions asked of Jean Aberbach whose acquaintance with Parker went back to when Parker was managing Eddy Arnold and the former was Arnold's music publisher. The answer was short—an unequivocal yes.

"The quickest way to lose your job was to even say hello to Elvis on the set or in the Colonel's office," says Sandy Lieberson, now president of Goldcrest Films, who had been one of the bright young mailroom boys William Morris loaned out to Parker.

It applied to everyone. Songwriters like Leiber and Stoller were never able to penetrate the Memphis Mafia to get to Elvis. Doc Pommus and Otis Blackwell, two others of his best songwriters, never even got to meet him. Scotty Moore and Bill Black, who had been so crucial to the creation of Elvis' sound, were phased out. Directors like Don Siegel and Philip Dunne were never able to break through what Dunne called in Elizabethan terms "the fart-catchers" surrounding him to establish a rapport beyond what was called for in the immediate day's shooting.

Finally one can imagine how Hal Kanter's article in *Variety* affected Parker appearing as it did after the long vacation, so to speak. The deep and genuine human emotion that came through in the writing, along with the news that Wallis had chosen Kanter also to direct *Loving You*, the danger of Elvis forming a friendship not with flighty young actors but with an older and cleverer man—not only talented but experienced in the ways of Hollywood—meant only one thing: another pernicious influence.

And now the further news that Elvis really intended buying a farm, his very manner when he told him—*told* him—didn't ask him! And on top of *that* the fact that Vernon and Gladys were coming out to Hollywood and staying there a month. Another solid month of Elvis under Gladys' influence. What kind of trouble might she make then? You never knew with mothers. In the beginning of that year the Colonel didn't need his spies to tell him what was up. The signs were all here in Elvis' independent attitude and coldness towards him.

Parker lashed himself into a fury. Wasn't it always that way? The more you did for these people, the more of your life's blood you put into scheming and planning for them day and night; the more exposure you got them; the more money *you* got for them—the less gratitude you got.

Every time. It had happened with Eddy Arnold. But he was not going to let it happen again. For a while now he'd had an ace up his sleeve. He was gambling on it to win the game for keeps.

He had already ruminated a good deal about how to play this one most effectively. It required the imaginative thinking and careful planning he was more than equal to. It also required him to manipulate some powerful people; but they were just the ones most eager to fall in with Elvis' acknowledged owner. Only time was of essence.

He was beginning to enjoy this; it used all his special talents. He would book a tour of one-night stands for Elvis starting in Chicago on March 27, 1957, and ending on April 6. This would leave Elvis with no more than three weeks back in Memphis in March after the completion of *Loving You* and keep his mind thoroughly diverted. And this time Parker himself would go on the tour to keep an eye on Elvis.

Elvis began by going to New York on January 6 where he did his final show for Ed Sullivan—the only one in which the cameras cut him off at the waist. Significantly, Elvis sang "Peace in the Valley." But Eisenhower had been re-elected and brinkmanship was the order of the day. January 12 found Elvis in California where some record sessions occupied him for a week. On January 21 he began the film *Loving You*.

Now that Elvis was gone, which no doubt exacerbated the discomfort of her ailments, Gladys was persuaded to go into the hospital for a two-week check-up. "She'd gotten all bloated again," says Lillian, "she had lots wrong with her insides and her metabolism wasn't right. Dr. Evans told me later he found she had gallstones. He wanted her to have an operation right then but she wouldn't hear of it. She was set on going to Hollywood. They put her on a diet and when she left the hospital she had the prettiest little figure you ever saw."

This added to her incentive to do Elvis proud and she went to a leading department store in Memphis to get herself fully outfitted for the occasion. Nattily attired, she and Vernon boarded the train for Los Angeles on February 12.

When Gladys and Vernon returned to Memphis she was still in high good spirits. If she'd had any worries about the way Elvis would be treated on the set of *Loving You* (he had confided to her about previous slights and ridicules and how certain people tried to put things over on him during *Love Me Tender*) her visit there put her mind at rest. In fact she told Lillian, "The way they kowtowed to him was a scream. There's always someone around especially to comb his hair for him and someone else to help him get dressed and there was one man with nothing else to do except knock on his door and ask him if he was *ready* to work!" Gladys got a big kick out of that. But one aspect of moviemaking disillusioned her sadly. "You know those big crowd scenes you're always seeing in the picture shows where you think there's thousands of people? Well, it isn't true. They never had more than twenty people there at the time and they can just make it look like a lot more."

Elvis would be returning soon, and meanwhile he had given her the go-ahead to start farm-hunting seriously. Of course now that they had gone on that tour of the movie stars' homes their conception of a farm had altered into something far grander.

Costing exactly the $100,000 Elvis had mentioned in September to Vernon, their newer and grander dream became a reality. The mansion which his parents had immediately coveted on sight was quickly approved of by Elvis on arrival.

Graceland, a neo-antebellum mansion built in 1939 out of Mississippi fieldstone, had at the time thirteen rooms and overlooked some thirteen acres of rolling land. It was in Whitehaven, a suburb of Memphis, but the area was then still undeveloped and the atmosphere was rural rather than suburban. The large house had been untenanted for some time. Its insides lying in ruins would give the Presleys unimaginable pleasure to reconstruct and redecorate it, making it closer to their heart's desire.

Loving You, chosen for the film's title from among the seven songs Elvis sings in it, sums up its whole approach to him. The film was angled so that in the end neither the actors on the screen nor the audiences in the theaters could help but come out loving Elvis. In no other film he made would he be so sympathetically treated. In no other story would his own story—the naive but talented youngster from a poor background relentlessly manipulated by publicity gimmicks into being regarded first a freak, then a force of evil by a clever manager (disguised in the silken body of Lizabeth Scott)—be presented so credibly. Also—probably just as important to Elvis-lovers or the merely Elvis-curious—in no other film would his performance of his musical numbers be as near to those he had performed in all his early road show days.

Lizabeth Scott, managing a small country band, is stuck in a small southern town with her ex-husband (Wendell Corey), a saxophone player who has skidded from the big time into a ragged country and western touring show, and comes across Deke Rivers (Elvis), a good-looking truck driver who, she notes, has an original way with a song. When she sees how he goes over with the teenage girls, she has him fired from his job and on his way to goose up the show. His rise to fame predicated on her publicity gimmicks, of which he is unaware, interspliced with her buttering him up so that he falls for her, eventually backfires. Disgusted, he takes off, she in pursuit. After a lot of last-minute explaining all around— Lizabeth was only exploiting Elvis in order to help Wendell back on his feet but in the process has recognized Elvis' real genius and gets him on a network TV show to prove it, Elvis finds he is really not in love with her anyway but with the ingenue, and all ends well. What saved pictures like this in the fifties was that the art of snappy repartee snappily delivered was still alive and well:

> Corey: "I wish I were twins. I'd have somebody to blame for this." Or:
> Lizabeth to Corey: "All you need is the right gimmick."
> Corey: "Gimmick? What gimmick? I play a quarter tone sharp and stamp my foot, what else do I have to do?" Or:
> Lizabeth to Corey (apologetically, after they realize they are not going to be paid): "Oh, Tex, I didn't know this would happen. I thought the governor was a *real* crook, that he would get somewhere."

Elvis plays himself at his most beguiling, with a tentative balance between ignorance and innocence, wistfulness and desolation. He displays an impressively fast mood swing from happy modesty to punk violence which culminates in a free-for-all in a jukebox joint. Such was the full range of the acting gifts his personal image-makers thought they had discerned. Strangely they overlooked his strongest one: his flair for comedy. But Elvis the singer, "so *exactly* the right shape for what he's doing—like Fred Astaire," as one person put it, is as mesmerizing on one level as Astaire, and on the other hand as Brando—or, as Elvis.

Only one more thing has to be said about it. Whether viewed in hindsight or at the time, whether or not we have learned that Hal Kanter rewrote the script after getting to know Elvis, it is as unambiguously clear, then as now, that Kanter's main message to Elvis was: Beware your manager's corny, carny publicity gimmicks taking you over. How, one wonders, did Parker take that?

On February 27, towards the end of all that loving, at a press conference at his home in Madison, Tennessee, the Colonel played his ace. Elvis' next film, he announced, would be made at MGM and for it he would receive $250,000 plus fifty percent of all profits. No, the film's title had not yet been set.

NINETEEN

Jailhouse Rock

We have all read enough books about the movie industry and seen enough of those Hollywood exposé movies Hollywood seems to relish making about itself not to need reminding of the lengths the old studio moguls would go, via their highly organized spy systems, to keep tabs on their stars. These included having a thorough knowledge of their past and present activities, and thorough knowledge as well of any embarrassing skeletons that might be rattling in the family closet. Prying into their private lives, the bosses would no doubt argue, was essential not only to keep their precious temperamental assets obediently in line but to "protect" them from blackmail—blackmail from the outside, that is. This would have been especially necessary in the fifties when a very nasty scandal sheet, *Confidential*, was in full bloom. *Confidential* was the kind of magazine characterized by the Kefauver Report as "scandal sheets which posed as legitimate but whose operations verged on blackmail." Kenneth Anger, in the first edition of *Hollywood Babylon*, explained how it worked. When *Confidential* uncovered information of a particularly compromising nature it was customary for its related agency, Hollywood Research, to visit the star involved with a copy of the story in hand. It was then suggested to the victim that the original might be purchased. Yet even stars who had given in to this blackmail several times in succession, when they finally refused, had to see their story in this tabloid's headlines. The worrying thing about the magazine was that it contained as much fact as fable.

It is not difficult to imagine that the Colonel, for the same reasons as the moguls, would see to it that he was privy to whatever secrets lurked in the Presleys' past: Vernon Presley was, after all, not a hundred miles from the damaging truth that had sent him to Parchman when he was twenty-two and had been out for only eighteen years. How would certain people, easily identifying Vernon both by his name and his face from the many photographs of the Presleys so often seen in newspapers, react toward his incredible family good fortune? When newspapers at the time were printing headlines such as ELVIS A MILLIONAIRE IN ONE YEAR, what sort of desire would this stir up in certain members in (or outside) society to share a bit of his good fortune?

There is always a point in biography where the biographer must try to reach a sound conclusion about facts which by their very nature depend on secrecy and concealment. How long the Colonel himself had known about Vernon's jail sentence and how he had found out creates just such a predicament. However, by examining all the available material—of which there is a great deal—it is possible to produce a sufficient amount of evidence to make an interpretation of how he used this information and the far-reaching effects it had on not only Elvis but his mother and father.

The very fact that Vernon's jail sentence was kept secret not only from the public but also from someone as close to Vernon as his second wife, Dee, during Elvis' lifetime, yet was headlined soon after his death in both the *Midnite Globe* ("The Darkest Secret in the Presley Closet") and the *Examiner* makes it safe to conclude that whatever pressures had been exerted when Elvis was alive to prevent the disclosure had been stopped when they were no longer deemed necessary.

One is reminded how often in the harsh unsparing plays of Ibsen, ghosts in the form of past indiscretions or transgressions turn up to confront the fragile happiness and shaky respectability of pillars of society and threaten to smash their doll's houses with social and public exposure.

Just so must this story now take its grim Ibsenesque turn. It is quite possible some fellow convict who served time with Vernon had suddenly shown up on Audubon Drive with a view to causing trouble. But there were many other paths that would lead to the courthouse in Tupelo where, buried in the records, was the information that on May 5, 1938, not only Vernon but Gladys' brother Travis Smith were sentenced on the charge of forgery to serve a term of three years in the state penitentiary. It only required knowing where to look.

It is inconceivable that Vernon, if being threatened with exposure,

would have been able to deal with a problem of this magnitude himself
and not have sought "help" from the Colonel. One says "a problem of this
magnitude" because suppose his secret did get out? The truth of the
matter, one might think, was surely not such as to damn a man for life;
or, more to the point, to damn the *son* of the man for life. Unless, of
course, the son was the notorious, morally suspect Elvis Presley. In any
case, who would believe the truth of the pettiness of the crime when
weighed against the evidence of the stiffness of the sentence? And we
must not forget that it involved not only Elvis' father but his uncle as
well. If some Americans had been persuaded to forgive the "uninhibit-
edness" of their new young erotic star because of his background of a
pious, God-fearing, close-knit, loving family, there would now be many
more who would find it impossible to forgive him for springing from a
family with such prison records. What a field-day hypocrisy would have
dusting off those wonderful old saws: "The fruit never falls far from the
tree" and "Lie down with dogs and you get up with fleas."

Added to this, powerful factions in America were morally in a celebrity-
punishing mood. Charlie Chaplin, on his way to London, was informed
in mid-Atlantic that the U.S. Attorney General had instructed immigration
authorities to deny him a re-entry visa unless he submitted to an inquiry
of his "moral worth." And because Ingrid Bergman had gone to Italy to
live openly with Rossellini, the chief film censor in Memphis had banned
the reissue of the Tracy/Bergman film *Dr. Jekyll and Mr. Hyde*, saying:
"Nothing wrong with the picture, I just don't want Bergman showing on
Memphis screens."

Hollywood, it is important to note, was working hard to clean up Elvis'
image "along the lines of an institutional build-up to recreate the rock 'n'
roller into an influence for good: particular accent will be on 'the kids'
with an eye to the juvenile delinquency problems. There is talk of ac-
centing Presley's churchgoing family background"—this from *Variety*
under the title "Halo, Everybody, Halo: The Latest Presley Pitch."

In his previous film, *Loving You* (which, incidentally, was not released
until *Jailhouse Rock* was completed), a great effort was made to close
the generation gap. Lizabeth Scott played out the scene in a courtroom
in which she defended the right to rock 'n' roll with the Fourth of July
zeal of someone defending the U.S. Constitution, insisting that the behavior of young people should not be blamed on music and pertly reminding the members of the court that thirty years ago they were doing
the Charleston and the Black Bottom. Could they not recall the time
when people were asking each other in alarm: "Is jazz a plot of disaster?
Did jazz put the sin in syncopation?" (laughter in court). Now, she ac-

cused the court of adopting the same attitude towards rock 'n' roll because "your children use it to let off steam." Concluding her peroration, she went historically highbrow, reached across the ocean to Lafayette's homeland, and grabbing Debussy's *Afternoon of a Faun* in one hand and Stravinsky's *Rite of Spring* in the other, pointed to the riots in the streets of Paris they caused when they were first performed: "Deke [Elvis]," she patriotically exhorts in conclusion, "is being condemned without a fair hearing which he has a right to under the American Constitution." (Cheers.)

The fair hearing takes place on a national television show. After a line of his old pals have come on to testify to what a hell of a good guy he is, Lizabeth announces to the audience in ringing tones, "America, judge for yourself!" By the time Elvis, in blue jeans and looking about sixteen, has finished his rousing "Got a Lot o' Livin to Do," delivered with those old-time religion handclaps before an audience of all ages—presto! The gap is closed. Elvis is trad; Elvis is folk; Elvis is OK. Don't worry about your daughter, Mrs. Jones, Elvis *is* Americana—he's part of the goddamn scene!

With this vigorous clean-up campaign under way, why was Elvis' new film called *Jailhouse Rock*, a title so indicative of its subject matter, with this juxtaposition of "jail" and "rock" that one could easily foretell what the film's effect was going to have on "concerned" parents; rather the same effect Mel Brooks' *Producers* had hoped for when they planned their musical *Springtime for Hitler*. Specifically, outrage.

And why choose for its story one in which our young teenage idol is shown not only as a regular at the local bar where he blows his paycheck every week, but who commits manslaughter for which he is sentenced to one-to-ten years in the pen; where he is stripped to the waist and brutally flogged after a prison riot and in which he emerges as an embittered young punk whose motto is "do unto others as they would do unto you—only do it first"; and who then carves out a sensationally successful rock career by following this motto? Is this really the way to build Elvis up into an "influence for good"? In what way can this be said to accent Presley's churchgoing background?

On the surface *Jailhouse Rock* seems to be a replay of Elvis' life as *Loving You* had been. But whereas *Loving You* had been a *film rose*, this was a *film noir*; a genre of film the French describe as characterized by a stark, somber tone and pessimistic mood with sets that suggest dingy realism, lighting that emphasizes deep shadows, and accents the mood of fatalism; where the dark tones and tense nervousness are further enhanced by the bleak choreography of the action and the doom-laden composition and camera angles. To all this one could add it is also a film in which all the characters immediately react with suspicion and dislike to all the others and can count themselves lucky to be given the right time of day. Though a decade off—the true *film noir* flourished in the forties—*Jailhouse Rock* nevertheless fits the definition like a glove.

Elvis in Maliceland.

Jailhouse Rock, within its framework, was a first-rate, realistic film except for one baffling question. It required the audience to get over one enormous hurdle, one suspension of belief: Namely the basic absurdity that the young man who has killed someone and spent time in a state penitentiary for it can become, almost immediately on his emergence from jail, a sensational rock star. And one who will be given his own show on a major network, who will have his records played on all the radio stations, and who will be welcomed by Hollywood with open arms and groomed for stardom, when Elvis—who in real life had *not* killed anyone and who had *not* spent any time in the state pen—was a figure controversial enough to be banned in places all over America. Just when (to choose a few examples out of thousands) after an Elvis concert, rock 'n' roll was outlawed in Corpus Christi, Texas; just when he was banned on the air in a town in Wisconsin and someone threw a rock through the station's front window reading: "I am a teenager—play Elvis Presley or we tear up the town" (the ban stood). Just when in Bennington, Vermont (the home, incidentally, of America's most famous progressive college), the high school PTA protested against showing *Love Me Tender* on Christmas Day, explaining it was not the film they objected to, nor the screaming, "but only what Presley represents on Christmas Day." Just when, a month before he began *Jailhouse Rock*, some college students threw eggs at him at a concert in Philadelphia. ("The egg who threw those eggs will never make the Yankees," shouted Elvis). And just when Elvis was hanged in effigy in Nashville, the dummy clad in a red shirt and blue jeans and its pockets bulged with phony money, an ambulance, probably summoned by a prankster, took the dummy away to a funeral home to the delight of a crowd of several hundred.

In the beginning of Elvis' career in movies the crafty old Dogcatcher spun a line—which he made sure got maximum exposure—that he would *not* involve himself with the actual making of Elvis' films. Those producers were the experts in a field which he didn't know a damn thing about, was his modest stand—so as long as the money was right, let them get on with it. He would not interfere. The revealing two-part, four-hundred-page guardian *ad litem* report in the *Presley* v. *Parker* suit filed in the probate court of Shelby County, Tennessee, in the early eighties arrives at the exact opposite conclusion.

By Parker's refusing to have any *written* agreement with the William Morris Agency concerning Elvis' film career, "this talent agency, though top in its field, was put in the incredible position of being forced to go along with Parker's plans for Elvis whether or not they were to Elvis' artistic advantage" (guardian *ad litem*, first report). The truth was Parker had *everything* to do with Elvis' film career and with every film Elvis ever made. And if he told producers—as one so often heard—not to bother sending him the script, one realizes how unnecessary that would have been. Abe Lastfogel, Elvis' agent and Parker's close associate, would certainly be sent it as a matter of course. As Parker controlled their dealings with Elvis, it was one and the same thing. Also, from Elvis' second film on, Parker was henceforth listed on the film credits as "technical adviser."

This film credit has always given film buffs a good laugh at the thought of the wily old Colonel in there picking up some extra bread for nothing; for what technical expertise would he have about car-racing, helicopters, or speedboats, around which most of the Elvis vehicles were constructed? But just as Parker was fond of expounding on the game of the artist-manager—one of his former William Morris mailroom minions, Jan Hartman, recalls his cavalier dictum: "A good manager has to believe there are no rules or regulations; you can make up your own rules as long as you can get away with it...that's what makes a good manager"[23]—so with the title technical adviser, Parker obviously made up his own rules which, as he saw them, allowed him to keep his eye on, and his oar in, what was happening daily on an Elvis set. In 1957 *Variety* spelled it out very clearly: *"Col. Tom Parker, Presley's manager, gets credit (for* Loving You) *as Technical Adviser, and take that literally and seriously. He's an expert property developer."* (My italics.)

Now we have a new definition of Technical Adviser as pioneered by Parker; no longer an expert on molecular biology or military maneuvers in the Crimean War, a technical adviser is more like, really *most* like, a sort of executive producer. Whether or not Parker was allowed to get away with his new definition as technical adviser in all Elvis' films, there is strong contention that he had a very great deal to do with Elvis' third film, *Jailhouse Rock*. For the deeper one gets into investigating this project from start to finish, the clearer it becomes that in *Jailhouse Rock* one could find the factor one had been looking for—the factor that was the

---

[23] *Elvis: A Biography*, by Jerry Hopkins.

glue, so to speak, that kept all the other factors stuck together—and kept Elvis stuck to the Colonel.

A habit of the Colonel's which has never been explored sufficiently, though endlessly written about, was a habit which from the very beginning was as compulsive and obsessive as his gambling at the tables in Las Vegas later on: his habit of playing practical jokes.

The term "practical joke" means precisely that. It is a joke with an underlying practical purpose, a purpose which can range from a gag played on someone in order to have a lighthearted laugh at his expense, to a more serious jest arranged to place the victim at a disadvantage or humiliate him in public, to—most seriously of all—a trick which serves as a reminder or a warning to the victim.

Our practical-joking Colonel, who, according to one former minion, insisted on his delivering by hand to the Jewish producer Hal Wallis a ham wrapped in greasy paper as a Christmas gift; who, according to Gabe Tucker, insisted on serving ham to Abe Lastfogel, also Jewish—the rest of the meal invariably consisted of pickles, cheese, canned pork and beans—every time they lunched together at Parker's offices and "would watch Lastfogel's every bite" saying "Goddamn, Abe, isn't that good ham?" and who, according to Bob Finkel, executive producer of Elvis' 1968 NBC Special, sent him a case of purportedly superb champagne which, when opened, turned out to be mineral water, would hardly be able to resist the playing of his ace by having Elvis do a movie in which, just like his daddy, he's a jailbird. It must have just tickled the hell out of his sense of humor. In this connection Gabe, seemingly noting down at random what he saw when describing the hodpepodge in the Colonel's office in 1965, noticed that the paper jailhouse used in *Jailhouse Rock* "had been moved squarely into the center of the reception room when Elvis was currently making *Tickle Me*." That was another thing that was good about the joke—its lasting power.

Elvis at twenty-two not only found himself re-enacting his daddy as a jailbird, but also re-enacting Vernon's experience at Parchman *when he was exactly the same age*. A further note for students of numerical co-incidence: When Elvis' cellmate is released from jail, he makes a point of saying he served eighteen years. When Elvis was making *Jailhouse Rock*, Vernon had been out of jail for exactly eighteen years.

There were signs of Elvis' reluctance to do this film and of the tremendous strain and emotional pressure he was under while doing it— signs which manifested themselves to his friends by alternate fits of rage, despair, arrogance and withdrawal. Though the reason remained a mystery, the symptoms exhibited themselves everywhere. In an interview at the start with the *Herald Tribune* feature writer Joe Hyams, who found Elvis uncharacteristically lunching alone in his dressing room, it comes out as confusion: "I'll tell you one thing. I sometimes get lonely as hell. A lot of times I feel miserable, don't know whichaway to turn. Even though I'm surrounded with people, I get lonely and stare at the wall. I don't know whichaway to turn next."

On May 1, the first day Elvis began working on *Jailhouse Rock* ended in behavior that, for him, was without precedent. It began at a recording session and ended with Elvis walking out.

Gordon Stoker of the Jordanaires, who was taking part in the session, remembers that day starting off ordinarily enough in the morning, with Elvis at the piano singing spirituals, his usual way of warming up with all the other musicians present, the Jordanaires, plus Blackie, Scotty, and D. J. Fontana joining in.

When they broke for lunch—as Stoker described the event to Jerry Hopkins in *Elvis*—a studio official called Stoker over and told him not to join in with Elvis in the afternoon if he tried singing spirituals again. They had to get down to work, he said. It was costing the studio a fortune. Stoker continues:

So we came back from an hour-and-a-half lunch break and Elvis went right to the piano again, starting right where he left off. I had talked with Hugh and Neal and Hoyt and we didn't join him. We refused to sing along. When that happened, Elvis stopped playing and looked at us. He called me over and asked me what was happening. I told him, "Elvis, they told us not to sing spirituals. They told us we have to cut the songs for the film." That did it. Elvis blew up. He didn't make a scene. When he blew up, he blew up inside. And he walked out, taking his six or seven cronies with him. The day was canceled. Elvis didn't come back.

But Stoker was not only deeply puzzled by this mute display of temperament on Elvis' part—Elvis who, of all performers he had ever worked with, was the most cooperative, easiest, most outgoing, and most sympathetic to his fellow musicians—he was puzzled by something else: the attitude of the studio officials. As he puts it:

It was really unfortunate. What the studio didn't realize was that Elvis hadn't sung in a studio in some while and this was his way of warming up, getting in the mood... he might have done all seven songs that afternoon, or perhaps by the end of the following day. In that way he still would have finished the tracking in far less time than most singers would. They should have given Elvis his head, let him do what he wanted... Elvis knew what he was doing and knew how he worked best. His schedule and style may have been unorthodox, but apparently Elvis thought everyone understood. Certainly there were enough of the regulars there—Freddy Bienstock, Steve Sholes, the Colonel, all his own musicians and backup singers. Someone should have said something. But no one did and Elvis blew up and walked out.

Now here is a puzzle indeed. Here we have the star of the production—who is in fact the only 'name' in the film and upon whose performance the success or failure of the film depends—upset to the point of walking out.

Here, certainly, is the moment that cried out for Parker to step in and do his personal management stuff. Here was the perfect opportunity to show what a personal manager was for: to look after his client; stand by him, protect him, explain him; above all, to see that the conditions he works under are the most comfortable and the best for him. But of course the Colonel didn't. Instead, he let Elvis blow up and walk out. The changes that came over Elvis, according to Red West in *Elvis: What Happened?*, during the making of *Jailhouse Rock* were alarming. "I don't mean that he was selfish and big-headed all the time," he says of this period, "but he took to fits of anger that none of us had ever seen before. He wanted to be treated as something special; of course he was something special, but he had never demanded that special attention. He was always one of the boys. He would often share the driving on long gigs. We had shared everything, even our women."

Of equal significance is that the shooting of this film also marked the beginning of his constantly making his friend Lamar Fike (at 300 pounds a good Colonel-substitute) the butt of his less than good-natured jokes. Fike had always been the court jester but now Elvis' sharp, "Get your fat ass out of here!" or "Get your fat ass in here!" expressed real impatience with that other person of similar circumference on whom he seemed unable directly to vent his anger.

Anne Neyland, the young actress in *Jailhouse Rock* whom Elvis was dating, saw he was under a terrible strain but ascribed it to fame. In an interview for *Photoplay* she said, "These last three years he's been so used to people tearing at him wherever he goes that he's drawn-into as hell. He's so used to being alone with a few close friends and going for drives and playing records that you can't get him out of it. I think he's at a stage now where he's just given up trying to make himself a little more normal life. He's one of those people who cannot be alone. He feels he has to surround himself with close friends as a sort of protection against loneliness because you can be very lonely in a mob of strangers." It was a nice try. She only got it wrong because she lacked that vital piece of information.

Just so it would be ten years hence when Red West tried to explain

Elvis' fits of destructive violence by describing him first lighting fire to and then bulldozing "a nice neat wooden house built into the northeast corner of Graceland." The significance of that house being where Uncle Travis lived—Vernon's partner in crime—and that Vernon himself was dozing on its porch before its demolition was a connection Red could not make. Close as he was to Elvis, he also seemed to lack that vital piece of information.

Shelley Winters recalls how Elvis would often go over to her house after filming and call up his mother and complain, "I don't like what I'm doing. I don't like this film, I don't like Hollywood. I don't like the Colonel. What'll I do?" And then he would turn to Shelley after he had spoken to Gladys and say miserably, "She says do what the Colonel says." In the light of all this, there are a number of other odd things about *Jailhouse Rock* itself that merit looking into.

Although it is an MGM film—produced on the MGM lot, distributed by MGM, roaring lion and all—on closer inspection it seems to be something of a stepchild. Early in 1957 MGM's two-page announcement of forthcoming productions in *Variety* makes no mention of *Jailhouse Rock*. Moreover, it is based on an original story by Ned Young, a blacklisted writer.

Aside from using a blacklisted writer, and giving him a credit in his own name—a risky business in those days if someone wanted to cause trouble—MGM didn't then do original stories. That wasn't their style. MGM did adaptations of best-sellers, classics, and successful Broadway plays, as for example during this period, *Tea and Sympathy, Ivanhoe, Raintree County*. Moreover, when they treated best-selling novels on juvenile delinquency, as in *Somebody Up There Likes Me*, it was with clear solutions to the problem. In the case of *Blackboard Jungle*, where their portrayal of juvenile delinquency might be thought so sensational as to bury the solution, it was not allowed to be shown at the Cannes Film Festival without an explanatory—or apologetic—preface assuring viewers that most schools in the United States were "tributes to their communities."

In *Jailhouse Rock*, the reform of our hero is tacked on very fast at the very end. Only a sock in the throat from an old buddy, which threatens our young hothead's voice, makes him see the errors of his ways. But the man who delivers this therapeutic sock, Hunk Houghton, Elvis' former cellmate, is played by Mickey Shaughnessy, an odd choice, one might think, to be signed up as Elvis' *buddy* in the film. A few months before shooting *Jailhouse Rock*, *Variety* had reported on Mickey Shaughnessy's act in a nitery in Omaha. It included "forty-five minutes of taking Elvis over the hurdles."

Forty-five minutes is inordinately long for a comic to take *anyone* over the hurdles. Why have Elvis' cellmate played by an actor who obviously hates his guts? A touch of *cinéma vérité* in this *film à clef*?

As to who set up *Jailhouse Rock* in the first place, all we know is that the deal was made by studio boss Benny Thau, with Abe Lastfogel acting for Parker.

Nor does Albert Goldman's interview, in his book *Elvis*, with its producer Pandro Berman, do much to clear things up. Berman, Goldman notes, "if left to his own devices, would never have thought of making a movie with Elvis Presley. He was engrossed at the time with more important things like his production of *The Brothers Karamazov*" (which, incidentally, flopped badly). It was Berman's wife, apparently, who liked the idea of "building a film around Elvis."

Now comes the interesting part. According to Albert Goldman, when Berman asked the Colonel if he should send the script to Elvis, the Colonel said *no*. "Do you want to read it?" persisted the surprised producer. Again, the Colonel said *no*. Suspecting a trap, Berman insisted: "What *do* you want?" The Colonel, no less surprised, replied: "I don't want nothin', except to get all the music I want in the picture and have it done by my boys." Now all these surprised reactions might be enough for Berman to have remembered this incident accurately over some twenty years, but his remarks do contrast strangely with *Variety*'s reporting on the spot: "Col. Tom Parker, Presley's manager, gets credit as technical adviser, and take that literally and seriously. He's an expert property developer." Needless to say, Parker was credited as technical adviser on *Jailhouse Rock*.

Elvis had walked off the set that first day of *Jailhouse Rock*. But he walked back on the next day, and so the film began being made. What was in store for him?

It is well known that in the mid-sixties, after Elvis had completed yet another in the series of dreadful films that were his burden to bear up under, he turned to the director and said, "Hey, there were some pretty funny things in this script. I'm going to have to read it some day." He wasn't smiling; nor was he using the word "funny" to mean amusing.

There were more than some funny things in *Jailhouse Rock*, this psychodrama plus parental trauma. There were a great many and some were quite clever. For instance, in *Love Me Tender*, after "Whoa!" which Elvis says to stop his plow horses, his first *real words*, as all Elvis fanatics devoutly know, were calling out to his brothers, "Vance!" and "Brett!"

Before the great vowel shift in eighteenth-century America, the "a" sound was pronounced as "i"—as in "innything" for "anything." Like all southerners, Elvis retained the earlier pronunciation, and "Vance" in his mouth became "Vince." So that playing off the vibrations of these famous two words, we have in *Jailhouse Rock* our hero called Vince Everett. Was also the name of his guitar-playing mentor, *Hunk* Houghton, amusingly struck off his first mentor, Mississippi *Slim*?

All round the scene, where Elvis first picks up Hunk's guitar, are little Elvis revelations—both known and unknown to the public. Known: Hunk to Vince, "Don't break the guitar strings." Known: Vince, "I had an uncle who had one of these things." But, unknown until now: Hunk to Vince, "You've got no rhythm in your bones"—which is of course the echo of Mississippi Slim's constant criticism of Elvis: "Your timing's off, kid. You've got to work on your timing."

More vibrations: In jail for manslaughter, Vince's cellmate Hunk is an old-time singer who recognizes Vince's singing talent and gives him some guitar lessons. In a talent show the prison holds, which gets broadcast on television, Vince steals the show and Hunk sees to it that the warden withholds all the fan mail Vince receives. (The Colonel withholding Elvis' *black*mail?) This enables Hunk to write out a contract between the two of them in which, for fifty percent of Vince's earnings, Hunk will be his co-partner and manager.

"How come you're willing to give me half of what you make?" Vince innocently queries.

"Alone you'll be a lamb in a pack of wolves," is the answer. (The Colonel's?) Vince signs.

Out of prison after a year, and having been given his sack of fan mail by the warden, Vince goes, as directed by Hunk, to a bar called the Florita where Hunk has assured him the owner will give him a job as a singer. This is in a sleazy downtown section of somewhere in urban America. Logically it should be Nashville, but no one speaks with a southern accent—no one except Elvis and one other person.

Before Vince goes to the Florita he takes a room in a rundown hotel (Heartbreak Hotel?). The maid comes in to make up the bed. She is a nice, motherly woman with a voice so precisely Tupelo-southern it immediately alerts one.

"Where's the nearest pawn shop?" he asks her. She gives him the information pleasantly enough (she is the only person in the film whose initial reaction to a stranger is simple courtesy) and adds as a little joke, "Whatcha gonna do? Buy yourself a diamond ring?" To which Vince sarcastically snarls back as he dashes to the door, "Naw, I'm gonna go and get me a guitar and sing love songs to you!" What Elvis must have felt playing this scene, with its evocation of Gladys as nurse's aide with a pile of sheets in her arms, and his having to snap those particular lines at her in this fashion, by now must be dreadfully clear.

The plot follows Elvis' own meteoric rise closely enough and the signposts of real events in his life loom often enough—his hopelessly hayseed ideas of showing a Hollywood starlet a good time by taking her to shooting galleries, amusement parks, hamburger stands, a sightseeing bus tour of the stars' homes, and stockcar racing. Throughout the film are references to his obsession with cars and their colors; his big break having a record played on the radio before the DJ's dog food commercial (in Dewey Phillips' case it was a commercial for cat food) A movie audience must conclude they are watching the real Elvis and that, like Vince, he ruthlessly clawed his way to the top stepping on everyone in his path. When the girl to whom he "owes everything" says of him: "When they make it big they generally go through a period of modesty, but he became a heel overnight," nine-tenths of the audience will assume it is Elvis she is talking about.

And for insiders were added, for their delectation, two other little nudges: Vince, the star, along with his cars and swimming pool, is the owner of two dogs: twin basset hounds. They receive quite a play in the film— and clearly serve not only as a reminder of that grisly moment when he found himself singing "Hound Dog" to a basset on the "Steve Allen Show," but the fact that, like the dogs, he too is a twin. The other appears at one of Vince's parties. Guarding the door is a black-suited, black-shirted, white-tie Mafia-type hood with an expression of evil stupidity and twitchy hands, which calls attention to him in case we missed this bit of "authenticity." And speaking of authenticity, what is to be made of the fact that Elvis himself, during the film, was actually rushed to the Cedars of Lebanon Hospital on May 15, not two days after the actual shooting of the film began? It was reported that he had inhaled a porcelain cap from one of his front teeth and it had become lodged in a lung and was removed. The film appears rewritten to accommodate this incident, as Vince too lands in the hospital. But if it was not and Elvis' accident followed the course of the film, we are getting into rough waters indeed.

For Elvis the actor, the waters would get rougher when the film was on general release all over America beginning in late October of 1957. That many critics watched it with an affronted sense of something being slipped over on the public was clearly reflected in their reviews. Some wondered how the Motion Picture Production Code had been bypassed to allow a teenage idol to swear on the screen—"I don't know what the hell you're talking about"—or let a scene stay in that showed Elvis and Judy lying across a bed, fully clothed it's true, but neither one with the obligatory foot on the floor at the same time.

The *New York Times* reviewer gave vent to his feelings by caustically referring to it being "reverently produced by Pandro S. Berman" and then by taking its scriptwriter to task with, "For reasons best known to Guy Trosper, who wrote the script, two delightfully capable people [Mickey Shaughnessy and Judy Tyler] are forced to hang on to the hero's flying mane and ego for the entire picture."

The main scapegoat was, and had to be, Elvis. And even though the *New York Times* critic pauses to wonder if "Presley fans may not like the idea of his being the churlish egotistical wonderboy of TV and screen for a good half of the picture," in the end his hostility really breaks out with: "And in the title song, done as a convict jamboree, Elvis breaks loose with his St. Vitus speciality. Ten to one, next time he'll make it—finally getting those kneecaps turned inside out and cracking them together like coconuts. Never say die, El."

Time magazine's critic (an inveterate Elvis-hater) concludes his attack with, "For moviegoers who may not care for that personality, Presley himself offers in the film a word of consolation: 'Don't worry,' he says, 'I'll grow on you.' If he does, it will be quite a depressing job to scrape him off."

It is, of course, too easy in this new wonderful age of porn and violence for all ages to smile at the quaint notions of what critics in those days thought permissible for suggestible youth to see on the screen. But without question their pain and, in some cases, alarm was genuine. In the same issue, *Time* writes despairingly about the whopping success of *Jailhouse Rock*'s title song, whose "movie-bred lyrics ... suggest a powerful argument for penal reform ..." Well, they had a point. The Leiber and Stroller lyrics, such as:

> *Number forty-seven said to number three,*
> *'You're the cutest jailbird I ever did see.*
> *I sure would be delighted with your company.*
> *Come on and do the Jailhouse Rock with me.'*

certainly suggest realistically what happens sexually to men cooped up together for long periods of time without women. And *The New Yorker* reviewed it by *not* reviewing it. Nor was it mentioned in the magazine's immaculately complete listing of films on in town.

Taking into account Memphis' chief censor's performance in the past—

he had banned *Blackboard Jungle* from the Memphis screens with the comment, "It's the vilest picture I've seen in twenty-six years as censor"—it seemed a certainty that *Jailhouse Rock* would not have been shown in Memphis. Yet *Jailhouse Rock* was not only shown in Memphis, it had its world premiere there. Its star, however, who in the normal course of events, as with *Loving You*, would certainly have been expected—not to say obliged—to show up for this honor, was conspicuously absent. "Elvis himself is not in town," the newspapers tersely informed their readers without further elaboration. Nor was Judy Tyler there. She had been killed in an automobile crash on her honeymoon a month after the film's completion.

The only person connected with the film who did attend was the starlet Anne Neyland. When asked by the *Memphis Press-Scimitar*, "Are you sorry Elvis is not in Memphis now?" she replied, "Let's just say it's too bad he can't be here for the premiere of his own picture." Clearly she, too, had been expecting him. Yes, too bad Elvis didn't attend the Memphis premiere and put his family through that? On the contrary, it would appear he had finally put his foot down. The only possible interpretation of his absence was his decision not to further associate himself with the film.

The *Press-Scimitar*'s film critic, Edwin Howard (the same Edwin Howard who was the first person ever to interview Elvis), wrote this in his review:

The new MGM film is the first which has to be carried solely by Presley—both his previous films had name performers to help out—and he carries it easily. Whether it was worth carrying at all is open to question, however. Elvis' advisers might have thought twice before allowing the idol of teenagers to be cast as one who frequents bars, beats a man to death, and remains a pretty unsavory character until a few minutes before the fade-out. I don't recall seeing the Vince Elvis portrays ever taking a drink, but the liquor flows freely at a party in his Hollywood apartment, and he offers to "mix a blast" for a latecomer.

The film's box office history is as odd as everything else about the picture. It opened to a "saturation launch" in a thousand cities at the end of October. By December it had grossed four million dollars and was placed number fourteen in the list of most successful films in 1957, having had only two months to get there. Yet, in 1958 there is no mention of it on the box-office lists *whatsoever*. This is curious considering *Love Me Tender*, made in 1956, was listed sixth in 1957, which indicates the normal life of a successful film. *Jailhouse Rock*'s abrupt disappearance from the lists suggests that forces such as the League of Decency were at work.

But that is mainly looking at the film from the public's point of view. Beyond the shock and panic and dread caused by the unearthing, the springing back to life of their eighteen-year-old secret—this debt to society that all three Presleys had long since repaid fully and with enough interest to warrant its burial forever—what presently concerns us is the effects its use in *Jailhouse Rock* had on each of them separately and immediately and for the rest of their lives.

For Gladys there must have been a sudden flooding back of memories of that terrible year of 1938: her fight for her own and her son's survival, her fight to secure Vernon's release from prison; the long and regular biweekly trips with Elvis to Parchman; those shorter but equally painful trips to the welfare office for her "commodities"; she and her son having to be taken in by relatives when her father-in-law made it impossible for them to remain in their house on the Old Saltillo Road. And, on Vernon's release there were the frightening "action" nightmares to which the three of them were communally prone. It was all summed up in that surprising statement of Gladys' after the Mississippi-Alabama Fair in 1956. "It made me feel bad coming back here like this to remember how poor we was."

Moving day to Graceland was the first of May. The builders had worked seven days a week to get the place ready for the Presleys to move in, lock, stock, and teddy bears (the two-hundred-odd sent to Elvis by fans) for the big day. Along with stuffed animals, Vernon had also supplied the "farm" with hogs and Gladys' beloved chickens.

One day, towards the end of that month Elvis was still in Hollywood making *Jailhouse Rock*, Frank Richards (that same cousin Frank who had taken Gladys and Elvis in when Vernon was in Parchman in 1938) suddenly turned to his wife Leona and said, "Let's drive up to Memphis and go see Gladys in her fine new mansion."

"She wouldn't want to see us," demurred Leona. "She'd be ashamed of us."

Frank was philosophical. "Well, if she won't see us we can look at the house anyway. Come on, we're going." They drove to Memphis and out to Whitehaven, parked their car near Graceland, and went up to the gates. Cousin Travis was on guard. Warm greetings were exchanged. They didn't want to trouble Gladys, Leona was quick to make clear— they just happened to be in the area and thought they'd say hello. Travis telephoned up to the main house and came out of the guard hut grinning. "She'd *love* to see you," he said, opening the gates. "Come right on in."

The Richards had only planned to call on Gladys for no more than an hour. At her insistence they stayed three days. Though the decorating had merely begun, Gladys, as the awed Richards described it to their friends, was surrounded by every imaginable luxury. Maids ran the water for her bath whenever she wanted one, changed the sheets every day, and washed and ironed her clothes the minute she discarded them. There were cooks making meals for them whenever she felt like eating—didn't matter what hour. MGM had just sent a stack of publicity pictures of Elvis to Graceland. Gladys, however, seemed reluctant to give Leona one of them when she asked for it. This puzzled Leona. Was there something wrong with it, she wanted to know, should she choose another? No, Gladys replied, that wasn't it. She just didn't like them. Leona got the feeling that the reason Gladys didn't want them circulated was that she felt there was something flawed about them, though studying them closely she was at a loss to say what. Instead, Gladys gave Leona a studio portrait taken before he had started in films. And speaking of photographs, you may see many of Elvis with the Colonel, a few perhaps of Vernon with the Colonel. But you never see any of Gladys with the Colonel.

"Well," said Frank to Gladys at the end of their stay, "I guess you must be about the happiest woman in the world." "No," she replied, "You got it wrong. I'm miserable. I'm guarded. I can't go buy my own groceries. I can't go to the movies. I can't see my neighbors. I'm the most miserable woman in the world."

Later, when they heard that Gladys had a drinking problem, they reasoned that must have been why.

"Gladys was proud and happy about Elvis' success at first, "says Annie Presley, "but after they moved to Graceland she was always saying how much she wished she was back here and poor again. "They won't let me see Elvis," she would say. "They're always keeping him working somewhere or other," or "They're just tearing my boy's clothes off and we don't know if he's going to come back alive." Later, after she'd been living in Graceland, coming down to visit Annie and her family seems to have been one of the few outings she was allowed. "And now I can't even feed my chickens," she complained to them during one of the last times they saw her. "It's supposed to be bad for his image."

To everyone close to her it seemed clear that Gladys was prey to imaginary fears which were causing her to fall apart. What no one besides Elvis and Vernon knew was that some of these fears were *not* imaginary, and that at least one was all too terrifyingly real. Again, they lacked that vital piece of information.

Not even to Lillian would Gladys' pride allow her to unburden herself about the way the Colonel (with the help of those movie people who didn't care for him any except for how much money he was making them) had gone about trapping her son for good. Therefore, what Lillian observed from May on were the *effects* rather than the basic *cause* of Gladys' crumbling hold on herself.

"When they bought Graceland in March," remembers Lillian, "it meant to Gladys that she'd have Elvis around for a while and they would decorate it together and she was really looking forward to it. He wasn't supposed to make another picture till May but then it turned out he was hardly there at all—he was on tour most of the time.

"It was when they moved into Graceland for good she started to get really depressed. I was working at the Fashion Curtain Company as an inspector and she would insist that I come out to Graceland every night to stay with her. Graceland was a long way from where I lived, but she insisted. She was lonely and Vernon was always off somewhere. So I came and sat with her. And then I heard from Alberta their maid[24] that a certain beautiful blonde movie star had come by to see Graceland and Vernon was showing her around, and maybe he was getting a bit too enthusiastic or something, but Gladys and Vernon had quite a row about that.

"From about July on, Gladys just seemed to lose interest in everything. Elvis was always buying animals for them but she had no time for any of them, except the chickens and the little Boston bulldog he gave her. She was all nerves. When he was away she'd say to me, 'He was supposed to phone last night and he didn't. I know something bad's happened to him.' And she'd be sure he'd been killed. You just couldn't get her to see it didn't make sense.

"She was getting real sick. She was drinking a lot. At the end she was drinking all the time. Vodka. Where'd she get it from? Vernon—he give it to her. Just to keep her quiet. It made Elvis very unhappy to see how unhappy she was. He was very considerate of her. He didn't fly because she was afraid of airplanes. And whenever he rode that motorcycle of his, he never revved it up until he was out of her hearing."

Gladys would have been less than human if she didn't begin to berate Vernon as the cause of all their troubles. And one can't help wondering why, instead of knuckling under to all the possibilities of blackmail, he didn't just come out with a public confession. A simply phrased statement revealing the reasons for his small forgery with its disastrous and out-of-proportion punishment and there wouldn't have been a dry eye in the

---

[24] Alberta, the Presleys' black maid, had been with them from 1956 at Audubon Drive. Considered one of the family from the beginning, she was one of the earliest recipients of Elvis' gift cars, presented to her when it was discovered she had to walk a mile from the bus stop to her home.

house. But unfortunately we are not dealing with a second-act curtain but real life. And in real life Vernon was not capable of such heroics. And in fact, as the years went by, his fear of disclosure would seem, if anything, to have increased.

In only one book—*The Complete Elvis*—does Elvis express himself on the burdensome secret. It was many years later, towards the end of his life, that he talked about it to his physician, Dr. Nick. And even then the need to whitewash Vernon's misdeed and subsequent disgrace reveals not only the continual pain Elvis felt about the secret but also the continuing protectiveness he felt towards his father (his "baby") by seeing that it was kept. According to Dr. Nick, Elvis told him that the Presleys had gone without food for a couple of days and Vernon stole some food from a grocery store and got caught and went to jail for several days. Adds Dr. Nick: "Elvis made me promise that I'd never say anything about that. He said, 'Nobody knows about this. I don't want anybody ever to know this, it would really hurt my daddy if people knew.'"[25] And yet to ascribe entirely selfish reasons to Vernon's silence is probably unfair. What would you have done in the situation had your son been Elvis—is where the question perhaps should be properly left to rest. There seems no doubt that Vernon's fear that the day his secret should become public was the exact day the money had to stop hardened his parsimonious inclinations. The changes within him clearly stamped themselves on the very cast of his features which, for the rest of his life, bore an expression that can only be described as sheepish.

Hardest of all, one imagines, far worse than Gladys and Vernon's own private anguish, must have been having Elvis, the beloved son they had tried so hard to protect in every way, finally knowing for the first time the whole truth of Vernon and Travis' transgression.

Elvis had walked off the set of *Jailhouse Rock* that first day. In those hours between then and when he returned, what influenced the decision? He was young, rich, at his peak. Over and over again the love, loyalty, and sympathy of his fans had been demonstrated in the face of all the furor and fury. But there was the grave issue of family pride and of family honor, grave realities to all southerners but graver still to Elvis, whose fight for these had been so hard won. If the sins of his father were being visited on him, so be it. Vernon was his daddy; the stain on the Presley escutcheon would be hid at all costs.

25. *The Complete Elvis*, edited by Martin Torgoff (New York: Delilah Books, 1982).

TWENTY

And After

The decision reached by the powers-that-be after *Love Me Tender* was that Elvis, a twenty-one-year-old singer who had never even been in a high school play, was *not* going to be trained to be an actor. Learning acting skills, it was decided, would ruin "his natural ability." This was easily the most depressingly shortsighted and self-defeating decision ever taken about his film career.

What should have been obvious to Elvis' management was that the development of his natural *singing* abilities had been the result of a lifetime's apprenticeship to the study of its demanding craft; starting as far back as his early childhood with mentors such as Mississippi Slim, with church groups and talent contests, and, not least, as part of a singing trio with Gladys and Vernon.

What did they think was taking place with Elvis, Scotty, and Blackie all through the long recording sessions for over a year under Sam Phillips? Exactly what, in any other apprenticeship, would be called "taking lessons." How does one dismiss two years of putting this lifetime's study into practice on the road?

In the first place, the new breed of actors Elvis would be competing with were not the toughs that stemmed from the Errol Flynn/Clark Gable school, like Burt Lancaster and Kirk Douglas, but the "tenders"—Marlon Brando, Montgomery Clift, Rod Steiger, Paul Newman, Ben Gazzara, and, of course, the not-so-late James Dean. All of these had had extensive method acting training, as well as Broadway stage experience, and their impact on Hollywood created a new kind of hero (or antihero, to use the popular fifties phrase) who now held the audience in his grip; this intense, inwardly tormented young man needed actors capable of revealing an inner life—capable of digging deep enough into the psyche to come up with the raw exposure of the soul. Both within and outside the profession the most talked-of-scene in the fifties was that prime example of Method-at-its-best, the famous "I could have been a contender" scene from *On the Waterfront* between Marlon Brando and Rod Steiger.

In this climate, Method teachers from the East had gone west and were welcomed with open arms; therefore, the kind of acting training Elvis would have received, had he been allowed or even instructed to "take lessons," would only have increased his natural emotional ability. His ability to put his heart in a piece of music was not so far removed from acting—certainly Elvis acted out his songs—but unlike music, acting is at least half *reacting*—or in the jargon, "relating"—to other actors, something he never mastered.

Besides deeming it unnecessary to teach him the disciplines needed to release his emotions without the help of music, or how to get to the heart of a role, Elvis' agents and managers also apparently wished him to remain innocent of the most basic camera technique, so that even in his fourth picture, *King Creole*, we find Elvis asking Carolyn Jones before a love scene which side of her face his nose was supposed to be on when they kissed. As he put it in an interview in 1957 when asked who "helped" or "aided" him on *Loving You*, "Well, there's nobody helps you out.... As far as acting and as far as singing and all, you're on your own. Nobody tells you how to do that, you have to do it yourself." And how did he rate himself as an actor? He was frank. "Pretty bad. I mean, that's something you learn through experience," he went on hopefully. "I think maybe... I might accomplish something at it through the years..." And so he went on through the years trying to invent the wheel all by himself, while on the screen he studied Brando and Dean, hoping by osmosis to pick up the trick.

They could at least have given him an acting coach. Any number of actors have depended on coaches to discuss the script with, to help break it down, and to clarify their characterizations—in short, to help them get the most out of a part. Isn't that, after all, what it's about? The guidance of an acting coach would, without question, have helped Elvis, so eager to learn new skills, be it karate or meditation, to quicken his interest in the art of acting, which would have given him the confidence to fight for good roles. Perhaps.

As it was, the singer who could express and compress so much emotion in a song was left "being his natural self" to wander around the screen, obviously restless, bored, and off-balance and in this way supposedly satisfying his most rabid fans, if no other audience.

Out of curiosity, in the early 1960s George Cukor dropped in on the set of an Elvis picture to watch him work. He did not intend to stay more than an hour. He remained the entire day. That evening, bubbling with enthusiasm, he said that Elvis was potentially one of the most remarkable and extraordinary acting talents that he had ever seen—in a class with Marilyn Monroe, no less. "He can do *anything*," were his exact words. "He would be a dream to direct. His comedy timing is faultless!" His ardor was such that one fully expected to hear that Elvis was appearing in Cukor's next picture—a good illustration of how totally innocent one was of the workings of Hollywood.

In the fall of 1956 Tennessee Williams had been working hard on *Sweet Bird of Youth*, using a semiprofessional theater group in Miami to test out the progress of his various drafts. Hal Wallis, who had successfully produced Williams' *The Rose Tattoo* the year before, arrived on his yacht and they spent the day together. Among other topics of conversation, could not one of them have been Williams' fellow Mississippian, the new sensation, Elvis Presley, who Wallis had under contract? The evidence certainly points that way for, from Gilbert Maxwell's *Tennessee Williams and his Friends*, one learns that soon after this meeting Williams abruptly stopped working on *Sweet Bird* and instead plunged feverishly into rewriting his first play, previously called *Battle of Angels* and now renamed *Orpheus Descending*. The setting remains the same, a small town in Mississippi. But the hero (Val Xavier), previously an itinerant young writer, undergoes a complete metamorphosis and emerges as an itinerant young ... guitar player. The source of the playwright's inspiration is indisputable.

And it may be that in the intensity of his vision of Elvis as Orpheus, the innocent youth doomed by his irresistibly erotic magnetism to stir the forces of corruption to fever pitch so that they tear him to shreds— or rather, as the play has it, the sheriff's dogs tear him to shreds—Williams has conferred upon his fellow Mississippian a poetic immortality. Study, for example, the stage directions by which Val's first entrance is enhanced to highlight his arrival. A moment before, a black man has begun emitting a piercing Choctaw cry; a young woman joins in the cry; the black man "throws back his head and completes it; a series of barking sounds that rise to a high sustained note of intensity. Just then, as though the cry had brought him, Val enters the store. He is a young man who has a kind of wild beauty about him that the cry would suggest. His remarkable garment is a snakeskin jacket, mottled white, black, and gray. He carries a guitar…"[26] This entrance, though considerably different from what was then Elvis' latest gimmick of getting himself on stage—gold-suited in a white Cadillac—was perhaps not so different in impact. And Williams' snakeskin jacket gets infinitely closer to the Elvis mystique—that complex of transcendental attitudes that was developing around him—than the heavy gold suit trimmed with rhinestones (courtesy of the Colonel) Elvis soon abandoned as being impossible to work in.

Orpheus Descending opened on Broadway in March 1957 with Cliff Robertson playing Val. It is interesting that in spite of the fact that almost everything about Val and everything he has to say—"I live in corruption but I'm not corrupted. Here's why. [Holds up guitar.] My life's companion! It washes me clean like water when anything unclean has touched me…" —have such strong resonances of Elvis, and in spite of the fact that only a few months before, the thirty-foot-high cut-out of Elvis and guitar in *Love Me Tender* was looming high over Broadway, of all the six major daily newspapers New York was able to boast of in those days, only one of the reviewers, Robert Coleman of the *New York Daily Mirror*, had noticed that Val was "an itinerant Elvis Presley." Were the other five, which included critics such as Brooks Atkinson and Walter Kerr, really so much part of another culture that Elvis had not intruded upon their consciousness, although Brando and James Dean certainly had? Or did they hope, by not *naming* him, he would just go away? In referring to Val wearily as "a variation of a sex symbol we've seen quite often before," and further remarking that Cliff Robertson "does an admirable job even seeming comparatively inoffensive when equipped with a snakeskin jacket and guitar," Wolcott Gibbs in *The New Yorker* obviously wished the whole bunch would get seriously lost.

Orpheus Descending received reviews that might be described not only as mixed but mixed-up. This had a good deal to do with the play which Tennessee Williams himself characterized as "overwrought and overwritten." There are, however, in *Orpheus*, as in all Williams' early and middle work, some rich rewards: passages that explode unabashedly and magnificently purple. And of the scenes between Val and Lady Torrance (Maureen Stapleton as the lady in her middle years in an ageless predicament), Brooks Atkinson wrote that "their humorous talk, their serious talk, the simplicity of their relationship after they had come to know each other—all this Mr. Williams has written in his best style of mood and lyricism and tenderness."

[26.] *Orpheus Descending*, by Tennessee Williams, Dramatist Play Service (renewed 1967).

Rereading the play today one hears so clearly in every line of Val's the voice of Elvis. Sidney Lumet, who later directed it as a film under the title *The Fugitive Kind* with Anna Magnani and Marlon Brando, has this to say: "Tennessee had always wanted Marlon to play the part and when Marlon said yes, no one else was even considered." But then Lumet goes on:

The funny thing is—years later, when I looked at the picture, I suddenly thought of Presley.

I began to wonder what would have happened to the piece without any of Marlon's overt sensitivity or the profound implications that Marlon brings to any sentence he utters. What would it have been like if Val had had Presley's simplicity, lyricism, and rather strange otherworldly quality? There's a speech in the play that I doubt whether Presley could have handled from an acting point of view. In the speech Val talks about his mythical bird that has no legs and can therefore never come to rest and just hovers in the sky until it dies because there was no place for it to land. In content it evoked such a memory of what I felt of Presley when I watched him work; something otherworldly, *un*human (not inhuman), a kind of restless spirit that could never rest anywhere. As I say, I don't know if he could have acted it, but the speech certainly reminded me of his personal quality when he performed. And I thought how extraordinary it might have been to hear it from someone exactly like that but totally unaware of his own separation from the rest of us. Would we have filled in all of the significance of that character because Presley himself would have been totally unaware?

Though the picture got mixed reviews and is a flawed picture but a very interesting one, as I look back on it now it would have been death to have cast Presley. There's snobbism in America that gets doubly vicious about its own.

Thanks to the brilliant management of Colonel Parker and Co., neither the old guard, Cukor, nor the up-and-coming Lumet would take a chance with Elvis. That left Norman Taurog, best known as a children's director, to direct nine of Elvis' films.

Was it in order to help him "be himself" that for the most part Elvis' films continued, like *Jailhouse Rock*, to be full of biographical detail? Of *G.I. Blues* Hal Wallis admits, "I decided to take advantage of the situation and do a picture based on his real-life experiences in the army..." and of *Blue Hawaii*, "Once again we tried to parallel his own life with his screen personality." Was this their way to reach the fans subliminally or consciously? In any case, what a perfect opportunity this approach could present for the irrepressible Parker to slip in his little practical jokes in the form of messages, digs, and innuendos so that in the end, one is left with a parody rather than a parallel of Elvis.

It becomes something of a game to see Elvis' movies now and notice all the little details of his life, picked up one way or another, that have been inserted in them. And something of a surprise to realize how much they knew. Why bother to bring the actor to the Method—seems to be the reasoning, when they could just bring the Method to the actor. Excluding two documentaries of his tours, Elvis made thirty-one films. To pluck out in each and every one of them, each and every reference to his life would be encyclophilism run mad, when even a random selection will do to note their recurrences.

There is, for instance, the recurring overreaching agent/manager who takes over Elvis' life and who first appears in *Loving You*, turns up again as the jailbird con in *Jailhouse Rock*, resurfaces as a nine-year-old Mexican boy in *Fun in Acapulco* (who nevertheless insists on—and gets—fifty percent of our hero's earnings for bookings), and, again, as his abrasive troublemaking buddy-cum-manager whose bad management, greed, and gambling losses get Elvis all snarled up with the Internal Revenue Service in *Speedway*.

The subliminal reminder that Elvis was a twin is sneaked in constantly in any number of ways. In *Loving You* there is first that line of dialogue "I wish I were twins, I'd have somebody to blame for this." In another shot in this film the camera pans over an audience to linger long enough over a pair of identical girl twins to make its point. *Jailhouse Rock* had its twin bassets. In *Girls! Girls! Girls!* when Elvis throws a big party to celebrate the wedding anniversary of his adoptive parents, in response to the father's "What have I done to deserve all this?" the reply that he has produced two gorgeous girls is followed by a shot of nubile identical twin sisters. One of the final shots in *G.I. Blues* shows Elvis among a mass of twin babies. And in *Kissin' Cousins* he is made to come right out and play twin roles, one in a blond wig.

That they, as well as Elvis, were aware of his Indian blood is obvious early on in *G.I. Blues* when he mentions, apropos of nothing, "My grandmother's a full Cherokee. They don't all sit around smoking corn-cob pipes, you know!" In *Flaming Star* he plays a half-caste (at a time when star parts were not Redskins) while Dolores Del Rio plays his full-blooded Indian mother. In *Stay Away Joe* he is again playing an Indian.

Speaking of the mother's role in Elvis films, it is fascinating to note that in both *King Creole* and *Wild in the Country* his mother has already died (and is sorely missed) before the film starts, although in both novels they were adapted from she is alive and well. In *Blue Hawaii*, in which, to quote Wallis again, they "tried to parallel his own life with his screen personality," Angela Lansbury as his mother bears a striking resemblance to Vernon's second wife Dee Presley both in her blonde good looks and southern belle personality.

Elvis' own well-known promiscuity gets such an airing in practically every one of his films, and the girls he ends up with could so easily have been any one of the others, the pursuit having been so passionless on his part—rarely going further than Elvis rushing after one or the other of them, puffing "You gotta forgive me, I can explain...." (often several times in the same film)—that one suspects it cannot be anything but deliberate. For the teenage girl fan the fantasy would be that since he's gotten around to so many of them up there on the screen it's just a matter of time before he'll get around to her. And for the teenage male fan, there is the fantasy that he too can attract girls like flies simply by buying the album of the movie and learning to sing it.

Elvis' love and understanding of children was genuine and reciprocated. He had a way with them that was magical. Philip Dunne, who directed him in one of his few good films, *Wild in the Country*, remembers: "Our rather shy eight-year-old daughter couldn't be made to shake hands. Elvis persuaded her to. He simply held out his hand and said in a direct order, 'Jessica, put her there.... Come on, stop stalling, you're going to shake hands.' And she did. And at that moment I saw what he might have become were it not for instant fame, the Colonel, and the stooges.... At that moment Elvis was charming." He also adds: "What I had against Parker was that he was a tasteless man who had power and used it. When he and Spyros Skouras put their heads together, I knew some disaster to the integrity of the film was being plotted."[27]

Elvis' way with children yielded far too great box-office potential for it not too be overexploited. Elvis' films in the 1960s were inundated with a monstrous regime of the old-fashioned, Hollywood-cute-type child actors, many of them saucily arch Lolitas, flirting, singing, and wiggling their bottoms alarmingly around an almost stationary Elvis. The depths were plumbed in *Paradise Hawaiian Style* by a little nine-year-old horror in a grass skirt, bumping and grinding her way through the great ragtime classic "Bill Bailey, Won't You Please Come Home," while Elvis, who could have turned it into gold, remained seated at the nightclub table (grinding his teeth, one imagines). And insult was added to injury when the little girl pertly announced to him she was not taking an encore because "Always leave them wanting more, isn't that what *you* always say, Rick?" (As a matter of fact it was what the Colonel always said.)

Yet if one had the guts and determination to follow through all of Elvis-with-kids films one would be strangely rewarded by two. In *G.I. Blues* his scenes with the baby, which range from knockabout farce to lullaby, are

[27.] Letter to author from Philip Dunne, September, 1982.

an enchantment. And in *Change of Habit*, in his long, harrowing scene as a doctor treating an autistic child by forcing her to scream out her emotions, he strikes an impressive note of rapport and reality. However, this film, in which he turns in one of his best performances, being one of his last, was treated with the same general contempt that had been given those from *Kissin' Cousins* (1964) on. And even the *Elvis Monthly* had stopped running articles about his films, calling them "puppet shows for not overbright children." True, they may have seemed so on the surface, yet more than one writer has observed along with Linda Ray Pratt in *Southern Quarterly* (1979) that Elvis' movies "were sprinkled with off-color jokes and plays on words." *Girls! Girls! Girls!* is squirmingly full of them: the "heavy," for instance, looking directly at Elvis' crotch and sneering, "Your butterfly is open—both buttons," or the girl, trying to extract $2,000 from her father to buy a boat, protesting over the telephone "*No, daddy, not* for medical expenses," in such a way that the audience is left in no doubt as to the going price for an abortion. Even without such cracks to alert us, the Chinese meal sequence, from the girl picking up a limp shrimp and glaring significantly at Elvis, to the painfully obvious double-entendres delivered by the Chinese couple over the dinner table ("Chinese proverb say, 'All men remember small things very big,' and, 'They say Chinese meal is like a date: after you have one, an hour later you want another'")—come across as smut aimed at Elvis' sexuality.

How many of these plays on words did Elvis catch? For catch them of course he did, although with the piecemeal way films are shot, often out of sequence, new pages given daily to the actors when the star is not around, etc., he might not have caught them until the whole film was put together for release. Vernon, in his interview in *Good Housekeeping* in 1978, has these incredible words to say: "[Elvis] had never had script approval or control over the songs in his pictures or over *anything else*." (My italics.) No wonder Elvis, in 1968, openly stated his dislike for his films, always avoided seeing them. Some, he said, had made him physically ill to make.

Finally, there is the recurrent theme of Elvis on trial. In *Loving You*, though Lizabeth Scott presents the defense, it is Elvis and his music on trial. In *Jailhouse Rock* it is Elvis himself who is on trial for manslaughter. In *Blue Hawaii* he is arrested in a general free-for-all and his father bails him out. *Follow That Dream* ends with a trial scene: the Kwimper family (Elvis') fighting for and winning the repossession of their land. In *Roustabout*, socking a snotty Ivy League bully lands him a week in the slammer. In *Speedway* a scene is set in an Internal Revenue Service office where his tax exemptions are on trial. In *Wild in the Country* he is twice on trial: in the beginning in a juvenile court as a potential delinquent and at the end for being provoked into punching a guy who, it turns out, had a weak heart, so that he is acquitted as not being the prime cause of the guy's death. The judge presiding over this case, incidentally, is called Judge Parker.

With the amount of trial scenes injected into Elvis' films (in the novel *The Last Country* from which *Wild in the Country* was adapted, there are no trial scenes) it is little wonder that so many of the nightmares he confided to his friends centered around himself on trial. It was as if what had begun as Vernon's trial had grown into trials warning Elvis about his own culpabilities—his increasingly uncontrollable temper, for example—or just any incriminating evidence of whatever nature Parker would have access to that might land Elvis in the dock.

Early in *Jailhouse Rock* there is a shot of the prison barber hacking off our hero Vince's hair, sideburns and all. Yet when Vince returns to his cell ruffling his ill-shorn locks, he is far from glum. He is in fact grinning from ear to ear. What can he be so happy about? Certainly not the prospect of a year in the cooler with an irascible cellmate. The answer is simple. Because of the haircut this scene had to be shot out of sequence at the end; so, for Elvis, it was his last day's work on the picture. It was over. Having served his time on the screen he was now free to have time serve him—for two months, that is—back in Memphis, home to Gladys.

On June 3, 1957, not long before Elvis' return, Lillian had as much need of Gladys' support as Gladys had had of Lillian's. It was the day of Lillian's husband Charlie Mann's funeral. Together Gladys and Lillian went back to Mississippi, back to that cemetery in Spring Hill where their mother and father were buried so many years before and where Charlie Mann, too, had asked to be laid to rest. A funeral, as always, had brought together a gathering of friends as well as of kin—of the Mitchells, the Lummuses, the Irwins, and the Harrises as well as Smiths, Mansells, and Manns. Cully Mitchell in particular noticed the dramatic change in Gladys since he had last seen her not a year before. It was not just that she was heavier and moved more slowly, but she appeared remote and burdened with cares. And when she talked of Elvis coming home in a couple of weeks, it was not only with anticipation but with relief. Yet when they exchanged a joke or two, as people will at funerals, her soft face lit up and she became the Gladys of yore—friendly and affectionate.

What an awesome thrill of satisfaction the sight of Graceland, stately and serene, its grounds now lush green in the summer, must have presented to its young master. Having bought it so quickly before dashing

off on tour again in March, now in mid-June for the first time driving up
the curving approach to its porticoed entrance, Elvis was fully able to
appreciate the great height to which he had raised his family, from their
shifting beginnings to the solid mansion they would inhabit for the rest
of their lives. Weigh that against any sacrifice and surely they had come
out the winners.

When they had first moved in, sometimes, after a particularly reassuring
call from Elvis the night before, Gladys would take herself in hand, get
dressed, and wander down to what would become the music gates, where
either Vernon's brother Vester or her brother Travis would be chatting
with the handful of fans who had found their way out there. And if the
group was small enough and the fans particularly well-behaved, Gladys
would take them up to the house to see the renovations. Then around
sunset she would amuse herself feeding her chickens, watching the downy
little ones tumble over each other, and afterward shooing them off the
front lawn.

But then had followed those terrible days when Elvis was in the Cedars
of Lebanon Hospital. Gladys was ready to go immediately to her son in
California and just as quickly this plan was defeated by one and all. That
he was back at work three days later did not reassure her. But what
lingered on in the aftermath of her initial fright was the thwarting of her
will. It left Gladys the Gladiator of the dogwood broom unarmed, de-
fenseless. She got into the habit of staying in her housecoat all day, either
keeping to her room or wandering through the large empty ones, frightened and overwhelmed by them, unable to accustom herself to their
strangeness.

Now that Elvis was home at last, she was up and about wearing a fresh
summer dress in which to greet him. But as they sat down to the meal
Gladys had cooked of all the food Elvis loved, they were uneasy in each
other's company. Whereas before Elvis would be eager to tell his parents
of the various happenings on the film he'd just completed, now, as if by
some unspoken agreement, there was no mention of it. After *Jailhouse
Rock*, nothing was the same between them. Everything had changed but
they had to go on as if nothing had changed. Each saw the other differently and more distinctly than ever before but was less able to do anything
with their own selves except give in more and more to their inner needs
and temptations. Gladys had her secrets and Elvis had his. Their conversation was entirely about Graceland, the renovations done so far, and
the decorator from Goldsmith's department store who was coming the
next day to present further ideas and drawings, samples, and swatches.

If Gladys—and especially Vernon the artisan, "who could do anything with wood" and who had a knowledge of and concern with "getting things done right"—had looked forward to a leisurely period of family discussions and decisions before choosing and matching colors and designs and furniture room by room, it soon became clear that this was not Elvis' way. He wanted it all done *now, immediately,* he told the decorator, if possible, *yesterday.* His solution to everything, it became obvious, lay in the baroque. Given a free hand the walls would be purple and gold and the ceilings would be skies painted with clouds, and all the chandeliers would be long glass tubes with lights on the end like shooting stars or fireworks. When the decorator, perhaps thinking of his reputation, assured Elvis that those sorts of things took time—months and months at least—Elvis was so impatient that he accepted most of the decorator's ideas if they were sumptuous enough. There is also a story, vouched for by Elvis' friends—this in 1965—that Vernon came to him one day saying, "I just went by Donald's Furniture Store and they've got the ugliest furniture I've ever seen in my life." After he described it, Elvis said "Good! That sounds like me." At Donald's it took Elvis just thirty minutes to furnish his den.

When *Loving You* opened in Memphis in July, Gladys sat there between Elvis and Vernon watching it unfold. There on the screen was the son she knew and loved so much. And then—the added excitement just before the end of the film—Elvis singing "Got a Lot o' Livin' To Do," coming down off the stage still singing and walking up the aisle while the screen audience clapped as if it were Sunday at a First Assembly of God church, and, if you looked quickly enough, there *she* was up on the same screen sitting right on the aisle as Elvis ended up singing right to her. They exchanged a split-second smile, and as the camera panned on him going back to the stage, you saw not only her graceful hands clapping in encouragement and undeniably perfect rhythm, but her dainty foot encased in a high-heeled pump, stamping for all its worth.

It is said that Elvis never watched the picture after Gladys' death because she was in it, but perhaps it was the remembrance of her at that moment, so happy as she watched them both on the screen, that he was unable to expose himself to again.

Shortly after this, Parker let Elvis know he'd booked him on a northwest tour beginning at the end of August—Vancouver, Spokane, Tacoma, Seattle, Portland—ending in Hollywood in September for another recording session which would serve as the basis of his Christmas album.

His few weeks at home might be said to have pulled Gladys around, temporarily halting her downward course. Then came Elvis' surprise. As he was about to go on tour—as his job, in short, was starting up again—

he decided to take himself and his gang to Biloxi for a couple of weeks' vacation at the Sea and Sand Hotel.

Those weeks he *chose* to spend away from his mother—not because of work but on vacation—can be seen as crucial to her equilibrium. Only days before, the tragic death of Judy Tyler, Elvis' co-star in *Jailhouse Rock*, had increased in Gladys her sense of the film's power for evil and her fear for Elvis' safety. In short, she was not able to look on his trip as a well-earned holiday by the sea but, painfully, as a willful filial rebuff. From then on, Graceland became not her monument but her mausoleum. For what difference did it make if he was at Graceland when again he had begun turning the days upside down so that she rarely saw her dutiful son except for the few hours of the evening between his waking up and his taking off on his all-night adventures and his motorcycling, now done with a wildness and recklessness that even alarmed his friends, as did his uncertain temper and spurts of explosive behavior.

All Gladys saw was that the part of his life the Colonel was not running, Elvis was running in a way that excluded her and into which all her efforts to re-enter were in vain. Biloxi was the port right next to Pascagoula where they had lived when Vernon was working in the shipyards. Would Elvis remember that? He was not much more than a baby, only four or five, but the way he insisted on toting that little cousin of his, Diane, around everywhere on his hip.... She would have loved to have talked to him about those days. But she didn't. Pascagoula was just after Vernon's release from jail. It was too close to that taboo subject and, therefore, was itself taboo.

Incapable of dealing with both the present and the future, Gladys depended more and more on vodka to block them out and return her to the only place she felt safe—the past. Lillian who had up till then dropped in to visit at Gladys' invitation was now turning up daily at Vernon's command.

In October Milton Bowers announced that because of reduced draft quotas, Elvis would probably not get his call for another year. And life went on: Elvis toured; Hal Wallis announced his plans for his second Elvis picture, an adaptation of Harold Robbins' bestselling novel, *A Stone for Danny Fisher*, retitled *King Creole*. The decorating at Graceland hurried to completion. The music gates and walls went up. And a house on the grounds was built for the Travis Smiths and their sons.

From the end of August when Elvis began his northwest tour to December when he returned for Christmas, Gladys did not see him at all except for those brief days around September 27, when he returned for his second benefit concert at the Mississippi-Alabama Fair in Tupelo.

Then he was off again. October, spent on the West Coast, climaxed in two performances at the Pan-Pacific Auditorium in Los Angeles. The first, held October 28, was deemed the most notorious Elvis had ever given. His critics vented their fury not only on Elvis' Dionysian rites— his "playing up to the mike with gestures expressly forbidden by the police in every burlesque show in Los Angeles County"—but in the finale, "Hound Dog," when, it was reported, "He got down on the floor with a huge replica of the singing dog and made love to it as if it were a girl. Slowly he rolled over and over on the floor." Whose gloriously gross idea was *that*? One theory is that the practical-joking Colonel sneaked it into Elvis' preperformance mind. Actually, the stuffed RCA dog, Nipper, had for some time shared the stage with Elvis during his act—Parker pushing him on stage at the appropriate moments from the wings and even putting him back on stage from the front of the house if Elvis accidentally knocked him off—but presumably things had never gone as far as this.

Elvis professed innocence at the outrage he had caused: "Man, when I sing I go into a complete trance from which I don't come out at all."

But the next day, for the second Pan-Pacific performance, with the police in full force armed with movie cameras to record evidence of obscenity, it was noted that he "reduced the orbit of the gyrations."

Around this time Frank Sinatra, from the height of his impeccable morality and his vested interest in the great show tunes of the past, took the opportunity to pronounce on the new music: "Rock and roll is played and written for goons for the most part by goons." Then, in case he hadn't made himself as clear as he wished, he went on in this fashion for a French magazine: "Rock and roll is the most brutal, ugly, degenerate, vicious form of expression—sly, lewd—in plain fact, dirty—a rancid-smelling aphrodisiac and the martial music of every sideburned delinquent on the face of the earth."

Nice words for a mother to hear about her son's music. The great Frankie's opinion taking up its own space in the press would certainly have gotten back to her. Less likely to have done so would be this small item tucked in the *New York Post*, dateline Davenport, Iowa:

"The rock and roll music of Elvis Presley is good therapy for mental patients," a specialist reported today. These words came from Florence Chambers at the Independence Mental Health Institute, who told a staff meeting that "his music is very good for the patients. The mentally ill have lost their rhythm and are out of step with the world," Dr. Chambers said. "We use music to give them back their rhythm."

The best songs for them she added are optimistic but without sentimental lyrics. The majority of Elvis hits at the time, like "Hound Dog" or "Blue Suede Shoes" or "Shook Up" perfectly filled the bill.

The beginning of November found Elvis as far away as Hawaii where the Colonel had booked him for two performances at the Honolulu Stadium. And the rest of the month was spent on the West Coast where preparation for *King Creole* had begun. Then finally in December, Elvis returned home.

"In 1957 the first Christmas at Graceland was quite different from any other Christmas I had known before. It was like being in fairyland and Santa Claus was my first cousin," is the way Billy Smith, Elvis' first cousin and Travis' youngest son, then aged fourteen, begins his recollection[28] of the last Christmas Gladys would ever have. "Inside Graceland was beautiful as always. It was like a dream. Elvis had a big white Christmas tree decorated with red ornaments.... Then, all the carpet in the living room was white."

On December 20, into this dream and onto the white carpet stepped Milton Bowers to deliver Elvis' induction notice in person. Dated December 18, it ordered Elvis to turn up at 198 South Main Street at 7:45 A.M. on January 20 to begin his army career.

What can have happened since October to make the draft board suddenly turn around and reduce the period from twelve months to two? On this subject there is a surfeit of opinion, but of the deciding factor no one can say with any certainty. Every veterans' organization and congressional representative's squeal or howl was printed and echoed around the country and there were congressional lobbies of irate parents. But one event must certainly be given its full importance. By early November *Jailhouse Rock* was on nationwide distribution—among the Establishment, it would seem, consensus had taken place.

That the unexpectedness of this sudden bringing forward of Elvis' induction caught even Hal Wallis totally by surprise is underlined by the fact that by November the producer was deep in preproduction activities for *King Creole*—the script prepared, actors and director already assigned to the project, songs selected and locations arranged, all involving the allocation of large sums of money. Even the month of the actual shooting had been set—January, the month Elvis was due to enter the army.

Wallis' ignorance of this seems all the more surprising since Hollywood, one of America's major industries, had always had close and patriotic ties with the U.S. government, especially Wallis' former studio, Warner Brothers. Who will forget one of Wallis' own musicals, *Footlight Parade*, with its wonderful finale of all the girls holding up cards which formed a

[28]. *Elvis: The Record*, Vol. 1, No. 7.

mammoth picture of President Roosevelt—the American flag, the bald eagle, and the appropriate New Deal symbols filling in the grand design? Was the present Eisenhower administration not talking to Wallis? How come he was the last to know?

On December 21, quick as a flash, a letter was sent from Wallis' production chief to the Memphis Selective Service requesting a two-month deferment for Elvis, implying that Elvis' first patriotic duty was to save a dying industry. The draft board's reply was that the request had to come from the star himself before they could consider it. With all this back-and-forthing, it was Christmas Eve by the time Elvis sat down to write his letter.

Whatever emotions he might have had about being drafted—and surely one of them must have been relief that the shoe had finally dropped—*Jailhouse Rock* had left Elvis itchingly eager to be involved in what he would consider a "legitimate" project. *King Creole* was to be what they like to call "a major motion picture" in lieu of just a plain movie. It had originally been bought for Elvis' idol, James Dean, and had now been especially tailored for Elvis with a cast full of carefully selected first-rate actors with the famous Michael Curtiz (*Yankee Doodle Dandy, Casablanca*) directing. That he desperately wanted to do this film comes out in the letter Elvis finally sent off to the draft board. Although his request for deferment begins by stating that it originates not from him personally but from Paramount "so these folks will not lose so much money," it ends on the personal plea that his desire to go along with this request is because they helped him so much at the start of his career, thereby calling the board's attention to the fact that they were cutting him off in the middle of a successful one.

He was informed that the decision would not be reached until the draft board reconvened after the holidays. That moment on December 20, when the dreaded "war thing" finally became a reality—whether in one month's time or three months hence—must have been for Gladys the ultimate of all those mixed events that had made her in Lillian's phrase "all nerves" during the past three years.

This particular mixed event, emotionally geared higher than all the others, had started off as the Christmas of her dreams—Elvis coming home to her to the new house he was so proud of—then a knock on the door or a ring on the bell and enter the army to snatch away her son for two years. Was there something familiar in this that somehow made two dissimilar things fuse in her mind—the apprehending of Elvis by the army and the apprehending of Vernon and his being sent away to prison?

By all that's holy in psychiatry, this should have been the moment of her total and final collapse, sending her to bed to center the attention on herself as she had watched her mother do while growing up. However, this did not happen. There was to be a houseful of people to cater to—family and friends; a Christmas Eve party to cook for; and a Christmas Day banquet to prepare. As always, when the occasion demanded, she rose to it.

But the crisis *had* come and the time to fulfill this need to collapse could only be delayed, allowed to fester within her until it dragged her into her final illness.

By now Elvis must have known about Gladys' drinking problem—all Memphis seems to have known.

That devastating axiom, much quoted in medical circles, that "a physician must devote most of his efforts toward *keeping the relatives from killing the patient* and then trust in God and occasionally the surgeon" is particularly applicable where a serious drinking problem is concerned. Over and over again medical experts have noticed a whole family unconsciously working in collusion with the particular member's illness of this kind. It is a mutual deception that the drinking is but a passing phase, a temporary weakness that, when external circumstances calm down and, they believe, with the exertion of a little more self-control, discipline, and determination on the part of this member, it will all blow over. That they genuinely do believe it is because they want to.

But to go back to the then fourteen-year-old Billy Smith's account of that Christmas. Far from noticing anything amiss with Gladys, he is constantly aware of her normal activities; his eyes as big as saucers as he "looked at all the food Aunt Gladys had cooked," and so on.

Though Elvis was left dangling on Christmas Eve about whether or not he would be able to make *King Creole*, he knew that at all events it was likely to be the last Christmas he would have at Graceland for two years—draftees get shipped overseas. In following him from early morning till 3 A.M. the next day, one sees him give full rein to all the complex and opposing elements of his personality heightened by the turbulence of this Yuletide. The day began with Elvis suddenly deciding to buy some last-minute gifts for his mother and father. Billy, his brother Bobby, and Elvis jumped into his black limousine and drove off to the recently built Whitehaven Plaza just a few blocks from Graceland. There Elvis did his shopping in his usual lightning fashion and they hurried back to Graceland to put the gifts under the tree.

Then Elvis told Vernon to withdraw twenty $1,000 bills and ten $100 bills out of the bank. At this, both Vernon and Gladys protested that their son didn't need to carry that much money on him. "Don't question me," he said. "I have a very good reason for this." So much for past obedience. Elvis and his cousins then got back into the limousine and, crossing the state line into Mississippi to buy fireworks (outlawed in Tennessee), they cleaned out the first store of its Roman candles and different types of bombs and rockets to the tune of eight hundred dollars.

"What're you going to do?" asked the salesman. "Start World War II all over again?"

Elvis told him, "I'm thinking about it."

It seemed to Billy that those were enough fireworks to set half of Memphis on fire, but it was only the beginning. Elvis then went to three other places purchasing more of the same fireworks for a grand total of $1,800. On the way back Elvis, stopping to buy a paper, gave the paper boy a $100 bill and told him to keep the change.

When he returned to Graceland, reports Billy, "Elvis was in such a good mood he even let reporters from the local newspaper come up to take pictures of him with his draft notice under the Christmas tree." And in these photographs one sees Elvis as he holds up the document for all the world to read, passive and powerless but grinning and bearing it. That he could have enlisted and thereby been able to pick the branch or specific job he was to have for the next two years (as Sal Mineo had done in choosing the Engineering Corps), but refused to do so, suggests that this passivity might have been accompanied by a secret gratification. Passivity is useful in pointing up the results of external influences. Smiling under the Christmas tree could have been Elvis' way of saying to his fans, "Look what they've done to me." But that was only part of him, the public person, responding to a public situation. Privately he had other responses.

In the afternoon people starting dropping in and the party began. Elvis took aside six of his employees (who were mainly made up of his kin) and gave them each a $1,000 bill while hugging them and wishing them a merry Christmas. To Billy and Bobby he gave one hundred dollars each. Whatever name we choose to give this breathtaking generosity—whether we deem it saintly, kingly, feudal, buying love, or showing off—to forget that the recipients were a lot better off for it is rather like concentrating on the manure and forgetting the rose garden.

Later on in the evening, by which time the party was in full swing, Elvis began to ask his guests to come upstairs with him one by one to his bedroom. On his bed were twelve $1,000 bills neatly laid out. "At some point," Billy relates, "Elvis would make some excuse to go into his bathroom or another room, leaving each one alone with the money. Then he would return a few minutes later and tell the person to wait downstairs to get ready to shoot fireworks a little later. Then he would count the money on the bed to see if any of it was missing.... I didn't know until years later what his motive was; this was just one of the ways Elvis had of testing to see which ones could be trusted. One of the bills did come up missing and Elvis, of course, knew exactly who took the money but just let him keep it thinking he had pulled a good one. Even though the person came to Graceland on other occasions, Elvis always kept a watchful eye on him and he was not made to feel welcome at Graceland again."

The slyness of this loyalty test, as well as the cruelty of tempting people as needful as most of his guests would then have been with such a sum of money, cannot escape comment. No doubt there was provocation for it (he carried a lot of money around with him and was careless about where he left it), but would he have thought up this Christmas trick a year ago? Now the need to be suspicious of his circle seemed to be as great as his need to trust them wholeheartedly had been years ago. The evidence is plain that this Christmas, Elvis was not so "nice," not so simple as he had been the Christmas before. But then—neither was his private world such a nice one, as the success of this ploy proved. Gladys' crumbling, Vernon's ineffectuality, suspicions about his friends and relations had all served to erode his trust as well. For so long Elvis had been at the center of so many tugs of war. His filial duty toward his mother tugged him in one direction, the Colonel's lasso around his neck dragged him in another; obligations to his fans in a third way, and his music in a fourth. And now the army hovered over his life, whispering into his ear the equivalent of Hamlet's "If it be not now, yet it will come. The readiness is all."

Not a whit had he defied augury; it had come. And it triggered off in Elvis a readiness to unlock the whole baggage of hostility he had been carrying around with him—a lifetime of stored-up, shored-up feelings— and transform these fantasies of aggression, rage, and violence into one glorious burst of actuality. Bringing it all back home to the grounds of Graceland.

The game he had especially invented for the grand finale of his Christmas Eve festivities he simply called War. And its rules were as simple and apt as its name. Without actual guns it is hard to see how he could have come closer to the real thing.

With no explanation, Elvis, along with Billy and Bobby, got most of the fireworks out of the car and distributed them equally among the family and friends now gathered outside. The rest were left in a pile as an ammunition supply. They then followed him down to the pasture behind the house, where Elvis set out the rules of the game. First they must choose sides. Then the boundaries were set. The big tree in the middle of the pasture served as the center line dividing the opposing teams and the fences around the pasture were the boundaries. Anyone who went outside these boundaries was automatically out of the game. After that, it was simply a matter of lighting up the rockets and Roman candles and hurling them at each other. "When one of the fireballs or rockets hit you, it gave you a pretty good lift and would sting like crazy," says Billy about these proceedings, from which there was not just the possibility but the strong likelihood that serious physical injury could result, "but we were having so much fun no one seemed to mind."

There he was wrong. At least one person minded a great deal. While they were having a ball at War, Cliff Gleaves arrived all unknowing and wandered into the pasture to see what was going on. Both sides thought they would have some fun with him, so they all turned their Roman candles in his direction. Cliff's jacket caught fire, not unnaturally causing him, in a blind panic, to yell and run around beating his chest. The game was interrupted briefly while they caught him and pulled off his by now blazing coat and shirt. His skin injuries were shrugged off as "a few scorched places on his chest and no serious burns" by everyone except the victim, "who even today would have you think he was badly burned," Billy insists.

Things heated up a lot more later on when cousin Junior Smith, drunk, went back to the ammunition supply. By that time the smoke from the fireworks was so thick he needed his cigarette lighter to see which ones he was getting out. Accidentally he dropped the lighter into the pile causing the whole arsenal to explode. The warriors in the pasture hit the ground—there was no place to escape that was not out of bounds. The spectators all made a dash for the house. "Some were lucky and some were not" is the succinct way Billy dismisses the injured civilian population, while he gleefully remembers Elvis and company laughing like crazy as they saw the hill "lit up like a giant Christmas tree. Boy! What a sight!"

Included in the sight were the animals of Graceland—also casualties of war; a ball of fire hit one of the horses' flanks and he bucked and snorted all the way to the barn. "I can remember seeing the rockets go into the chicken house and the chickens coming out," continues Billy. "As the feathers flew, Elvis raised his head and said, 'Mama is going to have a bunch of bald chickens.'" Nearby Christmas church bells pealing out "Peace on Earth" at midnight must surely have been drowned out by the bombs bursting in air. It was not until 3 A.M. that War was over.

"Everyone headed for the house," concludes Billy. "We sat downstairs in the basement den drinking sodas and reliving the game we had just finished. Elvis liked the game so much it became an annual affair at Graceland."

TWENTY-ONE

The Death of Gladys

After War, victory—of a sort. The draft board did grant Elvis a six-week deferment amidst, it can be imagined, cries of "It's not fair!" exploding from both sides in its wake. From January 1 to March 20, immersing himself in the making of *King Creole*, Elvis was better able to cope with headline-grabbing outbursts from backwoods statesmen than Gladys, slowly succumbing to her terminal illness, was able to cope with her bald chickens.

Red West recalls the last time he visited Gladys in Graceland. It was in February, 1958. As he describes it in *Elvis: What Happened?*, Elvis was in Hollywood and "Mrs. Presley and I sat down and talked some.... I knew there was something wrong with her. I couldn't put my finger on it, but it was just the way she talked. Man, that dear lady knew she was dying. She never said anything like that but the way she was talking it was as if it was all over.... When I got up to say goodbye, she just sort of called me back and she said what I heard her say a hundred times... 'Look after my boy.' When she said it this time it was different. There was a sort of, I don't know, a sort of finality to the sound of her voice, like as if it was the last time she would ever say it to me."

Red's perception of Gladys tallies absolutely with the mental state that invariably accompanies the onslaught of hepatitis, the most insidious of diseases, that would lead to Gladys' death.

Hepatitis is a confusing umbrella word that is used to cover any in-flammation of the liver caused by a variety of toxic agents from viral infections to alcohol, anesthetics, drugs, and a category simply lumped together as "poisons." Delving deeper into its pathology and consulting physicians in that field, one would be surprised not only by the multiplicity of categories of this common disease but by the extreme difficulty in diagnosing any of them at any time. In one of its most serious forms, known as chronic active (aggressive) hepatitis, for example, though it often results in liver failure and/or cirrhosis, in most cases the etiology is unknown. So if the sufferer does not mention to the doctor a history of alcohol or drugs it could be months or even years before the doctor would necessarily have noticed liver damage. But by whatever means the types eventually get sorted out, the symptoms at the onset are universally similar, clinically described as nonspecific malaise—lassitude, weakness, drowsiness, nausea, abdominal discomfort, headaches, and susceptibility to trauma. The symptoms are close enough to flu often to be diagnosed as such.

As anyone who has ever had hepatitis knows, for "nonspecific malaise," the layman's term would be a *very* specific depression, almost suicidal in its intensity. Unless you are lucky enough for your skin immediately to turn the telltale yellow—which is not common enough to be described as a primary symptom and sometimes only occurs when the illness is well under way—it is so illogical for you just suddenly to feel like that, that you tend to fix on some specific problem that has been giving you trouble and blow it up all out of proportion. In this way your "susceptibility to trauma" becomes a daily occurrence because these traumas seem to appear every day and over it all hangs the flu-like pall and the lassitude which again, in its intensity, seems like no other lassitude ever experienced. This often has the further effect of preventing you from making the effort of seeking medical aid for a long while.

One victim described a symptom of his prediagnosed state of hepatitis as taking the form of staring at a coffee pot for hours on end trying to beat down his nausea in order to get up enough energy to walk the three steps necessary to pour himself a cup. This made him consider that it was his mind, not his body, that was failing. Nor is it uncommon to drag oneself from doctor to doctor only to be told either that there is nothing the matter with you, or that you are undergoing a particularly virulent strain of flu, or to be prescribed medicines which make you feel sick. If, however, the doctor recognizes your symptoms and performs a liver biopsy or liver-function blood tests, a prompt and correct diagnosis of hepatitis can be expected to turn up.

In Gladys' case, what was happening was that not only her whole family but, by now, she herself was regarding her depression as increasing anxiety about Elvis and the army, and Dr. Evans' visits to her at Graceland were frustrated by not being furnished with the one vital clue she and her family kept secret: her alcoholic intake. Even if he had suspected it and had taken some liver-function blood tests, they still might have proved unremarkable.

However much discomfort Gladys was in, she held out stubbornly in Graceland throughout those sixty days that Elvis was filming. The effort to get dressed was beyond her and she appeared mostly in the new pink housecoat Elvis had bought her that Christmas. Though her route had narrowed from bedroom to kitchen and back, she saw to it that this routine was followed daily, though because of her increasing nausea, she had to be helped more and more in her cooking chores.

That Gladys might unconsciously be seeking to die, that she was in danger of joining hands with those forces now attacking her from within, was a view she would have flatly rejected. A visit to a hospital meant to her not the possible strengthening of her life but the weakening of it. No matter how poorly she was feeling, it meant a selfish and public succumbing to her own frailties just when Elvis needed least to be disturbed by added worry, needed most, in fact, to retain his childhood illusion of her strength.

Dr. Evans was convinced that her illness was due to her gallstones. He felt them to be causing her habitual bloating and told Lillian they might eventually lead to cancer if not attended to. Again Gladys was urged to go to the hospital. Again she procrastinated. At least he insisted those around her made sure she took the bile-acid medicines he prescribed which could dissolve gallstones. But when Gladys drank she would forget to take them.

What it cost her *not* to succumb to her illness by being hospitalized can be seen by the series of photographs taken of her with Vernon and Elvis on the eve of his induction.

The intrusion of cameras and press at this moment was one she deeply resented. Plainly enraged well beyond "grinning and bearing it," or even "cooperating" she pointedly declined to smile for the folks or even to look into the camera. In one photograph she is seated staring grimly into space, refusing to play up to Elvis' kiss; in the next, she stands but makes no effort to disguise the fact that it is only with the support of Elvis' hand holding on to the back of her head that she is able to do so. And in what was no doubt the last shot of that unhappy session, she is in total collapse, her face now swollen as if with tears recently shed, the black circles under her eyes deepened. Now she has disassociated herself entirely from everyone, including Elvis seated next to her, overtaken by a pain that no anesthetizing agent could numb.

All the more miraculous that in the very early hours of the morning of Monday, March 24, when Elvis arrived at his local draft board accompanied by his parents, Gladys, seen through the rarely flattering Movietone newsreel cameras, emerges as a figure of dignity. Wearing a new spring coat in honor of this important public occasion, she looks gentle but alert as she and Vernon walk into the building, witness Elvis being sworn in, and exit with no apparent effort. The swelling of her face has magically disappeared, revealing the delicacy of her features at their best.

Amid the friends gathered to see him off, reported by the press as cousin Patsy Presley, Judy Spreckles, Janet Hall, Bonnie Underwood, Cliff Gleaves, Lamar Fike, and Anita Wood (noted simply as "a Memphis entertainer" though she had been Elvis' steady girl since the July before), Gladys stood watching as Elvis and his fellow recruits got on the bus which was to drive them to Kennedy Hospital for their shots. Only then do we see her gently wipe away the few tears that have fallen. And only afterwards does she collapse.

As Elvis arrived at Fort Chaffee, Arkansas, to receive his indoctrination, physical examination, army fatigues, aptitude tests, and haircut, Colonel Parker was on hand for three days, his nuisance value at its peak as he steered the traffic of media to make sure that every publishable inch of Elvis' body, as well as his bodily functions, his actions, and reactions, were ruthlessly recorded until he and his circus were firmly ejected by Lieutenant Colonel Marjorie Schultern at Fort Hood.

At Fort Hood, where Elvis arrived at the end of March, the army announced the first part of what it had in store for him. It was strictly routine. He would be going through the basic combat training there with "A" Company, Second Medium Tank Battalion, Second Armored Division, for eight weeks. Upon its completion he would be given the usual fourteen-day furlough. At that point the authorities further divulged that Elvis would have another eight weeks in advance training as an armored crewman for tank warfare, followed by several more weeks of training with his unit, which would be shipped to Germany as a replacement for the Third Armored Division.

From the very beginning—and for obvious reasons the first eight weeks are the toughest—Elvis' behavior surprised, pleased, and relieved everyone on base. Army officials cautiously sang his praises declaring themselves impressed by his attitude and his exemplary conduct. Humes High was not so far away that he could not slip back into his well-learned lessons of how to comport himself when faced with authority, bringing into play his native politeness, modesty, humor, and that almost overdeveloped sense of "trying hard." The situation also brought out his flexibility and encouraged his already intense physical orientation, so that calisthenics, drill, long marches, and shooting practice were things he could take in his stride. Off base, to his friends, he might gripe and complain about how much he hated the army, but in this case it might be just as well to look at what Elvis *did* rather than what he *said*. And what he did on base for the months that he was there, in what could have been a very sticky predicament, was not to put a foot wrong. Perhaps, for the first time, he came closest to being liked for himself alone.

It helped, of course, that Fort Hood was an open base, which meant that he could receive visitors when off duty. A former disk jockey from nearby Waco, Eddie Fadal, opened his house and his wife's cooking to Elvis, and friends, including Anita Wood, visited him every weekend.

His fourteen-day furlough back in Memphis started on May 31, and he drove there in his Lincoln Continental with Anita Wood and the Colonel. Rumors of Elvis and Anita being secretly married were denied by both. He had returned looking tanned and fit in his well-cut uniform sporting his markmanship medals, his hair grown out to its natural brownish blond and his face fined down to that of a classic Greek beauty.

He attended a preview of *King Creole* with his parents, a print having been flown in especially for him in Memphis. *King Creole* is one of those films old-time Hollywood used to relish making—heavy with gangster menace and murder. "[Elvis'] numbers offer only remittent relief from the calculated violence and viciousness [of the film] and he can do little to balance the disagreeable story," wrote the *Monthly Film Bulletin* of the British Film Institute when they reviewed it. This, however, was a minority report. On the whole the film was popular with both critics and audiences and for the first time the critics singled out Elvis for praise. "The boy can act," commented the surprised *New York Times* reviewer.

But what of Gladys watching the film's beginning—watching the Fisher family, the son Danny (Elvis), his sister, and father, disrupted, disunited, and still desolated by the mother's death which had taken place a year before? A cold wind of prophecy must have chilled her to the marrow of her bones.

Parties at the Rainbow Rollerdome were still in order, and though on the whole they were of a more lighthearted nature with Anita Wood in attendance, at least one must have been a continuation of the Christmas war game, for UPI reported that Elvis returned to base on June 14 "with a black eye he picked up, he said, during a rollerskating game with friends."

The recording session that Elvis had done in Nashville on June 10—

11—it was to be his last for two years—yielded three hits: "A Big Hunk o' Love," "A Fool Such as I," and "I Got Stung."

Elvis' popularity was riding a crest. No longer the bad boy who made good but the bad boy who went straight, all factions in America united to claim him as a hero for being such an incontrovertible symbol of American democracy at its best. Even his more thoughtful admirers, such as Griel Marcus, confessed he "felt a great relief when Elvis was drafted because he made demands on me." The music he had unleashed *was* disturbing, unnerving. And a large part of the population who had hitherto been indifferent to the whole Elvis phenomenon found they were not indifferent to the curious feeling that in some way the gods had been appeased and Pandora's box shut. Only his legions of fanatic fans—and his mother—mourned his induction as a tragedy.

At that point Elvis himself was brimming with optimism: He had a girlfriend he was perhaps in love with (a girl, it must be noted, as unlike Gladys as can be imagined: blonde, petite, with aspiring ambitions for a career) and the money from RCA, from his merchandise, from his movie percentages which kept rolling in. He had proved himself a good soldier and a promising actor and he had, at last, everyone's goodwill. With his faith in God everything was bound to come out all right—didn't Mama always used to say that? And he was hopeful he could solve the problem of his mama's feeling so poorly by the best way he knew—by keeping her close by his side. After basic training, all soldiers at Fort Hood had permission to live off base if they had dependents, and though this usually meant wives and children, a literal interpretation could also include dependent parents. Elvis rented first a trailer and then a more comfortable three-bedroom house in the nearby town of Killeen.

A week after Elvis returned to base, in late June, he was joined by Gladys, Vernon, Minnie Mae, and Lamar Fike. With less than two months to live, Gladys was driven over four hundred miles through the heat into the height of a blazing, broiling Texas summer so that she and Elvis could be united. What can be more perplexing than a mother and her son reasoning only with their emotions?

For the last few months, withdrawing more and more into the protective confines of her bedroom, Gladys, in common with other victims of hepatitis, subjected herself endlessly to morbid fantasies of her death. Her religious beliefs had promised her eternal peace, freedom from suffering, and the welcoming arms of Jesus....

Now, for the first time in years, Gladys found herself in totally new surroundings, the bustle of an army-based town. But Elvis was again within her orbit. The shock of change may be said to have temporarily startled her back into her senses. The morbid fantasies were put aside for the moment as her spirit began fighting back against her fate. She raged against the rented house as she clumsily tried to find her way around while its furniture loomed unexpectedly to trip her; she raged against the strange kitchen where nothing was where it was supposed to be and she couldn't find anything. As for the household goods they had taken, they were the very ones she didn't want. She unleashed her rage on Vernon and in another form she unleashed a complaining anxiety upon Elvis. No one and nothing was spared the irascibility of this dying woman fighting for her life. Then, filled with remorse and self-reproach for the pain she was causing and the pain she was feeling, she would drink herself into the safety of oblivion.

The beginning of the end came in the first week of August. By now Gladys' condition was sufficiently serious to require immediate medical attention. Although her skin was jaundiced, the local doctor was unable to determine the cause of her illness. Her own doctor was telephoned, but he could not attend her as he had no license to practice outside Tennessee. Gladys must return to Memphis as soon as possible. Time was wasted—a whole day—while Gladys refused to go by plane and Elvis unsuccessfully tried to get a weekend pass to accompany her home by train. On Friday, August 8, Elvis drove his parents to Fort Worth and put them on the train to Memphis.

Immediately on their arrival home at 2 P.M. on Saturday, Gladys was taken to her doctor's office, then admitted to the Methodist Hospital late that afternoon. Four specialists were brought in and tests were run, but aside from coming to the rather obvious conclusion that she had hepatitis, they still could not agree on its cause.

From that moment on, daily bulletins on Gladys were issued to the press. Her age was given as forty-two, her illness first as "jaundice and a kidney ailment," and her condition, "very sick but in no danger."

Sunday and Monday passed with each bulletin increasingly more grave. In daily contact with her doctors and with Gladys' condition worsening, Elvis applied again for emergency leave. The leave was maddeningly delayed by having to pass through official channels and by the fact that Elvis had only one week left of his advanced training which, if he left, would seriously disrupt his army schedule. On Tuesday Elvis threatened to go AWOL if his request was not immediately granted; strings were pulled and he promptly flew to his mother's side, arriving there at 7:45 P.M. that same evening. "Because of his mother's fear of flying, it was only the second time Elvis had flown in two years," reported the newspapers.

The doctors now announced that Gladys was suffering from acute hepatitis and severe liver damage and that her condition was critical. When Elvis entered her room she was heard to cry out, "Oh, my son" as they embraced. When Elvis left her room briefly he told reporters, "Mama's not doing well right now. Not well at all." There were tears in his eyes and he was drawn and haggard. He had given his friends assembled in the waiting room only a brief greeting as he returned. Except for their immediate family no visitors were allowed and the door was guarded by a police officer. A cot was set up so that Vernon could remain in her room.

From Tuesday evening till Wednesday evening, Elvis stayed at his mother's bedside. At 9 P.M. on Wednesday, Gladys insisted that Elvis go back to Graceland and get some sleep. When he left that night he told reporters, "She's talking good and feeling so much better." He would come back in the morning, he said, and take some of the flowers home.

Elvis was asleep when the phone rang in the early hours of Thursday, August 14. He knew what it was before he answered it. Vernon told him Gladys had died at 3:15. "She woke me up struggling. She was suffering for breath. I got to her as quick as I could and the nurse and doctor put her in an oxygen tent. But it was too late."

In the shock of disbelief Elvis rushed to the hospital. The guard stood aside as he entered her room. Then, piercing the night time silence of the hospital and reverberating through its corridors, the wild despairing wails of Elvis and Vernon were heard as they wept and prayed, long and loud, over Gladys' lifeless body.

Dr. Charles Clarke, Gladys' physician in attendance, announced that Mrs. Presley's death was "apparently caused by a heart attack"[29] and the news was broadcast to the world. Gladys' remains were taken down to the hospital morgue, where the death certificate was registered, and from there to the National Funeral Home which was in charge of the obsequies. It was announced that the casket would arrive at Graceland at 2 P.M. that day.

When the news got out, family, friends, fans, and the press gathered outside at the Graceland gates. But in before all of them was the Colonel, of course, ready to take charge. Elvis' private bereavement was soon to become a public circus. Soon after Parker's arrival the Graceland gates

[29]. Though the heart attack was probably the result of the metabolic changes caused by cirrhosis or liver failure, both Elvis and Vernon refused to allow an autopsy to be performed; the cause of Gladys' death was never fully established.

were ordered to be opened to the press. They came upon a dazed father and son sitting on the front steps of the house, hardly aware of the intrusion, and alternately comforting each other and staring off into space: Elvis was wearing a white frilled shirt, Gladys' favorite, and white pants. His white buck shoes were unbuckled and would remain so the entire day. Vernon's shoelaces were also untied and neither had combed his hair.

The local newsmen plunged in:

At Graceland in mid-morning, Elvis told the *Press-Scimitar* the death "broke my heart." Tears streamed down his cheeks. He cried throughout the interview.
"She's all we lived for," he sobbed. "She was always my best girl."

Elvis struggled to answer their questions. Yes, he had spent the day in her hospital room, had kissed her goodnight when he left there late last night, and told her he would come back early this morning. Again he told how he planned to take some of the flowers home; again he said she had been talking good and feeling so much better, she was even well enough to talk to her doctor—to show him through the hospital window her pink Cadillac parked on the street and say, "There's my pink Cad. My boy gave it to me. I'll never take anything for it." But when he began to talk about the early-morning telephone call and how he already knew what it was going to be, he cried suddenly, "It just can't be true!" and then fell silent. It was left to Vernon to finish the story.

"Elvis cried without shame," reported the *Tupelo Daily Journal*. "He and his father sat on the steps of the big house looking down the big driveway leading to the iron gates where the curious assembled..." The newsmen waited. "When Mama was feeling bad," Elvis mumbled, "we used to walk her up and down the driveway to help her feel better.... Now it's over." Again, Vernon took over. "There were a lot of days when I would go out looking for jobs and get discouraged. I always knew if I could get back home to Gladys everything would be all right. She would always say, 'Things will get better.'" Photographs of the two sobbing men with their arms around each other about wrapped it up, and the journalists retired to fill in the rest of their copy with the rise of Elvis and his devotion to his mother.

When the hearse did arrive at two that afternoon, the Graceland gates opened again to admit it, along with close friends and more of the family.

Gladys, in a beautiful dress of baby blue that Lillian had never seen before (she whose father had had no winding sheet of his own), lay in a living room the size of a ballroom in a beautiful silver casket with its lid open.

Lillian watched while Elvis flung himself at his mother in her coffin,

hugging and kissing her, rocking her back and forth, weeping endear-
ments, and crying out to her in their own special language to come back
to him. "They couldn't get him to stop touching her," says Lillian, "until
they were afraid for him, you know, and they finally had to cover over
the coffin with glass. Then Elvis grabbed a hold of her pink housecoat—
the one he give her that Christmas, the one she wore all the time—and
he went tearing up and down the stairs, hanging on to it and fondling it
and kissing it, and it was the most pitiful sight you ever saw." Suddenly
Elvis stopped midstairs and cried out, "Oh *no* . . . not *you*!" Following his
line of vision Lillian saw it was Dixie Locke who had arrived to pay her
respects—with her husband.

Meanwhile the funeral arrangements had been made. The funeral
services were to be held where Gladys and Vernon's forebears had always
held them—in their own home. The Presleys' pastor at the First Assembly
of God Church, the Reverend James E. Hamill, would officiate and Gladys'
favorite gospel quartet, the Blackwoods, would sing her favorite hymns.
Food would be specially prepared for the guests, many of whom would
bring their own specially cooked dishes in honor of the occasion.

Suddenly these plans were changed! The Memphis morning paper,
the *Commercial Appeal*, made the announcement in good time.

Services for singer Elvis Presley's mother will be at 3:30 this afternoon in the
National Funeral Home. . . .

Original plans for the funeral to be at Graceland were canceled on advice of
his manager, Col. Tom Parker of Nashville.

"Elvis said his mother loved all of his fans," Colonel Parker said. "He wanted
them to have a last chance to see her."

The Colonel feared damage from curiosity seekers.

But the singer's wish to have his mother at home so he and his father might
be with her in the last hours before the services was granted. The casket will
remain at the home until nine this morning, when it will be returned to the
funeral home.

No need to read between the lines here. The Colonel had decided to
tamper with the rites and rituals of death. Keep Elvis hidden in the privacy
of his four walls when the opportunity of exhibiting him at just this
moment would have all the emotional appeal of a public hanging? Not
on his carny life!

Could the Colonel really have believed that the fans would rip up Elvis'
house even if allowed in on this occasion? If so, his conversion to south-
ernism must have been very superficial indeed. Fans might attack Elvis
after a performance, might collect and save leaves that had fallen from
Graceland trees, might attempt to climb over the not-very-high wall that

surrounded it, but where religious ceremonies were concerned they would behave appropriately—we are talking about the Bible Belt—and they would no more damage the house to which they had come to pay their respects to Gladys than they did when they came to pay their respects to Elvis. In any case, the Memphis police that had been organized could certainly have been counted on to keep the peace.

So instead of being able to release his feelings among intimate friends and family in his own home, the Colonel's plan subjected him to the long drive from Whitehaven to downtown Memphis to the funeral home's chapel. There where, in the 95° F. of a Memphis summer afternoon, three hundred people managed to jam their way in to watch Elvis finally lose control as the Blackwoods sang Gladys' favorite hymn, "Precious Memories." And all the while the numbers collecting in the parking lot outside swelled, so that by the time the service was over nearly three thousand people, according to the *Press-Scimitar*, had streamed through the funeral parlor to pay their respects, and the numbers of cars following the original five to the Forest Hill Cemetery where Gladys was to be laid to rest had multiplied to the point where a posse of sixty-five police was needed to move the procession down Bellevue Boulevard.

By this time Elvis' emotional pitch was such that the four men who had helped him out of the car were unable at the cemetery to stop him crying out at the final moment within the hearing of the pressing mob, "Goodbye, darling, goodbye. I love you so much. You know how much. I lived my whole life for you!" and then, "Oh, God! Everything I have is gone." The marker Elvis had placed on Gladys' grave read NOT MINE BUT THY WILL BE DONE.

He was given an extension of his emergency leave and was due back at Fort Hood on Monday, August 25.

"After attending funeral services for his mother," reported UPI, "Elvis was confined to bed temporarily with a virus infection and a slight fever." In fact Elvis spent most of those nine days in his bedroom, rarely emerging until nearly the end of his leave. A terrifying truth was closing in on him. He'd had a premonition of it before when he told Joe Hyams of his conflicting feelings that sometimes "scares the hell out of me"—how sometimes he felt that he was grown up and had been around, yet at others, as if he was still "a little kid that has to have someone to watch over me."

"I lived my whole life for you!" he had cried out at Gladys' graveside; but now there rose to contradict him sharp, painful, loving memories of the protection, the support, the sacrifice, and suffering she had lavished on him through the years. It was she who had lived her whole life for him. And on his account had died. No longer the proud, providing father of his earliest illusions, and later reality, Elvis was a little kid again. His only protection now would be provided by that particular ring of people he would control rather than trust; who—as he had learned at Christmas—would always need to be tried and tested.

On August 21 Elvis' dentist, Lester Hofman, and his wife Sterling received a call asking if they would come to see him. They had been Elvis' guests several times before and the atmosphere of Graceland had always been informal and full of activity. When they arrived and were ushered into the living room, they were confronted by what looked to Sterling as though "all Humes High, silent as statues, had taken up permanent residence there."

Finally one of them spoke. "He won't come down. We've been waiting a week for him to come out of his room."

"Send word we're here," Sterling said gently.

Five minutes later Elvis was there. "It's just a plain fact that you felt his presence in a room before you saw him," said Sterling. He pulled up a stool close to the Hofmans and first began talking about the funeral, his eyes never leaving the floor. Had they been there? No? He was glad. It was...it was just a circus. A silence. Then suddenly he looked right at Sterling with "those eyes that look up at you from the pillow," and grinned. "You've never seen my whole house, have you, Mrs. Hofman? Come on." He was smiling. "Let me show it to you."

The three of them rose. Elvis gave the merest flick of his head in the direction of his band of faithful and, to Sterling's utter astonishment, they vanished like obedient mice. The King had dismissed his jesters.

"Every time he returned to Graceland after Gladys' death," says Lillian, "he was depressed. He wouldn't talk to anybody for a couple of days. He was sitting outside on the lawn one day, after he got back from the army, looking so sad and with his head down, like I'd often seen him, and I went up to him and asked him, 'Have you been along to the cemetery?' 'I can't, Aunt Lillian,' he said, 'I can't go in....I can't hardly pass there.' And then he got up and just walked down to the fence and stood there looking out at nothing—just missing her.

"After Gladys died, he changed completely," says Lillian, thinking back to the boy she had known. "He didn't seem like Elvis ever again."

Epilogue

My chronicle of Elvis and Gladys is finished, but his power to haunt one compels me to make a few observations on the nineteen years as he lived them after Gladys' death.

For two years after Elvis' army service, Lillian, now working at answering fan mail in the small office Vernon had set up for that purpose in Graceland, was perhaps in a special position to notice how the prolonged mourning for his mother affected Elvis each time he came back after finishing a film. For him, "homesick" had taken on another dimension; he sickened for home even while he was in it. If she saw him at his lowest and most inconsolable at these times, she saw him once at his angriest.

Elvis had arrived back at Graceland one morning in June 1960 from Hollywood where he had just finished *G.I. Blues*. Lillian and a maid were sitting in the kitchen over a cup of coffee. Suddenly they heard a door upstairs violently slamming and Elvis shouting at the top of his lungs, "Don't you come out! Just don't come out!" Then followed footsteps racing down the stairs and into the big front room and the sound of furniture being hurled about. Terrified yet curious, the two women crept softly in the direction of the noise. They discovered Elvis in the act of ripping down all the curtains. In view of what had been happening while Elvis was away, a reaction of some sort came as no surprise to Lillian. She knew the difficulty Elvis had had in accepting the fact that, so soon after his mother's death, Vernon intended to marry Dee Stanley, a woman he had met while overseas. But what had prodded Elvis to take action was finding that Vernon had settled down with Dee where Gladys had once reigned, while Dee herself—when Elvis was away—had taken over the role of mistress of Graceland so thoroughly as to rearrange the furniture and replace the very curtains that Gladys had approved of.

Not until the afternoon had Elvis cooled down enough to send for Vernon and have it out with him. Soon after, a van arrived from Goldsmith's department store, accompanied by one of the decorating assistants, Don Johnson, and all Dee's household's goods, clothes, "improvements," and her own menagerie of pets, were loaded on—"We stuffed cats into that van for fifteen minutes!" recalls Don—while Vernon, Dee, and her three children went by car to a nearby house on Hermitage until they finally settled into a house on Dolan Drive which ran alongside Elvis' estate.

"He didn't seem like Elvis ever again," Lillian had said from her vantage point. But on the surface he remained precisely the same—as though in maintaining the status quo he could still keep Gladys alive. What had been operating in the past remained in operation; the wish to be one with her, the wish to please her still fighting with the other part of his nature, his desire to escape her; to be the triumphant surviving twin, the Captain Marvel, Jr., who flew above everyone into a stratosphere of his own. But the untraversable difference was that she was no longer there in the flesh as the pivotal object of his orbit.

And sensing her always inside him, and the wound inflicted by her loss increasing rather than healing, Elvis began an active search to understand the workings of this God who, it seems, had bestowed everything upon him only to take so much away. In the epitaph NOT MINE BUT THY WILL BE DONE his immediate reaction to her death (only later was added the more conventional SHE WAS THE SUNSHINE OF OUR HOME), feelings of anger, resentment, and confusion surged up from his seeming submission, which drove him in many directions to seek an answer.

Through his hairdresser, Larry Geller, serving as his guru, Elvis' quest led him through the study of all religions from Judaism to Buddhism and the teachings of theosophy with its beliefs in pantheistic evolution, reincarnation, the mystic, the psychic, the spiritual, and the occult—in short, all the Aladdin lamps that lit up the 1960s. But before we roll about with laughter at the spectacle of this young man from the Bible Belt, raised on fundamentalism and comics, though apparently already well versed in polypharmacy—struggling to master the Wisdom of the East, we might pause a moment to note the names of George Bernard Shaw, Louis Lumière, Thomas Edison, Yeats, Havelock Ellis, Maeterlinck, the educator Rudolf Steiner, Krishnamurti, and Gandhi, all of whom had been influenced by or involved in theosophy at one time or another and would, no doubt, have welcomed Elvis with open arms as a fellow traveler in the belief that magic is inherent in us all.

Numerology—the study of the occult significance of numbers—was of particular interest to Elvis and, one might say, with good reason. Numbers in general, often followed by five or six zeros, had been made to play such a significant part in his life. Since the age of twenty, more than anyone in his time, had his name in the papers been followed by a series of digits: the number of records sold, the number of records recorded, the numerical place of records on the charts, and above all, the money plus the percentages he was receiving per project. But he was delving deeper. Elvis, coming across the declaration that "in the science of numbers there is no chance. All is law and mathematical order—God geometrizes" would be sufficiently magnetized to read on; to figure out that he was an "eight," as was Red West, and so on.

And in fact, I find that already in the very first sentence of this epilogue, my mind has begun playing its own kind of numbers game: No sooner do I write "the nineteen years as he lived them after Gladys' death" than I am reminded that Elvis was nineteen years old when he embarked upon the career that would lead to her death.

The month of August always found Elvis at his most vulnerable. Under the scare-heading of August 15, enough unhappy events seemed to have collected to deserve mention. August 15, 1955, was the date of the first contract Elvis signed with the Colonel; August 15, 1958, was the date of Gladys' funeral; on August 15, 1972, the termination of his marriage agreement with Priscilla was filed; on August 15, 1974, he signed an agreement (at considerable financial disadvantage to himself) to transfer all the Elvis Presley commercial rights to the Colonel's company, Boxcar; and August 15, 1975, was, according to the guardian *ad litem* report, the date of one of his hospitalizations after collapsing in Las Vegas.

And what would Elvis have made about another numerical coincidence had he still been alive in 1979—his father's death on June 26, which was also the Colonel's birthday.

Five months before Elvis' death, while he was waiting in his car outside Graceland for the gates to open, his eyes fell upon a woman standing in the crowd. He invited her into his house and the following letter stamped with a sworn affidavit, on display at the Elvis Presley Museum in Memphis, tells us the rest of her story:

I met Elvis in early March 1977. In his own words I was a reincarnation of his mother (Gladys Love Presley). Love was also his name for me. In April 1977 he gave me this ring. It was a gift to his mother from him in 1955.

These were Elvis Presley's own words. I never doubted him one moment. It is one of the first gifts for her.

Sincerely,
Ellen Marie Foster
May 20, 1980,
St. Charles, Ill.

Also on display is the ring referred to in the letter. It is of eighteen-karat gold with a small square-cut diamond surrounded by diamond chips resting in a delicate filigree setting. We don't know what the proud nineteen-year-old gave his delighted mother as a birthday gift that April in 1955 twenty-two years before. If it was the same ring—and from its design nothing seems more appropriate—he had treasured it all this while. In giving it to her "reincarnation," perhaps he recaptured for a fleeting moment the pleasure he had felt in giving it the first time.

Between March and April, when Ellen Marie Foster received the ring, Elvis had made his will, toured the country for five concerts, collapsed on his sixth, and was taken for the last time to the Baptist Hospital on April 1. He checked himself out after a few days, returning to Graceland to prepare for his next series of concerts which were to start on April 21.

Two more tours followed his April one, in May and June, and the last performance he gave was in Indianapolis on June 26. By now there was no longer any question about how desperately ill he was: Elvis knew it and his public knew it.

August 4 was the publication date of *Elvis: What Happened?*—the first of what Elvis fans were to call "the bodyguard books." It caused a furor by being followed only twelve days later by Elvis' death. Its unflattering version of every aspect of Elvis' character, and his problems as seen through the eyes of three bodyguards he had fired a year before, seemed to have blinded its readers to what to me is the most interesting feature of this book. Though highly critical of Elvis' every thought and action, it is just the reverse whenever the Colonel makes his entrance in these pages. Indeed, every time he does, it is a signal that you are in for several paragraphs of undiluted raves about "the instant magic worked by the all-knowing Colonel Parker"—this "showbiz guru of all time"—this "cigar-chomping *southern* Colonel" who, in negotiating "top dollars" for his client, was "*southern* enough to remind the yankee [Ed] Sullivan of what he had once said about his boy" (italics mine)—and who doesn't deny "the more outrageous stories about himself" simply because "virtually all his time has been spent promoting Elvis."

Not only does the ex-dogcatcher emerge with his reputation immaculate but even his driveway, the bodyguards swear, is so clean you could eat a three-course meal off it. This could well be true; it could also be true that the driveway was all they were allowed to see of Parker's residence for, according to Gabe Tucker, although the Colonel was not above catching a ride from Hollywood to Palm Springs with the Memphis Mafia, he never invited them into his home once they had arrived, though he "might pitch a five-dollar bill inside the car."

"Tom Parker was and is amazing. With Elvis and him it was like a joint and socket who had been looking for each other. Man, I got a great respect for that ole boy." Here, as throughout the book, Red West displays a nice touch of Christian charity toward the Colonel, apparently forgiving him for not allowing him to be present at Elvis' wedding ceremony and substituting the black actor Redd Fox in his place. Truly, the Colonel could not have been provided with better character references if he had written them himself! Suddenly a flurry of questions rise and circle the air. Why didn't the "all-knowing" Parker, who was certainly as aware as Elvis that these bodyguards were hawking their confessions around, work his "instant magic" and have the book stopped simply by paying the boys off?

Elvis died at forty-two on August 16, 1977. It was two days after the anniversary of his mother's death. It has been pointed out that Gladys was in fact forty-six when she died but it was not until later, when Elvis had erected for her grave a marble monument, that the secret of her real age, validated only by school records, emerged. Forty-two was her age as reported throughout the media in 1958; the age she had chosen to be; the age Elvis believed her to be in the initial shock of her death. That age that would never be dislodged from his loyal mind.

Bibliography

(ELVIS BOOKS)
The following are books about Elvis or contain references to him which, for a variety of reasons, I have read more carefully than the others.

Carr, Roy, and Mick Farren. *Elvis Presley: The Complete Illustrated Record.* New York: Harmony Books, 1982.

Crumbaker, Marge, and Gabe Tucker. *Up and Down with Elvis Presley.* New York: G. P. Putnam, 1981.

Escott, Colin, and Martin Hawkins. *Elvis: An Illustrated Discography.* New York: G. P. Putnam, 1981.

———. *Sun Records: The Brief History of the Legendary Record Label.* London: Omnibus Press, 1980.

Goldman, Albert. *Elvis.* New York: McGraw-Hill, 1981; Avon, 1982.

Hopkins, Jerry. *Elvis: A Biography.* New York: Simon & Schuster, 1971.

———. *Elvis: The Final Years.* New York: Berkley, 1983.

Lacker, Marty, Patsy Lacker, and Leslie S. Smith. *Elvis: Portrait of a Friend.* New York: Bantam Books, 1980.

Lichter, Paul. *The Boy Who Dared to Rock: The Definitive Elvis.* New York: Doubleday, 1978.

Mann, May. *The Private Elvis.* New York: Pocket Books, 1977.

Marcus, Greil. *Mystery Train: Images of America in Rock 'n' Roll Music.* New York: E. P. Dutton, 1982.

Marsh, Dave. *Elvis: Life of Elvis Presley.* New York: Times Books, 1982.

McKee, Margaret, and Fred Chisenhall. *Beale Black & Blue.* Baton Rouge and London: Louisiana State University Press, 1981.

Presley, Dee, Rick Billy, and David Stanley as told to Martin Torgoff. *Elvis, We Love You Tender.* New York: Dell, 1980.

Presley, Vester. *A Presley Speaks.* Memphis: Wimmer Books, 1978.

Rolling Stone Press. *The Rolling Stone Illustrated History of Rock & Roll, 1950–1970*. New York: Random House, 1980.

Shaw, Arnold. *Honkers and Shouters: The Golden Years of Rhythm & Blues*. New York: Macmillan, 1978.

Smith, Bill, ed. *Elvis: The Record* (magazine).

Stearn, Jess, with Larry Geller. *The Truth About Elvis*. New York: Jove, 1980.

Torgoff, Martin, ed. *The Complete Elvis*. New York: Delilah Books, 1982.

West, Red, Sonny West, and Dave Hebler as told to Steve Dunleavy. *Elvis: What Happened?* New York: Ballantine Books, 1977.

Worth, Fred L., and Steve D. Tamerius. *All About Elvis*. New York: Bantam Books, 1981.

(GENERAL BOOKS)

Barnes, James. *From Then Till Now*. New York and London: D. Appleton-Century, 1934.

Bartlett, Richard A. *The New Country: A Social History of the American Frontier, 1776–1890*. New York: Oxford University Press, 1976.

Boorstin, Daniel J. *The Americans: The Colonial Experience*, Vol. 1. New York: Penguin Books, 1965.

Clark, Thomas D., and A. D. Kirwan. *The South Since Appomattox: A Century of Regional Change*. Westport, CT: Greenwood Press, 1980.

Du Maurier, George. *Peter Ibbetson*. London and New York: Harper & Brothers, 1891.

Dunne, Philip. *Take Two: A Life in Movies & Politics*. New York: McGraw-Hill, 1980.

Eaton, Clement. *The Growth of Southern Civilization, 1790–1860*. New York: Harper & Row, 1963.

Erickson, Charlotte, *Invisible Immigrants: The Adaptation of English and Scottish Immigrants in 19th Century America*. Miami: University of Miami Press, 1972.

Francis, W. Nelson. *The Structure of American English*. New York: Ronald Press, 1958.

Gill, Frances McLaughlin, and Kathryn McLaughlin Abbe. *Twins on Twins*. New York: Crown, 1980.

Hamilton, Virginia Van der Veer. *Alabama, Bicentennial History*. New York: W. W. Norton, 1977.

Handy, W. C. *W. C. Handy: Father of the Blues*. New York: Da Capo, 1985.

Kefauver, Estes. *Crime in America*. Westport, CT: Greenwood Press, 1951.

La Farge, Oliver. *Pictorial History of the American Indian*. London, Deutsch, 1958.

Lentz, Henry Jackson. *The Diary of Henry Jackson Lentz (1819–1869) of Limeston County, Alabama and Itawamba County, Mississippi* (recently discovered). Lee County Library, Tupelo, Mississippi, 1980.

McKenney, Thomas L., and James Hal John Grant. *History of Indian Tribes of North America* Vol. 3 (Philadelphia: F. W. Greenough, 1838–44.

Morison, S. E., and H. S. Commager. *The Growth of the American Republic*. New York: Oxford University Press, 1930.

Morse, Jedidiah. "A report to the secretary of war of United States, on Indian affairs." Washington, D.C.: S. Converse, 1822.

Remini, Robert V. *Andrew Jackson and the Course of American Empire, 1767–1821*, Vol. 1. New York: Harper & Row, 1977.

Scheinfeld, Amram. *Your Heredity and Environment*. New York: J. B. Lippincott, 1965.

Scholes, Percy A., ed. *The Oxford Companion to Music*, 10th Edition. New York: Oxford University Press, 1970.

Snow, Jimmy. *I Cannot Go Back*. Plainfield, NJ: Logos International, 1977.

Wallis, Hal, and Charles Higham. *Star Maker*. New York: Berkley, 1981.
Young, Stark, ed. *A Southern History of Life and Literature*. New York: Charles Scribner, 1937.

(ARCHIVAL SOURCES)

British Film Institute, London.

Commercial Appeal and *Press Scimitar* newspapers' archives, Memphis, Tennessee.

Guardian ad litem reports on Presley vs. Parker. First report filed September 29, 1980, in Probate Court of Shelby County, Tennessee; second report filed July 31, 1981, idem.

Lee County Library, Tupelo, Mississippi.

Lincoln Center Film and Music Library, New York.

Tupelo Journal archives, Tupelo, Mississippi.

United States Embassy Library, London.

University of Texas, Austin, Texas.

Index